Contents

WORLD BANK OPERATIONS EVALUATION DEPARTMENT

Addressing the Challenges of Globalization

An Independent Evaluation of the World Bank's Approach to Global Programs

2004
The World Bank
Washington, D.C.

http://www.worldbank.org/oed

1818 H Street, NW
Washington, DC 20433
Telephone: 202-473-1000
Internet: www.worldbank.org
E-mail: feedback@worldbank.org

Manufactured in the United States of America
First edition December 2004

Cover photo courtesy of the World Bank Photo Library.

ISBN 0-8213-6065-5
e-ISBN 0-8213-6066-3

Library of Congress Cataloging-in-Publication data have been applied for.

World Bank InfoShop
E-mail: pic@worldbank.org
Telephone: 202-458-5454
Facsimile: 202-522-1500

Operations Evaluation Department
Knowledge Programs and Evaluation Capacity Development (OEDKE)
E-mail: eline@worldbank.org
Telephone: 202-458-4497
Facsimile: 202-522-3125

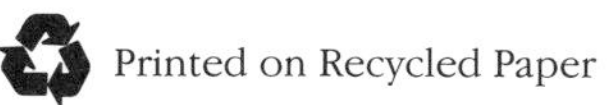
Printed on Recycled Paper

Tables

Figures

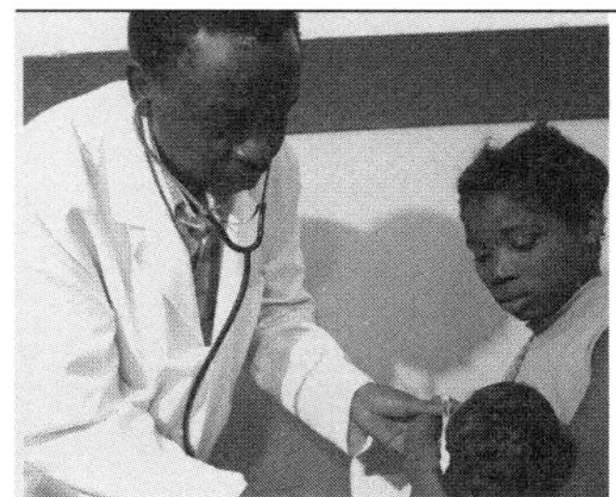

Acknowledgments

This report was written by Uma Lele and Chris Gerrard and builds on case-study analyses by the OED Global Team. The Team included Manmohan Agarwal, Yusuf Ahmad, Caroline Bahnson, Edward Bresnyan, Tomas Caspellan, Jozefina Cutura, Ramesh Govindaraj, Maisha Hyman, Jeffrey Jordan, Kristina Kavaliunas, Lauren Kelly, Yianni Konstantopoulos, Kavita Mathur, Karin Perkins, Saeed Rana, Naveen Sarna, Kirsten Spainhower, David Spielman, and Rod Stubina. The report benefited from the editorial contributions of Caroline McEuen, Brian Fitzpatrick, William Hurlbut, and Rachel Weaving.

The OED Team would like to acknowledge the valuable contributions of OED management and colleagues—Martha Ainsworth, Rema Balasundaram, Lily Chu, Laurie Effron, John Eriksson, Alice Galenson, Madhur Gautam, Roy Gilbert, Patrick Grasso, Catherine Gwin, Andres Liebenthal, Fernando Manibog, Ridley Nelson, Keith Pitman, and Yvonne Tsikata—to the earlier drafts of this report and to the case studies.

The authors and contributors also appreciate the perspectives and inputs from World Bank Group Executive Directors Tanwir Ali Agha, Jaime Alvarez, Yahya Alyahya, Gino Alzetta, Carole Brookins, Alieto Guadagni, Louis Kasekende, Jonathan Olsson, Chander M. Vasudev, Pietro Veglio, Jacob Waslander, and Niklaus Zingg, and from IMF Executive Directors Wei Benhua, Alexander Barro Chambrier, Roberto Junguito, Vijay L. Kelkar, Cyrus D.R. Rustomjee, Rosemary Stevenson , and J. de Beaufort Wijnholds.

The team also benefited from the information and insight provided by Managing Directors Jeffrey Goldstein, Mamphela Ramphele, Sven Sandstrom and Shengman Zhang; from Senior Vice Presidents Francois J. Bourguignon, Jean Louis Sarbib, and Nicholas Stern; from the Vice Presidents in charge of Operations, Networks, and External Relations, including James Adams, Ian Goldin, Ian Johnson, Motoo Kusakabe, Geoffrey Lamb, Frannie Leautier, Gobind Nankani, Jozef Ritzen, Nemat Shafik, and Anil Sood; and from the Director of the Quality Assessment Group, Prem Garg.

The OED Team thanks the following Country Directors: Michael F. Carter, Mats Karlsson, Edward Lim, Andrew Steer, and Vinod Thomas. We also thank numerous Bank staff from many programs and units, including the *Global Programs and Partnership Group* and the *DGF Secretariat:* Paul Hubbard, Jane Kirby-Zaki, Sophia Drewnowski, Judy Lu, Randall Purcell, and Anju Sharma; and the *Trust Fund Operations and Trust Fund Quality Assurance and Compliance Unit:* Arif Zulfiqar, Dale Hill, Paul Cadario, Diana Corbin, and Caroline Harper.

Environment and Agriculture: Kevin Cleaver, Sushma Ganguly, and Kristalina Georgieva. *Consultative Group on International Agricultural Re-*

search Meta-Evaluation: Jock Anderson, Shawki Barghouti, Derek Byerlee, Cees de Haan, Odin Knudsen, Eija Pehu, and Francisco Reifschneider. *Global Environmental Facility Case Study:* Kulsum Ahmed, Dinesh Aryal, Robin Broadfield, Gonzalo Castro, Christophe Crepin, Mohammed El-Ashry, Len Good, Jarle Harstad, Rohit Khanna, Kenneth King, Kanta Kumari, Kathleen MacKinnon, Amedee S. Prouvost, Susan Shen, Karin Shepardson, Lars Vidaeus, Claudio Volonte, Samuel Wedderburn, and Aaron Zazueta. *Multilateral Fund for the Implementation of the Montreal Protocol Case Study:* Helen Chan, Charles di Leva, Mary-Ellen Foley, Steve Gorman, Erik Pedersen, Neeraj Prasad, Bilal Rahill, Sandra Siles, Horacio Terraza, and Laura Tlyaie. *Prototype Carbon Fund Case Study:* Veronique Bishop, Hinderkus Busz, Denis Clarke, David Freestone, Johannes Heister, Franck Lecocq, Kenneth Newcombe, Neeraj Prasad, Juan Searle, Chandra Sinha, and Charlotte Strek. *Critical Ecosystems Partnership Fund Case Study:* Philip Brylski, Kerstin Canby, Michael Carroll, David Cassells, Gonzalo Castro, James Douglas, Malcom Jansen, Agi Kiss, Kathleen MacKinnon, Christian Peter, Jeanette Ramirez, Susan Shen, John Spears, Martien van Nieuwkoop, Chris Warner, and Anthony Whitten. *Global Water Partnership Case Study:* Masood Ahmad, Shawki Barghouti, John Briscoe, Salah Darghouth, Yoko Eguchi, and Karin Kemper. *Global Integrated Pest Management Facility Case Study:* Osmane Badiane, Charles di Leva, Gershon Feder, Doug Forno, David Freestone, Laurent Granier, Agi Kiss, Abdelaziz Lagnaoui, Stephen Lintner, Matthew McMahon, Tawhid Nawaz, Ridley Nelson, Eija Pehu, Malik Saifullah, Ethel Sennhauser, Susan Shen, Tjaart Schillhorn-Van Veen, John S. Wilson, and Willem Zijp.

Health, Nutrition, and Population: Jacques Baudouy, Robert Hecht, and Chris Lovelace. *Global Health Programs Case Study:* Lawrence Barat, Amie Batson, Peter Heywood, Bernhard Liese, L. Richard Meyers, Janet Nassim, Tawhid Nawaz, Ok Pannenborg, Helen Saxenian, Alfredo Sfeir-Younis and his office staff in Geneva, Richard Skolnick, Susan Stout, Nandita Tannan, Zafiris Tzannatos, Jagadish Upadhyay, Christopher Walker, Diana Weil, and Debrework Zewdie.

Infrastructure and Private Sector Development: Anwar Ravat, Anne Simpson, and Nigel Twose. *Infrastructure Case Study:* Henri J. Bretaudeau, Vivek Chaudhry, Jacqueline Dubow, Barbara Evans, Charles Feinstein, Mark Hildebrand, Parameswaran Iyer, Dominique Lallement, Bruno Lanvin, Kevin Milroy, Russel Muir, Cynthia Nunez-Ollero, Jordan Schwartz, Kazim Saeed, and Walter Stottman. *Consultative Group to Assist the Poor Case Study:* Tamara Cook, Carlos Cuevas, Elizabeth Littlefield, and Ousa Sananikone.

Trade and Finance: *Integrated Framework for Trade-related Technical Assistance Case Study:* Ataman Aksoy, Amar Bhattacharya, Nancy Benjamin, Uri Dadush, Bernard Hoekman, Nadir Mohammed, John Panzer, Axel Peuker, Miguel Saponara, Leendert Solleveld, and Su Yong Song. *Financial Sector Assessment Program and the Financial Reform and Strengthening Initiative Case Studies:* Julie Knowles, Susan Marcus, Larry Promisel, Dafna Tapiero, and Margery Waxman.

Social Development and Protection: *Post-conflict Fund Case Study:* Ian Bannon, Rajna Cemerska, Lisa Campeau, Paul Collier, Steve Holtzman, Steen Lau Jorgensen, Barbara Kafka, Pamphile Kantabaze, Barbry Keller, Kazuhide Kuroda, Ana Paula Lopes, Peter Miovic, Colin Scott, and Natalia Zakharina. *Understanding Children's Work Case Study:* David Harding, Robert Holzmann, Amit Dar, Bonna Kim, and Zafiris Tzannatos.

Information and Knowledge: *Global Development Network Case Study*: Paul Collier, Ishac Diwan, Ines Garcia-Thoumi, Alan Gelb, Benno Ndulu, Guillermo Perry, Samuel Wangwe, and Jacek Wojciechowicz. *World Links Case Study:* Samuel Carlson, Prema Clark, and Robert Hawkins.

External Relations: OED also acknowledges with thanks the contributions of Joseph Ingram, who chaired the meeting on the OED report on the Global Health Programs in Geneva; of Carlos Braga, Senior Advisor, International Trade Department, for his contributions to the consultations with the World Trade Organization and the working group of the Integrated Framework for Trade-related Technical Assistance program; and of other staff of the Geneva office, including Sophie Bolard, Isabelle Taylor, and Fabrizio Zarcone, who provided support during consultations with WHO, GAVI, WTO, and ILO relating to the UCW program.

In addition, the following staff gave us enormously helpful insight and information: Anders Agerskov, Thomas Duval, Arna Hartmann, Olga Jonas, Kathleen Mikitin, Sophie Smyth, John Todd, Hasan Tuluy, John Underwood, and Christine Wallich.

A complete list of persons consulted on each of the supporting cases is included in Annex G.

Interviews were also conducted with staff of the International Monetary Fund, the United States Agency for International Development, the World Health Organization, the International Labor Organization, UNAIDS, UNDP, UNEP, UNHCR, UNICEF, UNIDO, the Department for International Development (U.K.), the Swiss Agency for Development and Cooperation (SDC), the Canadian International Development Agency, and the Swedish Ministry of Foreign Affairs.

Director-General, Operations Evaluation: *Gregory K. Ingram*
Director, OED: *Ajay Chhibber*
Senior Adviser and Team Leader: *Uma Lele*
Task Manager: *Christopher Gerrard*

ENGLISH

FOREWORD

This Phase 2 report is based on case studies of 26 (of a total of 70) Bank-supported global programs that accounted for 90 percent of the Bank's global program expenditures in 2002.[1] It follows on the phase 1 report completed in 2002 and the meta-evaluation of the CGIAR completed in 2003 that evaluated Bank involvement in global programs. The phase 1 report addressed strategic and programmatic issues facing the Bank's global program portfolio. The meta-evaluation of the CGIAR evaluated the Bank's performance as a co-founder and lead partner in addressing the challenges posed by the rapidly changing external and internal environment facing this oldest—and the largest—program supported by the Development Grant Facility.

Since 2002, global program financing has grown rapidly. Annual disbursements to global and regional activities increased by $400 million, to $1.2 billion in 2004. A significant portion of this increase was for a new program—the Global Fund to Fight AIDS, Tuberculosis, and Malaria—for which the Bank is a trustee. Excluding the Heavily Indebted Poor Countries (HIPC) Initiative and International Finance Corporation (IFC), 64 percent of the Bank-managed trust fund balance ($7.1 billion in 2004) supported global and regional programs, compared with 57 percent in 2003. The Bank has been

ESPAÑOL

PRÓLOGO

Este informe de la fase 2 se basa en el estudio de casos de 26 programas mundiales (de un total de 70) respaldados por el Banco, que en 2002 representaron el 90 por ciento del gasto del Banco destinado a programas mundiales.[1] Este informe es la continuación del informe de la fase 1 finalizado en 2002 y de la metaevaluación del GCIAR que se completó en 2003, destinados a evaluar la participación del Banco en los programas mundiales. El informe de la fase 1 abordó las cuestiones estratégicas y programáticas que ha enfrentado la cartera de programas mundiales del Banco. La metaevaluación del GCIAR examinó el desempeño del Banco, en su carácter de cofundador y asociado principal, al abordar los retos que enfrenta este programa, el más antiguo y el de mayor envergadura respaldado por el Fondo de Donaciones para el Desarrollo, debido a los rápidos cambios en los entornos externo e interno.

Desde 2002, el financiamiento de los programas mundiales ha crecido rápidamente. Los desembolsos anuales con destino a actividades mundiales y regionales aumentaron en $400 millones a $1.200 millones en 2004. Una porción importante de este aumento se destinó a un nuevo programa, el Fondo Mundial de Lucha contra el SIDA, la Tuberculosis y la Malaria, en el cual el Banco se desempeña como depositario. Si se excluyen

FRANÇAIS

AVANT-PROPOS

Ce rapport sur la phase 2 se base sur des études de cas de 26 (sur un total de 70) programmes mondiaux financés par la Banque mondiale qui représentaient 90% des dépenses des programmes mondiaux en 2002[1]. Ce rapport fait suite au rapport sur la phase 1 clôturé en 2002 et à la méta-évaluation du GCRAI terminée en 2003 qui évaluaient la participation de la Banque mondiale à des programmes mondiaux. Le rapport sur la phase 1 abordait les problèmes stratégiques et programmatiques que rencontrait le portefeuille de programmes mondiaux de la Banque mondiale. La méta-évaluation du GCRAI a évalué l'efficacité de la Banque mondiale en tant que cofondateur et en tant que partenaire important pour aborder des problèmes que pose l'environnement interne et externe en rapide changement à ce programme, qui est le plus ancien et le plus grand programme financé par la DGF (Development Grant Facility).

Depuis 2002, le financement des programmes mondiaux a rapidement augmenté. Les décaissements annuels pour des activités régionales et mondiales ont augmenté de 400 millions de dollars pour atteindre 1,2 milliards de dollars en 2004. Une partie importante de cette augmentation était destinée à un nouveau programme, le Fonds mondial de lutte contre le SIDA, la tuberculose et le paludisme (GFATM), dont la Banque mondiale

ENGLISH

working well with external partners on a program-by-program basis. It now needs to improve the linkages between priorities for global programs and Bank client needs.

Management introduced a number of reforms in response to the recommendations of the earlier reports, including: establishing the Global Program and Partnership Council, instituting stronger ex ante and external reviews of proposals, and requiring more regular external evaluations of programs. While improving the management of the ongoing portfolio is necessary, OED believes that more remains to be done—particularly in the area of strengthening the strategic framework for the Bank's involvement in global programs. Steps taken to improve portfolio management will help identify errors of commission, but not errors of omission—such as the need for greater attention to global trade and health issues.

The phase 2 report's recommendations therefore stress two key elements:

- The need for a global strategy for the Bank that will focus Bank support on high-priority, well-funded global public goods programs and that will be based on a consultative process involving key partners
- Better routine management of the global portfolio in order to set international standards for quality, add value, and enhance returns to Bank country operations and clients.

ESPAÑOL

la Iniciativa para los países pobres altamente endeudados (PPAE) y la Corporación Financiera Internacional (CFI), el 64% de los fondos fiduciarios administrados por el Banco ($7.100 millones en 2004) se destinó a respaldar programas mundiales y regionales, en comparación con un 57% en 2003. El Banco ha trabajado satisfactoriamente con los asociados externos por programa. Ahora es preciso mejorar los vínculos entre las prioridades de los programas mundiales y las necesidades de los clientes del Banco.

La administración introdujo una serie de reformas en respuesta a las recomendaciones de los dos informes, entre las que se incluyen la creación del Consejo de Asociaciones y Programas Mundiales, el establecimiento de exámenes iniciales y externos más rigurosos de las propuestas, y la exigencia de que se realicen evaluaciones externas de los programas con mayor regularidad. Si bien es necesario mejorar la gestión de la cartera de programas en curso, el DEO considera que aún quedan cosas por hacer, en particular con miras a fortalecer el marco estratégico de la participación del Banco en los programas mundiales. Las medidas para mejorar la gestión de la cartera ayudarán a identificar errores por acción, no así por omisión, como es la necesidad de prestar mayor atención al comercio y la salud mundiales.

Por lo tanto, las recomendaciones del informe de la fase 2 hacen hincapié en dos elementos principales:

FRANÇAIS

est administrateur. En dehors de l'Initiative PPTE (pays pauvres très endettés) et de la SFI (Société financière internationale), 64% des fonds fiduciaires gérés par la Banque mondiale (7,1 milliards de dollars en 2004) ont été utilisés pour financer des programmes régionaux et mondiaux, contre 57% en 2003. La Banque a bien travaillé avec des partenaires extérieurs programme par programme. Il faut à présent renforcer les liens entre les priorités des programmes mondiaux et les besoins des clients de la Banque mondiale.

La direction de la Banque mondiale a introduit un certain nombre de réformes en réponse aux recommandations des rapports précédents, notamment l'établissement du Conseil des programmes et des partenariats mondiaux (GPP), l'institution de révisions externes et ex ante renforcées des propositions et l'exigence d'évaluations externes plus régulières des programmes. S'il faut améliorer la gestion du portefeuille actuel, l'OED pense qu'il reste encore beaucoup plus à faire, en particulier dans le domaine du renforcement du cadre stratégique de la participation de la Banque mondiale à des programmes mondiaux. Les mesures adoptées pour améliorer la gestion du portefeuille contribueront à identifier les erreurs de commission, mais pas d'omission – comme la nécessité de prêter une plus grande attention aux problèmes de santé et de commerce au niveau mondial.

ENGLISH

Some key elements of a Bank global strategy would likely include an understanding and exploitation of the comparative advantage of the Bank and its key partners, including U.N. agencies; a clear focus on key global public goods and global policies that adversely affect developing countries' prospects for growth and poverty alleviation; and support of poverty reduction activities that complement rather than compete with Bank country operations.

With respect to the improvement in the portfolio, OED recommends that the Bank:

- Separate oversight from management.
- Improve standards of governance and management of individual programs.
- Revisit selection and exit criteria.
- Strengthen evaluations of global programs and their review within the Bank.

ESPAÑOL

- La necesidad de una estrategia mundial para el Banco que se centre en el apoyo del Banco a programas de bienes públicos mundiales de alta prioridad y con suficiente financiamiento, y que se base en un proceso consultivo con la participación de los asociados principales.
- Una mejor gestión de rutina de la cartera mundial a fin de establecer normas internacionales de calidad, agregar valor y mejorar los resultados de las operaciones del Banco por país y de los clientes.

Algunos elementos principales de una estrategia mundial del Banco probablemente incluyan la comprensión y el aprovechamiento de la ventaja comparativa del Banco y sus asociados principales, incluidos los organismos de las Naciones Unidas; un enfoque claro en políticas mundiales y bienes públicos mundiales esenciales que afectan en forma adversa las probabilidades de crecimiento y erradicación de la pobreza en países en desarrollo; y la promoción de actividades para reducción de la pobreza que complementan en lugar de competir con las operaciones del Banco por país.

En relación con la mejora de la cartera, el DEO recomienda al Banco:

- Separar la función de supervisión de la gestión.
- Mejorar las normas de gobierno y gestión de los programas individuales.
- Revisar los criterios de selección y de salida.

FRANÇAIS

Les recommandations du rapport sur la phase 2 soulignent donc deux éléments essentiels:

- La nécessité d'une stratégie mondiale pour la Banque mondiale qui concentrerait l'aide de la Banque mondiale sur des programmes de biens publics mondiaux bien financés et à haute priorité et qui se baserait sur une procédure de consultation impliquant les principaux partenaires;
- Une meilleure gestion courante d'un portefeuille mondial qui contribue à établir des normes internationales pour la qualité et la valeur ajoutée et augmente les revenus pour les opérations nationales de la Banque mondiale et pour les clients.

Certains éléments essentiels d'une stratégie mondiale de la Banque mondiale pourraient être, entre autres, la compréhension et l'exploitation de l'avantage comparatif de la Banque et de ses principaux partenaires, y compris les agences de l'ONU; l'accent clair sur les principaux biens publics mondiaux et sur les politiques mondiales qui nuisent aux perspectives des pays en développement en matière de croissance et de réduction de la pauvreté; et le financement d'activités de réduction de la pauvreté qui complètent les opérations nationales de la Banque mondiale au lieu d'être en concurrence avec elles.

Concernant l'amélioration du portefeuille, l'OED recommande que la Banque mondiale:

ESPAÑOL

- Fortalecer las evaluaciones de los programas mundiales y su examen dentro del Banco.

FRANÇAIS

- Sépare le contrôle de la gestion;
- Améliore les normes de gouvernance et de gestion de programmes individuels;
- Réexamine des critères de sélection et de sortie;
- Renforce les évaluations des programmes mondiaux et leur révision au sein de la Banque mondiale.

Gregory K. Ingram
Director-General, Operations Evaluation

ENGLISH

PREFACE

This report completes the second phase of the Operations Evaluation Department's independent evaluation of the World Bank's involvement in global programs. The approach paper for the overall evaluation was presented to the Committee on Development Effectiveness (CODE) of the World Bank's Board of Executive Directors in January 2001. The draft Evaluation Strategy Paper was discussed at a June 19, 2001, workshop in Washington that brought together representatives of Bank management and policymakers from developing countries, U.N. organizations, international and regional financial institutions, nongovernmental organizations, and the private sector. The workshop proceedings and the final Evaluation Strategy Paper were distributed to participants in July 2001. The paper was then posted on the study Web site (http://www.worldbank.org/oed/gppp).

The Evaluation Strategy Workshop produced two changes in the evaluation design. First, at management request, the Operations Evaluation Department (OED) agreed to do the evaluation in two phases, with the first phase timed to inform the Bank's budgeting processes. Second, at the demand of the workshop participants, OED included a substantial meta-evaluation of the Consultative Group on International Agricultural Research (CGIAR) among the 26 cases to be examined in the study's second phase.

The Phase 1 report, *The World Bank's Approach to Global Pro-*

ESPAÑOL

PREFACIO

Este informe completa la segunda fase de la evaluación independiente del Departamento de Evaluación de Operaciones (DEO) sobre la participación del Banco Mundial en los programas mundiales. El documento de enfoque para la evaluación general se presentó ante el Comité sobre la Eficacia en Términos de Desarrollo (CODE) del Directorio Ejecutivo en enero de 2001. La versión preliminar del Documento de Estrategia de Evaluación se analizó en un taller organizado en Washington el 19 de junio de 2001, el cual reunió a representantes de la administración del Banco y a los responsables de la formulación de políticas en los países en desarrollo, los organismos de las Naciones Unidas, las instituciones financieras internacionales y regionales, las organizaciones no gubernamentales y el sector privado. Las actas del taller y la versión final del Documento de Estrategia de Evaluación se distribuyeron a los participantes en julio de 2001. El documento se publicó luego en el sitio web (http://www.worldbank.org/oed/gppp).

El taller de estrategia de evaluación produjo dos cambios en el diseño de la evaluación. En primer lugar, a solicitud de la administración del Banco, el Departamento de Evaluación de Operaciones (DEO) aceptó realizar la evaluación en dos fases, programando la primera fase para dar información a los procesos de presupuestación del Banco. En segundo lugar, a instancia de los participantes del taller, el DEO incluyó una metaevaluación significativa del

FRANÇAIS

PRÉFACE

Le rapport met un terme à la deuxième phase de l'évaluation indépendante, par le Département de l'évaluation rétrospective des opérations (OED), de la participation de la Banque mondiale à des programmes mondiaux. Le document d'orientation pour l'évaluation générale a été présenté au Comité pour l'efficacité du développement (CODE) du Conseil des administrateurs de la Banque mondiale en janvier 2001. L'avant-projet de document de stratégie d'évaluation a été débattu lors de l'atelier du 19 juin 2001 à Washington, qui a rassemblé des représentants de la direction de la Banque mondiale et des responsables politiques des pays en développement, des organisations de l'ONU, des institutions financières régionales et internationales, des organisations non gouvernementales et du secteur privé. Le compte rendu de l'atelier et le document final de stratégie d'évaluation ont été distribués aux participants en juillet 2001. Le document a ensuite été publié sur le site web de l'OED (http://www.worldbank.org/oed/gppp - en anglais).

L'atelier sur la stratégie d'évaluation a amené deux changements dans la conception de l'évaluation. Tout d'abord, à la demande de la direction de la Banque mondiale, le Département de l'évaluation rétrospective des opérations (OED) a convenu de procéder à l'évaluation en deux phases, le moment de la première phase étant choisi pour contribuer aux procédures de budgétisation de la Banque mondiale. Ensuite, à la demande des partici-

ENGLISH

grams, focused on the strategic and programmatic management of the Bank's global portfolio of 70 programs in five Bank networks (each of which covers a cluster of closely related sectors). The Phase 2 report, which is based on case studies of 26 global programs, derives additional lessons for such broad management; it also derives lessons for the design and management of individual programs.

The first and largest case study, of the CGIAR, was completed in April 2003. The remaining case studies have been undertaken in parallel with the Phase 2 report. OED circulated most of the case studies internally and externally to partners for comments and has received comments on many of them from both sources. All publicly disclosed reports are being posted on the study's external Web site.

The study has benefited from an external advisory committee consisting of Rolf Lüders, Professor and Editor, *Cuadernos De Economía*, Pontifical Catholic University of Chile; Wolfgang Reinicke, Managing Director, Galaxar SA, Geneva, and Director, Global Public Policy Project; Nafis Sadik, former Executive Director, United Nations Population Fund; and Adele Simmons, Vice Chairman and Senior Executive, Chicago Metropolis 2020, and former President of the MacArthur Foundation. (Biographical summaries are available on the study Web site.) The Phase 2 study design benefited from the contributions of Robert Picciotto, Director-General of OED until October 2002.

The evaluation was also informed by a joint UNDP/World Bank workshop, held in July 2000 in Washing-

ESPAÑOL

Grupo Consultivo sobre Investigaciones Agrícolas Internacionales (GCIAI) entre los 26 casos que se examinarían en la segunda fase del estudio.

El informe de la fase 1, *The World Bank's Approach to Global Programs (El Banco Mundial y su abordaje de los programas globales),* se centró en la gestión estratégica y programática de la cartera global del Banco integrada por 70 programas en 5 redes (cada una de las cuales comprende un grupo de sectores estrechamente relacionados). El informe de la fase 2, basado en el estudio de 26 programas mundiales, recoge nuevas lecciones para la gestión de programas en general como así también para el diseño y la gestión de programas individuales.

El estudio del caso del GCIAI, que fue el primero y de mayor envergadura, concluyó en abril de 2003. Los demás estudios de casos se han llevado a cabo en forma simultánea con el informe de la fase 2. El DEO difundió la mayoría de los estudios en el seno del Banco y, en el ámbito externo, entre los asociados del Banco para que éstos hicieran los comentarios pertinentes, y de hecho ha recibido comentarios sobre muchos de los estudios, tanto de fuentes internas como externas. Todos los informes que se dan a conocer al público se colocan en el sitio web externo del Banco.

El estudio se ha enriquecido al contar con un comité de asesoramiento externo integrado por Rolf Lüders, Profesor y Editor, *Cuadernos De Economía*, Pontificia Universidad Católica de Chile; Wolfgang Reinicke, Director General, Galaxar SA, Geneva, y Director, Proyecto de política pública mundial; Nafis Sadik,

FRANÇAIS

pants de l'atelier, l'OED a inclus une méta-évaluation importante du Groupe consultatif pour la recherche agricole internationale (GCRAI) des 26 cas à examiner au cours de la deuxième phase de l'étude.

Le rapport sur la phase 1, *L'approche de la Banque mondiale sur les programmes mondiaux,* s'est concentré sur la gestion stratégique et programmatique du portefeuille mondial de la Banque mondiale, composé de 70 programmes répartis dans 5 réseaux de la Banque mondiale (chacun couvrant une série de secteurs étroitement reliés entre eux). Le rapport sur la phase 2, qui se base sur des études de cas de 26 programmes mondiaux, tire des leçons supplémentaires pour une vaste gestion de ce type; il tire également des leçons pour la conception et la gestion de programmes individuels.

La première étude de cas, et la plus grande, du GCRAI a été terminée en avril 2003. Les autres études de cas ont été entreprises parallèlement au rapport sur la phase 2. L'OED a distribué la plupart des études de cas au niveau interne et externe à des partenaires pour observations et il a reçu des deux sources des observations sur la plupart de ces études. Tous les rapports rendus publics sont publiés sur le site web de l'OED.

L'étude a bénéficié d'un comité consultatif externe composé de Rolf Lüders, éditeur de *Cuadernos De Economía* et professeur à l'Université catholique pontificale du Chili; de Wolfgang Reinicke, directeur général de Galaxar SA, Genève, et directeur du Projet de vision de l'ONU sur les réseaux mondiaux d'inter-

ENGLISH

ton, DC, which gathered together some of the foremost analysts of global public policies and goods and the designers and implementers of global programs. The proceedings of that workshop were published by the World Bank. The Swiss Agency for Development and Cooperation has provided generous funding, contributed to the design of the OED review, and enabled broad-based consultations in conducting the case studies. Findings of the Phase 1 report and the CGIAR meta-evaluation were disseminated at the meeting of the U.N. Interagency Working Group in June 2002; the U.N. High Level Committee of Programs in September 2002; the CGIAR Annual General Meetings in Manila in October 2002; the Allied Social Sciences Association meetings in Washington, DC, in January 2003; the journal *Science*; the USDA Ministerial Conference on Agricultural Science and Technology in Sacramento in June 2003; and the Canadian Evaluation Society in Saskatoon in May 2004.

This report has three distinguishing features. First, it looks across the global programs to draw crosscutting lessons about the design, implementation, and evaluation of global programs. Second, it identifies sector-specific lessons. Third, it focuses on the Bank's role in the global program partnerships. Evaluating those partnerships' global activities entailed a meta-evaluation of the various self-evaluations and monitoring done by the partnerships themselves, by the networks, and by the Trust Fund Quality Assurance and Compliance Unit (TQC).

Each of the case studies involved extensive interviews and information-

ESPAÑOL

ex Director Ejecutivo, Fondo de Población de las Naciones Unidas; y Adele Simmons, Vicepresidente y Ejecutivo Principal, Chicago Metropolis 2020, y ex presidente de McArthur Foundation. (Las reseñas biográficas están disponibles en el sitio Web en donde se publica el estudio). El diseño del estudio en la fase 2 contó con el aporte del Sr. Robert Picciotto, Director General del DEO hasta octubre de 2002.

La evaluación también se informó en un taller conjunto del PNUD/Banco Mundial, organizado en julio de 2000 en Washington, DC, en donde se dieron cita algunos de los analistas de políticas y bienes públicos mundiales más prestigiosos y los encargados del diseño e implementación de los programas mundiales. Las actas de ese taller fueron publicadas por el Banco Mundial. La Agencia Suiza para la Cooperación y el Desarrollo proporcionó un importante financiamiento, contribuyó con el diseño del examen del DEO y facilitó un amplio proceso consultivo durante el estudio de casos. Las conclusiones del informe de la fase 1 y de la metaevaluación del GCIAI se han dado a conocer en la reunión del Grupo Interinstitucional de Trabajo de las Naciones Unidas en junio de 2002, el Comité de Alto Nivel sobre programas de las Naciones Unidas en septiembre de 2002, las Asambleas Generales Anuales del GCIAI en Manila en octubre de 2002, las reuniones de la *Allied Social Sciences Association* en Washington, DC, en enero de 2003, la publicación *Science*, la Conferencia Ministerial sobre Ciencia y Tecnología del Departamento de Agricultura de EE.UU. en Sacramento en junio de 2003, y la Sociedad de Evaluación Canadiense

FRANÇAIS

vention (UN Vision Project on Global Public Policy Networks); de Nafis Sadik, ancien directeur général du Fonds des Nations Unies pour la population; et de Adele Simmons, vice-présidente et cadre supérieur de Chicago Metropolis 2020 et ancien président de la Fondation McArthur (des résumés biographiques sont disponibles sur le site web de l'OED). La conception de l'étude sur la phase 2 a bénéficié des contributions de Robert Picciotto, directeur général de l'OED jusqu'en octobre 2002.

Cette évaluation a également bénéficié des contributions d'un atelier mixte Banque mondiale/PNUD, qui s'est tenu en juillet 2000 à Washington D.C. et qui a réuni certains des plus éminents analystes des politiques et produits publics mondiaux ainsi que les concepteurs et les personnes chargées de l'application des programmes mondiaux. Le compte rendu de cet atelier a été publié par la Banque mondiale. La Direction du développement et de la coopération (DDC) a apporté des fonds importants, a contribué à la conception de l'examen de l'OED et a permis de vastes consultations en réalisant les études de cas. Les conclusions du rapport sur la phase 1 et de la méta-évaluation du GCRAI ont été distribuées lors de la réunion du Groupe de travail interagences de l'ONU en juin 2002, lors de la réunion du Comité de haut niveau chargé des programmes de l'ONU en septembre 2002, lors de l'assemblée générale annuelle du GCRAI à Manille en octobre 2002, lors de la réunion de l'Allied Social Sciences Association à Washington D.C. en janvier 2003, dans la revue *Science*,

ENGLISH

gathering fieldwork. Interviews were held with members of the Board of the World Bank and International Monetary Fund; senior managers at the World Bank Group; DGF Council members and staff involved in Strategic Resource Management, Concessional Financing, and Global Partnerships; the Global Programs and Partnership Group; the Development Grant Facility (DGF) Secretariat; Trust Fund Operations; Bank Operations; the World Bank Institute; the International Finance Corporation; the World Health Organization; the Food and Agriculture Organization; UNICEF; the United Nations' Development Program; the International Labor Organization; the United Nations Environment Program; UNAIDS; UNHCR; the Department for International Development (U.K.); the Swiss Agency for Development and Cooperation (SDC); and the Swedish Ministry of Foreign Affairs. Field visits were made to Botswana, Bulgaria, China, the Czech Republic, Ethiopia, Ghana, India, Latvia, Morocco, the Philippines, Poland, the Russian Federation, Singapore, South Africa, Thailand, Turkey, and Vietnam. Annex F lists the study sources, and Annex G lists the people consulted.

ESPAÑOL

en Saskatoon en mayo de 2004.

Este informe tiene tres características distintivas. Primero, analiza los programas mundiales para recoger lecciones interdisciplinarias sobre el diseño, la implementación y la evaluación de los programas mundiales. Segundo, identifica lecciones específicas para cada sector. Tercero, se centra en la función del Banco en las asociaciones de colaboración para programas mundiales. Para evaluar las actividades mundiales de tales asociaciones de colaboración fue necesaria una metaevaluación de las diversas autoevaluaciones y seguimientos realizados por las asociaciones propiamente dichas, por las redes y por la Unidad de Garantía de Calidad y Cumplimiento de Fondos Fiduciarios.

En cada estudio de casos se realizaron entrevistas exhaustivas y trabajo de campo para la recopilación de información. Se entrevistó a miembros del Directorio del Banco Mundial y del Fondo Monetario Internacional, gerentes principales del Grupo del Banco Mundial, miembros del Consejo del Fondo de Donaciones para el Desarrollo y personal que participa de las operaciones de gestión estratégica de recursos, financiamiento concesionario y asociaciones mundiales; Grupo de Asociaciones y Programas Mundiales, la secretaría del Fondo de Donaciones para el Desarrollo, las operaciones de fondos fiduciarios, las operaciones del Banco, el Instituto del Banco Mundial, la Corporación Financiera Internacional, la Organización Mundial de la Salud, la Organización de las Naciones Unidas para la Agricultura y la Alimentación, UNICEF, el Programa de las Naciones Unidas para el Desarrollo, la Organi-

FRANÇAIS

lors de la conférence ministérielle sur la science et la technologie dans l'agriculture du Département de l'Agriculture des États-Unis à Sacramento en juin 2003 et lors de la réunion de la Société canadienne d'évaluation à Saskatoon en mai 2004.

Ce rapport présente trois caractéristiques distinctives. Tout d'abord, il examine les programmes mondiaux pour tirer des leçons transversales quant à la conception, à l'application et à l'évaluation des programmes mondiaux. Ensuite, il identifie des leçons spécifiques aux secteurs. Enfin, il se concentre sur le rôle de la Banque mondiale dans les partenariats des programmes mondiaux. L'évaluation des activités mondiales de ces partenariats a généré une méta-évaluation des différentes évaluations et des contrôles réalisés par les partenariats eux-mêmes, par les réseaux et par le Trust Funds Quality Assurance and Compliance Unit (TQC).

Chacune des études de cas a impliqué un important travail de collecte d'informations sur le terrain ainsi que des entrevues de grande envergure. Les entrevues ont été réalisées avec des membres du Conseil de la Banque mondiale et du Fonds monétaire international, des cadres supérieurs du Groupe de la Banque mondiale, des membres du Conseil de la DGF (Development Grant Facility) et du personnel travaillant dans la gestion des ressources stratégiques, des membres des partenariats mondiaux et du financement concessionnel; du Secrétariat de la DGF, du Département des opérations du Trust Fund, du Département des opérations de la Banque mondiale, de l'Institut de la Banque

ESPAÑOL

zación Internacional del Trabajo, el Programa de las Naciones Unidas para el Medio Ambiente, ONUSIDA, ACNUR (Alto Comisionado de las Naciones Unidas para los Refugiados), el Departamento para el Desarrollo Internacional, la Agencia Suiza para la Cooperación y el Desarrollo, y el Ministerio de Relaciones Exteriores de Suecia. Se realizaron visitas a Botswana, Bulgaria, China, Etiopía, Federación de Rusia, Filipinas, Ghana, India, Latvia, Marruecos, Polonia, República Checa, Singapur, Sudáfrica, Tailandia, Turquía y Vietnam. El anexo F incluye un listado de las fuentes de los estudios y el anexo G un listado de las personas consultadas.

FRANÇAIS

mondiale, de la Société financière internationale, de l'Organisation mondiale de la santé, de l'Organisation des Nations Unies pour l'alimentation et l'agriculture, du Programme des Nations Unies pour le développement, de l'Organisation internationale du travail, du Programme des Nations Unies pour l'environnement, de l'UNAIDS, du HCR de l'ONU, du Department for International Development (Royaume-Uni), de la Direction du développement et de la coopération (DDC), et du ministère des Affaires étrangères suédois. Des visites ont été réalisées sur le terrain en Afrique du Sud, au Botswana, en Bulgarie, en Chine, en Éthiopie, en Fédération de Russie, au Ghana, en Inde, en Lettonie, au Maroc, aux Philippines, en Pologne, en République tchèque, à Singapour, en Thaïlande, en Turquie et au Vietnam. L'annexe F donne la liste des sources des études et l'annexe G donne la liste des personnes consultées.

Executive Summary

The accelerated pace of globalization has stimulated dramatic changes in trade, finance, intellectual property, private investment, information and communications technology, health, environment, security, and civil society. Addressing the challenges posed by globalization often requires collective action at the global level. Increasingly, global programs are used as a means to organize global collective action, particularly for providing global public goods.

Global programs have also gone beyond providing global public goods to serve other objectives that the World Bank has traditionally addressed through its country-level operations. Such multicountry and "corporate advocacy" programs aim to take advantage of economies of scale and scope in providing country-level services and advocating policies that benefit developing countries.

Meeting the increased demand for global programs is difficult, absent a global government with the authority to establish and enforce policy regimes and rules, collect taxes, and raise revenues. Stagnation in official development assistance (ODA) compounds the challenge, though global programs—both global public-goods and multicountry programs—are now taking a larger share of ODA.

The World Bank is an important participant in these global activities because its global reach, its convening power, its ability to mobilize resources, and its multisectoral expertise position it well to deal with the challenges of globalization. The Bank's Board of Executive Directors has raised a variety of issues and concerns about the Bank's growing global partnership programs. These issues have guided OED's evaluation of the Bank's involvement in global programs. The Phase 1 report addressed several strategic and programmatic issues. The meta-evaluation of the CGIAR illustrated the challenges that a global program faces in this changed internal and external environment. This Phase 2 report synthesizes results from OED's review of 26 programs.

The specific objectives of this report are:

- To assess how well these case study programs measure up to the selectivity and oversight criteria and priorities for global programs established by the Development Committee and the Bank, particularly the Bank's Development Grant Facility (DGF)
- To derive crosscutting lessons for the Bank on program selectivity, design, implementation,

governance, management, financing, and evaluation
- To assess progress in implementing the recommendations of OED's 1998 grant program review, Phase 1 report, and meta-evaluation of the CGIAR, with respect both to the Bank's strategic and programmatic management and to the choice, design, and implementation of individual programs (box ES.1).
- To identify areas where further Bank action on its global-level strategy and programming is needed to improve global program effectiveness.

Management of Bank involvement in global programs. The architecture for Bank involvement in global programs has been evolving since 2000. The selectivity, oversight, and eligibility criteria (figure ES.1 and box ES.2) were developed at different times and in different contexts, and are applied in different ways. The Phase 2 evaluation applied these 3 sets of criteria as appropriate to the 26 programs and developed lessons for the future strategic directions for the Bank's involvement in global programs.

The scope of Bank involvement in global programs has also been increasing. Today, global partnerships have become an important line of Bank business. At the time this was being written, the Bank was engaged in more than 200 partnerships; about 70 of these meet the definition of a global program. The Bank also manages the largest amount of trust fund monies ($7.1 billion as of June 2004) of any international organization; 64 percent of this support goes to global and regional programs (compared with 57 percent last year). Trust fund disbursements to global and regional activities increased by $400 million to $1.2 billion in FY04. Much of this was directed toward the Global Fund to Fight AIDS, Tuberculosis, and Malaria (GFATM).

Brief Overview of the 26 Case Study Programs

In 2002, the 26 programs represented 90 percent of the annual expenditures of Bank-supported global programs. The programs vary by subject area; institutional location; number and types of partners; and organizational design, financing, and implementation. They range in age from 2 to 32 years, and in size from $560,000 to $447 million in annual expenditures.

The selected programs are concentrated in the Environmentally and Socially Sustainable Development (ESSD) Network (71 percent of total program expenditures and 67 percent of DGF grants in FY03). This is comparable to the overall distribution of global programs. The next-largest concentration is in health (22 percent of total program expenditures, excluding GFATM). The health, trade, and social protection programs are housed in the concerned U.N. agencies. All infrastructure programs and some others (in environment, finance, and social development) are housed in the Bank. A few programs involved in capacity building have recently been spun off from the Bank. Figure ES.2 summarizes the activities of the 26 evaluated programs.

Box ES.1 OED's Phase 1 Recommendations and Management Action

Since OED's Phase 1 report, Bank management has adopted several organizational and procedural changes in the management of global programs. Management has established a Global Programs and Partnerships Council (chaired by two managing directors), reconstituted a Concessional Financing and Global Partnerships Vice Presidency, and formed a Global Programs and Partnerships Group within this vice presidency. Management also indicated that it would strengthen oversight to enhance the strategic focus of the Bank's global portfolio and apply the subsidiarity principle more rigorously. The Development Grant Facility has instituted an external peer-review process for new programs seeking grant support. In response to OED's meta-evaluation of the CGIAR, Bank management accepted the principle of independent oversight by assigning oversight of the CGIAR to the Bank's chief economist. This last change is still being implemented.

Figure ES.1 Selectivity and Oversight of Global Programs

Selectivity Criteria for Bank Involvement in Global Public Goods: Endorsed by Development Committee (September 2000)[a]

1. An emerging international consensus that global action is required
2. A clear value added to the Bank's development objectives
3. The need for Bank action to catalyze other resources and partnerships
4. A significant comparative advantage for the Bank.

Approval Criteria for Bank Involvement in Partnership Initiatives beyond the Country Level, Established by Bank Management (November 2000)[b]

1. A clear link to the Bank's core institutional objectives and, above all, to the Bank's country work
2. A strong case for Bank participation based on comparative advantage
3. A clear assessment of the financial and reputational risks to the Bank and how these will be managed
4. A thorough analysis of the expected level of Bank resources (both money and time) required and the contribution of other partners
5. A clear delineation of how the new commitment will be implemented, managed, and assessed
6. A clear plan for communicating with and involving key stakeholders and for informing and consulting the Executive Directors.

Global Public-Goods Priorities[c]

Communicable diseases
- HIV/AIDS, tuberculosis, malaria, and childhood communicable diseases, including the relevant link to education
- Vaccines and drug development for major communicable diseases in developing countries

Environmental commons
- Climate change
- Water
- Forests
- Biodiversity, ozone depletion, and land degradation
- Promoting agricultural research

Information and knowledge
- Redressing the digital divide and equipping countries with the capacity to access knowledge
- Understanding development and poverty reduction

Trade and integration
- Market access
- Intellectual property rights and standards

International financial architecture
- Development of international standards
- Financial stability (incl. sound public debt management)
- International accounting and legal framework

Strategic Focus for Oversight of Global Programs: Established by Bank Management (March 2003)

a. Provide global public goods

b. Support international advocacy for reform agendas that in a significant way address policy framework conditions relevant for developing countries

c. Are multicountry programs that crucially depend on highly coordinated approaches

d. Mobilize substantial incremental resources that can be used for development

Corporate Advocacy Priorities[c]

Empowerment, security, and social inclusion
- Gender mainstreaming
- Civic engagement and participation
- Social risk management (including disaster mitigation)

Investment climate
- Support to both urban and rural development
- Infrastructure services to support private sector development
- Regulatory reform and competition policy
- Financial sector reform

Public sector governance
- Rule of law (including anti-corruption
- Public administration and civil service reform (including public expenditure accountability)
- Access to, and administration of, justice (judicial reform)

Education
- Education for all, with emphasis on girls' education
- Building human capacity for the knowledge economy

Health
- Access to potable water, clean air, and sanitation
- Maternal and child health

a. From the Development Committee Communiqué issued on September 25, 2000. Both the Development Committee and Bank Management envisaged global programs as being the principal instrument for Bank involvement in providing global public goods.

b. Global programs are expected to meet all six approval criteria.

c. These are the five corporate advocacy priorities and the five global public goods priorities (and bulleted sub-categories) from the *Strategic Directions Paper for FY02-04* (World Bank 2001b). Within the Partnership Approval and Tracking System (PATS), global programs are expected to identify, for tracking, their alignment with at least one of these 10 corporate priorities.

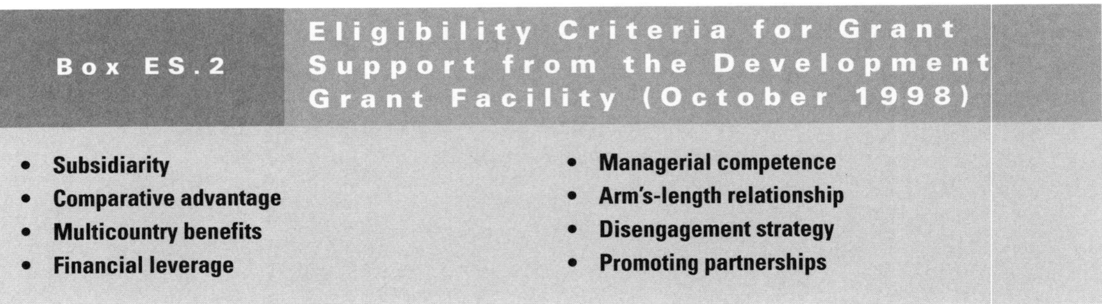

Box ES.2 Eligibility Criteria for Grant Support from the Development Grant Facility (October 1998)

- **Subsidiarity**
- **Comparative advantage**
- **Multicountry benefits**
- **Financial leverage**
- **Managerial competence**
- **Arm's-length relationship**
- **Disengagement strategy**
- **Promoting partnerships**

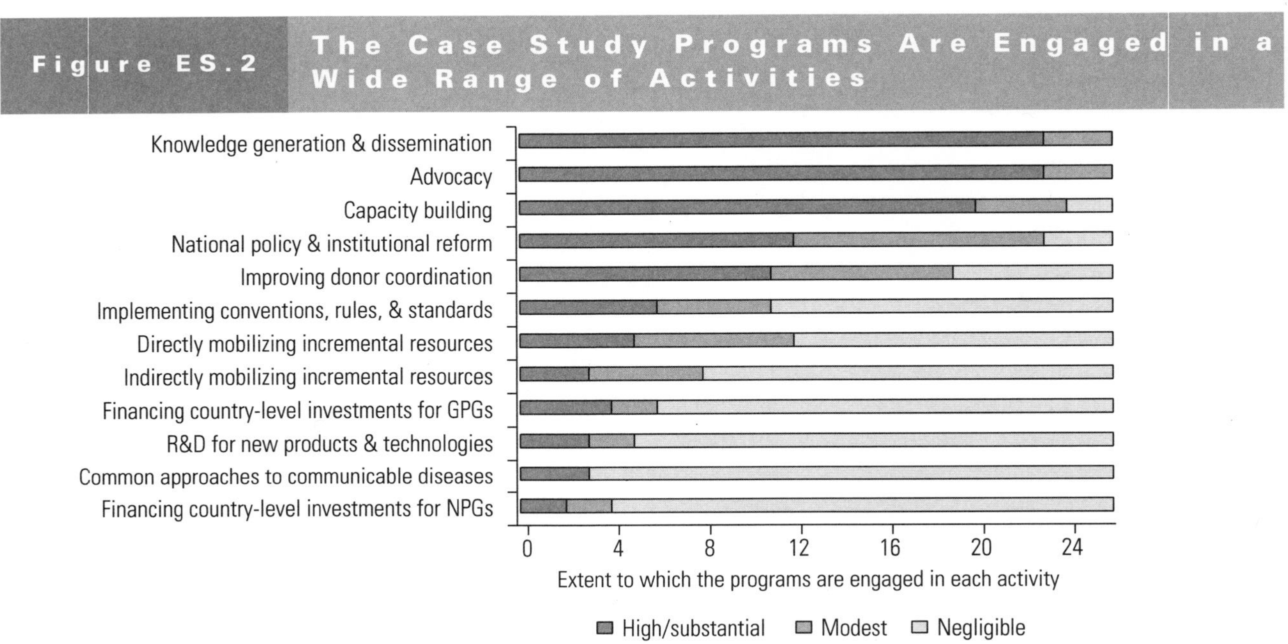

Source: Table H.8: OED assessment of programs' actual activities.

Each program conducts many different kinds of activities, but two dimensions of global programming are important from a strategic and programmatic perspective:

- Whether each program primarily aims to provide global public goods that require global collective action or to engage in "corporate advocacy" in support of the provision of national and local public, private, or merit goods. Programs in this latter category must pass the test of subsidiarity. That is, the benefits of collective action relative to the transaction costs of global partnerships to partners (including developing countries) must exceed the net benefits of the Bank acting through its normal instruments.
- Whether the programs have their own financing mechanism or rely on the investments or technical assistance of others (for example, Bank loans and credits, or donor or national funding).

Global public goods represent a minority of programs, but a majority of funds. When their most essential characteristics are considered, only 11 programs (including a part of the Global Alliance for Vaccines and Information—GAVI) provide global public goods (figure ES.3). Of these, only seven finance global or country investments. Only GAVI finances such investments on a significant scale at both levels, and hence is included in both global and national public-goods programs. The other four global public-goods programs promote common approaches to mitigating major communicable diseases or research on the diseases of the poor. They *advocate increased public investments by others* to combat communicable diseases, but, unlike GAVI, they do not finance investments at either level. The seven global and the two national public-goods programs that do finance investments (with GAVI being included in both) undertook 83 percent of the total expenditures of the case study programs in FY04 (figure ES.4). The remaining 18 *programs not financing investments* (including the 4 programs in health mentioned above) primarily finance activities related to information and knowledge, advocacy, capacity building, and technical assistance.

Figure ES.3 Corporate Advocacy Programs Dominate in Numbers

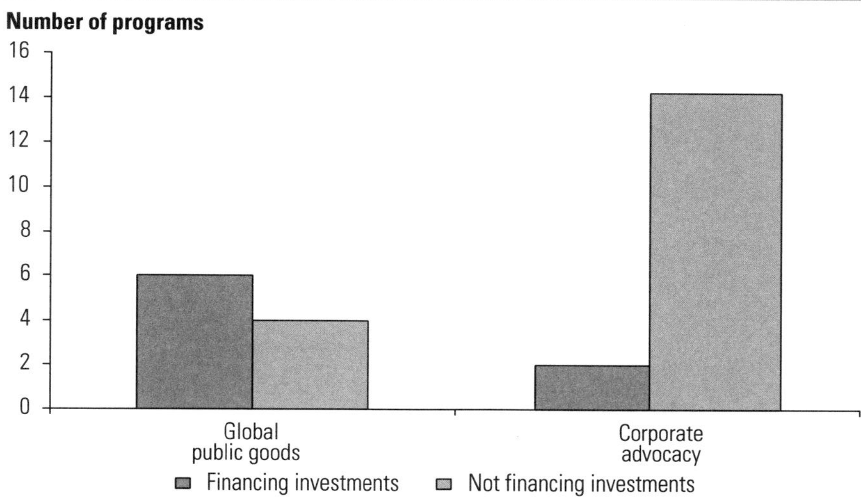

Figure ES.4 Global Public Goods Command Major Share of Expenditures

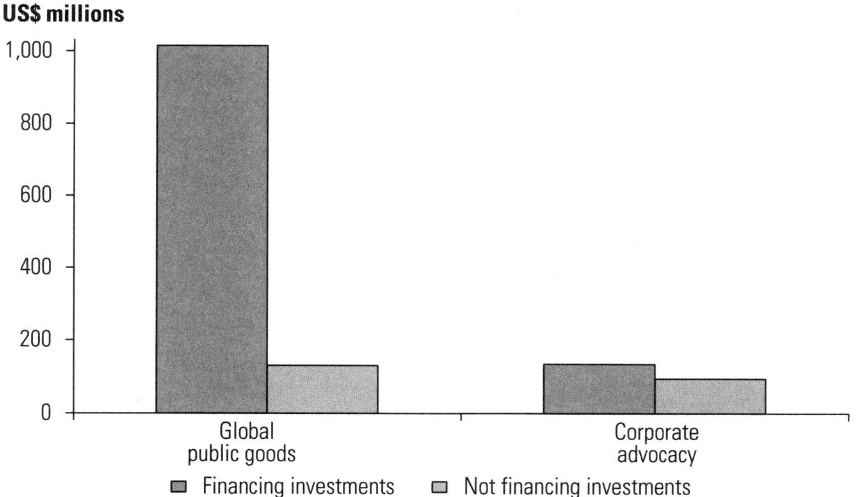

These programs stimulate country demand for additional technical assistance, training, and capacity building, but lack resources to meet it. The programs thus rely on donors, including the Bank, for complementary investments. While the programs expect that complementary activities will be included in Poverty Reduction Strategy Papers (PRSPs) and Country Assistance Strategies (CASs), such inclusion has thus far been limited, reflecting the weak link between multicountry advocacy programs and country activities.

OED Findings

Selectivity

"Letting a thousand flowers bloom" and experimenting with many new programs has helped the Bank understand the diversity and complexity of global challenges and provided opportunities to learn about the intricacy of global-country links. This has informed both the formulation and the refinement of the Bank's selectivity criteria.

Global public-goods programs meet most criteria. While largely supply-driven, most Bank-supported global public-goods programs, including the Multilateral Fund for the Implementation of the Montreal Protocol (MLF), the Global Environmental Fund (GEF), Prototype Carbon Fund (ProCarbFund) and Critical Ecosystem Partnership Fund (CEPF), CGIAR, the Special Program for Research and Training in Tropical Diseases (TDR), the Joint United Nations Program on HIV/AIDS (UNAIDS), Stop TB, Roll Back Malaria, the Global Forum for Health Research, and the Global Alliance for Vaccines and Immunization's (GAVI's) Global Research Funding, *largely meet the four Development Committee criteria for selectivity*. Most global programs also *largely meet* the approval and eligibility criteria for Bank involvement. CGIAR does not meet the arm's-length criterion; the Bank did not involve developing country stakeholders in CEPF's establishment or its global-level governance; the Bank did not do a thorough analysis of the expected level of Bank resources required for the health programs, or of how to implement and manage this new commitment. These are exceptions to the general rule, however.

The corporate advocacy programs meet the Development Committee selectivity criteria. This is largely because the criteria are broad and difficult to apply precisely. For example, the first criterion—"an international consensus that global action is required," which all programs claim as their raison d'être—provides no basis for selectivity because the concept of international consensus is amorphous and loosely applied. The case studies illustrate that the consensus is often driven by constituencies in donor countries and the staff of international agencies. At the same time, few of the networks demand links to country operations, one of the most important criteria, before approval, nor do they track them during implementation.

The Bank deploys its comparative advantages more at the global level than at the country level. Financial and reputational risks and budgetary and staffing implications are rarely sufficiently assessed. The international consensus on the existence of a problem is usually strong; consensus on what collective action is required is often weak. Many global programs are implicitly (sometimes explicitly) established to promote consensus, to "harmonize" donor approaches to specific problems, to delineate donor comparative advantages in addressing those problems, and to give the donors specialized knowledge to use on the problems. Capacity building in the recipient countries is secondary in such projects.

Evidence is lacking that the programs are exploiting economies of scale and scope in such activities as knowledge creation and dissemination, capacity building, technical assistance, and donor coordination. It is also not clear whether the knowledge they disseminate is sufficiently evidence-based, quality-tested, and contextual to add value to what the Bank's client countries themselves do, need, or want, or what the Bank can achieve working through country-level partnerships. Performance indicators to assess changed donor or international agency behavior do not exist. Performance indicators, when they exist at all, are focused on the behavior of developing countries. OED was able to identify only a few program-specific indicators of changed Bank and donor practices, procedures, and actions in response to the advocacy of global programs. In the case of corporate advocacy programs, the needs of the Bank's client countries should be the prime consideration for Bank involvement.

The voices of developing countries, or even those of the Bank's operational Regions, are inadequately represented in the international consensus. Case studies of many of these corporate advocacy programs show that including developing-country voices at the concept stage enhances program ownership, makes the organizational design more effective, and increases program impacts. Based on the evidence OED has provided so far, management has acknowledged the need to strengthen the role of developing countries and the Bank's operational Regions in global programs.

Value Added to the World Bank's Development Objectives

Evidence varies on the value added to the Bank's development objectives, but it is growing. Some programs lack clearly defined objectives, and others have many unstated objectives; this makes it difficult to judge what value they have added. It is difficult to assess many young programs that have not had time to demonstrate impacts. However, evaluations are increasing, in part prompted by the DGF, and are beginning to affect program design and implementation. When programs do not meet all three requirements for effective evaluation—clear, shared, and measurable objectives; appropriate methodology; and measurable evidence—their global impacts remain unclear.

Programs delivering global public goods often add value. Global public-goods programs (CGIAR, TDR, MLF, parts of GEF, and even some new global health programs) rate well in their impacts on reducing poverty or on focusing on the policy, institutional, infrastructural, or technological constraints developing countries face in achieving sustainable economic growth. Adding value on the ground in client countries is typically a joint product of global and country-level activities. For example, CGIAR, like TDR, has demonstrated impressive poverty-reducing impacts in part because the Bank, donors, and some governments made complementary investments at the country level. However, as country-level investments have shrunk, donors have tried to compensate by encouraging CGIAR to move downstream. They have offered funding tied to research programs that demonstrate immediate impacts to push CGIAR toward more national- and local-level applied and adaptive work. Management agrees that the activities of several CGIAR research centers now resemble those that regular Bank instruments would support through country-level investments.

Programs close to the Bank currently add more value. Not surprisingly, the programs for which the Bank is an implementing agency are more closely linked with Bank operations than are other programs. This is in part because the Bank is better at absorbing and using information and findings produced internally or nearby. The Bank needs to devise ways to increase its links to programs more distant from it. Keeping the governance of global programs at arm's length from the Bank and maintaining clear accountability for program performance offer the greatest potential for bringing new information and fresh perspectives to Bank operations.

Global programs have revealed major investment gaps. Evidence indicates that investments in health research have substantial poverty-reducing impacts. The current global policy and aid environment has huge *investment gaps at the global level* in the provision of global health research, as well as *gaps in complementary investments at the country level*. Health research, like agricultural research, is a long-term activity that the private sector is unlikely to address on the scale needed.

Global programs have also revealed gaps in global public policy. Several global programs highlight the existence of global public-policy gaps—often involving developed-country policies in trade, aid, finance, and intellectual-property rights—that affect developing countries. Few programs regard it as within their mandate to address these policy gaps. If changing the international ground rules is the objective of the programs, and if advocacy is the means to achieve it, then the programs should be assessed on their ability to deliver changed policies or a changed global environment from the perspective of the poor.

Governance, Management, and Financing

Governance is weak in several programs. While pure shareholder models of program governance are being replaced by stakeholder models, programs are still struggling to balance legitimacy and accountability for results with efficiency in achieving them. The permanent members of the programs' governing bodies, who tend to be the major international organizations and donors, have greater de facto responsibility, relative to the rotating members, to ensure that programs are successful. But such responsibility and accountability are rarely clearly articulated. Lack of effective governance and management must be addressed if the Bank's financial support is to continue.

Management arrangements can alter perceived and actual responsibilities. When the Bank or another international organization chairs programs that they house, this reduces the responsibility for shared governance. When programs are housed in the Bank or other international organization, the program manager often reports both to the programs' governing body and to a line manager in the housing organization. This situation often places responsibility for both management and oversight in the same management chain, which in turn creates real or perceived conflicts of interest in monitoring performance.

Global programs have increased overall aid very little. At the aggregate level, global programs have added little new money to ODA. Exceptions include funds from private sources for the Prototype Carbon Fund; from the Gates Foundation for health; and small amounts from pharmaceutical companies through new public-private partnerships for drug and vaccine development. Given the opportunity cost of ODA funds, the Bank's involvement in programs with important goals but little demonstrated value needs reconsideration. In some cases, too close an association with the Bank has hampered mobilization of other funds for these programs. It is time to move from "letting a thousand flowers bloom" to assessing which programs deserve continuing Bank support, and which do not.

World Bank Performance

Bank performance in global programs is better at the global than at the country level. Other partners view the Bank's leadership role, its financial clout, its access to policymakers, its operational support, and its fiduciary oversight as a seal of approval, giving them the confidence to invest in global programs, both in-house and externally managed. Even at the global level, though, the Bank's performance can be improved, particularly with respect to strategy, independent oversight, and global-country linkages.

The recent reforms are promising. The establishment of the Global Programs and Partnership Council, together with the GPP Group, is a positive development. In line with the Phase 1 report's recommendation, the GPP Council could help oversee the development of the Bank's global strategy, anticipate changes in the global environment, and help set priorities and funding strategies. It can move global programs from the current network perspective to a Bankwide perspective and establish Bankwide standards for global programming and performance. The Bank still needs to strengthen its appraisal of new programs and to make its selectivity, oversight, evaluation, and exit strategies more transparent and results based. Finally, assessment and oversight of complex global partnerships requires expert knowledge and *input*, not only from the program managers who promote them, but also from other partners, developing countries, and experts in the field.

Independent oversight is needed. The Bank needs to institute independent oversight of all its programs—in the case of in-house programs, by senior managers outside the line management of the vice presidency handling the program. Oversight of both externally managed and in-house programs needs to be guided by clear terms of reference and have the necessary budget and accountability for performance. Independent oversight is particularly important early on to ensure that programs get off to a good start. Bank management also needs to institute routine procedures of quality assurance, internal audits, risk assessment, and risk management.

Exit strategies of programs are not working well. The Bank's record in managing the separation of in-house programs from the Bank needs improvement. For example, the mechanical, hands-off, three-year rule for DGF Window 2 programs has not facilitated orderly financial exits. More attention needs to be paid to strengthening governance and sustainable financing of the programs being spun off.

The Bank's strategy for global programs is poorly defined. The Bank has lacked, but clearly needs, a global strategy that is developed in conjunction with its key partners and draws on the capacity of its central vice presidencies, network anchors, and Regions to do so. The strategy needs to address the coherence, or lack thereof, between global expectations (particularly in the donor community) and the needs of developing countries. At its center, the global strategy needs a clear focus on sustainable, poverty-reducing growth in the Bank's client countries; on global policy issues that prevent such growth; and on mobilizing incremental, unrestricted funding to address global issues that are of high priority for developing countries. Such a strategy will not simply emerge from improved selectivity or oversight of individual global programs—it must be worked out. Furthermore, strengthening oversight in the absence of an overall strategy risks micromanaging the global program portfolio.

OED Recommendations

Strategic Framework for the Bank's Involvement in Global Programs

1. In consultation with U.N. agencies, donors, developing countries, and other partners, management should develop a global strategy for the Bank's involvement in global programs, approved by the Board and periodically updated, that:
   - Exploits the Bank's comparative advantage as a multisectoral development financing institution with a global reach and strong capacity in policy analysis
   - Gives greater prominence to alleviating poverty and to addressing global public policies that limit developing countries' prospects for rapid, sustainable, poverty-reducing growth
   - Fosters stronger links between global programs and the Bank's Regional and country operations in prioritizing its global programming activities
   - Ensures that global programs add value beyond what the Bank can accomplish through partnerships at the country level.

Linking Financing to Priorities

2. Management should develop a financing plan for high-priority programs, particularly for those providing genuine global public goods, whether in the form of global policies, new products, technologies, knowledge, or practices that benefit the poor. This requires:
   - Identifying under-funded long-term global public-goods programs that benefit the poor—such as a global health research and a product-development network for diseases that disproportionately affect the poor—and using the Bank's convening power to mobilize additional resources for them
   - Improving the criteria and procedures relating to the DGF's Window 2 to create a more rational and informed approach to funding "venture capital" programs, in which the DGF only provides initial support
   - Developing a policy on the use of trust funds in the context of the overall strategy for global programs.

Selectivity and Oversight of the Global Program Portfolio

3. Management should establish approval, oversight, evaluation, and exit/reauthorization cri-

teria and procedures for Bank-supported global programs that will help them to add value to the Bank's mission. This includes:

- Streamlining and clarifying the eligibility and approval criteria for Bank selectivity and grant support and instituting a two-stage approval process for global programs at the concept and appraisal stages
- Sharpening and more rigorously applying the subsidiarity criterion for approval and grant support
- Separating Bank oversight from the implementing management and, for Bank staff serving on the governing bodies of global programs, clarifying their roles, responsibilities, and accountabilities through standard terms of reference and training
- Allocating money for oversight and money that the network anchor and Regional staff can use to operationalize global programs in the Bank's Regional operations
- Instituting clear, well-planned, and well-executed reauthorization/exit processes and ensuring that the programs the Bank spins off have an independent identity, accountability for results, and a good chance of succeeding.

Governance and Management of Individual Programs

4. Management should work with its global partners to develop and apply universally accepted standards of good governance, management, results-orientation, and evaluation to all Bank-supported global programs. These include:
   - Legal status and/or written charters as appropriate
   - Transparent selection criteria and processes for board chairs and board members; clarifying their roles, responsibilities, accountabilities, and constituencies; and giving them authority to direct and oversee the program, its policies, and its budget
   - Voice of the Bank's client countries on the governing bodies of global programs for better balance between developed and developing countries
   - Guidelines on conflicts of interests, on the roles of NGOs and the private sector in governing bodies, and on the roles and quality of advisory boards
   - Designation of evaluation and auditing as functions of the governing body, not the program management, with results that should routinely be made available to program financiers and other stakeholders.

Evaluation

5. OED should include global programs in its standard evaluation and reporting processes. This includes:
   - Working with the Bank's global partners to develop international standards for the evaluation of global programs
   - Reviewing selected program-level evaluations conducted by Bank-supported global programs (both internally and externally managed), much as OED reviews other self-evaluations at the project and country levels.

Résumen ejecutivo

El ritmo acelerado de la globalización ha promovido cambios drásticos en el comercio, las finanzas, la propiedad intelectual, la inversión del sector privado, la tecnología de la información y las comunicaciones, la salud, el medio ambiente, la seguridad y la sociedad civil. Para poder enfrentar los desafíos que presenta la globalización normalmente se requiere la acción colectiva en el ámbito mundial. Los programas mundiales se utilizan cada día más como un medio para organizar la acción colectiva, en particular para la provisión de bienes públicos mundiales.

Los programas mundiales también han trascendido la provisión de bienes públicos mundiales para cumplir otros objetivos que tradicionalmente eran abordados por el Banco Mundial mediante operaciones específicas para países. Los programas dirigidos a varios países que "promueven el desarrollo institucional" se proponen aprovechar las economías de escala y de alcance en la provisión de servicios específicos en cada país y promover políticas que redunden en beneficio de los países en desarrollo.

Resulta difícil satisfacer la creciente demanda de programas mundiales, debido a la ausencia de un gobierno mundial con autoridad para establecer y hacer cumplir políticas y normas, cobrar impuestos y recaudar ingresos. El estancamiento de la asistencia oficial para el desarrollo (AOD) acrecienta el desafío, aunque los programas mundiales, tanto los que se centran en la provisión de bienes públicos mundiales como los programas dirigidos a múltiples países, absorben una mayor proporción de la AOD.

El Banco Mundial es un participante importante de estas actividades mundiales dado que su alcance internacional, su poder de convocatoria, su capacidad para movilizar recursos y su conocimiento práctico de múltiples sectores hacen que esté en condiciones de enfrentar los desafíos de la globalización. El Directorio Ejecutivo del Banco ha planteado diversos temas e inquietudes acerca de los programas de asociaciones mundiales en franco aumento. Estos temas han servido de guía para la evaluación del DEO sobre la participación del Banco en tales programas. El informe de la fase 1 abordó diversos aspectos estratégicos y programáticos. La metaevaluación del GCIAI puso de manifiesto los desafíos que enfrenta un programa mundial en este entorno interno y externo modificado. Este informe de la fase 2 sintetiza los resultados del examen de 26 programas realizado por el DEO.

Los objetivos específicos de este informe son los siguientes:

- Evaluar hasta qué punto estos programas tomados para el estudio de casos cumplen con los criterios de selectividad y supervisión y con las prioridades de los programas mundiales, definidos por el Comité para el Desarrollo y por el Banco, en particular el Fondo de Donaciones para el Desarrollo.
- Recoger lecciones interdisciplinarias sobre la selectividad, el diseño, la implementación, el gobierno, la gestión, el financiamiento y la evaluación de programas.
- Medir el avance realizado en la implementación de las recomendaciones del examen de proceso realizado por el DEO en 1998, y de la metaevaluación del GCIAI, en relación con la gestión estratégica y programática del Banco y la elección, el diseño e implementación de programas individuales (recuadro RE.1).
- Identificar áreas en donde se requiere una mayor intervención del Banco en su estrategia y programación mundial a fin de mejorar la eficacia de los programas mundiales.

Gestión de la participación del Banco en los programas mundiales. La arquitectura de la participación del Banco en programas mundiales ha ido evolucionando desde 2000. Los diversos criterios de selectividad, supervisión y admisibilidad (figura RE.1 y recuadro RE.2) se desarrollaron en diferentes momentos y contextos, y se aplican de diferentes maneras. La evaluación de la fase 2 aplicó estos tres grupos de criterios, según su pertinencia, a los 26 programas, y extrajo lecciones para las futuras orientaciones estratégicas de la participación del Banco en los programas mundiales.

El alcance de la participación del Banco en los programas mundiales ha ido en aumento. En la actualidad, las asociaciones mundiales se han transformado en una línea de actividad importante del Banco. A la fecha de elaboración de este informe, el Banco participaba en más de 200 asociaciones, 70 de las cuales cumplían con la definición de un programa mundial. Además, el Banco administra la mayor cantidad de fondos fiduciarios (US $7.100 millones en junio de 2004) de toda organización internacional, de los cuales el 64 por ciento se destinan a programas mundiales y regionales (frente a 57 por ciento el año anterior). Los desembolsos de los fondos fiduciarios con destino a actividades mundiales y regionales aumentaron en US $400 millones a US $1.200 millones en el ejercicio fiscal 2004. Gran parte de estos fondos se destinaron al Fondo Mundial de Lucha contra el SIDA, la Tuberculosis y la Malaria.

Recuadro RE.1 Recomendaciones de la fase 1 del DEO y respuesta de la administración

A partir del informe del DEO de la fase 1, la administración del Banco ha incorporado varios cambios en la organización y en los procedimientos de la gestión de los programas mundiales (estos cambios se describen en el memorando de marzo de 2003 dirigido a los directores ejecutivos, "Update on Management of Global Programs and Partnerships" [Actualización sobre la gestión de los programas y asociaciones mundiales]). La administración ha creado un Consejo de Asociaciones y Programas Mundiales (presidido por dos gerentes generales), ha restablecido la vicepresidencia de Financiamiento Concesional y Asociaciones Mundiales, y creado el Grupo de Asociaciones y Programas Mundiales que depende de dicha vicepresidencia. La administración también declaró que fortalecería la supervisión para potenciar el enfoque estratégico de la cartera mundial del Banco y aplicar el principio de subsidiaridad de manera más rigurosa. El Fondo de Donaciones para el Desarrollo ha establecido un proceso de revisión externa de pares para los nuevos programas que procuran la asistencia de donantes. En respuesta a la metaevaluación del GCIAI que realizó el DEO, la administración del Banco aceptó el principio de supervisión independiente, asignándole la supervisión del GCIAI al Primer Economista del Banco. Esta última modificación aún está en proceso de implementación.

Figura RE.1 Selectividad y supervisión de los programas mundiales

Criterios de selectividad para la participación del Banco en los bienes públicos mundiales: Respaldado por el Comité para el Desarrollo (septiembre de 2000)[a]

1. Consesnso internacional que requiere de acción global
2. Un valor agregado claro para los objectivos de desarrollo del Banco
3. Necesidad de acción del Banco como catalizador de otros recursos y associaciones
4. Una ventaja comparativa significativa para el Banco

Criterios para la aprobación de la participación del banco en las iniciativas de asociación que trascienden el nivel de país, establecidos por la dirección del Banco (noviembre de 2000)[b]

1. Un vínculo claro con los objetivos institucionales básicos del Banco y, por sobre todo, con el trabajo del Banco por país
2. Argumentos sólidos para la participación del Banco en función de su ventaja comparativa
3. Una evaluación clara de los riesgos financieros y para la reputación del Banco, y de la manera en que se gestionarán
4. Un análisis claro del nivel previsto de recursos del Banco (de tiempo y dinero), y de la contribuciones de los otros asociados
5. Un descripción clara de la implementación, gestión y evaluación del nuevo compromiso
6. Un plan claro para comunicarse con las principales partes interesadas, y promover su participación, así como para informar y consultar a los directores ejecutivos

Prioridades de bienes públicos mundiales[c]

Enfermedades transmisibles
- VHI/SIDA, tuberculosis, malaria y enfermedades transmisibles en menores, incluido el vínculo relevante con la educación
- Desarrollo de vacunas y medicamentos para las principales enfermedades

Aspectos de medio ambiente
- Cambio climático
- Agua
- Bosques
- Biodiversidad, degradación de la tierra y agotamiento de la capa de ozono
- Promoción de la investigación agropecuaria

Información y conocimiento
- Cómo cerrar la brecha digital y dotar a los países con la capacidad para acceder al conocimiento
- Desarrollo y reducción de la pobreza

Comercio e integración
- Acceso a mercados
- Derechos de propiedad intelectual y normativa

Arquitectura financiera internacional
- Elaboración de normas internacionales
- Estabilidad financiera (incluida la gestión responsable de la deuda pública)
- Marco internacional de normas contables y legales

Enforque estatégico para la supervisión de programas mundiales: establecido por la administración del Banco (marzo de 2003)

a. Proveer bienes públicos mundiales

b. Respaldar la promoción internacional para la reforma de la agendas que, de alguna menara, abordan las condiciones del marco normativo relevante para los países en desarrollo

c. Son programas destinados a múltiples países que dependen necesariamente de enfoques estrechamente coordinados

d. Movilizar recursos incrementales sustanciales que pueden emplearse con eficacia para el desarrollo

Prioridades de promoción del desarrollo institucional[c]

Empoderamiento, seguridad e inclusión social
- Integración del género
- Compromiso cívico
- Gestión del riesgo social (incluida la mitigación de desastres)

Clima de inversión
- Apoyo para el desarrollo urbano y rural
- Servicios de infraestructura para apoyar el desarrollo del sector privado
- Reforma normativa y política de competencia
- Reforma del sector financiero

Gobierno del sector público
- Estado de derecho (incluida la lucha contra la corrupción)
- Reforma de la administración y la función pública (incluida la rendición de cuentas del gasto público)
- Acceso y administración de la justicia (reforma judicial)

Educación
- Educación para todos, con especial énfasis en la educación de las niñas
- Fortalecimiento de la capacidades para la economía del conocimiento

Salud
- Acceso a agua potable, aire puro y sanidad
- Salud materna e infantil

a. Del Comunicado del Comité para el Desarrollo emitido el 25 de septiembre de 2000. Tanto el Comité para el Desarrollo como la administración del Banco conciben a los programas mundiales como el instrumento principal de la participación del Banco en la provisión de los bienes públicos mundiales.

b. Los programas mundiales deben cumplir con los seis criterios de aprobación.

c. Estas son las cinco prioridades en la promoción del desarrollo institucional y las cinco prioridades en la provisión de bienes públicos mundiales (y sus subcategorías ordenadas con viñetas) que se definen en el *Documento de Orientación Estratégica 2002-2004* (Banco Mundial 2001b). Dentro del Sistema de Seguimiento y Aprobación de Asociaciones (*Partnership Approval and Tracking System o PATS*), los programas mundiales deben identificar, para fines de seguimiento, su alineación con al menos una de estas 10 prioridades institucionales.

Recuadro RE.2

Criterios para recibir apoyo del Fondo de Donaciones para el Desarrollo (octubre de 1998)

- Subsidiaridad
- Ventaja comparativa
- Beneficios para múltiples países
- Apalancamiento financiero
- Competencia de gestión
- Relación de independencia
- Estrategia de salida
- Promoción de asociaciones

Breve descripción de los 26 programas tomados para el estudio de casos

En 2002, los 26 programas representaban el 90 por ciento del gasto anual de los programas mundiales respaldados por el Banco. Los programas varían en función del área temática, la ubicación institucional, el número y clase de asociados, y el diseño, financiamiento e implementación de la organización. Tienen una antigüedad de dos a 32 años y el volumen de gasto anual oscila entre US $560.000 y US $447 millones.

Los programas seleccionados se concentran en la red de Desarrollo Ambiental y Socialmente Sostenible (ESSD) (71 por ciento del gasto total de programas y 67 por ciento de las donaciones del Fondo de Donaciones para el Desarrollo en el ejercicio fiscal 2003). Esta proporción es semejante a la distribución general de los programas mundiales. La segunda concentración en importancia es en el sector de salud (22 por ciento del gasto total destinado a programas, excluido el Fondo Mundial de Lucha contra el Sida, la Tuberculosis y la Malaria). Los programas para la salud, el comercio y la protección social tienen su sede en los órganos de las Naciones Unidas pertinentes. Todos los programas de infraestructura y algunos otros (de desarrollo ambiental, financiero y social) tienen su sede en el Banco. Recientemente, algunos programas para el fortalecimiento de capacidades se han separado del Banco. La figura RE.2 resume las actividades de los 26 programas evaluados.

Cada programa lleva a cabo gran variedad de actividades, pero en los programas mundiales hay dos dimensiones importantes desde la óptica estratégica y programática:

- Si el objetivo primordial del programa es proveer bienes públicos mundiales para los cuales se requiere la acción colectiva mundial, o bien "fomentar el desarrollo institucional" para respaldar la provisión de bienes públicos, privados o de mérito, en el ámbito nacional o local. Los programas que se encuadran en esta segunda categoría deben cumplir con el requisito de subsidiaridad. Es decir que, para los asociados (incluidos los países en desarrollo), la relación entre los beneficios de la acción colectiva y los costos de transacción de las asociaciones mundiales, debe exceder los beneficios netos que se obtendrían si el Banco actuara mediante sus mecanismos habituales.
- Si los programas tienen su propio mecanismo de financiamiento o si dependen de inversiones o de la asistencia técnica de terceros (por ejemplo, préstamos y créditos del Banco, financiamiento nacional o de donantes).

Los programas de bienes públicos globales representan una minoría, pero absorben la mayor parte de los fondos. Al evaluar sus características fundamentales, se observa que apenas 11 programas (incluida una parte de la Alianza Mundial para Vacunas e Inmunización, GAVI) proveen bienes públicos mundiales (figura RE.3). De estos, sólo siete financian inversiones mundiales o en un país. Únicamente la Alianza GAVI proporciona financiamiento en gran escala para tales inversiones, en ambos niveles, y por ello se encuadra en los programas de bienes públicos mundiales y nacionales. Los otros programas de bienes públicos mundiales promueven enfoques comunes para mitigar las principales enfermedades transmisibles, o la investigación de las enfermedades que afligen a los pobres. *Promueven mayores inversiones públicas de terceros* para luchar contra las enfermedades transmisibles, pero a diferencia de la GAVI, no financian las inversiones en

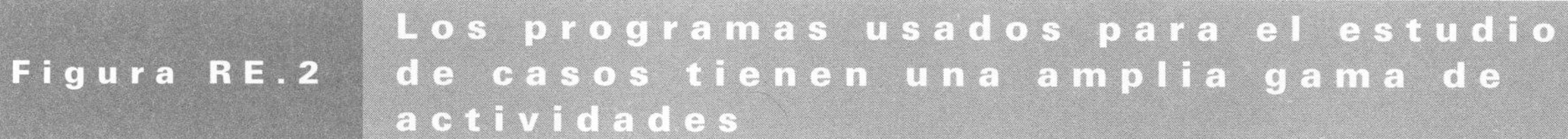

Figura RE.2
Los programas usados para el estudio de casos tienen una amplia gama de actividades

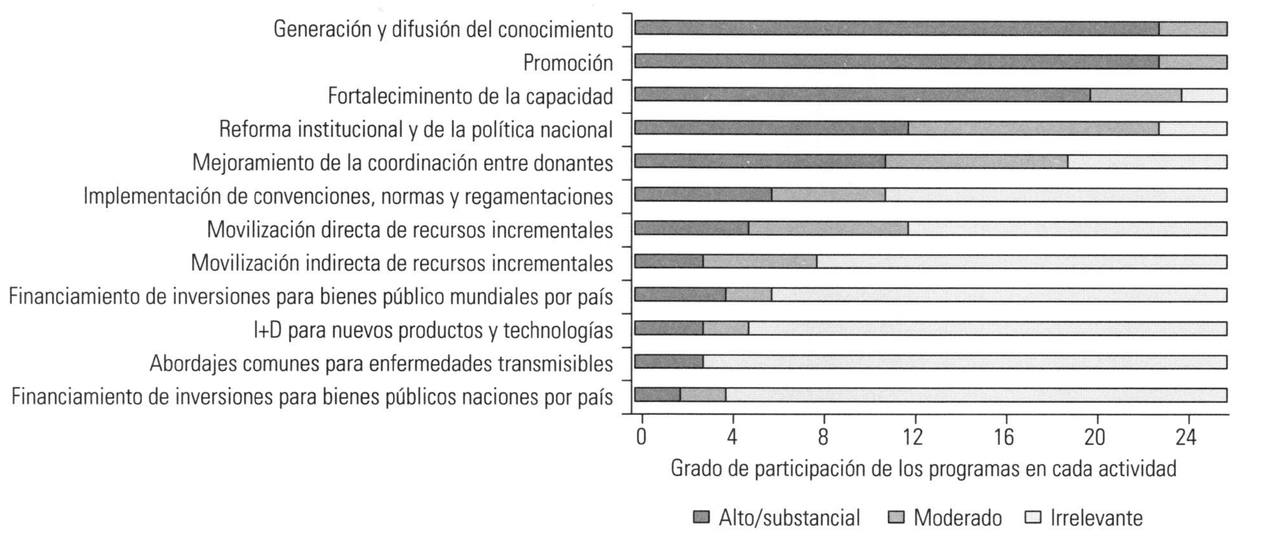

Fuente: Cuadro H.8: Evaluación del DEO sobre las actividades de los programas.

Figura RE.3 Los programas de promoción son amplia mayoría

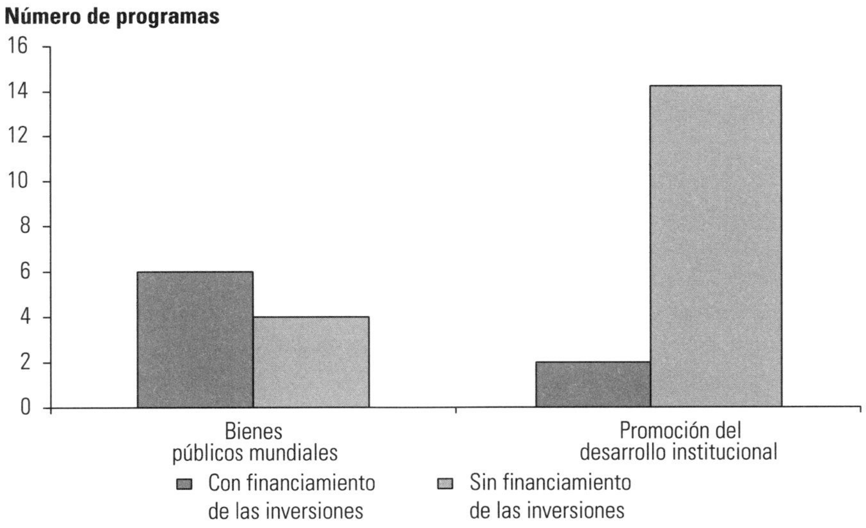

ningún ámbito. Los siete programas de bienes públicos mundiales y los dos de bienes públicos nacionales que efectivamente financian inversiones (incluido el GAVI en ambas categorías) comprometieron el 80 por ciento del gasto total de los programas usados para el estudio de casos en el ejercicio fiscal 2003 (figura RE.4). Los 18 *programas restantes que no financian inversiones* (incluidos los cuatro programas de salud antes mencionados) fundamentalmente financian actividades relacionadas con la información y el conocimiento, la promoción del desarrollo

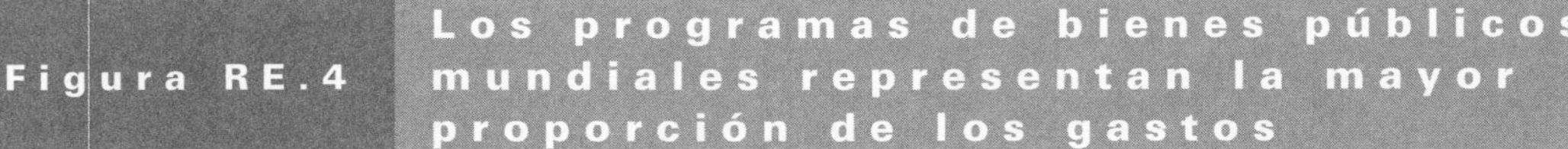

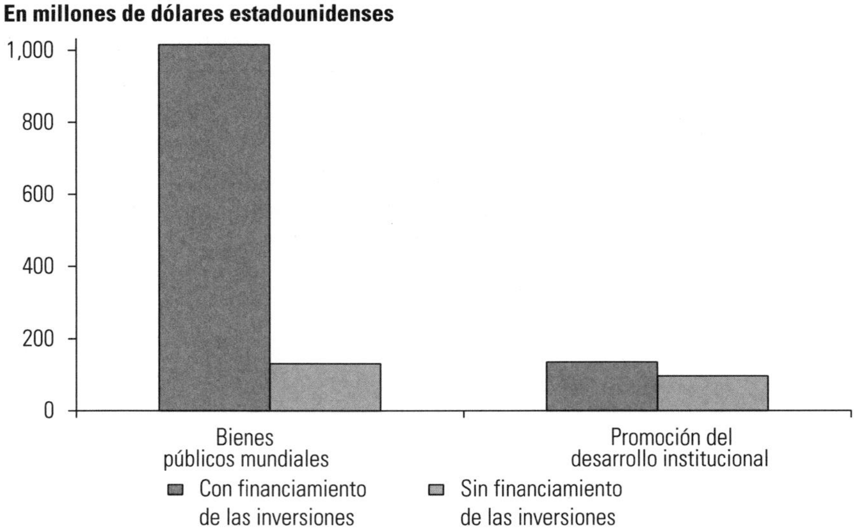

institucional, el fortalecimiento de las capacidades y la asistencia técnica.

Estos programas estimulan la demanda de mayor asistencia técnica, capacitación y fortalecimiento de las capacidades por parte de los países, pero carecen de los recursos para satisfacerla. Por esa razón dependen de los donantes, incluido el Banco, para que realicen las inversiones complementarias. Si bien los programas pretenden que las actividades complementarias se incluyan en los DELP y los EAP, hasta el momento su inclusión se ha visto limitada, lo que refleja el vínculo débil que existe entre los programas dirigidos a varios países y las actividades por país.

Conclusiones del DEO

Selectividad

La "proliferación" y experimentación con muchos programas nuevos ha permitido que el Banco comprendiera la diversidad y complejidad de los desafíos que se plantean en el ámbito mundial, y ha generado oportunidades para aprender los intrincados vínculos que existen entre la esfera mundial y la nacional. Esto ha sido instructivo tanto para la formulación como para el perfeccionamiento de los criterios de selectividad del Banco.

Los programas de bienes públicos mundiales cumplen con la mayoría de los criterios. Pese a estar impulsados fundamentalmente desde la oferta, la mayoría de los programas de bienes públicos mundiales respaldados por el Banco (el Fondo Multilateral, Fondo para el Medio Ambiente Mundial, Fondo Tipo del Carbono y el Fondo de Asistencia para Ecosistemas Críticos, el Grupo Consultivo sobre Investigaciones Agrícolas Internacionales, programa de investigación de enfermedades tropicales, ONUSIDA, la iniciativa Alto a la Tuberculosis, la iniciativa Hacer Retroceder la Malaria, el Foro Mundial para la investigación de salud y el Financiamiento de la investigación mundial de la GAVI) *cumplen mayormente con los cuatro criterios de selectividad del Comité para el Desarrollo*. La mayoría de los programas mundiales también cumplen en gran parte con los criterios de aprobación y admisibilidad para la participación del Banco. El GCIAI no cumple con el criterio de independencia; el Banco no promovió la participación de partes interesadas de países en desarrollo en el establecimiento del Fondo para Alianzas Estratégicas en Ecosistemas Críticos (CEPF, por sus siglas en inglés) ni en su gobierno en el ámbito mundial; el Banco no analizó en forma exhaustiva el nivel estimado de recursos del Banco que serían necesarios para los programas de salud, ni la forma de implementación y gestión de este nuevo compromiso. Sin embargo, éstas son excepciones a la regla.

Los programas de promoción del desarrollo institucional cumplen con los criterios de selectividad del Comité para el Desarrollo. Esto obedece en gran medida a que los criterios son generales y no es fácil aplicarlos con precisión. Por ejemplo, el primer criterio - "consenso internacional sobre la necesidad de acción mundial", que todos los programas proclaman como su razón de ser – no constituye una base para la selectividad del programa, ya que el concepto de consenso internacional es amorfo y se aplica con poca rigurosidad. Los estudios de casos indican que el consenso normalmente surge de los representantes de países donantes y del personal de los organismos internacionales. Por otra parte, pocas redes requieren vínculos con las operaciones para países, uno de los criterios más importantes, antes de la aprobación, y no hacen un seguimiento durante la etapa de ejecución.

El Banco aprovecha sus ventajas comparativas más en el ámbito mundial que en el nacional. Prácticamente nunca se evalúan lo suficiente los riesgos financieros y para la reputación, como así tampoco las repercusiones presupuestarias y de personal. El consenso internacional sobre la existencia de un problema suele ser fuerte; el consenso sobre la acción colectiva necesaria suele ser débil. Muchos programas mundiales se establecen en forma implícita (en ocasiones explícita) para promover consenso, "armonizar" la forma en que los donantes abordan los problemas específicos, describir las ventajas comparativas de los donantes al abordar tales problemas, y dotar a los donantes de conocimiento especializado para usar en la resolución de los problemas. En esos proyectos, el fortalecimiento de las capacidades en los países beneficiarios pasa a ocupar un segundo plano.

No hay pruebas suficientes de que los programas exploten economías de escala y de alcance en actividades como la creación y difusión del conocimiento, el fortalecimiento de las capacidades, la asistencia técnica y la coordinación de los donantes. No queda claro si el conocimiento que difunden se fundamenta en pruebas, se someten a control de calidad y se define conceptualmente, en forma suficiente, para añadir valor a las acciones, necesidades u objetivos de los países clientes del Banco, o a los logros que puede alcanzar el Banco trabajando mediante asociaciones para países. Se carece de indicadores de desempeño para evaluar el cambio de actitud de los donantes o de los organismos internacionales. Los indicadores de desempeño, en caso de existir, se centran en el comportamiento de los países en desarrollo. El DEO pudo identificar únicamente unos pocos indicadores específicos por programa que miden el cambio en las prácticas, procedimientos y acciones del Banco y de los donantes, en respuesta a la promoción de los programas mundiales. En el caso de programas de promoción del desarrollo institucional, las necesidades de los países clientes del Banco deberían ser la consideración primordial para decidir la participación del Banco.

La ingerencia de los países en desarrollo, o incluso de las regiones operativas del Banco, no está adecuadamente representada en el consenso internacional. Los estudios de casos de muchos de estos programas de promoción del desarrollo institucional indican que la inclusión de los países en desarrollo en la etapa de desarrollo conceptual potencia la identificación con el programa, aumenta la eficacia del diseño orgánico y los impactos en el programa. En función de la evidencia presentada por el DEO hasta el momento, la administración ha reconocido la necesidad de fortalecer la función de los países en desarrollo y las regiones operativas del Banco en los programas mundiales.

Valor agregado para los objetivos de desarrollo del Banco Mundial

El valor agregado que se ha comprobado para los objetivos de desarrollo del Banco varía según el programa, pero está en franco aumento. Algunos programas carecen de objetivos claramente definidos, y otros tienen muchos objetivos no declarados; por ello es difícil determinar su valor agregado. Resulta difícil evaluar muchos programas recientes que no han tenido tiempo suficiente para demostrar sus impactos. Sin embargo, las evaluaciones están aumentando, en parte inducidas por el Fondo de Donaciones para el Desarrollo (DGF, por sus siglas en inglés), y comienzan a afectar el diseño y la implementación de programas. Cuando los programas no cumplen con todos los requisitos de una evaluación eficaz – objetivos claros, compartidos y mensurables; metodología adecuada; y evidencia mensurable – su impacto en el ámbito global sigue siendo poco claro.

Los programas que proveen bienes públicos mundiales suelen agregar valor. Los programas de bienes públicos mundiales (el GCIAI, el Programa de investigación de enfermedades tropicales (TDR), el Fondo Multilateral, partes del Fondo para el Medio Ambiente Mundial, e incluso algunos nuevos programas mundiales de salud) logran tener un impacto satisfactorio en la reducción de la pobreza o concentrarse en las limitaciones normativas, institucionales, de infraestructura y tecnología de los países desarrollo que dificultan la consecución de un crecimiento económico sostenible. El hecho de agregar valor en los propios países clientes normalmente es producto de las actividades en el ámbito mundial y nacional. Por ejemplo, el GCIAI, al igual que el TDR, han demostrado tener un impacto significativo en la reducción de la pobreza, en parte porque el Banco, los donantes y algunos gobiernos realizaron inversiones complementarias en el ámbito nacional. Sin embargo, dado que las inversiones en el ámbito nacional se han reducido, los donantes han procurado contrarrestar esta situación alentando al GCIAI a ocuparse de actividades secundarias. Han ofrecido financiamiento reservado para programas de investigación con impactos inmediatos evidentes, para llevar al GCIAI a un trabajo más adaptativo con aplicación en el orden nacional y local. La administración coincide en que las actividades de varios centros de investigación del GCIAI actualmente se asemejan a aquellos que los instrumentos normales del Banco respaldarían mediante inversiones en programas para países.

Los programas cercanos al Banco actualmente tienen mayor valor agregado. Como es de esperar, los programas en donde el Banco es el organismo ejecutor tienen vínculos más estrechos con las operaciones del Banco. Esto se debe, en parte, a que el Banco incorpora y utiliza mejor la información y las conclusiones que se originan en el ámbito interno o cercano. El Banco debe implementar mecanismos para aumentar sus vínculos con programas que son menos cercanos. El gobierno independiente de los programas mundiales fuera del seno del Banco y la rendición clara de cuentas para el desempeño de programas ofrecen enormes posibilidades de incorporar información nueva y otros puntos de vista a las operaciones del Banco.

Los programas mundiales han dejado al descubierto grandes brechas de inversión... Se ha comprobado que las inversiones en investigación en el sector de salud tiene gran impacto en la reducción de la pobreza. La política mundial actual y el contexto de la ayuda presentan *enormes brechas de inversión en el orden mundial* para la investigación mundial en materia de salud, como también *brechas en las inversiones complementarias en el ámbito nacional.* La investigación en el sector de salud, al igual que la investigación en el sector agrícola, es una actividad de largo plazo que el sector privado difícilmente emprenda en la escala necesaria.

... como así también brechas en la política pública mundial. Varios programas mundiales hacen hincapié en la existencia de brechas en la política pública mundial, que normalmente incluye las políticas comerciales, asistenciales, de finanzas y derechos de propiedad intelectual de países desarrollados - que afectan a los países en desarrollo. Son pocos los programas que incorporan dentro de su mandato la tarea de cerrar estas brechas. Si el objetivo de los programas consiste en modificar las directrices internacionales, y si la promoción del desarrollo institucional es el medio para lograrlo, entonces los programas deben evaluarse en función de su capacidad para lograr la modificación de políticas o del marco mundial, desde la perspectiva de los pobres.

Gobierno, gestión y financiamiento

El gobierno es débil en varios programas. Si bien los modelos de gobierno puramente accionario son reemplazados por modelos de partes interesadas, los programas aún pugnan por lograr el equilibrio entre la legitimidad y la rendición de cuentas de resultados, por un lado, y la eficiencia para su consecución, por el otro. Los miembros permanentes de los órganos de gobierno de los programas, que habitualmente son las principales organizaciones y donantes internacionales, tienen mayor responsabilidad de hecho que los miembros alternos, para garantizar el éxito de los programas. Pero dicha responsabilidad y rendición de cuentas pocas veces se definen con claridad. Es preciso abordar la falta de un gobierno y una gestión eficaces para que pueda continuar el apoyo financiero del Banco.

Las disposiciones en materia de gestión pueden modificar las responsabilidades reales y las percibidas. Cuando el Banco u otro organismo internacional ejerce la presidencia en programas que albergan en su propio seno, se reduce la responsabilidad de un gobierno compartido. Cuando los programas tienen su sede en el Banco u otros organismos internacionales, el gerente del programa suele estar bajo las órdenes del órgano de gobierno del programa y de un gerente de línea en la organización que sirve alberga el programa. Como consecuencia, la responsabilidad por la gestión y la supervisión tiende a recaer en la misma cadena gerencial, lo que a su vez crea conflictos de intereses reales o presuntos en el seguimiento del desempeño.

Los programas mundiales han aumentado muy poco la asistencia en general. En su conjunto, los programas mundiales han añadido pocos fondos nuevos a la asistencia oficial para el desarrollo. Entre las excepciones se incluyen fondos del sector privado para el Fondo Tipo del Carbono; de la Fundación Gates para programas de salud; y pequeñas sumas de dinero aportadas por empresas farmacéuticas mediante asociaciones de colaboración entre el sector público y privado para el desarrollo de vacunas y medicamentos. Dado el costo de oportunidad de los fondos de la AOD, debe reconsiderarse la participación del Banco en programas con objetivos importantes, pero de escaso valor probado. En algunos casos, la existencia de una asociación muy estrecha con el Banco ha obstaculizado la movilización de otros fondos para estos programas. Ha llegado el momento de pasar de "privilegiar la proliferación de programas" a evaluar qué programas merecen seguir recibiendo el apoyo del Banco y cuáles no.

Desempeño del Banco Mundial

El Banco ha tenido un mejor desempeño en el ámbito mundial que en el nacional en relación con los programas mundiales. Otros socios perciben la función de liderazgo del Banco, su peso en materia financiera, su acceso a los responsables de la formulación de políticas, su asistencia operativa y su supervisión fiduciaria como un sello de aprobación, que les inspira confianza para invertir en los programas mundiales que se administran dentro o fuera del seno del Banco. Sin embargo, incluso en el ámbito mundial es posible mejorar el desempeño del Banco, particularmente en lo que atañe a la estrategia, la supervisión independiente y los vínculos entre la esfera mundial y la nacional.

Las reformas recientes son prometedoras. El establecimiento del Consejo de Asociaciones y Programas Mundiales, junto con el Grupo GPP (Bienes Públicos Mundiales) es una medida positiva en ese sentido. En sintonía con la recomendación del informe de la fase 1, el Consejo GPP podría ayudar a supervisar el desarrollo de la estrategia mundial del Banco, prever cambios en el entorno mundial y contribuir a establecer prioridades y definir estrategias de financiamiento. Puede modificar la perspectiva de red que tienen actualmente los programas mundiales por una perspectiva integradora, y definir normas que rijan en todo el Banco para el establecimiento de programas mundiales y su desempeño. El Banco todavía necesita fortalecer la evaluación inicial de nuevos programas y dar mayor transparencia a sus estrategias de selectividad, supervisión, evaluación y salida, además de una mayor orientación a la obtención de resultados. Por último, la evaluación y supervisión de asociaciones mundiales complejas requiere el conocimiento de expertos y la opinión no sólo de los gerentes de programas que los promueven sino también de otros asociados, países en desarrollo y expertos en la materia.

Se requiere una supervisión independiente. Es preciso que el Banco establezca la supervisión independiente de todos sus programas; en el caso de tratarse de programas dentro el seno del Banco, la supervisión debe estar a cargo de gerentes principales ajenos a la línea gerencial de la vicepresidencia que tiene a su cargo el programa. La supervisión de programas con gestión externa e interna debe guiarse por términos de referencia claros, contar con el presupuesto necesario y rendir cuentas por su desempeño. La supervisión independiente es particularmente importante en las primeras etapas a fin de garantizar que los programas tengan un buen comienzo. La administración del Banco también tiene que establecer procedimientos de rutina para control de calidad, auditorías internas, evaluación y gestión del riesgo.

Las estrategias de salida de los programas no funcionan bien. El Banco debe gestionar mejor la escisión de los programas internos. Por ejemplo, la norma mecánica teórica de tres años para los programas de la Ventanilla 2 del Fondo de Donaciones para el Desarrollo no ha facilitado salidas financieras ordenadas. Debe prestarse más atención a fortalecer el gobierno y el financiamiento sostenibles de los programas que se escinden.

La estrategia del Banco para los programas mundiales no se define con claridad. El Banco carece, pero sin duda necesita una estrategia mundial que se formule conjuntamente con sus principales asociados y se nutra de las capacidades existentes en las vicepresidencias centrales, los coordinadores de las redes y las regiones. La estrategia debe abordar la coherencia, o incoherencia, entre las expectativas mundiales (particularmente en la comunidad de donantes) y las necesidades de los países en desarrollo. En esencia, la estrategia mundial necesita un enfoque claro en el crecimiento sostenible que ayude a reducir la pobreza en los países clientes del Banco; en los problemas de política mundial que impiden el crecimiento; y en la movilización de financiamiento incremental no sujeto a restricciones para abordar los problemas mundiales que tienen máxima prioridad para los países en desarrollo. Una estrategia con esas características no surgirá simplemente de mejorar la selectividad o la supervisión de cada programa mundial; es preciso reformularla. Por otra parte, con el fortalecimiento de la supervisión sin una estrategia general, se corre el riesgo de microgestionar la cartera de programas mundiales.

Recomendaciones del DEO

Marco estratégico de la participación del Banco en los programas mundiales

1. Previa consulta con los organismos de las Naciones Unidas, los donantes, los países en desarrollo, y otros asociados, la administración debería elaborar una estrategia mundial para la participación del Banco en los programas mundiales, aprobados por el Directorio y actualizada en forma periódica, que:
   - Aproveche la ventaja comparativa del Banco como institución de financiamiento para el desarrollo multisectorial con alcance mundial y sólida capacidad para el análisis de políticas.
   - Dé mayor prominencia al alivio de la pobreza y aborde las políticas públicas mundiales que limitan las posibilidades de los países en desarrollo para alcanzar un crecimiento rápido, sostenible y que reduzca la pobreza.
   - Fomente vínculos más fuertes entre los programas mundiales y las operaciones regionales y nacionales del Banco al priorizar las actividades de programación mundial.
   - Asegure que los programas mundiales agreguen valor más allá de los logros que pueda alcanzar el Banco mediante asociaciones de orden nacional.

Vinculación del financiamiento con las prioridades

2. La Dirección debe elaborar un plan de financiamiento para programas de alta prioridad, en particular para aquellos que proveen bienes públicos mundiales genuinos, ya sea en la forma de políticas mundiales, nuevos productos, tecnologías, conocimiento o prácticas que benefician a los pobres. Para ello es preciso:
   - Identificar programas de bienes públicos mundiales a largo plazo que beneficien a los pobres con financiamiento insuficiente,

como es la red mundial de desarrollo de productos e investigación en el sector de salud para aquellas enfermedades que afectan a los pobres en forma desmedida, y usar el poder de convocatoria del Banco para movilizar recursos adicionales.
- Mejorar los criterios y procedimientos relacionados con la Ventanilla 2 del DGF, a fin de crear un enfoque más racional e informado para el financiamiento de programas de "capital de riesgo", en donde el DGF se limite a proporcionar el apoyo inicial.
- Desarrollar una política que rija el uso de los fondos de fideicomisos en el marco de la estrategia general para los programas mundiales.

Selectividad y supervisión de la cartera de programas mundiales

3. La administración debe establecer criterios de aprobación, supervisión, evaluación y salida/nueva autorización, y procedimientos para los programas mundiales respaldados por el Banco, que le permitirán agregar valor a la misión del Banco. Esto conlleva:
   - Racionalizar y clarificar los criterios de admisibilidad y aprobación para la selectividad del Banco y el acceso a las donaciones, y establecer un proceso de aprobación de dos etapas para los programas mundiales, en las etapas de definición conceptual y de evaluación inicial.
   - Agudizar y aplicar con mayor rigurosidad el criterio de selectividad para la aprobación y el apoyo financiero mediante donaciones.
   - Separar la función de supervisión del Banco de la gestión de la ejecución; y para el personal del Banco que desempeña funciones en órganos de gobierno de los programas mundiales, clarificar sus funciones, responsabilidades y rendición de cuentas mediante términos de referencia estándar y capacitación.
   - Asignar fondos para supervisión, y fondos que podrán ser utilizados por el coordinador de la red y el personal regional a fin de operativizar los programas mundiales en la órbita de las operaciones regionales del Banco.
   - Establecer procesos de reautorización/salida claros, bien planificados y ejecutados, y garantizar que los programas que se escinden del Banco tienen identidad independiente, rinden cuenta por sus resultados y tienen buenas probabilidades de éxito.

Gobierno y gestión de los programas individuales

4. La administración debe trabajar con sus socios mundiales para desarrollar y aplicar normas de aceptación universal de buen gobierno, gestión, orientación a los resultados y evaluación a todos los programas mundiales respaldados por el Banco. Para ello se requieren:
   - Personalidad jurídica o actas constitutivas, o ambos, según corresponda.
   - Criterios y procesos de selección transparentes para los presidentes y miembros de directorios; clarificar sus funciones, responsabilidades, rendición de cuentas y representaciones; y facultarlos para dirigir y supervisar el programa, sus políticas y su presupuesto.
   - Ingerencia de los países clientes del Banco en los órganos de gobierno de los programas mundiales, para un mejor equilibrio entre los países desarrollados y en desarrollo.
   - Directrices que rijan los conflictos de intereses, las funciones de las ONG y del sector privado en los órganos de gobierno, y las funciones y calidad de los consejos de asesoría.
   - Determinación de las funciones de evaluación y auditoría dentro de las funciones del órgano de gobierno, no la dirección del programa; los resultados deben ponerse a disposición de las instituciones que financian el programa y de otras partes interesadas en periodicidad regular.

Evaluación

5. El DEO debe incluir los programas mundiales en sus procesos estándar de evaluación e información. Esto supone:
   - Trabajar con los socios mundiales del Banco para desarrollar normas internacionales para la evaluación de programas mundiales.

- Examinar evaluaciones de programas seleccionadas realizadas por programas mundiales respaldados por el Banco (con gestión fuera y dentro del seno del Banco), así como el DEO examina otras autoevaluaciones en el plano de proyectos y operaciones para países.

Résumé analytique

Le rythme de plus en plus rapide de la mondialisation a engendré des changements spectaculaires dans le domaine du commerce, des finances, de la propriété intellectuelle, des investissements privés, de la technologie de l'information et des communications, de la santé, de l'environnement, de la sécurité et de la société civile. Aborder les défis posés par la mondialisation requiert souvent une action collective au niveau mondial. Des programmes mondiaux sont de plus en plus souvent utilisés pour organiser l'action collective mondiale, en particulier pour fournir des biens publics mondiaux.

Les programmes mondiaux ont également été au-delà de la fourniture de biens publics mondiaux pour servir d'autres objectifs que la Banque mondiale a généralement abordés par le biais de ses opérations au niveau national. De tels programmes multinationaux et de « défense générale » cherchent à tirer profit des économies d'échelle et d'envergure en fournissant des services au niveau national et en défendant des politiques qui profitent aux pays en développement.

Il est difficile de répondre à la demande croissante de programmes mondiaux, en l'absence d'un gouvernement mondial habilité à établir et à appliquer des régimes et règlements politiques, à percevoir des impôts et à générer des recettes. La stagnation de l'aide publique au développement (APD) aggrave le problème, bien que les programmes mondiaux – tant les programmes de biens publics mondiaux que les programmes multinationaux – participent aujourd'hui davantage à l'APD.

La Banque mondiale est un acteur important de ces activités mondiales car sa portée mondiale, son pouvoir de rassemblement, sa capacité à mobiliser les ressources et son expertise multisectorielle la placent dans une bonne position pour aborder les défis posés par la mondialisation. Le Conseil des administrateurs de la Banque mondiale a soulevé une variété de problèmes et d'inquiétudes quant au nombre croissant de programmes de partenariat mondiaux de la Banque mondiale. Ces problèmes ont guidé l'évaluation de l'OED de la participation de la Banque mondiale à des programmes mondiaux. Le rapport sur la phase 1 a abordé plusieurs problèmes stratégiques et programmatiques. La méta-évaluation du GCRAI a illustré les problèmes que rencontre un programme mondial dans cet environnement interne et externe différent. Le rapport sur la phase 2 synthétise les résultats de l'examen des 26 programmes par l'OED.

Les objectifs spécifiques de ce rapport sont les suivants:

- Évaluer la mesure dans laquelle les programmes d'études de cas sont à la hauteur des critères et des priorités de sélectivité et de surveillance des programmes mondiaux établis par le Comité pour le développement et la Banque mondiale, en particulier la DGF (Development Grant Facility).
- Tirer des leçons transversales pour la Banque mondiale sur la sélectivité, la conception, l'application, la gouvernance, la gestion, le financement et l'évaluation des programmes.
- Évaluer les progrès dans la mise en œuvre des recommandations de l'examen de la procédure de 1998 de l'OED, du rapport sur la phase 1 et de la méta-évaluation du GCRAI concernant la gestion stratégique et programmatique et le choix, la conception et la mise en œuvre de programmes individuels (encadré RA.1).
- Identifier des domaines requérrant une action plus poussée de la Banque mondiale au niveau de la programmation et de la stratégie mondiale afin d'améliorer l'efficacité des programmes mondiaux.

Gestion de la participation de la Banque mondiale à des programmes mondiaux. L'architecture de la participation de la Banque mondiale à des programmes mondiaux a évolué depuis 2000. Les différents critères de sélectivité, de surveillance et d'éligibilité (tableau RA.1 et encadré RA.2) ont été développés à différents moments et dans différents contextes et ils sont appliqués de manières différentes. L'évaluation de la phase 2 a appliqué ces trois séries de critères selon le cas aux 26 programmes et a tiré des leçons pour les orientations stratégiques futures de la participation de la Banque mondiale à des programmes mondiaux.

L'ampleur de la participation de la Banque mondiale à des programmes mondiaux a également été de plus en plus importante. Aujourd'hui, les partenariats mondiaux sont devenus une ligne importante des activités de la Banque mondiale. Au moment de la rédaction de ce document, la Banque mondiale participait à plus de 200 partenariats, dont environ 70 répondent à la définition d'un programme mondial. La Banque mondiale est également l'organisation internationale qui gère la plus grande quantité de fonds fiduciaires (7,1 milliards en juin 2004), dont 64 % sont destinés à des programmes régionaux et mondiaux (contre 57 % l'année dernière). Les décaissements de fonds fiduciaires pour des activités régionales et mondiales ont augmenté de 400 millions de dollars à 1,2 mil-

Encadré RA.1 Recommandations et action de gestion de la phase 1 de l'OED

Depuis le rapport sur la phase 1 de l'OED, la direction de la Banque mondiale a procédé à plusieurs changements de procédure et d'organisation dans la gestion des programmes mondiaux (ces changements sont soulignés dans un mémorandum de mars 2003 à l'attention des directeurs exécutifs, « Mise à jour sur la gestion des programmes et des partenariats »). La direction de la Banque mondiale a instauré un Conseil des programmes et des partenariats mondiaux (présidé par deux directeurs généraux), a reconstitué une vice-présidence des partenariats mondiaux et du financement concessionnel et a créé un Groupe des programmes et des partenariats mondiaux au sein de cette vice-présidence. La direction de la Banque mondiale a également signalé qu'elle renforcerait la surveillance afin d'améliorer l'accent stratégique du portefeuille mondial de la Banque mondiale et qu'elle appliquerait le principe de subsidiarité de manière plus rigoureuse. La DGF a établi une procédure externe de révision par les pairs pour les nouveaux programmes à la recherche de subventions. En réponse à la méta-évaluation du GCRAI de l'OED, la direction de la Banque mondiale a accepté l'idée d'une surveillance indépendante en attribuant la surveillance du GCRAI à l'économiste en chef de la Banque mondiale. Ce dernier changement est toujours en cours d'application.

Tableau RA.1 Sélectivité et surveillance des programmes mondiaux

Critères de sélectivité pour la participation de la Banque mondiale à des biens publics mondiaux : Avalisés par le Comité pour le développement (septembre 2000)[a]

1. Un nouveau consensus international sur la nécessité d'une action mondial
2. Une valeur ajoutée claire aux objectifs de développement de la Banque mondiale
3. La nécessité que l'action de la Banque mondiale catalyse d'autres ressources et partenariats
4. Un avantage comparatif important pour la Banque mondiale

Critères d'approbation de la participation de la Banque mondiale à des initiatives de partenariat au-delà du niveau national, établis par la direction de la Banque mondiale (novembre 2000)[b]

1. Un lien clair avec les princiapux objectifs institutionnels de la Banque mondiale et, surtout, avec le travail de la Banque mondiale au niveau national
2. Des solides arguments en faveur de la participation de la Banque mondiale se basant sur un avantage comparatif
3. Une évaluation claire des risques financiers et de réputation pour la Banque mondiale et la manière dont ils seront gérés
4. Un analyse approfondie du niveau prévu de ressources nécessaires de la Banque mondiale (en temps et en argent) et de la contribution d'autres partenaires
5. Un exposé clair de la manière dont le nouvel engagement sera mis en œuvre, géré et évalué
6. Un plan clair de communication avec les principaux intervenants (avec la participation de ceux-ci) et d'information et de consultation des directeurs exécutifs

Priorités des biens publics mondiaux[c]

Maladies transmissibles
- VIH/SIDA, tuberculose, paludisme et maladies transmissibles de l'enfance, y compris le lien pertinent avec l'éducation
- Développement de vaccins et de médicaments pour les principales maladies transmissibles dans les pays en développement

Patrimoine environnemental commun
- Changement climatique
- Eau
- Forêts
- Biodiversité, baisse de l'ozone et dégradation des sols
- Promotion de la recherche agricole

Information et connaissances
- Combler le fossé numérique et équiper les pays en capacités d'accès aux connaissances
- Comprendre le développement et la réduction de la pauvreté

Commerce et intégration
- Accès aux marchés
- Normes et droits de propriété intellectuelle

Architecture financière internationale
- Développement de normes internationales
- Stabilité financière (y compris gestion saine de la dette publique)
- Comptabilité internationale et cadre juridique

Accent stratéguqie pour la surveillance des programmes mondiaux : établi par la direction de la Banque mondiale (mars 2003)

a. Fournir des biens publics mondiaux

b. Soutenir la défense internationale pour la réforme des programmes qui abordent de manière importante les conditions du cadre politique pertinentes pour les pays en développement

c. Être des programmes multinationaux dépendant essentiellement d'approches hautement coordonnées

d. Mobiliser d'importantes ressources supplémentaires qui peuvent être utilisées de manière efficace pour le développement

Prioriés de défense générale[c]

Autonomisation, sécurité et inclusion sociale
- Intégration de la dimension de genre
- Participation et engagement civiques
- Gestion des risques sociaux (y compris atténuation des caatastrophes)

Climat d'investissement
- Soutenir le développement urbain et rural
- Services d'infrastructures pour soutenir le développement du secteur privé
- Politique de concurrence et réforme des règlements
- Réforme du secteur financier

Gouvernance du secteur public
- État de droit (y compris anti-corruption)
- Réforme de l'administration publique et de la fonction publique (y compris responsabilité des dépenses publiques)
- Accès à la justice et administration *de la justice (réforme judiciaire)*

Éducation
- Éducation pour tous, en particulier pour les filles
- Renforcement des capacités humaines pour l'économie de la connaissance

Santé
- Accès à l'eau potable, à l'air pur et à l'hygiène
- Santé des enfants et des mères

a. Du communiqué du Comité pour le développement émis le 25 septembre 2000. Le Comité pour le développement et la direction de la Banque mondiale ont examiné les programmes mondiaux comme étant le principal instrument de la participation de la Banque mondiale à la fourniture de biens publics mondiaux.

b. Les programmes mondiaux devraient répondre aux six critères d'approbation.

c.Il s'agit des cinq priorités de défense générale et des cinq priorités des biens publics mondiaux (et sous-catégories non numérotées) du *Document d'orientation stratégique pour les exercices 02-04* (Banque mondiale 2001b). Dans le cadre du Système d'approbation et de suivi des partenariats (PATS), les programmes mondiaux doivent identifier, à des fins de suivi, leur alignement sur une des dix priorités générales au moins.

Encadré RA.2 Critères d'éligibilité pour l'octroi de subventions de la Development Grant Facility (octobre 1998)

- **Subsidiarité**
- **Avantage comparatif**
- **Bénéfices multinationaux**
- **Effet de levier financier**
- **Compétence en gestion**
- **Relation sans lien de dépendance**
- **Stratégie de désengagement**
- **Promotion de partenariats**

liards de dollars pour l'exercice 2004. Une grande partie de ces fonds était destinée au Fonds mondial de lutte contre le SIDA, la tuberculose et le paludisme (GFATM).

Bref aperçu des 26 programmes d'études de cas

En 2002, les 26 programmes représentaient 90 % des dépenses annuelles des programmes mondiaux financés par la Banque mondiale. Les programmes varient selon le domaine, l'emplacement institutionnel, le nombre et le type de partenaires et la conception, le financement et la mise en œuvre organisationnels. Leur ancienneté varie de 2 à 32 ans et leur taille de 560.000 à 447 millions de dollars en dépenses annuelles.

Les programmes choisis se concentrent dans le réseau du développement durable au niveau social et environnemental (71 % des dépenses totales des programmes et 67 % des subventions de la DGF au cours de l'exercice 2003). Cela est comparable à la distribution globale des programmes mondiaux. La santé arrive en deuxième place (22 % des dépenses totales des programmes, à l'exception du GFATM). Les programmes de santé, de commerce et de protection sociale sont intégrés dans les agences de l'ONU concernées. Tous les programmes d'infrastructure et certains autres programmes (dans le domaine de l'environnement, des finances et du développement social) sont intégrés dans la Banque mondiale. Quelques programmes dans le domaine du renforcement des capacités ont récemment été séparés de la

Tableau RA.2 Les programmes d'études de cas sont engagés dans un large éventail d'activités

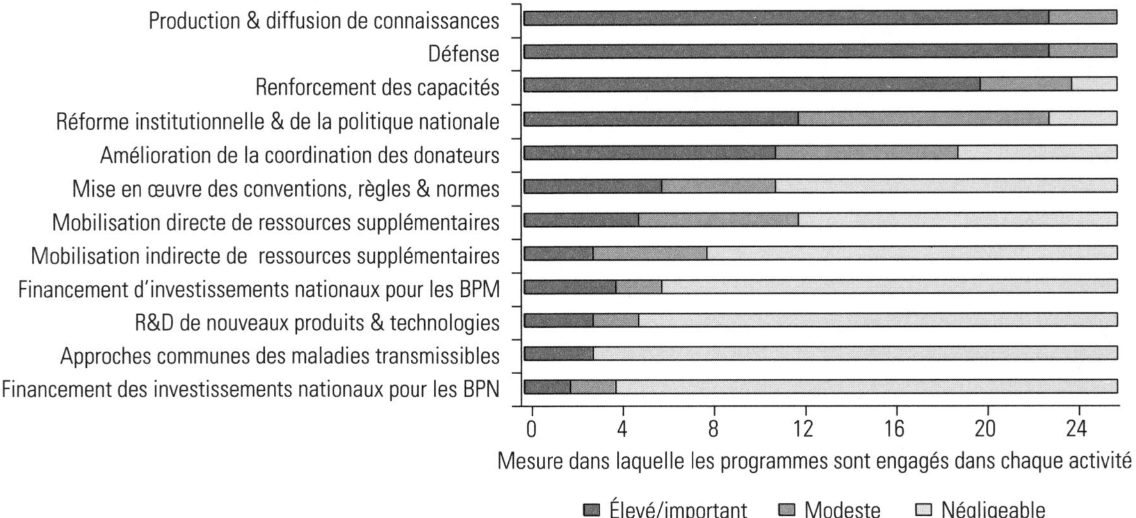

Source: Tableau H.8: Évaluation des activités annuelles des programmes par l'OED.

Banque mondiale. Le tableau RA.2 résume les activités dans lesquelles sont engagés les 26 programmes évalués.

Chaque programme réalise de nombreux types d'activités différents mais deux dimensions des programmes mondiaux sont importantes d'un point de vue stratégique et programmatique:

- Le fait de savoir si chaque programme vise essentiellement à fournir des biens publics mondiaux requérrant une action collective ou à s'engager dans une « défense générale » afin de soutenir la fourniture de biens privés, publics ou tutélaires locaux et nationaux. Les programmes de cette dernière catégorie doivent passer le test de la subsidiarité. En d'autres termes, les bénéfices d'une action collective relative aux frais de transaction des partenariats mondiaux pour les partenaires (y compris les pays en développement) ne doivent pas être supérieurs aux bénéfices nets d'une action de la Banque mondiale en utilisant ses instruments ordinaires.
- Le fait de savoir si les programmes ont leur propre mécanisme de financement ou s'ils se basent sur les investissements ou l'assistance technique de tiers (par ex., prêts et crédits de la Banque mondiale ou fonds nationaux ou de donateurs).

Les biens publics mondiaux représentent une minorité des programmes mais une majorité des fonds. Lorsque leurs caractéristiques les plus essentielles sont examinées, seuls 11 programmes (y compris une partie de l'Alliance mondiale pour les vaccins et la vaccination - GAVI) fournissent des biens publics mondiaux (tableau RA.3). Parmi ceux-ci, sept seulement financent des investissements mondiaux ou nationaux. Seule la GAVI finance de tels investissements à une grande échelle au niveau mondial et national et est donc reprise dans les programmes de biens publics mondiaux et nationaux. Les quatre autres programmes de biens publics mondiaux encouragent des approches communes pour atténuer les principales maladies transmissibles ou encouragent la recherche sur les maladies des pauvres. Ils *défendent des investissements publics accrus par des tiers* pour lutter contre les maladies transmissibles mais, contrairement à la GAVI, ils ne financent pas les investissements, à aucun niveau. Les sept programmes de biens publics mondiaux et les deux programmes de biens publics nationaux qui financent les investissements (la GAVI étant reprise dans les deux catégories) ont assumé 80 % des dépenses totales des programmes d'études de cas au cours de l'exercice 2003 (tableau RA.4). Les 18 autres *programmes ne finançant pas*

Tableau RA.3
Défense générale
Nombre concret de programmes

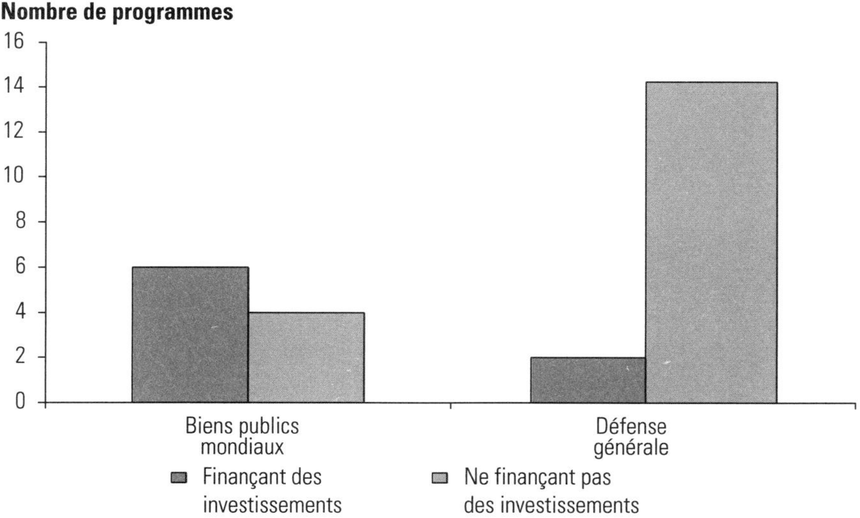

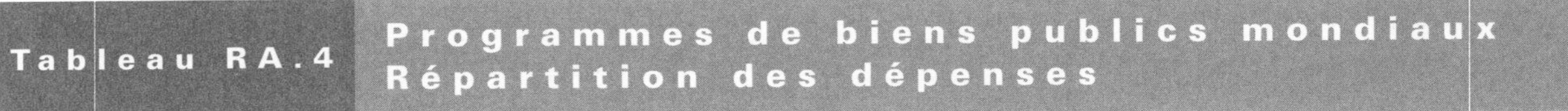

Tableau RA.4 Programmes de biens publics mondiaux Répartition des dépenses

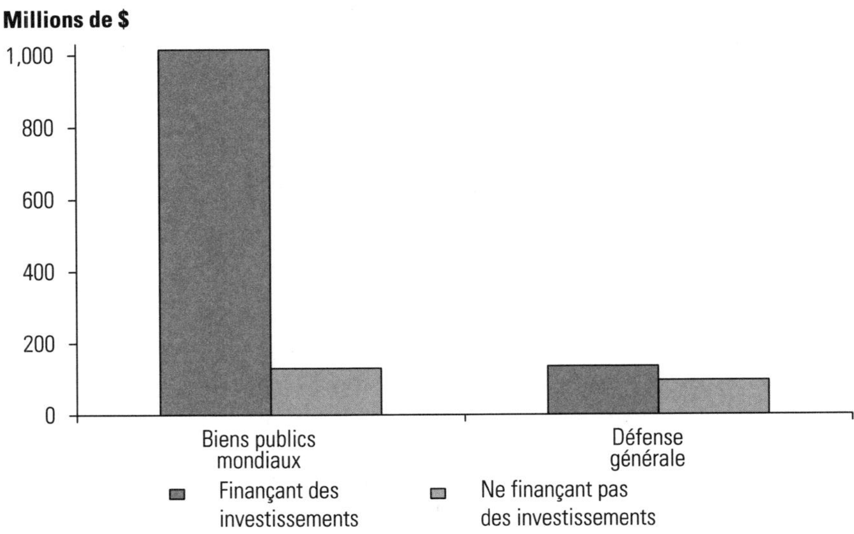

des investissements (y compris les 4 programmes précités dans le domaine de la santé) financent essentiellement des activités liées à l'information et à la connaissance, à la défense, au renforcement des capacités et à l'assistance technique.

Ces programmes stimulent la demande existante des pays en matière d'assistance technique, de formation et de renforcement des capacités mais ne disposent pas des ressources pour répondre à cette demande. Les programmes dépendent donc de donateurs, y compris la Banque mondiale, pour des investissements supplémentaires. Si les programmes espèrent que les activités complémentaires seront incluses dans les DSRP et dans les SAP, cette inclusion a été limitée jusqu'à présent, reflétant le faible lien existant entre les programmes de défense multinationaux et les activités nationales.

Conclusions de l'OED

Sélectivité

Le fait de « laisser un millier de fleurs éclore » et d'expérimenter de nombreux nouveaux programmes a permis à la Banque mondiale de comprendre la diversité et la complexité des problèmes mondiaux et a permis de tirer des leçons de la complexité des relations monde-pays. Cela a contribué à la formulation et à l'amélioration des critères de sélectivité de la Banque mondiale.

Les programmes de biens publics mondiaux répondent à la majorité des critères. S'ils dépendent en grande partie de l'approvisionnement, la plupart des programmes mondiaux de biens publics financés par la Banque mondiale (Fonds multilatéral, FEM, FPC et CEPF, GCRAI, TDR, UNAIDS, Halte à la tuberculose, Faire reculer le paludisme, Forum mondial pour la recherche en santé, Fonds mondial pour la recherche de la GAVI) *répondent en grande partie aux quatre critères de sélectivité du Comité pour le développement*. La plupart des programmes mondiaux *répondent en grande partie* également aux critères d'approbation et d'éligibilité pour la participation de la Banque mondiale. Le GCRAI ne répond pas au critère de pleine concurrence; la Banque mondiale n'a pas fait participer les intervenants des pays en développement à l'établissement du CEPF ou à sa gouvernance mondiale; la Banque mondiale n'a pas procédé à une analyse approfondie du niveau prévu de ressources de la Banque mondiale nécessaire pour des programmes de santé ni de la manière de mettre en œuvre et de gérer ce nouvel engagement. Ce sont toutefois des exceptions à la règle.

Les programmes de défense générale répondent aux critères de sélectivité du Comité pour le développement. Cela est en grande partie dû au fait que les critères sont larges et difficiles à appliquer précisément. Par exemple, le premier critère – « un consensus international sur la nécessité d'une action mondiale », que tous les programmes revendiquent comme leur raison d'être – ne fournit aucune base pour la sélectivité car le concept de consensus international est informe et appliqué librement. Les études de cas illustrent le fait que le consensus dépend souvent des intervenants dans les pays donateurs et du personnel des agences internationales. Parallèlement, peu de réseaux demandent des liens avec les opérations nationales, l'un des critères les plus importants, avant l'approbation, et ils ne les surveillent pas non plus pendant la mise en œuvre.

La Banque présente ses avantages comparatifs davantage au niveau mondial qu'au niveau national. Les risques financiers et de réputation ainsi que les implications budgétaires et de dotation en personnel sont rarement suffisamment évalués. Le consensus international sur l'existence d'un problème est généralement fort; le consensus sur l'action collective nécessaire est souvent faible. De nombreux programmes mondiaux sont implicitement (parfois explicitement) établis pour promouvoir le consensus, pour « harmoniser » les approches des donateurs quant à des problèmes spécifiques, pour déterminer les avantages comparatifs des donateurs pour résoudre ces problèmes et pour donner aux donateurs des connaissances spéciales à utiliser pour ces problèmes. Le renforcement des capacités dans les pays bénéficiaires est secondaire dans de tels projets.

Il n'y a pas de preuves que les programmes exploitent les économies d'échelle et d'envergure dans des activités telles que la création et la diffusion des connaissances, le renforcement des capacités, l'assistance technique et la coordination des donateurs. Il n'est également pas clair si les connaissances qu'ils diffusent se basent suffisamment sur des preuves, si leur qualité est éprouvée et si elles sont contextuelles pour apporter une valeur ajoutée à ce que les pays clients de la Banque mondiale font, nécessitent ou veulent eux-mêmes ou à ce que la Banque mondiale peut obtenir en travaillant par le biais de partenariats au niveau national. Il n'existe pas d'indicateurs de performance afin d'évaluer un changement de comportement des donateurs ou des agences internationales. Les indicateurs de performance, lorsqu'ils existent, se concentrent sur le comportement des pays en développement. L'OED n'a pu identifier que quelques indicateurs spécifiques aux programmes indiquant des changements dans les pratiques, procédures et actions des donateurs et de la Banque mondiale en réponse à la défense de programmes mondiaux. Dans le cas des programmes de défense générale, les besoins des pays clients de la Banque mondiale devraient être la première considération pour la participation de la Banque mondiale.

L'opinion des pays en développement, ou même celle des régions opérationnelles de la Banque mondiale, n'est pas bien représentée dans le consensus international. Les études de cas sur bon nombre de ces programmes de défense générale montrent que la prise en considération de l'opinion des pays en développement à l'étape de la conception améliore la possession des programmes, rend la conception organisationnelle plus efficace et renforce les impacts des programmes. Sur les bases de preuves que l'OED a fournies jusqu'à présent, la direction de la Banque mondiale a reconnu la nécessité de renforcer le rôle des pays en développement et des régions opérationnelles de la Banque mondiale dans des programmes mondiaux.

Valeur ajoutée aux objectifs de développement de la Banque mondiale

Les preuves de la valeur ajoutée aux objectifs de développement de la Banque mondiale varient mais sont de plus en plus importantes. Certains programmes n'ont pas d'objectifs clairement définis et d'autres ont de nombreux objectifs non déclarés, ce qui complique l'évaluation de la valeur qui a été ajoutée. Il est difficile d'évaluer de nombreux programmes récents qui n'ont pas eu le temps d'avoir des impacts. Toutefois, les évaluations sont de plus en plus nombreuses, en partie provoquées par la DGF, et elles commencent à affecter la conception et la mise en œuvre des programmes. Lorsque les programmes ne répondent pas aux trois exigences pour une évaluation efficace – des objectifs clairs, partagés et mesurables, une méthodologie appropriée et des preuves mesurables –, leurs impacts mondiaux restent flous.

Les programmes fournissant des biens publics mondiaux apportent souvent une valeur ajoutée. Les programmes mondiaux de biens publics (GCRAI, TDR, Fonds multilatéral, des parties du FEM et même certains nouveaux programmes mondiaux de santé) sont bien considérés quant à leurs impacts pour réduire la pauvreté ou se concentrer sur les contraintes politiques, institutionnelles, technologiques ou d'infrastructures auxquelles sont confrontés les pays en développement pour parvenir à une croissance économique durable. Ajouter une valeur sur le terrain dans les pays clients est en général un produit commun des activités au niveau mondial et national. Par exemple, le GCRAI, comme le programme TDR, s'est révélé avoir des impacts éprouvés impressionnants en matière de réduction de la pauvreté, en partie parce que la Banque mondiale, les donateurs et certains gouvernements ont réalisé des investissements supplémentaires au niveau national. Toutefois, comme les investissements au niveau national ont diminué, les donateurs ont tenté de les compenser en encourageant le GCRAI à se déplacer en aval. Ils ont proposé des fonds liés à des programmes de recherche qui ont des effets immédiats, afin de pousser le GCRAI vers un travail plus adaptatif et plus appliqué au niveau local et national. La direction de la Banque mondiale convient que les activités de plusieurs centres de recherche du GCRAI ressemblent à présent à celles que financeraient les instruments de la Banque mondiale par le biais d'investissements au niveau national.

Les programmes proches de la Banque mondiale apportent réellement une valeur ajoutée. Il n'est pas surprenant que les programmes dont la Banque mondiale est un organisme d'exécution sont plus étroitement liés aux opérations de la Banque mondiale. Cela est dû en partie au fait que la Banque mondiale arrive mieux à absorber et à utiliser des informations et des conclusions produites au niveau interne ou proche. La Banque mondiale doit concevoir des moyens d'augmenter ses liens avec des programmes qui sont plus distants d'elle. Le fait de conserver la gouvernance de programmes mondiaux sans lien de dépendance vis-à-vis de la Banque mondiale et de conserver une claire obligation de résultats des programmes donne une plus grande possibilité d'apporter de nouvelles informations et de nouvelles perspectives pour les opérations de la Banque mondiale.

Les programmes mondiaux ont révélé de grandes lacunes en matière d'investissements… Des preuves indiquent que les investissements dans la recherche en santé ont d'importants effets sur la réduction de la pauvreté. L'environnement mondial actuel en matière de politique et d'assistance présente de grandes *lacunes en matière d'investissements au niveau mondial* dans la fourniture de la recherche mondiale en santé, ainsi que des *lacunes dans les investissements supplémentaires au niveau national*. La recherche en santé, comme la recherche agricole, est une activité à long terme que le secteur privé est peu susceptible d'aborder à l'échelle nécessaire.

…ainsi que des lacunes dans la politique publique mondiale. Plusieurs programmes mondiaux soulignent l'existence de lacunes dans la politique publique mondiale – impliquant souvent les politiques des pays développés en matière de commerce, d'assistance, de finances et de droits de propriété intellectuelle – qui affectent les pays en développement. Peu de programmes considèrent que le fait de combler ces lacunes politiques fait partie de leurs missions. Si le changement des règles de base internationales est l'objectif des programmes et si la défense est le moyen d'y parvenir, les programmes devraient alors être évalués par rapport à leur capacité à fournir de nouvelles politiques ou un nouvel environnement mondial, du point de vue des pauvres.

Gouvernance, gestion et financement

La gouvernance est mauvaise dans plusieurs programmes. Si les modèles d'actionnaires purs de gouvernance de programmes sont actuellement remplacés par des modèles d'intervenants, les programmes luttent toujours pour mettre en équilibre la légitimité et l'obligation de résultats avec l'efficacité lors de l'obtention de ceux-ci. Les membres permanents des organes directeurs des programmes, qui sont généralement des donateurs et des grandes organisations internationales, ont *de facto* une plus grande responsabilité, par rapport aux membres tournants, pour garantir la réussite des programmes. Toutefois, une telle responsabilité est rarement clairement articulée. Le manque de gouvernance et de gestion efficaces doit être résolu si l'on veut que la Banque mondiale continue à apporter une aide financière.

Les accords de gestion peuvent altérer les responsabilités réelles et perçues. Lorsque la Banque mondiale ou une autre organisation internationale dirige les programmes dont elle s'occupe, cela réduit la responsabilité d'une gouvernance partagée. Lorsque les programmes sont intégrés dans la Banque mondiale ou une autre organisation internationale, le gestionnaire du programme fait souvent un rapport à l'organe directeur du programme et à un cadre responsable dans l'organisation hôte. Cette situation place souvent la responsabilité de la gestion et du contrôle dans la même chaîne de gestion, ce qui crée à son tour des conflits d'intérêt réels ou perçus pour le contrôle des performances.

Les programmes mondiaux ont augmenté l'aide globale de très peu. Dans l'ensemble, les programmes mondiaux ont ajouté très peu de fonds supplémentaires à l'aide publique au développement. Des exceptions englobent des fonds de sources privées pour le Fonds prototype pour le carbone; de la Fondation Gates pour la santé; et de petites sommes provenant d'entreprises pharmaceutiques par le biais de nouveaux partenariats public-privé pour le développement de médicaments et de vaccins. Vu le coût de renonciation des fonds de l'APD, la participation de la Banque mondiale à des programmes ayant de grands objectifs mais peu de valeur démontrée doit être réexaminée. Dans certains cas, une association trop étroite avec la Banque mondiale a gêné la mobilisation d'autre fonds pour ces programmes. Le temps est venu de passer du principe de « laisser un millier de fleurs éclore » à la détermination des programmes qui méritent d'être financés en permanence par la Banque mondiale.

Performances de la Banque mondiale

Les performances de la Banque mondiale dans des programmes mondiaux sont meilleures au niveau mondial qu'au niveau national. D'autres partenaires considèrent le rôle prépondérant de la Banque mondiale, son poids financier, son accès aux responsables politiques, son soutien opérationnel et son contrôle fiduciaire comme un sceau d'approbation, leur donnant la confiance pour investir dans des programmes mondiaux, tant gérés en interne qu'en externe. Même au niveau mondial, cependant, les performances de la Banque mondiale peuvent être améliorées, en particulier concernant la stratégie, le contrôle indépendant et les relations monde-pays.

Les récentes réformes sont prometteuses. L'établissement du Conseil des programmes et des partenariats mondiaux (GPP), et du Groupe des GPP, est un événement positif. Conformément à la recommandation du rapport sur la phase 1, le Conseil des GPP pourrait contribuer à surveiller le développement de la stratégie mondiale de la Banque mondiale, anticiper les changements de l'environnement mondial et contribuer à établir des priorités et des stratégies de financement. Il peut déplacer les programmes mondiaux de la perspective de réseau actuelle vers une perspective à l'échelle de la Banque mondiale et établir des normes de la Banque mondiale pour les performances et les programmes mondiaux. La Banque mondiale doit encore renforcer son évaluation des nouveaux programmes et rendre ses stratégies de sélectivité, de contrôle, d'évaluation et de sortie plus transparentes et davantage basées sur les résultats. Enfin, l'évaluation et le contrôle de partenariats mondiaux complexes requièrent les connaissances et les idées d'experts, pas seulement de gestionnaires de programmes qui les encouragent mais également d'autres partenaires, de pays en développement et d'experts dans le domaine.

Il faut un contrôle indépendant. La Banque mondiale doit établir un contrôle indépendant de tous ses programmes – dans le cas de programmes internes, par des cadres supérieurs en dehors de la gestion hiérarchique de la vice-présidence en charge du programme. Le contrôle des programmes internes et des programmes gérés en externe doit être orienté par un mandat clair, disposer du budget nécessaire et avoir une responsabilité en matière de résultats. Le contrôle indépendant est en particulier important au début afin de garantir que les programmes partent sur de bonnes bases. La direction de la Banque mondiale doit également établir des procédures de routine en matière d'assurance de la qualité, d'audits internes, d'évaluation des risques et de gestion des risques.

Les stratégies de sortie des programmes ne fonctionnent pas correctement. Les dossiers de la Banque mondiale concernant la gestion de la séparation des programmes internes de la Banque mondiale doivent être améliorés. Par exemple, la règle mécanique de non-intervention de trois ans pour les programmes en phase 2 de la DGF n'a pas facilité les sorties financières ordonnées. Il faut prêter davantage attention au renforcement de la gouvernance et au financement durable des programmes.

La stratégie de la Banque mondiale pour les programmes mondiaux est mal définie. La Banque mondiale ne dispose pas, et elle en a clairement besoin, d'une stratégie mondiale qui est développée en collaboration avec ses principaux partenaires et qui encourage la capacité qui existe dans ses principales vice-présidences, les points d'ancrage des réseaux et les régions à le faire. La stratégie doit aborder la cohérence, ou le manque de cohérence, entre les attentes mondiales (en particulier au sein de la communauté des donateurs) et les besoins des pays en développement. La stratégie mondiale doit se concentrer clairement sur la croissance durable réduisant la pauvreté dans les pays clients de la Banque mondiale, sur les problèmes de politique mondiale qui empêchent cette croissance et sur la mobilisation de fonds non affectés supplémentaires pour résoudre les problèmes mondiaux qui sont une grande priorité pour les pays en développement. Une telle stratégie ne découlera pas simplement d'une meilleure sélectivité ou d'un contrôle accru des programmes mondiaux individuels, elle doit être mise au point. Par ailleurs, le renforcement du contrôle en l'absence d'une stratégie globale risque d'entraîner la microgestion du portefeuille de programmes mondiaux.

Recommandations de l'OED

Cadre stratégique de l'implication de la Banque dans les programmes mondiaux

1. Après consultations auprès des agences des Nations unies, des donateurs, des pays en développement et d'autres partenaires, la direction devrait élaborer une stratégie mondiale pour servir de fondement à l'engagement de la Banque dans les programmes mondiaux, qui serait approuvée par le comité de direction, mise à jour de manière périodique et qui :
   - Exploite les avantages comparatifs de la Banque mondiale en tant qu'institution multisectorielle de financement du développement ayant une portée mondiale et une forte capacité d'analyse politique.
   - Se consacre davantage à réduire la pauvreté et à aborder les politiques publiques mondiales qui limitent les perspectives des pays en développement en matière de croissance rapide, durable et réduisant la pauvreté.
   - Encourage des liens plus étroits entre les programmes mondiaux et les opérations régionales et nationales de la Banque mondiale concernant l'établissement des priorités de ses activités de programmes mondiaux.
   - Garantisse que les programmes mondiaux apportent une valeur ajoutée au-delà de ce

que la Banque mondiale peut accomplir par le biais des partenariats au niveau national.

Relier le financement aux priorités

2. La direction de la Banque mondiale devrait élaborer un plan de financement pour les programmes à haute priorité, en particulier pour ceux qui fournissent de véritables biens publics mondiaux, que ce soit sous forme de politiques mondiales, de nouveaux produits, de technologies, de connaissances ou de pratiques qui bénéficient aux pauvres. Cela requiert :
   - L'identification de programmes mondiaux de biens publics à long terme sous-financés qui bénéficient aux pauvres – comme la recherche mondiale en santé et le réseau mondial de développement de produits pour des maladies qui affectent les pauvres de manière disproportionnée – et l'utilisation de pouvoir de rassemblement de la Banque mondiale pour mobiliser des ressources supplémentaires pour ces programmes.
   - L'amélioration des critères et procédures concernant la phase 2 de la DGF, afin de créer une approche plus rationnelle et plus approfondie du financement de programmes de « capital-risque », dans lesquels la DGF n'apporte que l'aide initiale.
   - Le développement d'une politique sur l'utilisation de fonds fiduciaires dans le cadre de la stratégie globale pour les programmes mondiaux.

Sélectivité et contrôle du portefeuille de programmes mondiaux

3. La direction de la Banque mondiale devrait établir des critères et des procédures d'approbation, de contrôle, d'évaluation et de sortie/nouvelle autorisation pour les programmes mondiaux financés par la Banque mondiale qui les aideront à apporter une valeur ajoutée à la mission de la Banque mondiale. Cela englobe :
   - La rationalisation et la clarification des critères d'approbation et d'éligibilité pour l'aide à la sélectivité et à l'octroi de subventions de la Banque mondiale et l'institution d'une procédure d'approbation en deux étapes pour les programmes mondiaux au moment de la conception et de l'évaluation.
   - L'affûtage et l'application plus rigoureuse du critère de subsidiarité pour l'approbation et l'aide aux subventions.
   - La séparation du contrôle de la Banque mondiale et de la gestion de la mise en œuvre; et, pour le personnel de la Banque mondiale travaillant dans les organes directeurs des programmes mondiaux, la clarification de leurs rôles et responsabilités par le biais d'une formation et d'un mandat standard.
   - L'allocation de fonds pour le contrôle et de fonds que le point d'ancrage du réseau et le personnel régional peuvent utiliser pour rendre opérationnels les programmes mondiaux dans les opérations régionales de la Banque mondiale.
   - L'établissement de procédures de sortie/nouvelle autorisation claires, bien planifiées et bien exécutées et la garantie que les programmes que la Banque mondiale a séparés ont une identité indépendante, une obligation de résultat et de bonnes chances de succès.

Gouvernance et gestion de programmes individuels

4. La gestion devrait travailler avec ses partenaires mondiaux pour élaborer et appliquer des normes universellement acceptées concernant la bonne gouvernance, la gestion, l'orientation des résultats et l'évaluation à tous les programmes mondiaux financés par la Banque mondiale. Il s'agit entre autres de :
   - Statuts juridiques et/ou chartes écrites le cas échéant.
   - Procédures et critères transparents pour la sélection des présidences et membres des conseils; précisant leurs rôles, responsabilités et structures de base; et leur donnant l'autorité d'orienter et contrôler le programme, ses politiques et son budget.

- Opinions des pays clients de la Banque mondiale quant aux organes directeurs des programmes mondiaux, pour un meilleur équilibre entre les pays développés et les pays en développement.
- Directives sur les conflits d'intérêts, sur les rôles des ONG et du secteur privé dans les organes directeurs et sur les rôles et la qualité des conseils consultatifs.
- Désignation de l'évaluation et de l'audit comme des fonctions de l'organe directeur, pas de la direction du programme, avec des résultats qui devraient être régulièrement mis à disposition des financiers du programme et d'autres intervenants.

Évaluation

5. L'OED devrait inclure les programmes mondiaux dans ses procédés standard d'évaluation et de rapport. Cela englobe le fait de :
   - Travailler avec les partenaires mondiaux de la Banque mondiale pour développer des normes internationales pour l'évaluation des programmes mondiaux.
   - Réviser les évaluations des programmes choisies réalisées par des programmes mondiaux financés par la Banque mondiale (tant ceux gérés en interne que ceux gérés en externe), comme l'OED révise d'autres auto-évaluations au niveau des pays et des projets.

List of Case Study Programs

Acronym/ short form	Full name	Operational start date	Size ($ millions)[a]
Environment & Agriculture			
1. CGIAR	Consultative Group on International Agricultural Research	1972	395.0
2. GEF	Global Environment Facility	1991	387.53
3. MLF	Multilateral Fund for the Implementation of the Montreal Protocol	1991	158.6
4. ProCarbFund	Prototype Carbon Fund	2000	6.5
5. CEPF	Critical Ecosystem Partnership Fund	2000	20.19
6. GWP	Global Water Partnership	1997	10.25
7. GIF	Global Integrated Pest Management Facility	1996	1.3
Health, Nutrition & Population			
8. TDR	Special Program for Research and Training in Tropical Diseases	Dec 1975	47.5
9. Global Forum	Global Forum for Health Research	Jan 1998	3.07
10. UNAIDS	Joint United Nations Program on HIV/AIDS	Jan 1996	95.0
11. RBM	Roll Back Malaria	Nov 1998	11.4
12. Stop TB	Stop TB Partnership	July 1999	20.8
13. GAVI	Global Alliance for Vaccines and Immunization	Oct 1999	124.1
Infrastructure & Private Sector Development			
14. WSP	Water and Sanitation Program	Mar 1978	12.4
15. ESMAP	Energy Sector Management Assistance Program	Jan 1982	7.58
16. CGAP	Consultative Group to Assist the Poor	Aug 1995	12.67
17. *info*Dev	Information for Development Program	Sept 1995	8.90
18. PPIAF	Public-Private Infrastructure Advisory Facility	Dec 1999	15.61
19. CA	Cities Alliance	Dec 1999	13.25
Social Development & Protection			
20. PostConFund	Post-conflict Fund	1998	10.60
21. UCW	Understanding Children's Work	2000	0.56
Trade & Finance			
22. IF	Integrated Framework for Trade-related Technical Assistance	1997	2.71
23. FSAP	Financial Sector Assessment Program	May 1999	10.46
24. FIRST	Financial Sector Reform & Strengthening Initiative	July 2002	4.64
Information & Knowledge			
25. GDN	Global Development Network	Dec 1999	8.67
26. World Links	World Links for Development	1998	6.52

a. FY04/CY03 expenditures. For the following cases, updated data were not readily available so the previous fiscal or calendar year expenditures were used: Global Integrated Pest Management Facility, Water and Sanitation Program, The Information for Development Program, Integrated Framework for Trade-Related Technical Assistance.

Abbreviations and Acronyms

Currency amounts are expressed in U.S. dollars (US$)

AERC	African Economic Research Consortium
AfDB	African Development Bank
AFTHD	Africa Region Human Development Unit
AIDS	acquired immunodeficiency syndrome
ARD	Agriculture and Rural Development Department
ARV	anti-retroviral
AsDB	Asian Development Bank
BB	World Bank administrative budget
CAS	Country Assistance Strategy
CBC	Committee of Board Chairs (CGIAR)
CBD	Convention on the Conservation of Biodiversity
CCD	U.N. Convention on Combating Desertification
CDC	Center Directors' Committee (CGIAR)
CEO	chief executive officer
CEPF	Critical Ecosystem Partnership Fund
CERG-EI	Center for Economic Research and Graduate Education of Charles University and Economics Institute of the National Academy of Sciences
CFP	Concessional Finance and Global Partnerships
CG	Consultative Group
CGAP	Consultative Group to Assist the Poor
CGIAR	Consultative Group on International Agriculture Research
CI	Conservation International
CIDA	Canadian International Development Agency
CODE	Committee on Development Effectiveness
CRC	U.N. Convention on the Rights of the Child
CY	calendar year
DANIDA	Danish International Development Agency
DC	Development Committee
DEC	Development Economics Vice Presidency
DECPG	DEC Prospects Group
DECRG	Development Economics Research Group
DFID	Department for International Development (U.K.)
DGF	Development Grant Facility
DOTS	Directly Observed Treatment/Therapy Short Course
DTIS	Diagnostic Trade Integration Study
EBRD	European Bank for Reconstruction and Development
ECOSOC	U.N. Economic and Social Council
ECSHD	Europe and Central Asia Region Human Development Sector Unit
EDU/SP	Education and Social Protection Department
EMRO	Eastern Mediterranean Regional Office
ENV	Environment Department
ESMAP	Energy Sector Management Assistance Program
ESSD	Environmentally and Socially Sustainable Development Vice Presidency and Network
EU	European Union

EWD	Energy and Water Department
EWDDR	Energy and Water Department, Office of the Director
ExCo	Executive Committee
FAO	Food and Agriculture Organization of the United Nations
FIRST	Financial Sector Reform and Strengthening Initiative
FSAP	Financial Sector Assessment Program
FSE	Financial Sector Vice Presidency and Network
FSE/OPD	Financial Sector Operations and Policy Department
FSEGP	FSE Global Partnerships
FY	fiscal year
GAMET	Global HIV/AIDS Monitoring and Evaluation Support Team
GAVI	Global Alliance for Vaccines and Immunization
GDN	Global Development Network
GEF	Global Environment Facility
GFAR	Global Forum on Agricultural Research
GFATM	Global Fund to Fight AIDS, Tuberculosis, and Malaria
GIF	Global Integrated Pest Management Facility
GPG	global public good
GPPs	global programs and partnerships
GTZ	Deutsche Gesellschaft für Technische Zusammenarbeit (GTZ) GmbH
GWP	global water partnerships
HDN	Human Development Vice Presidency and Network
HDNGA	Human Development Vice Presidency and Network Global HIV/AIDs Program
HDNHE	Human Development Vice Presidency and Network Health Nutrition & Population Team
HDNSP	Human Development Vice Presidency and Network Social Protection Team
HIPC	Highly Indebted Poor Countries Initiative
HIV	human immunodeficiency virus
HNP	Health, Nutrition, and Population Vice Presidency
ICT	information and communications technology
IDA	International Development Association
IDB	Inter-American Development Bank
IDRC	International Development Research Center
IF	Integrated Framework for Trade-Related Technical Assistance
IFAD	International Fund for Agricultural Development
IFPRI	International Food Policy Research Institute
ILO	International Labour Organisation
IMF	International Monetary Fund
*info*Dev	Information for Development Program
INF	Infrastructure Vice Presidency and Network
IOM	International Organization for Migration
IPEC	ILO/International Programme on the Elimination of Child Labour
IPM	integrated pest management
IPR	intellectual property right
ISEAS	Institute of Southeast Asian Studies
ITC	International Trade Center
IWRM	integrated water resources management
JCB	Joint Coordinating Board
LCR	Latin America and Caribbean Region
LCRCE	Latin America and Caribbean Region, Chief Economist Unit
LCSER	Latin America and Caribbean Region, Rural Development Family
LCSHE	Latin America and Caribbean Region, Education Sector
LDC	least-developed country

LICUS	low-income countries under stress
MAP	multicountry AIDS Program
MD	managing director
MDGs	Millennium Development Goals
MIGA	Multilateral Investment Guarantee Agency
MLF	Multilateral Fund for the Implementation of the Montreal Protocol
MMV	Medicines for Malaria Venture
MNA	Middle East and North Africa Region
MOU	Memorandum of Understanding
NARS	national agricultural research system
NGO	nongovernmental organization
NIH	National Institutes of Health (U.S.)
NORAD	Norwegian Agency for Development
NPG	national public good
ODA	official development assistance
ODS	ozone-depleting substances
OECD	Organisation for Economic Co-operation and Development
OED	Operations Evaluation Department
OEG	Operations Evaluation Group
OEU	Operations Evaluation Unit
OORG	Ozone Operations Research Group
OP	Operational Policy
OPCS	Operations Policy and Country Services Vice Presidency
OPEC	Organization of Petroleum Exporting Countries
PAN-UK	Pesticide Action Network, United Kingdom
PATS	Partnership Approval and Tracking System
PCB	Program Coordinating Board
PostConFund	Post-conflict Fund
ProCarbFund	Prototype Carbon Fund
POP	Stockholm Convention on Persistent Organic Pollutants
PPIAF	Public-Private Infrastructure Advisory Facility
PREM	Poverty Reduction and Economic Management Vice Presidency and Network
PREMEP	Poverty Reduction and Economic Management Economic Policy Division
PRMTR	Poverty Reduction and Economic Management International Trade Department
PRSP	Poverty Reduction Strategy Paper
PSI	Population Strategies International
RBM	Roll Back Malaria
R&D	research and development
ROSC	Reports on Observance of Standards and Codes
SADC	Southern African Development Community
SANEI	South Asian Network of Economic Institutes
SASRD	South Asia Sector Rural Development Department
SDC	Swiss Agency for Development and Cooperation
SDV	Social Development Department
SGP	Special Grants Program
SIDA	Swiss International Development Agency
SSP	Sector Strategy Paper
TA	technical assistance
TAC	Technical Advisory Committee (CGIAR)
TAG	Technical Advisory Group
TAP	technical assistance program
TB	tuberculosis
TDR	Special Program for Research and Training in Tropical Diseases

TEAP	Technical Economic Assessment Panel (UNEP)
TF	trust fund
TOR	terms of reference
TRIPS	trade-related intellectual property rights
TQC	Trust Fund Quality Assurance and Compliance Unit
TUD	Transportation and Urban Development Department
UCW	Understanding Children's Work
U.N.	United Nations
UNAIDS	Joint United Nations Program on HIV/AIDS
UNCDF	United Nations Capital Development Fund
UNCED	United Nations Conference on Environment and Development
UNDP	United Nations Development Program
UNEP	United Nations Environment Program
UNESCO	United Nations Educational, Scientific and Cultural Organization
UNFCCC	United Nations Framework Convention on Climate Change
UNFPA	United Nations Population Fund
UNHCR	United Nations High Commission for Refugees
UNICEF	United Nations Children's Fund
UNIDO	United Nations Industrial Development Organization
UNODC	United Nations Office on Drugs and Crime
USAID	United States Agency for International Development
VHAI	Voluntary Health Association of India
VPU	vice presidential unit
WBI	World Bank Institute
WFP	World Food Program
WHO	World Health Organization
WMO	World Meteorological Organization
WPRO	World Health Organization Regional Office for the Western Pacific
WSP	Water and Sanitation Program
WSSCC	Water Supply and Sanitation Collaborative Council
WTO	World Trade Organization

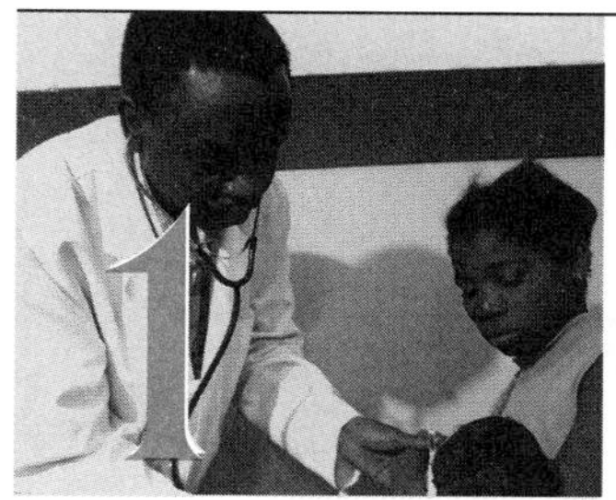

Introduction and Context: Global Challenges and the Need for Collective Action

Rapid changes in the Bank's external and internal environment and the growth of global issues relevant to developing countries have accelerated the Bank's involvement in global and regional programs since 1998. While the Bank's Board of Executive Directors has recognized the need for the Bank to be involved at the global level, the growing number of activities has also prompted concerns among Board members that the objectives and procedures for such involvement have not been clear.

Board members' concerns about partnership proliferation, development impact, and related reputational risks led them to call for prioritizing. The goal would be to increase selectivity, clarify responsibilities and accountabilities, more rigorously monitor the use of Bank resources, and improve reporting to the Board on the development impact of global programs (defined in box 1.1).

To help guide the prioritization process, the Board asked the Operations Evaluation Department (OED) to evaluate the Bank's global activities. The evaluation has been conducted in two phases. OED's Phase 1 report focused on the Bank's overall portfolio of 70 global programs (OED 2002c). It clarified concepts with regard to global programs and partnerships and their management and assessed the Bank's internal decisionmaking processes, including its internal and external responsibilities and accountabilities. Taking into account the recommendations of OED's 1998 internal review of the Bank's grant programs (OED 2002a) and the Bank's comparative advantage in relation to its partners, the Phase 1 report derived lessons for the strategic and programmatic management of the Bank's involvement in global programs, including decisionmaking processes with regard to the Bank budget, the Bank's Development Grant Facility (DGF), trust funds, and links between global programs and country operations. Management has acted on several of the report's recommendations. (See table 1.1 at the end of this chapter, and Annexes A and B.)

Phase 2 carried out 26 case studies of global programs, including a review of the Consultative Group for International Agricultural Research (CGIAR), which was the first global program to receive grants from the Bank and is still the largest recipient of grants from the DGF.[1] The meta-evaluation of the CGIAR presented OED's assessment of CGIAR's impact and drew some implications for the Bank's leadership and oversight of this

Box 1.1 Definition and Management of Global Programs by the World Bank

Global programs are defined as partnerships and related initiatives whose benefits are intended to cut across more than one region of the world and in which the partners:

- Reach explicit agreements on objectives
- Agree to establish a new (formal or informal) organization
- Generate new products or services
- Contribute dedicated resources to the program.

Approval of global programs. Since November 2000, all new global and regional programs have had to be approved at the initial concept stage, based on the six approval criteria that were shown in figure ES.1 in the Executive Summary, by the managing director responsible for the vice presidential unit (VPU) advocating the Bank's involvement. Such approval then authorizes the respective VPU to enter into agreements with partners and to mobilize resources for the program—whether from the DGF, trust funds, or the Bank's administrative budget. Both before and after November 2000, the Bank's participation in some high-profile programs—such as the Global Environment Facility, the Multilateral Fund for the Implementation of the Montreal Protocol, the Prototype Carbon Fund, and the Global Fund to Fight AIDS, Tuberculosis, and Malaria—has been considered and approved by the Bank's Executive Board.

Oversight and management of global programs. Once programs have been approved at the initial concept stage, the network vice presidencies are responsible for their oversight, management, and quality assurance. This includes establishing priorities among programs, ensuring their coherence with the Bank's sector strategies, sponsoring applications for DGF grants, managing programs that are housed in the Bank, fostering links to the Bank's country operations, and promoting synergy among programs, both internally and externally. While regional programs are not covered in this OED evaluation, many global programs have strong regional dimensions (which are addressed in the case studies), in addition to their links to the Bank's country-level economic and sector work, policy advice, and lending.

The Global Programs and Partnership Council has been established in response to one of the recommendations of OED's Phase 1 report. Consolidating the functions of the former Partnership Council and DGF Council, the new council is the management committee responsible for overseeing the strategic framework and operational policies for global programs and partnerships (GPPs). Composed of 19 Regional, network, and central vice presidents and co-chaired by two managing directors, its current terms of reference are:

- To set the Bank's vision and priorities for its engagement in GPPs
- To review VPU portfolios and the Bank's institutional partnerships
- To set and oversee criteria for selection and evaluation of GPPs, including governance structures, risk management, exit strategies, and best practices.

program, in light of CGIAR's changing environment and the growing competition for the Bank's limited grant resources (OED 2003b).

Based on these foundations, and as proposed in the evaluation design, this report synthesizes the case study findings of 26 of the Bank's 70 global programs. It summarizes the practical lessons for the design and implementation of individual global programs and for the development of a strategic framework within which to approve and oversee these programs.

The specific objectives of the Phase 2 evaluation are:

- To assess how well the case study programs measure up to the selectivity and oversight criteria and the priorities for global programs established by the Development Committee and the Bank, particularly the DGF
- To derive crosscutting lessons for the Bank on program selectivity, design, implementation, governance, management, financing, and evaluation
- To assess progress in implementing the recommendations of OED's 1998 review, the Phase 1 report, and the meta-evaluation of the CGIAR, with respect to the Bank's strategic and programmatic management and to the choice, design, and implementation of individual programs
- To identify areas where further Bank action is needed.

The OED team used 20 questions (listed in Annex C) in each case study to assess the relevance, efficacy, efficiency, and Bank performance of each global program. Chapters 3 through 7 of this report roughly correspond to the following four standard OED criteria, adapted by drawing upon the Bank's eligibility and approval criteria for global programs:

- Relevance (chapter 3) – assessing the international consensus for the 26 global programs
- Efficacy (chapter 4) – assessing the outcomes, impacts, and value-added of global program activities, both to developing countries and to the Bank's country operations
- Efficiency (chapters 5 and 6) – focusing on governance, management, financing, partnerships, and participation (since these influence efficiency and the programs' value-added)
- Bank performance (chapter 7) – in the numerous roles that the Bank plays in these global programs.

The case studies were based on meta-analysis of available program evaluations,[2] OED's review of the related literature, and its analysis of the programs' objectives, design, implementation, results, and Bank oversight. OED also interviewed stakeholders,[3] including Bank managers and program partners, and visited partnering agencies and developing countries. Not all stakeholders have equal knowledge about the partnerships, making analysis of stakeholders' perspectives and roles complex.

As with CGIAR, the other case studies evaluate each partnership as a whole and focus on the Bank's role and performance in realizing its comparative advantage in each program (box 1.2). The Bank acts variously as a convener, trustee, and donor and typically is the largest lender for activities related to the global programs. In the case of the Global Environment Facility (GEF), the Bank is a trustee and an implementing agency. For the Multilateral Fund for the Implementation of the Montreal Protocol (MLF), the Bank is an implementing agency but not a trustee. The Bank's financial support to global programs comes from the Development Grant Facility (DGF), from the Bank's net administrative budget, and from Bank-administered trust funds. Thus, the assessment of Bank performance includes the use of the Bank's convening power, the Bank's trusteeship, Bank financing and implementation of global programs, and, where appropriate and necessary, links to the Bank's country operations. Bank oversight of this set of activities is an important aspect of the Bank's strategic and programmatic management of its portfolio of global programs.

The Bank acts variously as a convener, trustee, and donor and typically is the largest lender for activities related to the global programs.

Issues and Trends in Global Programs

Global programs have become an important Bank activity, supplementing its lending and advisory work. The Bank is now engaged in more than 200 global and regional partnerships. Of these, about 70 programs fit the definition of global programs (box 1.1).[4] Their total expenditures were about $1.2 billion in FY01. That year the Bank spent $30 million of its administrative budget on global programs,

Box 1.2 What Is the World Bank's Comparative Advantage with Respect to Global Programs?

Comparative advantage **describes the ability of one economic actor to produce a good, a service, or knowledge at a lower opportunity cost than another economic actor.**

Opportunity cost **is the cost of forgoing one activity in favor of another, measured in terms of the goods, services, or knowledge whose production is forgone.**

The Bank's *Strategic Directions Paper* for fiscal 2002–04 identified three comparative advantages for the Bank at the global level—global mandate and reach, convening power, and ability to mobilize financial resources—and three at the country level—multisectoral capacity; expertise in country and sector analysis; and in-depth, country-level knowledge.

provided $120 million in grants from the DGF, and disbursed another $500 million from Bank-administered trust funds. Although DGF grants represent less than 10 percent of the total expenditures, these grants signal the Bank's priorities and de facto set standards for Bank-supported global programs.

Strategic planning and priority setting are difficult because issues requiring global collective action have been multiplying.

The Bank remains by far the largest manager of donor trust funds among international agencies. The stock of trust funds held by the Bank increased from $3.8 billion at end of FY02 to $7.1 billion at the end of FY04. Almost two-thirds of these trust funds were committed to global and regional programs. Disbursements to global and regional activities increased by 6 percent, from $495 million in FY02 to $526 million in FY03. CGIAR, GEF, and the Global Fund to Fight AIDS, Tuberculosis, and Malaria (GFATM) accounted for 56 percent of these disbursements.[5]

Global program priorities are changing. The programs reviewed represented 90 percent of Bank-supported global programs expenditures in 2001 (when the Phase 1 evaluation was launched). At that time, environmental programs had the highest share of expenditures of Bank-supported global programs. Since then, health's share has increased dramatically. GFATM disbursed about $200 million during its first two years of operation (in 2002 and 2003) and plans disbursements of about $750 million in 2004—equivalent to about 60 percent of the total expenditures of the Bank's global program portfolio in 2001.

Global, national, and local issues increasingly interact, requiring considerable thought about where and how global collective action can be most useful.

Strategic planning and priority setting are difficult because issues requiring global collective action have been multiplying. The diversity of issues that programs face reflects diverse views of globalization. To some, globalization means the liberalization of international trade and investment or setting global rules and standards with respect to air and sea navigation, to trade in endangered species of plants and animals, or to the trafficking of women and children. To others, it means the spread of ideas, values, and norms consistent with the principles of democracy and equal rights for all. Moreover, thanks to the communications revolution, global, national, and local issues increasingly interact, requiring considerable thought about where and how global collective action can be most useful (Scholte 2000). The programs are responding to the emerging consensus that dramatic changes in areas such as trade, finance, intellectual property, investment, technology, health, environment, and security offer both opportunities and threats that spill over national borders.

Global programs provide global public goods, and more. Awareness of cross-border spillovers and the need for collective action has helped produce a specialized vocabulary related to global public goods (box 1.3). The Bank has defined global public goods as "commodities, resources, services—and also systems of rules or policy regimes with substantial cross-border externalities that are important for development and poverty reduction, and that can be produced in sufficient supply only through cooperation and collective action by developed and developing countries" (World Bank 2000, p. 2). Pure global public goods are few: peace and security; information and knowledge; trade and traffic rules; and the mitigation of climate change, financial contagion, and communicable diseases.

The global program agenda has widened beyond the provision of pure global public goods requiring supra-national action. The agenda increasingly includes multicountry "corporate advocacy" programs that aim to exploit economies of scale and scope in the provision of national and local public goods, private goods, and merit goods, such as empowerment, social inclusion, gender, education for all, maternal and child health, and water and sanitation—all areas in which the Bank is active at the country level. The conception of some goods as public or private has also changed. For example, research on

Box 1.3 Global Public Goods, Merit Goods, and the Logic of Global Collective Action

Public goods are distinguished from private goods by nonrivalry and nonxcludability. Nonrivalry means that many people can consume, use, or enjoy a public good at the same time: one person's consumption does not reduce the benefits that others can derive from consuming the same good at the same time. Nonexcludability means that it is difficult to exclude from consumption those who do not pay for or otherwise contribute to the cost of supplying the good.

Global public goods are distinguished from national and local public goods by their reach. Their nonrivalry and nonexcludability spill across national boundaries. People in more than one country can benefit from the provision of a global public good, whether or not they contributed to the cost of supplying the good. For national and local public goods, only those who live in a given country or in a given locality can benefit from the provision of such public goods.

The distinctions between public and private and between local, national, and global vary in practice, depending on such factors as the level of economic development, prevailing technology, and social choices.

Market mechanisms tend to undersupply public goods and to oversupply public "bads" such as air and water pollution. While large countries sometimes find it in their own interest to supply a global public good, in the absence of a global government with taxation powers, some kind of global collective action or partnership is generally necessary to supply them. Partners contribute grants, again because there is no global government to lend to.

Merit goods are goods whose value derives from the activities or consumption patterns of others or, in the case of foreign assistance, individual nations. The concept of merit (or demerit) goods should not be confused with that of public goods, since it transcends the distinction between public and private goods. When donors direct development assistance to certain uses, rather than providing pure, untied assistance to developing countries, they are implicitly attaching merit to their own preferences, whether the assistance is tied to the provision of public or private goods. (See Musgrave 1998.)

child work and labor issues, which arose in relation to international trade discussions, has fostered awareness of the global benefits of moving children from work to school (Basu and Tzannatos 2003). Because the size of official development assistance (ODA) has been relatively stable in recent years (figure 1.1), the increased spending on global programs translates into a larger share of ODA going to such programs.

Demand for new organizational forms is spawning global programs. The growing popularity of global programs reflects the concern that established international organizations and the governments that constitute them lack the capacity to address these complex, multilayered, and increasingly multisectoral issues by themselves. Addressing these issues requires the voices of multiple stakeholders. The traditional international organizations do not sufficiently incorporate the perspectives and comparative advantages of stakeholders such as civil society organizations, nongovernmental organizations, and the private sector. Global programs seek more agile organizational forms to reflect these perspectives and to bring fresh approaches to the challenges of globalization. They also aim to mobilize additional resources from unconventional sources; exploit the various actors' comparative advantages; and provide speedier, more targeted responses.

The needs of Bank clients are becoming more diverse. Establishing coherence between global program priorities and country priorities poses a challenge because the relative importance of the constraints that the Bank's client countries face varies considerably. Communicable diseases, climate change and conflict afflict the poorest of the Bank's

The growing popularity of global programs reflects the concern that established international organizations and the governments that constitute them lack the capacity to address these complex, multilayered, and increasingly multisectoral issues by themselves.

Figure 1.1 Official Development Assistance Has Fluctuated, but Not Grown, since 1990

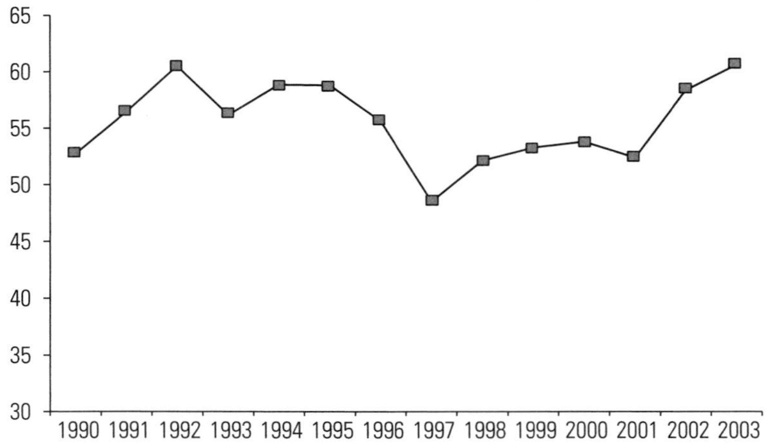

Source: OECD, net official development assistance from Development Assistance Committee member countries, in real terms, adjusted for inflation and fluctuations in exchange rates.

186 members more than they do others. Intellectual property rights and private capital flows affect the countries with large industrial bases and domestic markets differently than the resource- and import-dependent countries. Yet the scope for cooperation among the Bank's client countries, for example in the production and trade of drugs and vaccines, has also increased considerably.

The World Bank's involvement in global programs is responding to the new global reality. Like many other international organizations, the Bank has recognized that, in an era of aid harmonization, it cannot singlehandedly address many global issues that affect its clients. Nor should it be perceived by the key opinionmakers in the donor countries to be acting alone. The Bank has been adjusting to this new reality. But how well is it using global programs to shape and manage this new external environment for the benefit of the poor in its client countries? Because of its global reach and the multisectoral nature of its analytic and lending activities at the country level, the Bank is, in principle, in a unique position to influence the relevance and content of individual global programs and to set clear priotities among them. Moreover, through its support for, and active involvement in, global programs, the Bank can help bring new global knowledge, technologies, products, practices, and standards to its client countries. Is the Bank exploiting its comparative advantage well?

The World Bank's involvement in global programs is responding to the new global reality.

Table 1.1 Management Actions Following OED's Phase 1 Report

OED Phase 1 recommendations	Management actions
Organization	
Management should strengthen strategic planning and oversight of global programs and partnerships. While the networks would continue to have the primary responsibility for task management and partner relations, management should task a central vice presidential unit (VPU) to: • Set standards, oversee programming and budgeting, perform quality assurance functions, and report annually to senior management and the Board on program implementation. • Provide intellectual leadership, monitor and anticipate changes and emerging opportunities in the global environment, and draw partnership implications for the Bank. • Identify constraints in the global policy environment that need to be addressed to improve development outcomes for the Bank's clients.	A Global Programs and Partnerships (GPP) Council, composed of key Regional, network, and central vice presidents and co-chaired by two managing directors, has been established and is becoming operational. A GPP Group has been established to support and advise teams involved in GPPs and to provide an anchor for coordination and analysis across the Bank.
Strategy	
Management should articulate a strategy for Bank involvement in global programs and policies that establishes overarching objectives, oversight responsibilities, and the Bank's comparative advantage. The central VPU should: • Develop and monitor performance indicators to ensure that networks and Regions are linking global programs, country assistance strategies, and sector strategies. • Develop clear and transparent criteria and guidelines for resource allocation; budgeting, accounting, and auditing practices; and information systems for global programs.	GPPs are being incorporated into the business planning processes of network anchors, Development Economics, and the World Bank Institute. Tracking of spending on GPPs is being improved by more uniform use of business processes and product lines related to GPPs. Rules have been clarified for allowable use of Bank budget and grants for support of GPPs.
Selectivity	
The central VPU should establish and monitor standards for networks to follow for global programs relating to verifiable objectives, dedicated Bank resources, appropriate organizational and funding arrangements, and some form of cost-benefit or other ex ante criteria for Bankwide prioritization and quality assurance. The central VPU should: • For programs above a threshold size, help institute a transparent identification, preparation, appraisal, Board approval, supervision, and evaluation process. • For new small programs of a merit-goods nature that are not presented to the Board, help improve approval, monitoring, and auditing in the DGF, in particular by introducing independent reviews that are external to the programs. • Help adapt to global programs the standards and procedures applied to innovative lending operations such as learning and innovation loans and adaptable program loans.	External ex ante review by peers outside the Bank has been instituted for new GPP proposals for DGF funding. During the vetting and prioritization process for the FY04 DGF budget, sector boards were more thorough in reviewing applications than in the past. The Bank's chief economist has been designated responsible for oversight of CGIAR.
Program Implementation	
Management should clarify the responsibilities and accountabilities of the Board, Regions, networks, and task managers and provide each with the resources needed to fulfill the Bank's commitments with its partners, including: • Introducing a more systematic and regular approach for task-manager monitoring of program performance • Ensuring independence of program evaluations • Including global programs in the standard evaluation and reporting processes of OED.	Standardized governance models are being developed. More early-stage advisory support is being provided to new programs. Improved terms of reference have been developed for evaluations of DGF-supported programs.

Overview of the Case Study Programs

The programs are very heterogeneous. Their diversity poses a challenge not only for evaluating individual programs and for deriving crosscutting lessons, but also for equipping the Bank to develop an effective global strategy and program selectivity.

The programs vary widely in size. They range from Understanding Children's Work (UCW), with expenditures of $560,000 in CY02, to the Consultative Group on International Agricultural Research (CGIAR), with expenditures of $395 million in CY03. As shown in table H.1, only six of the programs, or 23 percent of the programs reviewed, had annual expenditures of more than $21 million in CY03/FY04.[1] These programs represent 82 percent of the total FY04/CY03 expenditures of the case study programs. Another eight programs had expenditures between $10 and $21 million in the same period.

The programs also vary in age. They range from the CGIAR, which began in 1972, to the Financial Sector Reform and Strengthening Initiative (FIRST), which began in December 2002. Only six programs are more than 10 years old (figure 2.1). Although less can be said about the outcomes and impacts of the newer programs, reviewing them offers lessons about establishing clear and shared objectives, a sound strategy, good governance, and resource mobilization. This report thus reviews these dimensions of the programs, in addition to their outcomes and impacts.

The programs are heavily concentrated in a few of the Bank's networks and sectors. The Environmentally and Socially Sustainable Development Network accounts for the bulk of total program expenditures and DGF grants from the programs in FY03 (table 2.1), with the Human Development Network a distant second.[2] These network and sector shares are representative of the Bank's global program portfolio, but they differ greatly from the sector distribution of Bank lending commitments, since the latter reflect country and Regional priorities arising from the Poverty Reduction Strategy Paper (PRSP) and Country Assistance Strategy (CAS) processes.[3]

Divergence between the Bank's global programs and country lending priorities is to be expected in the case of global programs that provide global public goods because of externalities, spillovers, and the differences between global and local costs and benefits. Such a divergence would prevail whether the

The Environmentally and Socially Sustainable Development Network accounts for the bulk of total program expenditures and DGF grants.

Figure 2.1 Age of Case Study Programs

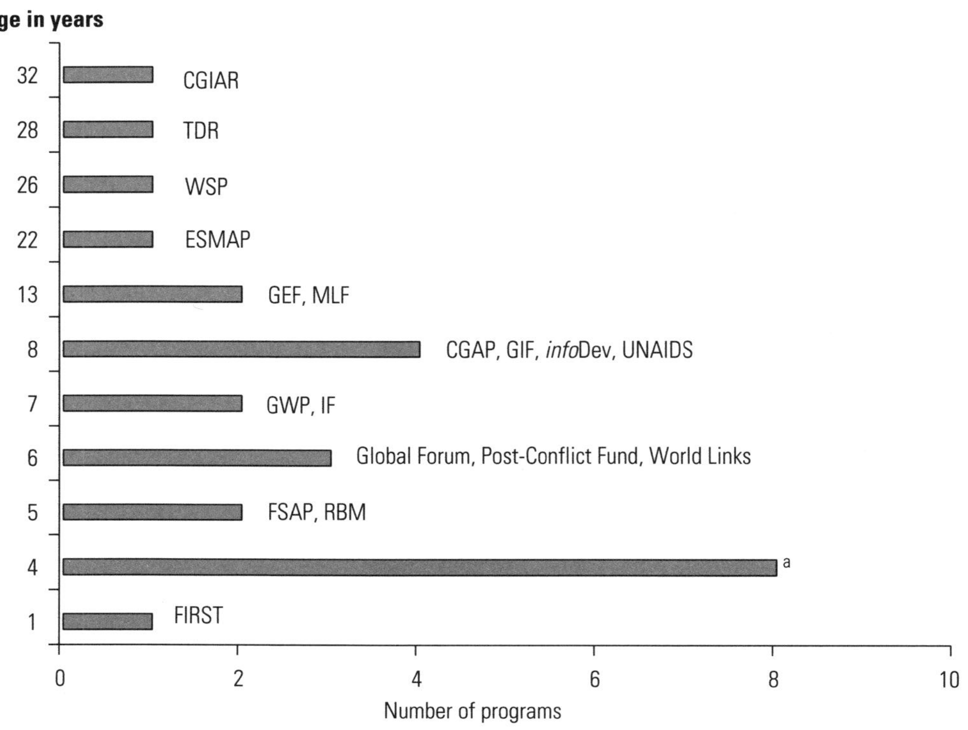

a. CEPF, Cities Alliance, GAVi, GDN, Prototype Carbon Fund, PPIAF, Stop TB, and UCW.

Table 2.1 Environment and Agriculture Are the Largest Case Study Programs

Network	Sector	Programs	FY04 program expenditures [a] $Millions	FY04 program expenditures [a] Percent	FY04 DGF grants [b] $Millions	FY04 DGF grants [b] Percent
ESSD	Environment (ENV)	GEF, MLF, ProCarbFund, CEPF	572.8	40.8	4.0	4.0
	Agriculture & Rural Development (ARD)	CGIAR, GWP, GIF	406.6	29.0	50.0	50.3
	Social Development (SDV)	PostConFund	10.6	.8	9.2	9.3
HDN	Health, Nutrition, & Population (HNP)	TDR, Global Forum, UNAIDS, RBM, Stop TB, GAVI	301.8	21.5	16.2	16.3
	Education & Social Protection (EDU/SP)	World Links, UCW	4.5	.3	1.6	1.6
INF	Infrastructure	WSP, ESMAP, *info*Dev, PPIAF, Cities Alliance	57.7	4.1	6.4	6.4
FSE	Finance	CGAP, FSAP, FIRST	27.8	2.0	6.7	6.7
PREM	Poverty Reduction & Economic Management	IF, GDN	21.4	1.5	5.3	5.3
	Total		**1,403.2**	**100.0**	**99.4**	**100.0**

a. Or most recent fiscal year.

b. Grants from the Bank's Development Grant Facility (DGF). Eight programs—GWP, GIF, GEF, MLF, ProCarbFund, WSP, ESMAP, and FSAP—did not receive DGF grants in FY04.

global public goods affect both industrial and developing countries (as does climate change), or benefit mostly the world's poor (as do vaccines and drugs). The issue of divergence is more complex in the case of the multicountry corporate advocacy programs that promote policy reforms at the national and local levels.

Moreover, global programs often have as an implicit or explicit objective the coordination of donor approaches and practices in a sector, and the shifting of country priorities toward the approaches and activities being advocated at the global level. The necessary links between global and country programs depend on program design objectives, activities, and intended outcomes and must be adapted to account for country needs and priorities. When global programs are not well linked to country priorities, country needs, and country activities, they raise issues about country demand and ownership, and about exactly whose needs and priorities are being advocated.

Program Objectives

The programs vary in their objectives, their activities, and whether they produce primarily global or national, public, private, or merit goods. Generating and disseminating information and knowledge about best practices in a sector, advocating approaches to development in a sector, capacity building, and supporting national-level policy and institutional reforms are the most common activities among the case study programs (figure 2.2).[4] Few programs provide global public goods or mobilize substantial incremental resources.

Notwithstanding this range of activities, two aspects of global programs are of particular interest for the Bank from a strategic and programmatic perspective:

- *Whether each program aims primarily to provide global public goods for which global collective action is required, or to engage in "corporate advocacy" in support of the provision of national and local public, private, or merit goods.* The latter try to use multicountry programming to exploit economies of scale and scope in developing and promoting consensus on how to address national and local problems. Programs in this category must pass the subsidiarity test (box 2.1).

Figure 2.2 The Programs Are Engaged in a Wide Range of Activities

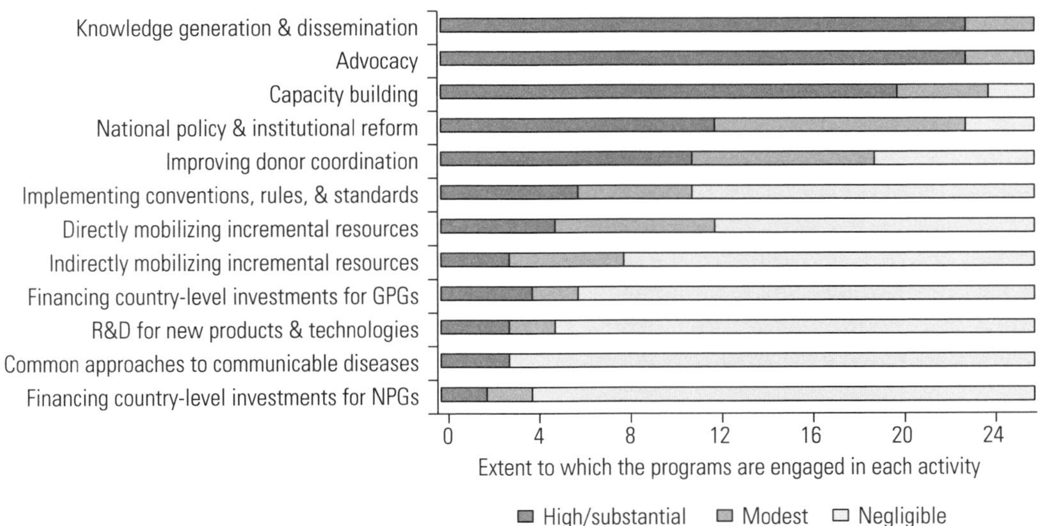

Note: GPG = Global Public Good; NPG = National Public Good.
Source: Table H.8: "OED Assessment of Actual Program Activities."

Of the 26 programs, only 2 and part of a third are financing global-level investments to deliver global public goods by mobilizing the best of science with a view to developing new technologies and processes for the benefit of the poor in developing countries.

- *Whether the programs have their own financing mechanism* or rely on the investments or technical assistance activities of others, such as Bank loans and credits and donor or national funding. The programs that lack a direct investment component pose by far the most complex issues in determining what constitutes a "global program." Does a program comprise only the activities of the global program secretariats, or does it also include the supporting—particularly the investment—activities of the partners? The latter activities are typically not considered part of global programs, since they are not under the program's direct control.

When the 26 programs are classified according to these 2 criteria (table 2.2), only 2 programs (CGIAR and the Special Program for Research and Training in Tropical Diseases [TDR]) and part of a third (the Global Alliance for Vaccines and Immunization [GAVI]) are financing *global-level investments* to deliver *global* public goods by mobilizing the best of science with a view to developing new technologies and processes for the benefit of the poor in developing countries.[5] Moreover, because of increasingly restricted donor funding, CGIAR's activities have moved downstream to include applied and adaptive research of a national and local public-goods nature, as well as agricultural development. If they have enough Bank and donor assistance, developing countries could conduct these latter types of activities more cost-effectively and sustainably, while freeing up global resources for those activities that are best done at the global level.[6] In short, at least a portion of the $50 million allocated to CGIAR from the DGF has violated the DGF's subsidiarity principle by financing Center activities that regular Bank instruments could support better and longer.[7]

For TDR as well, donor funding has become more restricted. Pressures on TDR have increased to deliver downstream results, rather than to conduct long-term health research that might benefit the poor, which is best done at the global level (TDR, Third External Review Committee). Moreover, unlike the situation for agriculture, neither donors nor governments have financed much *national-level* health research in borrowing countries (though Bank experience, based on the limited health research it has financed, suggests that it has high returns).[8] GAVI, which is primarily a child vaccination program, also finances global-level research and development for vaccine and drug development and, indeed, has now become the largest source of funding for global research and development on the health issues of the poor. It is also helping to stimulate global spending on research and development by others.

Four environment programs—the Global Environment Facility (GEF), the Multilateral Fund for the Implementation of the Montreal Protocol (MLF), the Prototype Carbon Fund,

Box 2.1 Subsidiarity: Who Does What

The subsidiarity principle addresses the issue of selecting the most appropriate level at which activities should be carried out. Management has posited this issue for global programs as "whether an activity should be carried out by a global program rather than, as the preferred option, implemented through country operations." Global programs would be the appropriate level for an activity when the benefits of collective action relative to the transaction costs of the global partnership exceed the net benefits from the Bank, using its normal instruments.

Table 2.2 Most Programs Primarily Address National Public Goods or Capacity

	Financing global investments	Financing country-level investments	Fostering country-level approaches, standards	Financing country-level technical assistance[a]	Strengthening country-level capacity	Number of programs
Delivering global public goods	CGIAR (1972), TDR (1975)	GEF (1991), MLF (1991), ProCarbFund (2000), CEPF (2000)	UNAIDS (1996), RBM (1998), Global Forum (1998), Stop TB (1999)[c]			10
Delivering national public goods		PostConFund (1998), GAVI (1999)[b]	CGAP (1995), GIF (1996), GWP (1997), UCW (2000)	WSP (1978), ESMAP (1982), IF (1997), PPIAF 1999), Cities Alliance (1999)	*info*Dev (1995), World Links (1998), GDN (1999), FSAP (1999), FIRST (2002)	16
Number of programs	2	6	8	5	5	26

Note: Each program is classified by OED according to only one category, corresponding to its primary activity. Programs are listed chronologically by start date within each category.

a. With the intent of stimulating public or private investments in the sector.

b. The GAVI Vaccine Fund also finances research and development of new vaccines and promotes strategies to address the constraints to R&D investment.

c. Stop TB also has a small drug facility that is financing country-level investments in the form of drugs for the treatment of tuberculosis.

and the Critical Ecosystem Partnership Fund (CEPF)—finance *country-level investments* to deliver *global* public goods, such as preserving biodiversity, protecting international waters, and reducing emissions of carbon dioxide and other ozone-depleting substances.[9] One social development program and one health program—the Post-conflict Fund and GAVI—finance *country-level investments* to deliver *national* public goods.[10] Even though peace and security are global public goods, OED concluded that the Post-conflict Fund, *as the program is currently designed and implemented,* is delivering primarily national, at best regional, public goods.[11] The eight programs with investment components represented 83 percent of the case studies' total FY04 expenditures.

Three health programs—the Joint United Nations Program on HIV/AIDS (UNAIDS), Roll Back Malaria (RBM), and the Stop Tuberculosis Partnership (Stop TB)—promote common approaches to mitigating communicable diseases, and a fourth program—the Global Forum for Health Research—is advocating increased global research on the diseases most prevalent in developing countries. While these four programs advocate political mobilization for increased public investment in these areas, they do not provide a significant level of financing for investment.[12] Rather, they are designed to encourage countries to follow the program's advice or approach in their ongoing activities.[13] But each program also calls on donors and countries to invest more in their respective health activities. Partly thanks to their advocacy, Bank lending for communicable diseases grew by an average of 7.6 percent annually between 1993 and 2003, and for HIV/AIDS alone by 17.6 percent annually, while overall health sector lending remained constant.

Of the remaining 14 programs, 5 finance country-level technical assistance for reforms to stimulate public and private investments in their respective sectors. These are the Water and Sanitation Program (WSP), the Energy Sector

Some of these same programs are also geared to improve donor practices and to harmonize the standards they use and the approaches they promote.

Management Assistance Program (ESMAP), the Integrated Framework for Trade-Related Technical Assistance (IF), the Public-Private Infrastructure Advisory Facility (PPIAF), and the Cities Alliance. The programs do not finance investments, because the benefits of such investments would largely be national or local. It is assumed that the respective national, subnational, or local governments would be prepared and able to borrow funds or receive grants to finance such investments. As demonstrated below, evidence does not always bear out this assumption. In addition, for the Integrated Framework for Trade-Related Technical Assistance, PPIAF, and the Cities Alliance, to finance country-level technical assistance could also violate the DGF subsidiarity criterion. The extent to which these programs replace or compete with regular Bank technical assistance will be addressed in the later chapters.

Four programs—the Consultative Group to Assist the Poorest (CGAP), the Global Water Partnership (GWP), the Global Integrated Pest Management Facility (GIF), and UCW—promote approaches and standards (box 2.2) for addressing global concerns at the country level. Some of these programs are also intended to help deliver global public goods indirectly by providing information and knowledge to improve national capacities and practices in areas where it is not easy to distinguish between a national and a global public good, such as financial management or food safety. Some of these same programs are also geared to improve donor practices and to harmonize the standards they use and the approaches they promote—for example, through policy advice, institutional development, and financial assistance in the areas of microfinance, or through safeguards with regard to the uses of pesticides.

Three programs—the Information for Development Program (*info*Dev), World Links for Development, and Global Development Network (GDN)—are intended to build capacity in information and communication technologies, education, and socioeconomic research. Their activities are primarily at the national level, although, once again, some of their intended activities are to promote national capacity to share knowledge across countries and across regions. The final two programs—the Financial Sector Assessment Program (FSAP) and FIRST—strengthen

Box 2.2 Both "Approaches" and "Standards" Raise Practical Issues: The Devil Is in the Details

Standards are developed to deal with cases where the goods or services being produced are so complex that the users cannot fully evaluate the product for themselves. The objective of standards, such as the Basel Core Principles for Effective Banking Supervision and the Bank of International Settlements Principles on Payment and Settlement Systems, is to specify what must be done at a minimum to achieve objectives held by those who use, and those who are affected by, the standards.

However, there are frequent differences of opinion among respected professionals about particular standards, which can have large consequences for development. For example, Wilson and Otsuki (2002) find that, if the world were to adopt the more stringent European Union standard on the use of pesticides in the production of bananas rather than the less stringent one suggested by Codex (the body charged with setting global standards in this area), world exports of bananas could be reduced by $5.3 billion annually.

Approaches refer to strategies such as the commercialization and privatization of energy, community-based management of natural resources, integrated water management, and integrated pest management. But approaches are not silver bullets for solving particular development problems. To implement them effectively requires considerable multisectoral and contextual information and knowledge on policies, institutions, and human resource capacities, combined with the ability to adapt approaches to specific circumstances.

country-level capacity for macroeconomic management; the banking system; and the securities, insurance, and other financial markets—FSAP by diagnosing strengths and weaknesses in these financial systems, and FIRST by providing technical assistance to strengthen them.

Governance and Management

The programs are complex partnerships with multiple partners at both the governance and activity levels—international and regional organizations, bilateral donors, private foundations, developing countries, nongovernmental organizations (NGOs) and other civil society organizations, and the private sector.[14] While most programs have now evolved to include stakeholders beyond the traditional donors on their governing bodies, international organizations and donors still have large roles and an overwhelming share of the responsibility to ensure effective partnerships—issues discussed in chapter 5.

Where programs are located and how they are governed and managed influence incentives for performance and accountability for results. The pros and cons of an arm's-length relationship with the Bank, specifically its effects on program independence, accountability, and performance, have been debated in the Bank since OED's 1998 process review (OED 2002a). OED argued that the lack of an arm's-length relationship creates potential conflicts of interest that could hurt program performance. (This is also an issue for programs housed in other international organizations.) The review emphasized the importance of maintaining such distance. Since then, the number of in-house programs has increased, though recently the Bank has also begun to implement program exit strategies—issues discussed in chapter 7.

Twelve programs are located inside the Bank or shared between the Bank and other organizations; eight are located in other organizations; and six are independent legal entities (table 2.3 and table H.3). Two programs—the Post-conflict Fund and FSAP—do not have a formal governing body, so that the Bank's Executive Board is the effective governing body of both programs. (Indeed, the Bank's Executive Board approved both.) They are managed by Bank program managers who report to their line managers within the Bank's management chain.

For the Post-conflict Fund, the Bank is the only partner at the governance level, though the program does have some partners who have contributed trust funds and others (such as UNHCR and UNICEF) who have had responsibility for implementing particular activities. Both the U.N. High Commission on Refugees and the U.N. Children's Fund raised the issue with OED of whether there should be a global program in post-conflict reconstruction, involving external partners, rather than just an internal Bank program. The Steering Committee of the Post-conflict Fund, chaired by the director of the Bank's Social Development Department and composed entirely of Bank staff, is responsible for approving applications for grants for activities in conflict-affected countries. The Fund is in many respects similar to some other Bank-managed programs that are supported by multidonor trust funds, but the Bank classified it as a global program in April 2000 because it receives DGF funding (after the CGIAR, the second-largest DGF grant to a global program).

Where programs are located and how they are governed and managed influence incentives for performance and accountability for results.

The Financial Sector Assessment Program (FSAP) is a closely coordinated parallel activity with the International Monetary Fund (IMF). The Financial Sector Liaison Committee is co-chaired by the Bank and the IMF and is composed of three staff members from each organization. The two program managers for the Bank and the IMF report to their respective line managers. The two organizations contribute their own financial and human resources to the program without pooling these resources into a common fund.

The Bank chairs or co-chairs all but two of the programs that have secretariats located inside the Bank (table 2.4). These secretariats

Table 2.3 Governance and Management Arrangements Are Diverse

Major classification	Subclassification	Number of programs	Programs[a]
Line management within the Bank	Standard multidonor trust fund	1	PostConFund
	Programmatic trust fund[b]	0	
	Carefully coordinated parallel partner activities	1	FSAP (with IMF)
Secretariat inside the Bank	Bank as lead partner	7	ProCarbFund, WSP, ESMAP, CGAP, *info*Dev, PPIAF, CA
	Independent governance structure	1	GEF
Secretariat functions shared between Bank and an external organization		2	CGIAR (with FAO)[c] FIRST (with DFID)[d]
Secretariat inside an external organization	External organization as lead partner	6	CEPF (Conservation International), GIF (FAO), RBM (WHO), Stop TB (WHO), UCW (UNICEF in Florence), IF (WTO)
	Independent governance structure	2	GAVI (UNICEF), TDR (WHO)
Independent external entity	Not a legal entity[b]	0	
	Legal entity	4	MLF (Montreal), GWP (Stockholm), Global Forum (Geneva), UNAIDS (Geneva)
	Legal entity with close identification with the Bank	2	GDN (Washington, moving to New Delhi), World Links (Washington)

Note: This classification scheme follows work on governance and management arrangements done in the Legal Department of the World Bank. GDN = Global Development Network.

a. Location of program in parentheses—organization or city—if not located in the World Bank.

b. Although none of the case study programs falls into these two categories, some other Bank-supported global programs do.

c. The CGIAR Secretariat is located in the Bank, and the Science Council (previously TAC) Secretariat is located in the Food and Agriculture Organization.

d. The Management Unit (under management contract with DFID) is located in London, and the Coordination Unit is located in the World Bank in Washington.

report to governing bodies composed of donors and other partners. Most were designed as such or were modified, typically in a period of financial crisis, to give more voice and accountability to the donors and other external partners. The Bank's vice president of infrastructure (INF) is the chair or co-chair of the six infrastructure programs' governing bodies, and the respective program managers are managers or directors of units in the INF vice presidency (table 2.4). The program manager thus reports to the Bank INF vice president, both as his Bank manager and as chair of the governing body. This sets up a potential "two masters" problem (Davis and Stark 2001), which has implications for program performance, accountability, and risk management, as discussed in chapter 5.

While the six infrastructure programs have many common features, the Prototype Carbon Fund and the GEF are more idiosyncratic. The Prototype Carbon Fund's program manager and head of the fund management unit (the secretariat) chairs the Fund Management

Table 2.4 Unlike Programs Housed outside the Bank, Those Housed inside the Bank Tend to Be Chaired by the Bank

Governance model	Chaired or co-chaired by the World Bank	Chaired by other organization	Rotating chair among member partners	Independent chair[a]
Line management within the Bank	Post-conflict Fund, FSAP[b]			
Secretariat inside the Bank	WSP, ESMAP, CGAP,[c] *info*Dev, PPIAF, Cities Alliance[d]		Prototype Carbon Fund[e]	GEF
Shared secretariat between Bank and external organization	CGIAR, FIRST			
Secretariat inside external organization	CEPF[f]	GIF (FAO) UCW (UNICEF) [g]	RBM, Stop TB, GAVI, TDR, IF[h]	GWP, Global Forum
Independent external entity			MLF, UNAIDS, GDN, World Links	
Number of programs	11	2	10	3

a. The chair, selected specifically for the position, is an eminent person who does not represent one of the members of the program.
b. World Bank and IMF co-chair the Financial Sector Liaison Committee.
c. World Bank chairs the Council of Governors. Chair of the Executive Committee rotates among bilateral member donors.
d. World Bank and UN-Habitat co-chair both the Consultative Group and the Steering Committee.
e. The chair of the Participants' Committee rotates annually among the public and private sector participants. World Bank chairs the Fund Management Committee.
f. The World Bank chairs the Donor Council. Conservation International chairs the Working Group.
g. Unclear protocol on chair of the GIF Governing Group and UCW Steering Committee.
h. Chair of the Steering Committee rotates. WTO chairs the Working Group.

Committee, which prepares projects for approval. The Participants' Committee approves the projects, and its chair rotates annually among the 6 public sector and 17 private sector participants in the program.

Although the GEF Secretariat is housed in the Bank, and although the Bank is both the trustee and one of the three implementing agencies, the program has a completely independent governing structure separate from the Bank (box 5.1 below). Of the 12 programs that are fully or partially housed inside the Bank, the GEF has perhaps the clearest responsibility and accountability structure. However, the reasons why accountability for performance remains a challenge for GEF are discussed in chapters 4 and 5.

The two programs partially housed in the Bank—CGIAR and FIRST—have even greater ambiguity on responsibilities and accountabilities, since a Bank vice president chairs the CGIAR and a managing director currently chairs FIRST, while the Bank shares the secretariat functions with an external entity. The CGIAR Secretariat is located in the Bank and the Technical Advisory Council (TAC)/Science Council Secretariat is located in the Food and Agriculture Organization (FAO) of the United Nations. Nonetheless, OED's meta-evaluation of the CGIAR concluded that responsibility for managing the CGIAR system has accrued over time to the Bank—an issue discussed further in chapter 5.

For FIRST, the Coordinating Unit is located in the Bank, and the management unit is contracted out by the U.K. Department for International Development (DFID) to a private entity in London. The Coordination Unit is responsible for non-private-sector-implemented projects, helping to generate projects from the Bank and IMF, the Information Exchange,

> *Most programs located in external partner organizations have chairs that rotate among member partners, thus distancing them somewhat from the organizations that house them.*

and the due diligence process. The Management Unit processes and classifies all projects, recruits private sector consultants, and manages other projects.

Most programs located in external partner organizations have chairs that rotate among member partners, thus distancing them somewhat from the organizations that house them. A notable exception is CEPF, which is housed in Conservation International (an NGO) and chaired by the World Bank President. This is the only case among the 26 programs in which an organization that does not house the secretariat is designated the chair of the governing body.

Few programs are independent legal entities. Of the six cases that are, the chair rotates among members in four cases and is an eminent person specifically selected for the purpose in two cases. Two of these programs—GDN and World Links—have been spun off from, but remain financially dependent on, the Bank. How and how well the Bank has applied exit strategies is discussed in chapter 7.

> *Twelve of the 26 global programs brought in almost $90 million in FY03 that supplemented the Bank's administrative budget. This can itself become an unstated incentive for partnerships.*

The Bank's Roles

The Bank plays 11 different roles in these programs (table 2.5 and table H.4). Noteworthy among the various roles, discussed in chapter 7, is that of a lender to activities related to the objectives of all 26 programs, and that of a founder or co-founder of 25 of the programs. Furthermore, the Bank is on the governing bodies of 23 of the programs. Unlike other international organizations where global programs are housed, the Bank chairs all but two of the programs housed in the Bank. In addition, 12 of the 26 global programs brought in almost $90 million in FY03 that supplemented the Bank's administrative budget (table 2.6). The infrastructure vice presidency is the largest beneficiary of these supplementary resources. This can itself become an unstated incentive for partnerships. As stated in chapter 1, the Bank is the largest manager of trust funds among international organizations. It currently manages a stock of more than $7 billion in trust funds, almost two-thirds of which is devoted to global and regional programs.

Given this substantial demonstrated potential for Bank influence, how successful has the Bank been in contributing to the programs' strategic direction and oversight; in promoting synergy between global and country activities; and in ensuring their accountability, value added to the Bank's operations, and impacts in client countries? Are the incentives for program selectivity distorted by the fact that some programs clearly bring in considerable additional funds for program implementation? These issues are discussed in chapters 4 through 7.

Table 2.5 World Bank Plays Multiple Roles in Global Programs

Role	Number of programs Yes	Number of programs No	Programs where applicable
Lender to the sector[a]	26	0	
Founder or co-founder	25	1	All except MLF
Member of governing body	23	3	All except GEF, MLF,[b] ProCarbFund
Convener of initiatives in the sector[c]	23	3	All except MLF, GIF, UCW
Financial contributor (DGF or Bank budget)[d]	22	4	All except GEF, MLF, ProCarbFund
Trust-fund trustee	18	10	CGIAR, GEF, MLF, ProCarbFund, UNAIDS, Stop TB, WSP, ESMAP, CGAP, *info*Dev, PPIAF, CA, PostConFund, IF, FSAP, FIRST, GDN, World Links
Houses secretariat	12	14	CGIAR, GEF, ProCarbFund, WSP, ESMAP, CGAP, *info*Dev, PPIAF, CA, PostConFund, FSAP, FIRST
Implementing agency[e]	12	14	GEF, MLF, ProCarbFund, ESMAP, *info*Dev, PPIAF, CA, PostConFund, UCW, IF, FSAP, FIRST
Chair or co-chair of governing body[f]	11	15	CGIAR, CEPF, WSP, ESMAP, CGAP, *info*Dev, PPIAF, CA, PostConFund, FSAP, FIRST
Trust-fund manager[g]	10	16	ProCarbFund, WSP, ESMAP, CGAP, *info*Dev, PPIAF, CA, PostConFund, IF, FIRST
Co-sponsor	6	20	CGIAR, GWP, GIF, TDR, UNAIDS, ESMAP

a. "Lending" in this context includes all aspects of Regional operations, including PRSPs, CASs, economic and sector work, policy dialogue, and lending.

b. World Bank attends GEF and MLF meetings as an implementing agency.

c. The Bank takes the initiative to organize meetings and conferences in the sector on issues related to, but outside the scope of, the program in order to advocate change, reach consensus, or mobilize resources with respect to emerging issues in the sector.

d. Financial contributions to the program itself, not including Bank Budget resources spent on oversight and liaison activities.

e. The Bank's operational staff, not including the staff of in-house secretariats, is involved in either the supervision or the implementation of program activities.

f. While the Bank chairs the Fund Management Committee of the Prototype Carbon Fund, the chair of the higher-level Participants Committee rotates annually among public and private sector partners.

g. Involves responsibility for oversight and management of how the trust fund resources are used.

Table 2.6 Many Programs Contribute Financial Resources That Supplement the Bank's Administrative Budget

Sector	Program	FY03 contribution (US$ millions)	Comments
Environment	GEF	25.1	Administrative budget provided by GEF to the Bank for project-related expenses, program coordination, and trusteeship
	MLF	4.77	Administrative budget provided by MLF to the Bank for project-related expenses and program coordination
	Prototype Carbon Fund	4.09	Administrative expenses of the Prototype Carbon Fund, not including grant disbursements
Health	UNAIDS	2.47	Funds disbursed from UNAIDS trust fund (received from UNAIDS) for monitoring and evaluation activities
	GAVI	1.47	Funds disbursed from Gates and other trust funds for GAVI and child vaccination activities
Infrastructure	WSP	11.4	Total program expenditures, less Bank's administrative budget contribution
	ESMAP	5.46	Total program expenditures, less Bank's administrative budget contribution
	CGAP	3.90	Program expenditures funded from donor trust funds
	*info*Dev	5.81	Total program expenditures, less Bank's DGF and administrative budget contributions
	PPIAF	12.5	Total program expenditures, less Bank's DGF contribution
	Cities Alliance	7.97	Total program expenditures, less Bank's DGF contribution
Trade	Integrated Framework	1.29	Funds disbursed from UNDP trust fund (received from UNDP) for IF studies implemented by the Bank
Total		86.3	

Program Relevance to Global Challenges, Bank Priorities, and Country Priorities

Assessing relevance is by far the most challenging task in evaluating global programs, since resources, comparative advantages, benefits, costs, and priorities at the global and country levels do not always coincide. Indeed, the divergence of benefits and costs between the global and country levels is often a fundamental reason for the need for global public goods.

Evaluating the relevance of global programs to the Bank's client countries is nonetheless important, because the global development agenda has become congested and, with the few exceptions highlighted below, global programs have brought few extra resources to overall ODA. This is why being more selective among programs is important.

The Bank has established four major criteria for assessing the relevance of global programs at entry/approval and during implementation:

- *International consensus:* The program reflects an emerging international consensus that global action is required (endorsed by the Development Committee on September 25, 2000).
- *Clear link to the Bank's core institutional objectives and, above all, to the Bank's country operational work:* In its presentation to the Board on January 30, 2001, Bank management added that each program should have a clear strategic rationale consistent with the relevant sector strategy paper (established by Bank management in November 2000).
- *Subsidiarity:* The program does not compete with, or substitute for, regular Bank instruments (established by the DGF Council on October 28, 1998). Bank management also indicated in its March 2003 update to the Board that it would henceforth apply this criterion rigorously to all global programs.
- *Strategic focus:* Management also indicated (in its March 2003 update) that it would ensure that global programs comprise activities that (1) provide global public goods, (2) support international advocacy for reform agendas that significantly address policy frameworks relevant for developing countries, (3) are multicountry activities that *crucially depend on highly coordinated approaches*, and/or (4) mobilize substantial incremental resources that can be effectively used for development.[1]

Given the breadth of these criteria, it is possible for a wide range of partnership programs to claim eligibility to receive Bank support. In addition, these criteria are not appropriately applied either ex ante, to assess the initial relevance of new global programs, or ex post, during oversight of implementation, to ensure their continuing relevance.

First, even though many—but not all—global programs can provide evidence for consensus on what they are trying to achieve and how, this is typically a consensus among donors and international agencies. The Bank's developing-country clients have emphasized to OED that they have little voice in the consensus-building process about what objectives the programs should pursue or how to pursue them effectively.

Second, with rapid changes at the global level, the process of articulating sector strategies as consensus documents has become long and costly. Moreover, sector strategies have been weak in articulating global concerns, in providing strategic links between global programs and country operations, and in establishing clear principles for selectivity with respect to global programs of greatest operational relevance to the Bank's clients.

Third, while the subsidiarity criterion could, in principle, be applied strictly to limit global programs to those that do not compete or substitute for regular Bank instruments, the relationship between the provision of global and national public and private goods has rarely been adequately explored before a program is formed.

Fourth, by including both global public goods and corporate advocacy among the Bank's four strategic foci for global programs, the potential topics for a global program are essentially made limitless. Besides, management has indicated that they view the strategic foci only as descriptors to identify global programs that should be overseen during implementation.

Fifth, alleviating poverty is not an explicit criterion among the selectivity and oversight criteria for global programs. It is simply implied in the second Development Committee criterion (a clear value added to the Bank's development objectives), in the first approval criterion (a clear linkage to the Bank's core institutional objectives), and in the definition of corporate advocacy as "the critical enablers of poverty reduction that the Bank is particularly well-qualified to champion by sharing knowledge (both research and experience) and building awareness with clients, development partners, and other stakeholders." The links of each program's objectives and activities to sustainable growth and poverty reduction need to be well defined at the outset and monitored during implementation, from inputs through outputs to outcomes and impacts.

Alleviating poverty is not an explicit criterion among the selectivity and oversight criteria for global programs.

Sixth, the Bank is still essentially following a one-stage approval process for new global programs (box 1.1). This approval process does not provide an adequate assessment of operational relevance. To supplement this, OED recommended in its Phase 1 report that the Bank institute a transparent identification, preparation, and appraisal process, with Board approval for global programs above a threshold size and an independent external review in the DGF for programs below that size. In addition, OED suggested an appraisal template for global programs above the threshold size.[2] These recommendations have not yet been implemented, although in FY03 the DGF did institute an ex ante review by peers outside the Bank for new global programs seeking DGF funding.

Evidence of International Consensus

International consensus is articulated by stakeholders in the "global community" and is reflected in as many ways. The Millennium Declaration in September 2000 and the Millennium Development Goals (MDGs) are the most recent manifestations of a formally endorsed, broad-based international consensus on economic and social development that also has a strong poverty focus.

OED has classified the case study programs by how their creation reflects an international consensus (tables 3.1 and H.6). For example, two programs are formally responsible for implementing international conventions to which both industrial and developing countries are signatories—the Global Environment Facility (GEF)[3] and the Multilateral Fund for the Implementation of the Montreal Protocol (MLF).[4] These convention-based programs enjoy strong legitimacy thanks to their formal authorizing environments, strong participation of developing countries in their design and implementation, and equitable governance arrangements. These programs are unique in their acknowledgment of the differing priorities of developing and industrial countries. Developing countries sought and achieved financing mechanisms for the incremental compliance costs of achieving global environmental benefits.[5] Compared with the other programs OED has reviewed, these two

The GEF and the MLF are unique in their acknowledgment of the differing priorities of developing and industrial countries.

Table 3.1 Genesis Is One Indicator of International Consensus for a Program

Category	Number of programs	Programs	Convention, agreement, conference, or standards
A. The program is formally responsible for implementing an international convention	2	GEF	1992 U.N. Framework Convention on Climate Change (UNFCCC), 1992 Convention on Biological Diversity (CBD), 1994 U.N. Convention on Combating Desertification (CCD), and the 2001 Stockholm Convention on Persistent Organic Pollutants (POPs)
		MLF	1987 Montreal Protocol on Substances That Deplete the Ozone Layer
B. The program arose out of an international conference	5	UNAIDS	1994 Resolution of the United Nations Economic and Social Council
		IF	1996 WTO Ministerial Conference, Singapore
		WSP	1977 World Water Conference and Declaration, Mar del Plata, Argentina
		Cities Alliance	1996 Conference on Human Settlements (Habitat II) and Istanbul Declaration
		UCW	1997 International Conference on Child Labor and Oslo Agenda for Action
C. The program is facilitating the implementation of formal standards, international agreements, or formally agreed-upon approaches	5	FSAP, FIRST	Basel Core Principles for Effective Banking Supervision, IOSCO Principles of Securities Regulation, IAIS Insurance Core Principles, Bank of International Settlements Principles on Payment and Settlement Systems, IMF Principles on Transparency in Monetary and Fiscal Policies
		ProCarbFund	1997 Kyoto Protocol to the UNFCCC
		GWP	1992 Dublin Conference on Water and Environment and 1992 U.N. Conference on Environment and Development, Rio de Janeiro
		GIF	Agenda 21 and the 1992 Convention on Biological Diversity (CBD)
D. Donor partners collectively agreed to establish the program	9	CGIAR, TDR, Global Forum, RBM, Stop TB, GAVI, ESMAP, CGAP, PPIAF	
E. World Bank sought other partners after initially founding the program	5	CEPF, *info*Dev, PostConFund, GDN, World Links	

Note: Each program is assigned to only one category.

programs are large, significant, well conceived, and well organized, given the magnitude of the challenges they address.

Ten programs arose out of international conferences or are facilitating the implementation of formal standards and approaches (categories B and C in table 3.1). While these programs also focus on some of today's most important global challenges, they have not been directly formed by parties to implement an agreement. They represent a less explicit form of international consensus. None of these programs except the Prototype Carbon Fund has an attached financing mechanism. When programs are largely oriented toward advocacy and not complemented by financing for investments, they lack credibility and ownership in developing countries. Their objectives, even when broadly defined to include technical assistance, training, and capacity building, as well as their results, tend to be harder to assess. Even when financing arrangements are subsequently established in response to the expressed needs and concerns of developing countries and the experience of trying to do program activities, the funds tend to be insufficient, and the organizational arrangements tend to be weak.

The global programmatic responses to developing-country priorities in trade, finance, and infrastructure illustrate the problems of an inadequate response. Most programs remain small relative to the needs and demands of developing countries, and some involve high transaction costs.[6]

The Integrated Framework for Trade-Related Technical Assistance (IF) is an example of a program with a wide gap between its objectives and means and the expectations of developing countries. Its primary goal is to better integrate trade policy into the domestic planning process and into Poverty Reduction Strategy Papers (PRSPs). (See table H.2 for details on program objectives and strategy.) However, developing countries also seek open and fair markets for their products in industrial countries and investment finance from donors to address internal supply constraints, such as physical infrastructure, institutional capacity, and personnel training.[7] Programs such as the IF are inadequate instruments either for widening external market access or for loosening domestic supply constraints. Indeed, the IF seems to lack enough funds even to meet its more limited objectives. As an interim measure, the IF has begun providing a small amount of technical assistance as "bridging finance"—with a cap of $1 million per country—to follow up on the diagnostic studies, with the expectation that follow-up resources for technical assistance and investments will be provided through the PRSP process.[8]

Understanding Children's Work (UCW) was conceived in response to the need for strengthened cooperation and coordination between the Bank, the International Labour Organisation (ILO), and UNICEF, articulated at the 1997 International Conference on Child Labor and the Oslo Agenda for Action. There was a general recognition in Oslo that, despite a common policy framework in the form of ILO Conventions No. 138 and No. 182, and the U.N. Convention on the Rights of the Child (CRC), action on child labor was poorly coordinated across the three agencies. The program has provided significant support for informal, interagency technical coordination and has begun to address the lack of comparable data on child labor. To date, though, there remain varying definitions of child work and varying approaches stemming from the different institutional cultures and mandates of the three agencies.

Advocacy programs can direct attention and resources to daunting country realities. UNAIDS, for example, which arose from a 1994 U.N. Economic and Social Council resolution, is cosponsored by eight U.N. agencies and the Bank. UNAIDS has convinced the Bank and donors to pursue policy dialogue, increase their own financial commitments to communicable diseases, and contribute to the creation of GFATM in 2002. The new agreement on antiretroviral drugs among the Clinton Foundation, the World Bank, UNICEF, and the Global Fund demonstrates the power of global partnerships to achieve a global policy consensus. Bank partners have stressed to OED that no single actor, particularly the existing international agencies, could have done this alone. The agreement holds the potential for increasing the supply of affordable, quality drugs for poor countries, although operationalizing this agreement will be a major challenge and will take time. Having made considerable progress, AIDS programs face new challenges (box 3.1).

The remaining 14 programs (categories D and E in table 3.1) were established by groups of donors coming together to address a major global challenge or by the Bank, which then sought partner support. While "supply-led," some of these programs have acquired ownership among developing countries by demonstrating substantial impacts. Both CGIAR and TDR started as donor initiatives, but acquired considerable ownership by delivering new products, technologies, and knowledge that complemented the countries' own efforts. These programs illustrate that, if well conceived and implemented with appropriate partnerships, externally driven programs can deliver results and develop ownership (OED 2003b).

The global program agenda involves many donors (figure 3.1). Donors are using "international consensus" to deliver technical assistance and approaches to solving problems they consider important. Many donors have become disenchanted with traditional means of delivering development assistance. Driven by the need to be accountable to their own domestic constituencies in order to maintain support for aid programs, they are less well focused on linking global agendas to developing-country objectives, while developing-country governments are often unaware of many programs' objectives, scope, and means of operation.

The new agreement on anti-retroviral drugs demonstrates the power of global partnerships to achieve a global policy consensus.

Since the capacity of donors and international agencies has not kept up with the expanding global agenda, they often look to global programs to help build their own capacities—as in the cases of IF, UCW, and the Consultative Group to Assist the Poor (CGAP). The programs are often intended to improve aid coordination among donors and international agencies. A related objective is to mobilize resources for individual organizations through global aid programming. Yet these

Since the capacity of donors and international agencies has not kept up with the expanding global agenda, they often look to global programs to help build their own capacities.

Box 3.1 AIDS Programs Face Continuing Implementation Challenges

Recent progress has prompted new challenges for the implementation of HIV/AIDS programs:

At the global level:

- **How to deliver tools to political leaders to help achieve the necessary behavioral changes to prevent further spread of the disease**
- **How to deal with the different priorities of developing- and industrial-country governments for the containment of HIV/AIDS and communicable diseases, relative to other development priorities in health and other sectors**
- **How to address the inadequate, albeit increased, amounts of funding.**

At the country level:

- **How to address health-system capacity constraints, even with the support of private vendors, community organizations, and NGOs, to better assess needs and improve delivery in under-funded and overstretched health-delivery systems**
- **How to reduce the stigma of infection and increase the willingness and means of households to pursue testing or treatment**
- **How to address the information gaps on a variety of fronts, including monitoring and evaluation.**

Source: UNAIDS 2003.

programs rarely diagnose their partners' capacity to participate in program activities or to link the program activities to their own country work. The objectives and activities focus largely on improving the behavior of developing countries and less on improving the internal workings of the donor countries, donor agencies, or international organizations. For example, donor coordination is one of the four specific activities CGAP is supposed to pursue under its Phase III, and was also an explicit objective under Phases I and II. Yet the program's own Phase II evaluation cited weak achievement on this front, specifically with regard to program financing, information-sharing, and mainstreaming microfinance in donor agencies, even though these are explicit requirements of the participating donors (Fox, Havers, and Maurer 2002).

The Millennium Declaration in September 2000 and the resulting Millennium Development Goals (MDGs) reflect international consensus, have a strong poverty focus, and provide concrete targets for assessing progress. Not surprisingly, virtually all programs assert their alignment with the MDGs to enhance their own legitimacy. The objectives of half of the study programs are directly related to specific MDG targets, but their outputs are only some of the ingredients needed to achieve the respective MDGs (table H.7). The remaining programs' objectives are related to the MDGs only insofar as the goods and services the programs provide are necessary to achieve particular MDG targets. Though both industrial and developing countries have endorsed them, the MDGs represent a consensus on *what* needs to be done, rather than on *how* to do it. OED's consultations with partnering agencies indicate that the new global programs strain the limited financial and institutional capacity of even the partnering international organizations. The strain is worse in developing countries, particularly those with the greatest incidence of poverty and the least institutional and financial capacity.[9] This poses a risk of dashed expectations and cynicism.[10]

Figure 3.1 Donor Participation Varies in the Case Study Programs

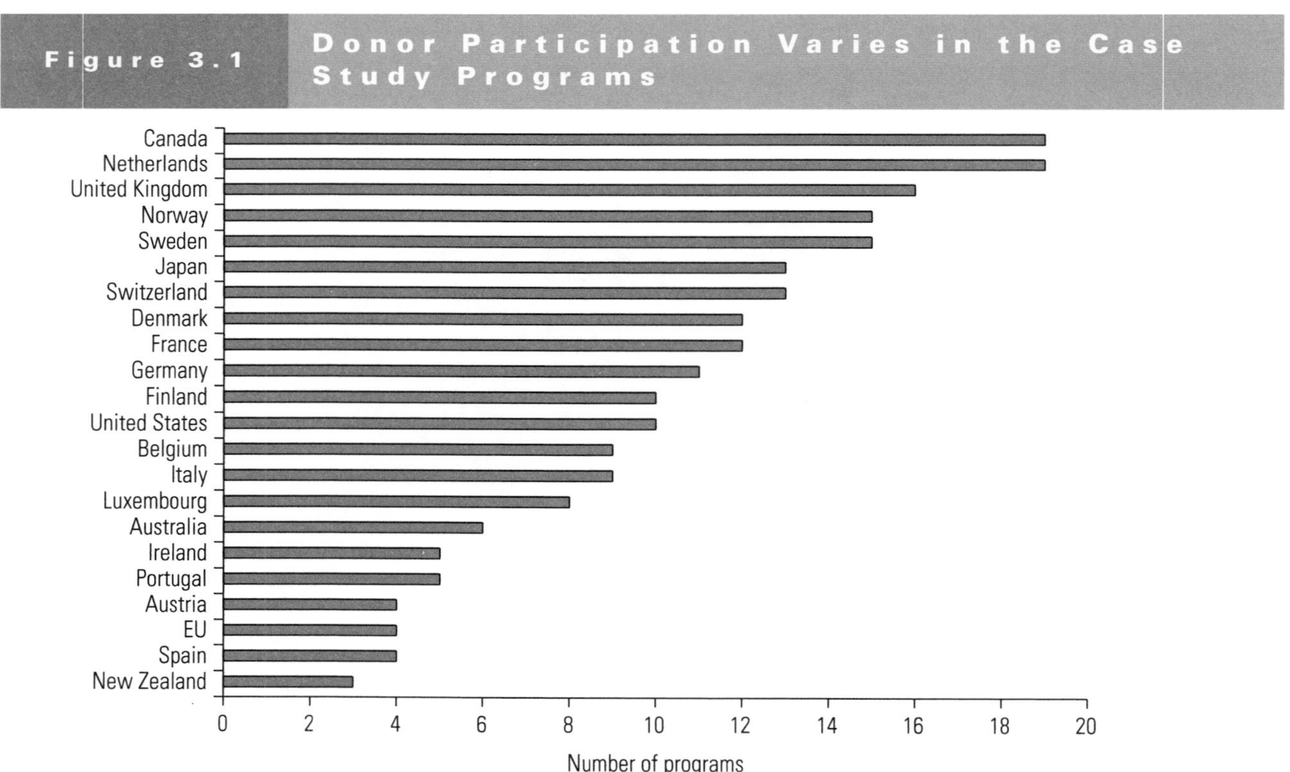

Overall, the voice of developing countries in determining what constitutes international consensus is weak, and needs to be reflected through links to Poverty Reduction Strategy Papers (PRSPs) and Country Assistance Strategies (CASs). OED has traditionally defined relevance in the context of investment projects as "the extent to which the project's objectives are consistent with the country's current development priorities and with current Bank country and sectoral assistance strategies and corporate goals (expressed in Poverty Reduction Strategy Papers, Country Assistance Strategies, Sector Strategy Papers, Operational Policies)."[11] In specific country PRSPs and CASs, OED evaluators found few mentions of the issues that the global programs address.[12] The relationship of global programs to PRSPs and CASs needs to be strengthened to reflect genuine international consensus and introduced as a criterion for Bank support of global programs.

Consistency with the Bank's Sector Strategies

As part of the approval process for involvement in new partnerships, Bank management requires that all partnerships should have a clear strategic rationale consistent with the relevant sector strategy paper. "If such strategies are not available in advance, a clear explanation should be provided about the relationship of a proposed partnership to an agreed upon work program."[13] As part of the annual DGF vetting and prioritization process, the Bank's sector boards are also expected to indicate how grant proposals are prioritized and coordinated within the context of their sector strategies.

These criteria and procedures do not provide a basis for selectivity, for four reasons. First, management has acknowledged that sector strategies have mostly become advocacy documents that are poorly aligned with country programs. Based on a review of 16 sector strategies, that paper concluded that, while they were strong on strategic relevance and analytic quality, they were weak on business focus (such as guidance to staff on priorities, choice of instruments, and business planning) and on monitoring of implementation (including establishing indicators of outcomes and clear monitoring responsibilities). Thus, even if global programs were aligned with the sector strategies, this would not guarantee alignment with the needs and priorities of the Bank's client countries. Given the challenges of matrix management, global programs managed by networks have weak links with Bank operations.

The voice of developing countries in determining what constitutes international consensus is weak.

Second, networks have little incentive or capacity to review and prioritize their annual grant proposals to the DGF Council across networks. Rather, their incentive is to retain as large a share of the DGF funds within their respective sectors as possible, even if several networks offer proposals on closely related topics. Their capacity to address the global-policy and country-capacity challenges facing the global programs and to explore their relationship to other proposals is limited and declining (as OED demonstrated in its CGIAR meta-evaluation). If Regional managers serving on the sector boards see no benefit in these global programs for their Regional operations, they dismiss them as the business of the sector and network anchors.

Third, global programs would serve the Bank and its clients better if they were more independent of the Bank and if they mobilized global knowledge and ground-level experience in developing countries so as to inform, not reflect, the Bank's investments and approaches. While alignment with the Bank's prevailing approach may prevent client countries from developing alternative viewpoints, it also reduces the programs' supposed value of marshalling independent thinking and knowledge. As the CGIAR meta-evaluation showed with respect to policy research, what developing countries need from global programs are proven options in policies, technologies and institutional arrangements, whether or not those options reflect the Bank's alignments.

Global programs would serve the Bank and its clients better if they were more independent of the Bank.

The infrastructure programs and the Global Development Network also illustrate this point. According to its 2000 evaluation, ESMAP has had a major impact on Bank thinking.[14] WSP, ESMAP, and *info*Dev staff contributed to the most recent water and sanitation business strategy (September 2003) and to the information and communications technology (ICT) and energy sector strategies (January 2001 and December 2001). Yet respondents to OED's survey of stakeholders involved in the governance of these programs expressed concerns about the Bank's domination of the programs and the difficulty of advocating viewpoints different from the Bank's.

Recent OED reports on the electric power and the water and sanitation sectors found that in both sectors the approaches that the Bank has advocated since the early 1990s to encourage private sector development have performed poorly, and that Bank lending commitments have declined precipitously (OED, OEG, and OEU 2003; OED 2003a). It is unclear to what extent ESMAP and WSP contributed global knowledge and best practices during this period that were independent of the prevailing Bank views on private-sector development—either to the Bank's own operational policy dialogue and advice to its client countries, or directly to the Bank's clients who faced the challenges of declining private investment (especially after 1997), disappearing donor aid flows, poor public sector performance, and mounting NGO criticism of the Bank's advice.

The lack of coordination of the content of global programs within a sector, the poor integration of their content into Bank country operations within a sector, and the lack of evidence of the Bank benefiting from independent thinking have led to lack of coherence across sectors in the messages emanating from Bank-supported global programs.

In the case of the GDN, external stakeholders view both the reality and the perception of independence from the Bank as essential to promote policy research that developing countries need, rather than what is aligned with the so-called Washington Consensus. Members of its governing board consider GDN's relocation, first outside the Bank and then outside Washington, to be one of several essential steps to provide it the independence needed for setting relevant research agendas for the Bank's clients. One of GDN's regional networks, the African Economic Research Consortium, established a governance structure, research priority-setting processes, and financing to ensure that it was not driven by donors (including the Bank and IMF) and was truly responsive, and seen to be so, to Africa's analytical needs.[15]

Fourth, the lack of coordination of the content of global programs within a sector, the poor integration of their content into Bank country operations within a sector, and the lack of evidence of the Bank benefiting from independent thinking have led to lack of coherence across sectors in the messages emanating from Bank-supported global programs. Thus, whereas the health programs promote broad access to pharmaceuticals, the Financial Sector Assessment Program (FSAP) promotes adherence to international financial management standards that, in practice, preclude sufficient spending on health and other social sector ministries.[16] OED's report on the Highly Indebted Poor Country (HIPC) Initiative points out the incoherence between debt management and social spending promoted by donors.[17]

Consistency with the Subsidiarity Principle and the Bank's Strategic Foci for Global Programs

The subsidiarity principle (box 2.1) and the Bank's strategic foci for global programs are closely related. Corporate advocacy programs (the second strategic focus) that do not provide global public goods may violate the subsidiarity principle by competing with or substituting for regular Bank instruments. Such programs need to justify the Bank's involvement in the global partnership based on the program's ability to do something more efficiently or effectively than the Bank can do acting through country-level partnerships.

The prime candidates for adding value are activities associated with the third and fourth strategic foci; that is, activities with substantial economies of scale and scope, such as knowledge creation and dissemination, capacity building, improving donor coordination, and mobilizing incremental resources. Advocacy programs that are truly "multicountry...that crucially depend on highly coordinated approaches" may add value, among other things, through mutual learning across developing countries or through the availability of increased global expertise based on comparative advantage. But the criterion does not explain what is meant by "multicountry programs that *crucially depend on highly coordinated approaches.*" Does it mean coordination among donors, among developing countries, or among sectors within a developing country?

To assess the consistency of the activities of the case study programs with the Bank's four strategic foci, OED has expanded each strategic focus, as follows:

(1) Providing global public goods:
- Implementing conventions, rules, or formal and informal standards and norms
- Financing research and development for new products and technologies
- Financing country-level investments to deliver global public goods
- Promoting common approaches to mitigating communicable diseases.

(2) Supporting international advocacy for reform agendas that in a significant way address policy framework conditions for developing countries:
- Advocacy
- Supporting national-level policy, institutional, and technical reforms
- Financing country-level investments to deliver national public goods.

(3) Multicountry programs that crucially depend on highly coordinated approaches:
- Generation and dissemination of information and knowledge
- Capacity building and training
- Improving donor coordination.

(4) Mobilizing substantial incremental resources that can be effectively used for development:
- Directly
- Indirectly.

OED found that all 26 programs are multicountry efforts that support international advocacy in one way or another (table H.8). As stated in chapter 2, 10 programs and part of GAVI's Vaccine Fund provide global public goods (not including knowledge creation and dissemination, whose global public-goods characteristics must be verified through empirical research, since useful knowledge tends to be contextual). Two financial-sector programs—FSAP and FIRST—also support national implementation of international standards relating to macroeconomic management; the banking system; and securities, insurance, and other financial markets. The goal of both programs is to strengthen countries' financial systems to help mitigate the risks and costs of global financial crises—a genuine global public good.[18]

Prime candidates for adding value are activities with substantial economies of scale and scope, such as knowledge creation and dissemination, capacity building, improving donor coordination, and mobilizing incremental resources.

Only five programs—CGIAR, GEF, MLF, the Prototype Carbon Fund, and GAVI—mobilize substantial incremental resources. Only two programs provide new money from nonofficial sources—the Prototype Carbon Fund from private commercial sources and GAVI from the Gates Foundation. While the GEF and MLF have been incremental to ODA resources, it has been difficult to demonstrate any such increment to overall development assistance. Thus, the growth of global programs appears to be coming at the cost of country-level assistance.

OED supports management in extending the subsidiarity principle to all (including non-DGF) programs, because the inclusion of corporate advocacy among the criteria for global programs stemmed from the interest of the Bank networks in ensuring that "their" activities are inside the global tent. However, management

The growth of global programs appears to be coming at the cost of country-level assistance.

has not yet established the capacity in the GPP Council or Group to do this. Applying the subsidiarity principle effectively is a complex and difficult issue for at least four reasons.

First, there is the sheer empirical difficulty of assessing whether the value added in organizing a multicountry global partnership to provide national or local public or private goods outweighs the costs, compared with using the Bank's regular operational instruments.

Second, the Bank's own financial and human resources to do economic and sector work have declined, while the range and complexity of country issues needing Bank involvement have increased. Corporate advocacy programs add value of a financial or technical nature, such as budgetary or trust fund resources or in-kind technical assistance on a scale that the Bank could not provide from its own administrative budget. Some programs may also help donors improve their own bilateral operations. CGAP, for example, is called upon frequently by donors to provide technical assistance for their operations.

Third, global programs may also add intangible value to the Bank, such as a presence in major global forums, interaction with opinion-makers in specific areas, and membership in the global development community. The last includes participating in conventions such as the GEF and MLF, improving the consensus and donor coordination on controversial global issues such as HIV/AIDS and trade, improving the understanding of its partners, and increasing the relevance of a program's content based on the Bank's knowledge of its client countries.

Fourth, global and local agendas have merged, and a variety of stakeholders want to have a voice and to influence the Bank to pursue their agendas. According to their proponents, global programs help to maintain aid levels (or even increase them in the case of AIDS) that would otherwise dwindle by demonstrating to the issues-oriented aid constituencies that their concerns are being addressed. They also create awareness and constituencies for reform—as in the cases of Organisation for Economic Co-operation and Development (OECD) agricultural trade subsidies and intellectual property rights for pharmaceuticals.

Global public policy issues that will affect program outcomes get little attention in most programs. This poses a major challenge.

Conclusions

The 26 global programs reviewed in this report, while diverse in their origins, relevance, and ownership in developing countries, generally meet the Bank's selectivity criteria for global programs. But this is not difficult: the existing criteria are sufficiently broad to permit the approval of almost any global program that is engaged in activities within the Bank's development mandate. It is time to adapt, modify, and apply many of the processes and tools that the Bank has developed for its country operations to global programs, including a two-stage approval process—at the concept and appraisal stages—based on a deeper understanding of the difficulty of applying the current criteria. While OED recommended this in its Phase 1 report (OED 2002c, Annex A), this has not yet been implemented by Bank management.

Other than those promoting information and knowledge, only a third of the programs provide global public goods. The remaining programs address one or more global concerns through corporate advocacy at the country level. They do so by providing country-level technical assistance, conducting country-level studies, and fostering country-level capacity building closely aligned with the Bank. Such work largely produces national public or private goods rather than bringing global knowledge to bear on countries or Bank operations in the countries. The programs in this latter category raise subsidiarity issues. What value (beyond budgetary resources) is the global program adding that the Bank cannot achieve through partnerships at the country level? Are the programs raising substantial additional resources?

Global public policy issues that will affect program outcomes get little attention in most programs. This poses a major challenge: Where and how to address such policy issues, which usually require agreements among sovereign nations, and what if any role global programs can play in this process, beyond advocacy. When there are policy failures at the country level, the Bank can shift its support from investments to policy reforms. When there are global policy failures, such a shift is more difficult, because the forums in which such reforms occur are not those in which decisions on global programs are made.

Striving for Results: Assessing the Outcomes and Impacts of Global Programs

This chapter assesses three aspects of the case study programs' performance: (1) the quality of their monitoring and evaluation activities, (2) their links to country-level activities and the Bank's country operations, and (3) their value added to the Bank's clients and to the Bank.

There are huge variations across the programs in the availability of independently validated outcomes and impacts, summarized at the end of this chapter in table 4.3 and in Annex E. The variation in performance is partly a function of age (figure 2.1) and the extent to which program activities have direct outcomes on the ground.

Though the absence of evidence of impact does not imply the absence of impact, absence of evidence is often due to the lack of a results-oriented culture. In some programs, it also results from a combination of poorly defined objectives, weak monitoring and evaluation processes, and poor links to country-level activities.

Demonstrating program impacts is complicated by the number of partners, the range of objectives, the levels and interconnectedness of activities, and externalities and cross-border spillovers. Accurate financial information is often unavailable for program activities and for the partner and country activities that the programs influence. The concept of the opportunity cost of resources is rarely used in assessing global programs.

Assessing the outcomes and impacts of corporate advocacy program activities (technical assistance, studies, capacity building and policy, institutional or technical reforms) is inherently more difficult. Outcomes are difficult to track and costly to monitor. Within the Bank, country priorities are increasingly determined at the national level, which further complicates monitoring. In any case, country priorities do not always coincide with the industrial countries' perception of country needs.

Though the absence of evidence of impact does not imply the absence of impact, absence of evidence is often due to the lack of a results-oriented culture.

Despite these challenges, the number and quality of program-level evaluations have both improved during the past few years (table 4.1). Twenty-one of the case study programs

Table 4.1 Most Recent Program-Level Evaluations

Year completed	Number of programs	Programs
1998	2	CGIAR, TDR
1999	0	
2000	1	ESMAP
2001	2	GIF, Global Forum
2002	6	UNAIDS, RBM, CGAP, *info*Dev, Cities Alliance, Post-conflict Fund
2003	5	CEPF, GWP, Stop TB, UCW, IF
Taking place in 2004	4	WSP, GDN, MLF, GEF
Programs not yet evaluated[a]	6	World Links (1998), GAVI[b] (1999), PPIAF[b] (1999), FSAP (1999), ProCarbFund (2000), FIRST (2002)

a. Program starting dates in parentheses.

b. The GAVI Board has commissioned a number of evaluations of specific aspects of its program, and PPIAF's Technical Advisory Panel has conducted ex post evaluations of selected program activities.

have now had at least one program-level evaluation. The DGF requirement (instituted in June 2000) for programs receiving more than $300,000 annually to be evaluated every three to five years and the issuance of guidelines for such evaluations[1] have encouraged these trends. The challenges in improving the quality of evaluations and their impacts are both procedural and methodological.

Quality of Monitoring and Evaluation Activities

OED assessed monitoring and evaluation according to the following five criteria:[2]

- Clear and coherent program objectives and strategies that give focus and direction to the program and provide a basis for evaluating the performance of the program
- The use of a results-based management framework with a structured set of (quantitative or qualitative) output, outcome, and impact indicators
- Systematic and regular processes for data collection and management
- Independence of program-level evaluations
- Effective feedback mechanisms to reflect evaluation findings on strategic focus, organization, management, and financing of the programs.

Partners often weigh objectives differently and have different expectations of what the program should deliver.

Clear and Coherent Objectives and Strategies

A number of programs have process objectives rather than outcome objectives—objectives such as "to assist," "to help," "to support," and "to promote" are very common (table H.2). For instance, one objective of the GEF is to assist developing countries in meeting their obligations to international environmental conventions, yet donors increasingly seek evidence of impacts on global environmental outcomes.[3]

There is more agreement on the need for action than on what the action should be. Governing board members and program managers have indicated that programs are often established to achieve consensus and harmonize partner approaches to development in a sector. Examples include addressing water resources management, HIV/AIDS, private participation in infrastructure, microfinance, financial sector reforms, and information and communications technology. But partners often weigh objectives differently and have different expectations of what the program should deliver. Donor-related objectives are often unstated and harder to evaluate. There are no indicators to assess "harmonization" (box 4.1).[4]

Box 4.1 UNAIDS-Funded and Bank-Administered Monitoring and Evaluation of HIV/AIDS Programs Face the Challenge of Donor Coordination

UNAIDS formed the Global HIV/AIDS Monitoring and Evaluation Support Team (GAMET) at the World Bank to facilitate efforts to build country monitoring and evaluation capacities. GAMET has made progress in its first year of operation, including the establishment of an advisory board to offer guidance across agencies. Also put in place are country support teams, a network of consultant experts (most from Africa) in building capacity for monitoring and evaluation, and training in several countries for the design and implementation of a new management development intervention to provide an accountability framework. Yet a recent Bank report on the MDGs in health notes that all of the agencies participating in the GAMET initiative face tensions between their internal requirements for monitoring and evaluation and their desire for a coordinated approach at the country level. The donors are under pressure to show impacts in the short term, which can undercut even the best intentions to rely on country-based systems. The tradeoff between donors spending staff time working on coordinating approaches and building country capacity and on fulfilling fiduciary responsibilities to monitor their own programs generates additional problems. Notwithstanding these obstacles, GAMET is a worthy experiment. It is worth watching whether the donors will be willing to put nationals in the driver's seats of these coordinated monitoring and evaluation approaches.

Sources: Human Development Network, staff and country interviews.

Program objectives and activities evolve over time, some in response to the changing external environment, some based on lessons learned, and others simply to maintain donor support. CGIAR's original objective was to develop technologies that would reduce hunger, WSP's was to develop appropriate small-scale technology, ESMAP's was to assist developing countries hurt by the second OPEC oil crisis, and CGAP's was to establish a $100 million multidonor microfinance facility. CGIAR has since shifted its focus toward policy, social science, and natural resource management research; WSP and ESMAP toward improving sector policies and institutions in developing countries; and CGAP toward establishing standards for microfinance and disseminating best practices.

Frequent changes in a program's goals and objectives, such as with the Global IPM Facility, make it difficult to determine what should and can be evaluated. A good evaluation should assess whether the new objectives reflect the program's comparative advantage and core competence. OED's meta-evaluation of CGIAR concluded that its increased focus on policy, social science, and natural resource management research relative to productivity-enhancement research did not reflect the group's comparative advantage, which lay in mobilizing global scientific work on global public goods that would help reduce poverty. Developing countries can rarely mobilize global science on their own, but they can do cost-effective, locally relevant research on policy and national resource management.

When program objectives are unclear, strategies and activities may reveal more about program intentions than the stated objectives do. Evaluation needs to explore whether global programs focus on the right issues or whether other instruments are more appropriate to achieve the stated (country-level) objectives. Underlying each program's interventions are analytical and interdisciplinary issues requiring diagnosis of the problem at hand and the choice of appropriate instruments, including whether a global pro-gram is needed and, if so, what net value the program adds (box 4.2).[5]

Use of a Results-Based Framework

As a management strategy, focusing on performance and achievement of outputs, outcomes, and impacts; results-based management; and results-based evaluation (box 4.3) are all relatively new ideas that

Frequent changes in objectives make it difficult to determine what should and can be evaluated.

Box 4.2 To Deliver Global Public Goods of Benefit to the Poor, Global Programs Need Analytical Foundations with a Results-Based Orientation

While much of the growing program activity at the global level is justified on the basis of cross-border spillovers and cross-border benefits, it has lacked strong analytical foundations and well-thought-out results chains in programs' strategies. Global programs in agriculture, health, trade, and child work illustrate the complexity.

In the agricultural and environment sectors, the CGIAR must weigh its research priorities between mitigating the effects of climate change and adapting to climate change. The latter has more potential to help the poor in the Bank's client countries to tackle shifts in rainfall variability, higher temperatures, new or more threatening pests and diseases, and higher atmospheric carbon dioxide (CO_2) levels. Of course, win-win strategies for both developing and industrial countries are desirable. When this is not possible, CGIAR needs to focus on research that benefits the world's poor more than the global community.

In the health sector, developing countries' timely access to drugs at affordable prices has been a major thrust of global program advocacy. Access depends on the quality and quantity of drugs available, intellectual property rights, production and trade issues, and a variety of domestic diagnostic- and delivery-capacity issues. What constitutes a *global* or *national, public* or *private* health sector good is situation-specific. Access to drugs, ostensibly a private good, has become an issue of global public policy at the WTO because of the inability of developing countries to develop and produce new drugs and vaccines affordably or on a large enough scale. Whether drug access should be a publicly or privately supplied good—and the policy and the operational implications of these options for the strategies that individual developing countries should pursue—calls for both policy and empirical analysis on a country and global level to draw implications for advocacy and advice. Such analysis has often been weak.

With respect to trade, the focus of the Integrated Framework for Trade-Related Technical Assistance (IF) has been on mainstreaming trade in the countries' overall development strategy by its inclusion in the national plans and PRSPs. Diagnostic trade integration studies of least-developed countries' trade have identified both domestic and external constraints. Domestically, these include the regulatory environment, access to competitively priced transport and communication services, functioning of the labor market, labor-force skills, legal services, management of import procedures, and customs. Externally, these include general and commodity-specific tariff and non-tariff barriers that limit trade options in specific export markets. Mauritania faces barriers to potential exports such as camel cheese. Malawi's sugar exports are excluded from American and EU trade initiatives for Africa. Senegal's phosphate fertilizers face significant tariffs in India, the major importing country. The U.S. tariff barrier on tobacco amounts to 88 percent, Canada's on liver preparations 65 percent, and Japan's on boneless beef 40 percent.

In the cases of child labor and pesticide use, what may appear to be universally desirable values become the basis for erecting barriers to trade with developing countries. The child labor issue is driven by the universalization of norms and values. Restricting the use of pesticides involves a complex trade-off between farm productivity and developing-country competitiveness vis-à-vis the safe handling of pesticides to minimize adverse health and environmental impacts. The way in which both issues are currently addressed in the global programs focuses too little on arriving at effective operational solutions to achieve measurable (quantitative or qualitative) poverty reduction, health, or environmental indicators, and demands too much of the poorest and too little of industrial countries.

have only recently been fully incorporated into the Bank's business practices. Their limited use in global programs is thus not surprising. Programs financing investments at the global or national levels have a longer record of results-based management.[6] A growing number of program-level evaluations—such as the recent RBM, Stop TB Partnership, Cities Alliance,[7] UCW,[8] and IF evaluations—are also using results-based frameworks that recommend that the programs adopt results-based management practices, develop performance indicators related to outcomes rather than outputs alone, and generally adopt more businesslike management practices, including better accounting. These are positive developments.

Box 4.3 Key Terms in Results-Based Management and Evaluation

Results-based management: A management strategy focusing on performance and achievement of outputs, outcomes, and impacts.

Results chain: The causal sequence for a development intervention that stipulates the necessary sequence to achieve desired objectives—beginning with inputs; moving through activities and outputs; and culminating in outcomes, impacts, and feedback. In some agencies, reach is a part of the results chain.

Inputs: The financial, human, and material resources used for the development intervention.

Outputs: The products, capital goods, and services that result from a development intervention. This may also include changes resulting from the intervention that are relevant to the achievement of outcomes.

Outcomes: The likely or achieved short-term and medium-term effects of an intervention's outputs.

Impacts: Positive and negative, primary and secondary long-term effects produced by a development intervention, directly or indirectly, intended or unintended.

Indicator: Quantitative or qualitative variable that provides a simple and reliable means to measure achievement, to reflect the changes connected to an intervention, or to help assess an actor's performance.

Performance monitoring: A continuous process of collecting and analyzing data to compare how well a project, program, or policy is being implemented against expected results.

Source: OECD 2002.

Systematic and Regular Processes for Data Collection and Management

Data collection and monitoring vary widely across programs. At one extreme, CGIAR has been exemplary in regularly assessing the impacts of its research on increasing agricultural productivity (mostly germplasm and crop improvement research) and contributing to methodological advances. The number, frequency, and quality of its independent external impact evaluations are unmatched by the agricultural research systems of even the most advanced countries (Gardner 2002). Following the OED meta-evaluation, CGIAR is also moving rapidly to do impact assessments in the more difficult to evaluate areas of policy research, natural resource management research, and capacity building.[9] TDR and MLF have assessed and demonstrated clear and substantial impacts, as described in table 4.3.

At the other extreme, a lack of clarity and consensus on program objectives and the lack of a results-based framework mean that performance indicators, when they are available, are not well focused, appropriate, or tracked. There is often an implicit assumption that the program's outputs (such as studies) will lead to outcomes (such as policy and institutional reforms) and that these, in turn, will automatically expand the poor's access to technologies, information, or finance and improve their incomes and livelihoods. Assessment of whether this will occur or what follow-up steps are needed to achieve this is rarely part of program design or implementation. Related partner activities are insufficiently ranked. For example, IF assumed that the program's diagnostic trade integration studies (DTISs) would help integrate least-developed countries into the multilateral trading system, enhance their ability to participate in and benefit from the system, and improve their export performance. The DTISs would also incorporate trade in the PRSPs. But all of this has been a challenge. GWP assumed that promoting partnerships at the country and regional levels would support countries in the

Focusing on performance and achievement of outputs, outcomes, and impacts; results-based management; and results-based evaluation are all relatively new ideas that have only recently been fully incorporated into the Bank's business practices.

sustainable development of their water resources. UCW assumed that reconciling data sources from three different international organizations will speed the elimination of child labor. CGAP assumed that developing guidelines for financial sustainability of microfinance institutions would help build financial systems that work for the poor. Yet CGAP's partners do not even agree on whether an impact assessment of the ultimate beneficiaries is needed (box 4.4).[10]

It is admittedly more difficult to assess the ultimate impacts of technical assistance of a policy or strategic nature that is upstream of project preparation and investments. However, PPIAF has demonstrated that it is possible to systematically assess outcomes. PPIAF appears to have the most advanced monitoring processes among the technical assistance programs, which includes the involvement of the members of its Technical Advisory Panel in ex post, on-site reviews of a range of its activities.[11]

Program efficacy is enhanced when incentives to measure and deliver results are embedded in the program design—for example, through accountability to shareholders. The Prototype Carbon Fund has been highly attentive to project design and measuring results precisely because it has to provide internationally certifiable results to its private sector shareholders. Good design is also a feature of GAVI, financed primarily by the Bill and Melinda Gates Foundation. Incentive structures can be complex, affecting the Bank as well as partners and beneficiaries.

Methodological Challenges

Impact measurement needs more methodological and empirical attention. In the health sector, for example, the impacts of TDR research have been thoroughly assessed and found to be enormous, even if they have not been quantitatively measured (box 4.5). Although this makes comparisons of ex ante benefits across programs difficult, leading programs such as the CGIAR to claim a large share of DGF resources, to obtain a fair share of the resources, all program appraisals should

Box 4.4 Partners in Poverty-Focused CGAP Disagree on Need to Verify Program Impact on the Poor

The U.S. Microenterprise for Self-Reliance Act of 2000 made available $310 million over a two-year period for grants to microfinance institutions. The 2002 reauthorization of the Act allocates an additional $176 million for FY03 and stipulates that USAID, in consultation with microfinance institutions and other organizations, should develop and certify at least two methods for measuring the poverty levels of microfinance clients served by microfinance institutions that receive USAID grants. These methods are meant to ensure that at least 50 percent of USAID microenterprise assistance is set aside for the "very poor," defined as those who either live on less than $1 a day or who are in the bottom half of those below a country's poverty line.

Prior to the reauthorization, an Internet-based forum for microfinance professionals (the Microfinance Gateway) hosted a virtual discussion. The goal was to "better inform [the microfinance community] on ground-level realities and thus enable us to take well-reasoned positions to promote a financial sector that serves the needs of the poor."

Six members of the CGAP Executive Committee, representing the partners, participated and offered their views on the subject. Five voiced opposition to the required outreach verification, saying it would "stifle [microfinance institution] freedom and growth," "increase compliance costs, deter investments," and result in "formulaic restrictions (to) choke private sector incentives to serve the poor."

The remaining discussant noted that this is not regulation, but rather an investment target for subsidies paid for by U.S. taxpayers and added, "Is there a cost to getting to know your clients? Yes. Is investing in that knowledge bad for business? Absolutely not! . . . That's the nature of the market for sourcing funds (both publicly and privately). If you need a subsidy and can provide some informed analysis about the wealth of your clients, go to USAID. If you don't feel knowing the wealth of your clients is worth the effort, go somewhere else."

try to systematically assess expected benefits.

Counterfactuals to assess outcomes and impacts are not explored enough in evaluations. Most CGIAR impact studies of its productivity-enhancement research have researched the counterfactual of what would have happened to agricultural productivity had there been no CGIAR research. They have explored less well whether productivity growth would occur without investments in national agricultural research systems (Gardner 2003). OED's meta-evaluation of the CGIAR explored this issue more fully by contrasting the CGIAR impacts in Sub-Saharan Africa with those in Brazil and India (Eicher and Rukuni 2003; Macedo and others 2003; Katyal and Mruthyunjaya 2003).

Measuring results is a challenge in some of GEF's focal areas, such as biodiversity conservation (also being addressed by CEPF).[12] Methodological challenges in assessing biodiversity loss loom large, because both the sources and the beneficiaries of loss tend to be external to the protected area. Baselines and outcomes require sophisticated assessment, involving several levels of aggregation, to demonstrate impact.

GEF and its implementing agencies, including the Bank, are under increasing pressure from donors to develop outcome and impact indicators for biodiversity conservation. Questions being posed are: Is GEF developing better models for biodiversity conservation than are developing countries? Is GEF funding increasing the quantity or quality of global investments in biodiversity conservation and achieving significant global-level impacts? Are implementing agencies monitoring and

Box 4.5 Impacts of Global Agricultural and Health Research

CGIAR: Expenditures of $395 million in 2003; TDR: Expenditures of $47.5 million in 2003.

CGIAR impact studies suggest that an investment of $150 million a year in germplasm improvement generates more than $1 billion yearly in output that is attributable to the CGIAR. OED concluded that the social rates of return to investment in improved cereal crop varieties derived from CGIAR centers are very large. This research has had huge poverty-reducing impacts through an increased and more secure food supply, increased employment, reduced prices, and environmental impacts through more diversified and efficient land use. Having now trained nearly 50,000 agricultural scientists in developing countries (a third of the total), CGIAR has played a key role in the development of the scientific capabilities of developing countries' agricultural systems. CGIAR's work on environmental protection—countering global warming, fostering biodiversity, and improving policies through social science research—is more recent, and assessment of its impacts, even quantification of the baseline situation, is often very difficult. Uncertainty of returns to these new activities would be acceptable if the expanded agenda were costless, but not if it diverts resources from activities with higher expected returns.

TDR's evaluations, while not estimating rates of return, have identified three known impacts on diseases of the poor: (a) development of new tools, (b) product development, and (c) strengthening of developing-country research capacity. TDR has contributed to the use of Ivermectin for the treatment of onchocerciasis, to multidrug therapy for leprosy, and to the use of fumigant canisters for the vector control of Chagas disease. TDR's efforts have fostered the development of candidate vaccines for malaria, leishmaniasis, and schistosomiasis. As the fourth-largest financer of malaria research, TDR has had 85 percent of its papers cited at least once—the highest number of acknowledgments per million dollars invested. TDR provides unique access to an international network of experts and institutions for increased collaboration in large-scale field trials and product development through increased networking between researchers in the industrial and developing world. It has strengthened developing-country research capacity through the training of individual scientists, the establishment of independent research units, the transfer of technology and methods to research groups in developing countries, and its wider contributions to disease control. However, its funding has declined in real terms over the past decade and has become more restricted, while the program's research mandate has expanded (from 8 tropical diseases to 10) and expectations have grown. The greatest pressures facing TDR are the unavailability of untied resources, the growing trend of public-private partnerships, and donor pressure to deliver results on a short schedule.

evaluating project performance to know if global outcomes are being achieved?[13] GEF has begun to address these evaluation challenges jointly with the Bank. The task of aggregating outcome data to demonstrate global impacts remains.[14] GEF and its implementing agencies need to invest the kind of intellectual capital in global impact assessments of the GEF portfolio that the CGIAR partnership initiated, soon after its formation, on germplasm impacts.

Evaluation Processes: Independence of Program-Level Evaluations

Ideally, both evaluation and audit should be functions of a program's governing body, not its managers. They should be commissioned and managed by the governing body as an input into improving the program's objectives, strategy, design, and implementation. At initial stages, until the program is well established and the governing body has developed the capacity to do so, the founders, co-sponsors, lead donors, and financiers often manage the first generation of evaluations.

Evaluation documents do not always indicate who commissioned and managed the evaluation, who financed it, how much it cost, how the external evaluation team was selected, to whom the evaluation team reported, or how the initial drafts were reviewed. All these aspects influence the independence of the evaluations. When external evaluations are managed by program secretariats and do not report to the board chairs, independence and coverage of issues is compromised.

Evaluations tend to be relatively strong on process and weak on the substantive issues relating to program objectives, strategies, allocation of resources, the program's comparative advantage, and implications for development impact.[15] Given the breadth and complexity of coverage in most evaluations, the evaluation teams need the triple complement of technical expertise, knowledge of development, and knowledge of how donor agencies function and partner. When such a combination is lacking, evaluation findings tend to focus on the team's area of expertise.

Ideally, both evaluation and audit should be functions of a program's governing body, not its managers.

OED has concluded that that 5 of the 20 recent program-level evaluations were highly independent of management. The health sector global programs have had the strongest tradition of independent external evaluations. UNAIDS, the largest of the six health programs, established a donor-appointed secretariat to manage its recent evaluation.

Whether independent or not, recent external evaluations have had significant influence on programs in helping to improve objectives, strategy, focus, governance, and management arrangements. An important evaluative issue highlighted in the UNAIDS evaluation is to determine what constitutes a "program." Is it simply the activities of the secretariat or the activities of the key partners in the areas related to the program? The independent external evaluation of RBM in 2002 was perhaps one of the strongest in identifying the realism of goals and objectives; clarity in the responsibilities of the partners; and progress in achieving country-level buy-in, political mobilization, and quality of technical advice. The RBM program has been restructured substantially on the basis of the 2002 evaluation. Yet, as in several other programs, there is more agreement on what *strategy* to follow than on how to apply the instruments that RBM promotes.

Overall Assessment of Monitoring and Evaluation

Figure 4.1 summarizes OED's ratings of the monitoring and evaluation activities of the case study programs. Overall, fewer than a third of the programs have clear objectives, systematic and regular processes of data collection, and management and systems for feedback on control systems, finances, and strategic focus. An additional third could be rated as substantial on these scores.

Variations in the programs' age, size, objectives, scope, design, financing, and implementation make it difficult to compare outcomes and impacts across programs.

Figure 4.1 Overall OED Assessment of Monitoring and Evaluation

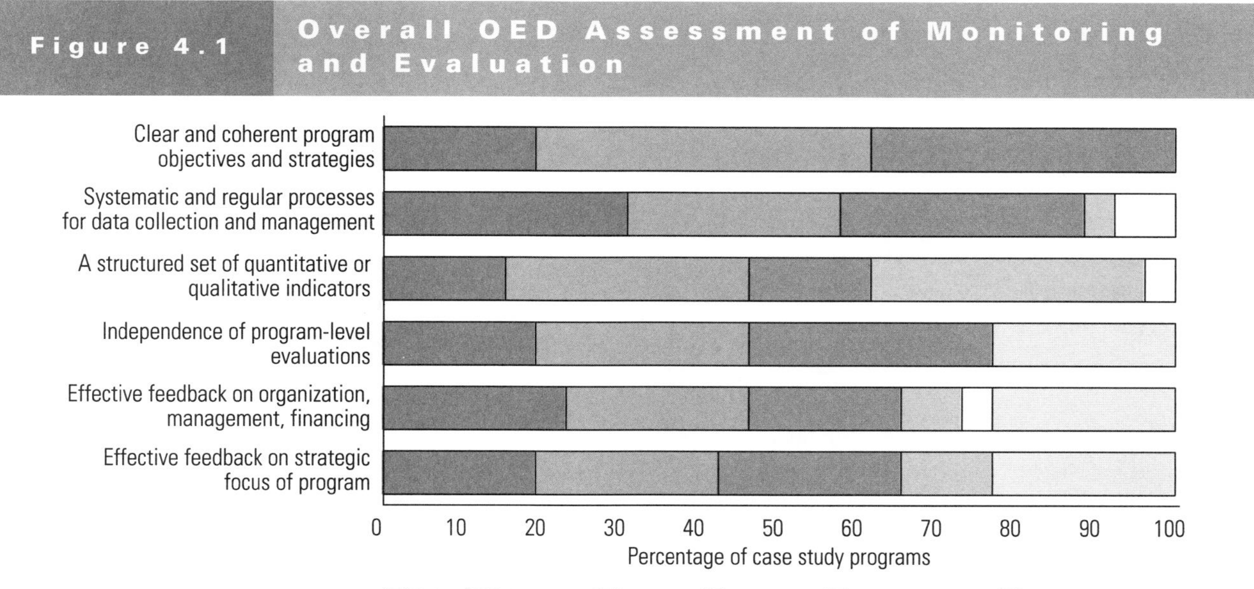

However, it is easy to determine which programs are being managed for results, once the objectives and desired results are clear and measures for evaluating them are in place.

Links Between Global Programs and Country Operations

As the preceding discussion indicates, value added on the ground in client countries is generally a joint product of global and country-level activities, but the desired nature of these links varies greatly according to the objectives, design, and implementation of the programs. As reported in OED's Phase 1 report, the Bank's operational task managers viewed enhancing the effectiveness of the Bank's country operations as potentially the most important value global programs can add to the Bank and its clients.

For the purpose of assessing the strength and value of global-country links, OED classified the 26 programs into three categories: (1) research programs, (2) programs for which the Bank is an implementing agency, and (3) programs for which the Bank is not an implementing agency (table 4.2).

Links are important in both directions. First, countries can add value to global programs, particularly for the technical assistance, advocacy, and capacity building programs that do not provide financing for investments. They can do this by identifying their constraints, needs, and priorities, thereby increasing relevance, focus, ownership, and impacts. Second, global programs can bring globally improved technologies and global best practices to the Bank's country operations and to the countries' own activities. They can also help mobilize additional investment resources.

Research Programs

While research programs do not require links to the Bank's country operations to achieve their objectives, complementary investments by the Bank and other donors in developing countries increase the programs' impacts. In the case of CGIAR, the Bank used its convening power well to *mobilize substantial resources at the global level* to establish a large global network of agricultural research centers with a clear poverty focus, and invested substantially at the national level to build developing-country capacity. CGIAR's capacity building activities have also strengthened national systems and increased the productivity of both the Bank's and the countries' own investments, leading to substantial and well-documented poverty-reducing impacts.

Table 4.2 The Bank Has Difficulty Linking Global Programs with Country Operations Where Bank Staff Are Not Implementing Global Program Activities

Classification	Number of programs	Programs	OED rating of current extent of country linkages
Research programs that do not require links to the Bank's country operations to achieve their objectives, but for which complementary investments by the Bank in developing countries would increase the effectiveness of the programs.	5	CGIAR[a]	Not applicable
		TDR[a]	
		Global Forum	
		UCW	
		GDN	
Programs for which the Bank is an implementing agency. The Bank's operational staff are involved in the supervision or implementation of program activities.	11	GEF[a,b]	High
		ESMAP[b]	High
		PPIAF[b]	High
		MLF[a,b]	Substantial
		ProCarbFund[a,b]	Substantial
		Cities Alliance[b]	Substantial
		PostConFund[a]	Substantial
		IF[a]	Modest, but improving
		*info*Dev[b]	Modest
		FSAP	Too early to rate
		FIRST[b]	Too early to rate
Programs for which the Bank is not an implementing agency. The Bank's operational staff are *not* involved in supervision or implementation of program activities.	10	UNAIDS[b]	Substantial
		WSP[b]	Substantial
		RBM	Modest-substantial
		The Stop TB Partnership	Modest-substantial
		CEPF[a]	Modest
		GWP	Modest
		GIF	Modest
		GAVI[a,b]	Modest
		CGAP[a]	Modest
		World Links	Modest

a. The program finances investments in developing countries (table 2.2).

b. The program provides resources that supplement the Bank's administrative budget (table 2.6)

Bank leadership is crucial to mobilize funding for health research, surveillance, and epidemiology, areas in which investments are low at both the global and the country levels. In part because of the efforts of the Global Forum, policymakers and donors are said to be more aware of the 10/90 gap in health research (only 10 percent of the world's funding for health research has been estimated to be devoted to the conditions responsible for 90 percent of the global disease burden).[16] Public-private partnerships have added about $200 million of health research for the development of drugs and vaccines over a 10-year period. A large share comes from the Bill and Melinda Gates Foundation, and some from pharmaceutical companies. Health experts stress that health-related MDGs cannot be realized without substantial, long-term, and predictable funding for research on the health problems of the poor. Most experts consulted by OED considered the annual allocation of $3 billion that the Report of the Commission on Macroeconomics and Health (WHO 2001) recommended in support of health research to be unachievable in the present climate, but most nonetheless stressed the huge funding gap and the need for more investments.

The Bank has not used its considerable convening power beyond the small level of DGF resources devoted to TDR and the Global Forum and occasional convening of stakeholders to help establish a global health research network. This will require working in partnership with the Bill and Melinda Gates Foundation, WHO, UNICEF, and others, as the Bank did so well in the past with the Rockefeller and Ford Foundations. Partners suggested that, to set an example to donors and governments, the Bank should allocate between 2 and 5 percent of all health sector loans to clients to build their national research capacity.

Programs Where the Bank Is an Implementing Agency

In 11 cases, Bank operational staff—beyond the secretariat staff of the programs that are located in the Bank—are involved in the supervision or implementation of program activities. For the three programs—GEF, MLF, and the Prototype Carbon Fund—that are financing country-level investments to deliver global public goods, the programs bring substantial additional investment resources beyond what the Bank can offer. However, mainstreaming these environmental programs in the Bank and its client countries remains an issue.[17] Their goals are not yet well reflected in the PRSPs or the CASs of specific countries, in part because country priorities are not the same as global priorities. The countries are nonetheless implementing these programs successfully because funding for investments is available.[18]

In the case of the Post-conflict Fund, Regional operational staff supervise the implementation by partners such as UNHCR, UNICEF, national governments, and NGOs of small-scale pilot reconstruction activities. More than half of the Fund's grants have been awarded to eight of the most conflict-affected areas.[19] The Post-conflict Fund's external evaluation observed that in many cases the watching briefs and pilot-scale grants established an effective basis for follow-on financing. Nevertheless, the evaluation stressed the need to (1) attract donor support, (2) become more proactive about funding projects, (3) improve implementation monitoring, and (4) strengthen knowledge generation and management. The PostConFund evaluation found that on project outcomes, the Fund's grants rated similarly to the Bank's 1990s norm. While Post-conflict Fund grants have been designed to be catalytic and support a larger international response in post-conflict situations, a lack of information about exactly how many individual projects actually secured additional follow-on financing makes it difficult to assess the program's overall impact.[20]

Bank leadership is crucial to mobilize funding for health research, surveillance, and epidemiology, areas in which investments are low at both the global and the country levels.

Among the technical assistance and capacity building programs, ESMAP, PPIAF, and Cities Alliance have developed synergy with the Bank's Regional operations. ESMAP requires the Bank's Regional operational team to contribute from 10 to 25 percent of the cost of country-level activities in order to ensure that the results are integrated into the country program and/or dialogue. PPIAF requires both the Bank's country director and the recipient government to sign off on all funding proposals to ensure alignment with the priorities of both the Bank and the client country. The Cities Alliance requires each funding request to be sponsored by at least one Cities Alliance member, with sign-off by the recipient country. The program gives priority to proposals with clearly documented links to follow-up investments in urban areas,

Health-related MDGs cannot be realized without substantial, long-term, and predictable funding for research on the health problems of the poor.

What value do these programs add for the Bank and its clients beyond the resources to finance technical assistance—which, in principle, could be financed as part of the Bank's regular country operations?

including the identification of the expected investment partners.[21]

An issue for these programs is what value they add for the Bank and its clients beyond the resources to finance technical assistance—which, in principle, could be financed from the Bank's administrative budget or lending as part of its regular country operations. The pro-grams do not finance project preparation activities. ESMAP, for instance, rations its support to upstream (ex ante) activities where there is a potential for policy formulation and strategy development, or to downstream (ex post) evaluation and dissemination of emerging best practice. The programs claim to have developed specialized expertise in their respective areas. According to the 2003 report of its Technical Advisory Panel, PPIAF has established itself as a niche player in private sector infrastructure participation through its ability to identify, disseminate, and customize emerging global good practices to country-specific situations. *info*Dev, however, has had weak links to the Bank's country operations and little impact at the country level beyond the direct beneficiaries, even though it is dominated by the Bank.[22]

A second issue for these programs is unclear responsibility for the quality of technical assistance and unclear accountability for performance. During OED field visits, developing-country representatives spoke of growing confusion and frustration in the eyes of the Bank's clients in differentiating among *global program activities*, *Bank activities,* and *Bank borrower activities*, particularly for programs that are housed in the Bank. International consultants working for in-house programs, who have Bank contracts, typically say that they are working for the World Bank, often expect the Bank's country offices to line up appointments for them, and write reports with the World Bank's logo on them. This blurring of the line between the Bank and its partners, and between Bank activities and global-program activities, entails potential liabilities and reputational risks for the Bank.[23] There is also the risk of the Bank's technical assistance being driven by what donors want to finance.

Developing-country representatives spoke of growing confusion and frustration in differentiating among global program activities, Bank activities, *and* Bank borrower activities, *particularly for programs that are housed in the Bank.*

Programs for which the Bank Is Not an Implementing Agency

The links between externally implemented global programs and the Bank's Regional operations tend to be weaker than for programs either housed in the Bank or managed by the Bank. This is natural. Among the externally housed and externally managed programs, however, links have been stronger for some programs, such as UNAIDS, than for others, demonstrating the scope for bringing external know-how and approaches into the Bank.

Although causality between advocacy and responses is difficult to establish, consistent with the UNAIDS advocacy, new commitments to HIV/AIDS and other communicable diseases have grown by an average of 8.18 percent a year since 1990 (figure 4.2). The Stop TB Partnership has made important contributions in developing a global network of professionals, bringing technical information and (through the Global Drug Facility) improved access to drugs at reduced prices, providing 1.9 million patient treatments to date, and influencing Bank lending to specific countries. Overall lending for communicable diseases increased by 7.5 percent annually. Links on TB have been strong in some area, particularly China, India, and Eastern Europe, but countries could not distinguish the activities of WHO from those of the Stop TB Partnership. Since malaria control requires diverse and multisectoral approaches, links are strong in some African countries, with respect to the import and subsidization of bed

Figure 4.2 New Commitments to HIV/AIDS and Other Communicable Diseases Have Grown Rapidly

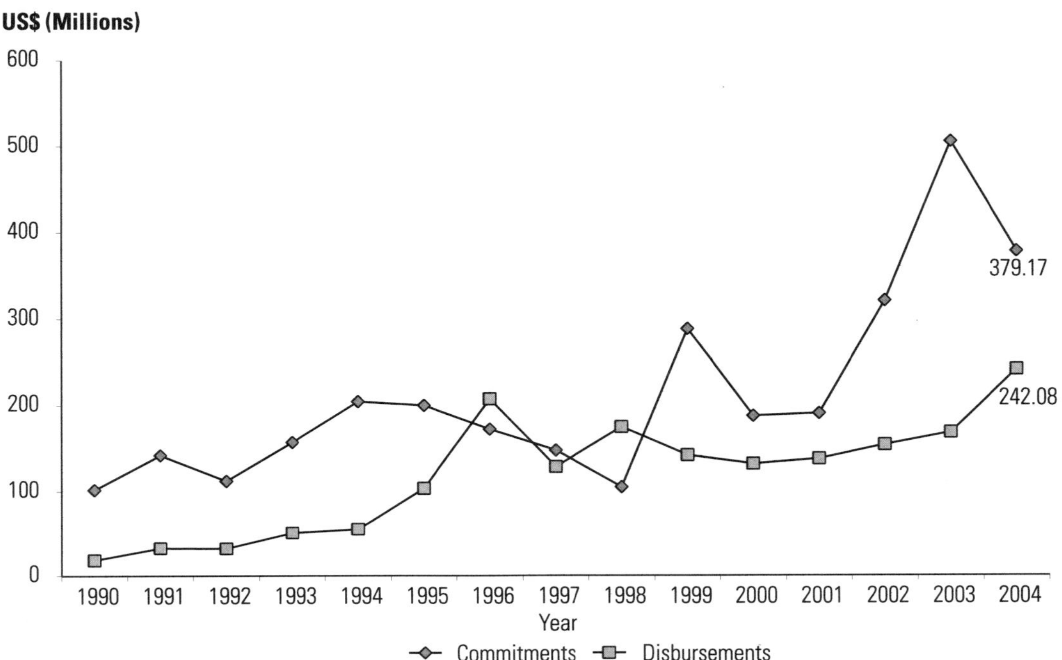

nets, but weak in others, such as China and India. Overall Bank lending to the health sector has fluctuated around $1.4 billion and places considerable pressure on health system capacities, because resources are increasingly being directed to deal with communicable diseases.[24]

Although a clear link to the Bank's country work is a criterion for approving new global programs, neither the networks nor the DGF demand that task managers of global programs provide evidence that global programs have added value to country and Bank operations. OED conducted its own investigations and found a mixed record. Even in those cases where the programs have had impacts, OED found little documented and reported evidence of effective links to Bank country operations. OED has concluded that the Bank is not exploiting its unique multisectoral comparative advantage at the country level.

Previous OED reviews have stressed the importance of the Bank's developing an arm's-length relationship with global programs to ensure their clear independence, accountabilities, and responsibilities. Therefore, the findings in this section present a challenge. To bring new knowledge and technologies to the Bank, programs need independence from the Bank. Yet externally implemented programs are as yet only weakly linked to the Bank.

OED has concluded that the Bank is not exploiting its unique multisectoral comparative advantage at the country level.

Conclusions

Although most programs invoke a poverty focus, only a few have demonstrated impacts on poverty reduction or on loosening the policy, institutional, or technological constraints that developing countries face. Several have the *potential* to add value to the poverty-reduction objective. In general, programs financing investments have more demonstrable impacts than other programs. The Bank's current tracking system is inadequate for the strategic manage-

The Bank's current tracking system is inadequate for the strategic management of its global portfolio from the perspectives of its ultimate clients.

ment of its global portfolio from the perspectives of its ultimate clients.

When programs do not meet all the requirements for effective evaluation—evaluable objectives, measurable indicators, and evaluable evidence—and do not have appropriate strategies, governance, or management, their global impacts remain unclear. CGIAR and TDR, which finance global-level investments for the benefit of the poor, have had strong evaluation cultures and produced evidence of high returns. But there remain huge investment gaps in agriculture and health research, both at the global level and in complementary investments at the country level.

Some of the programs that finance country-level investments to produce global public goods have achieved major global impacts. In the case of the MLF, Bank management reports that it has helped to reduce 85 percent of the ozone-depleting substances globally by using only 45 percent of the program's resources. Measuring results is a bigger challenge in some of GEF's focal areas, such as biodiversity conservation.

The programs that finance country-level investments to achieve national public goods, such as the Post-conflict Fund and GAVI, have had quite different impacts. The Post-conflict Fund's impacts have been small and difficult to document. GAVI and the Vaccine Fund together have brought more than $1 billion to 69 countries, with a vast increase in immunization coverage, but they pose issues of long-term financial sustainability. By working actively with the Bank, GAVI and the Vaccine Fund address health system financing capacity and reforms.

The programs that finance country-level technical assistance to stimulate public and private investments in their respective sectors provide examples of evolving or unshared objectives and raise subsidiarity issues. Impacts beyond the studies conducted, reports published, or individuals trained are lacking. But monitoring and evaluation is improving as programs put in place results-based management and evaluation systems. IF places greater emphasis on the internal policy and institutional constraints to expanded trade than on external barriers in industrialized countries, and it expects countries to seek investment funds from donors through the PRSP process to finance internal infrastructure improvements.

The impacts of advocacy programs that promote common approaches to mitigating communicable diseases are difficult to attribute to the programs. While they have certainly persuaded donors to increase investments in research, prevention, and treatment of these communicable diseases and contributed to increased information and knowledge, they require concrete country-level strategies and strong links with Bank operations, as well as more and longer-term investments in developing-country health system capacity.

The principal outcomes of the programs that promote approaches and standards to addressing issues of global concern at the country level are enhanced institutional and human-resource capacity with respect to microfinance, integrated pest management, water resources management, and child-labor institutions. Programs face changing or unclear objectives, insufficient Bank or country involvement, and lack of evidence of impacts on the intermediaries (such as donors, governments, and community organizations) or the ultimate beneficiaries (such as the poor in developing countries).

Programs to increase capacity to utilize information and communications technologies and to conduct socioeconomic research in developing countries have not yet demonstrated impacts beyond the direct beneficiaries of the programs' activities. The programs also raise issues concerning their objectives and strategies, the efficiency and scalability of their activities, their links to country operations (in the case of *info*Dev), and their exit strategies (in the cases of World Links and GDN).

Overall, programs are usually better coordinated at the global level than at the country level.

Indicators of this include weak links to the Bank's country operations and lack of synergy with Bank country operations in areas where there are similar activities. A problem for the Bank's Regions and its client countries is that there are too many global programs involving too many priorities relative to the capacity of many developing countries and that most of these priorities are not based on analysis of what is needed to address the most binding constraints to sustainable, poverty-reducing growth.

Programs are usually better coordinated at the global level than at the country level.

Table 4.3 Programs Financing Investments Have More Known Benefits to Developing Countries

Activities	Programs	Beneficiaries
Financing global-level investments to deliver global public goods	CGIAR	Agricultural research systems and poor households in developing countries, donors
	TDR	Health research systems and poor households in developin countries
Financing country-level investments to deliver global public goods	GEF	Global community, environmental institutions, environment ministries in developing countries, households in developir countries
	MLF	
	Prototype Carbon Fund	
	CEPF	
Financing country-level investments to deliver national public goods	Post-conflict Fund	Conflict-affected countries
	GAVI	Health institutions and children in developing countries needing immunization
Financing country-level TA to stimulate public or private investments in the sector	WSP, ESMAP, PPIAF, Cities Alliance, IF	Water and sanitation, energy, other infrastructure, urban, a their staff in developing countries
Promoting common approaches to mitigating communicable diseases	UNAIDS	Health sector institutions and households with communica diseases in the Bank's client countries
	RBM	
	Stop TB	
	Global Forum	Health research institutions and poor households in developing countries
Promoting approaches and standards to addressing global concerns at the country level	CGAP	Donors, microfinance institutions, poor households
	GIF	Agricultural and water resource institutions, farmers, other water users
	GWP	
	UCW	Child labor institutions

Known outcomes and impacts
Increased Bank access to international science and improved donor coordination. Developed a global research system and network. High returns to germplasm research. Positive impacts on reducing food prices, food productivity, employment, and incomes. Unknown impacts of policy and social science research and research on management of natural resources.
Notable success in mobilizing global science to conduct research and development on the underresearched, neglected tropical diseases.
Reduced ozone-depleting substances (ODS) in transition countries. Some success in promoting energy efficiency and renewable energy, improving management of standards for protected areas (to conserve biodiversity), promoting and implementing agreements on fresh water and marine ecosystems. Too early to assess results in areas of land degradation. Uncertain sustainability of global environment impacts.
Expended $1.48 billion to support 4,300 projects in 134 developing countries, which phased out consumption of 74% and production of 85% of ODS tons. Funded ozone offices in 129 developing countries, leading to institutional capacity. Qualitative indicators are weak but evolving.
Mobilized new resources to catalyze the market for project-based greenhouse-gas emission reductions, building institutional capacity in host countries. Increased knowledge on ER transactions, but grants are too small to exert a large change in greenhouse-gas concentrations.
Small grants focused on "hot spots" are raising awareness of conservation and resulting in positive conservation outcomes in these areas, but the cumulative impact of relatively small grants on ultimate conservation of the ecoregion is uncertain.
Small-scale reconstruction activities in conflict-affected countries. Support for innovative work and some activities have established effective ground for follow-on projects, but most grants are too small and have few and uncertain (documented) impacts.
Benefits totaling more than $1 billion to immunize children and families in 69 countries. 35.5 million children vaccinated against hepatitis B; 6 million against Haemophilus influenzae type b; 2.7 million against yellow fever; and an additional 8 million have access to basic vaccines. Assistance to develop immunization system delivery capacity. Support for global health research for new vaccines and technologies.
Diagnostic, policy, and strategic studies. Sector reforms, laws, regulations, and institutions, privatizations and concessions. Increased institutional and human resource capacity. Few and uncertain (documented) impacts.
Increased strategic information, technologies, and tools, and some formation of multisectoral strategies. Increased capacity of local authorities and NGOs through funding for training, policy planning, technical support, and institutional development. Helped develop national strategic AIDS plans. Unclear prevention success because of attributional difficulty.
Providing political and technical support. Provision of insecticide-treated nets, Intermittent Prevention Treatment and therapy. Some success in advocacy, resource mobilization, and consensus building, but slow progress in achieving objectives and making an impact.
Built and sustained a network of partners, heightened political support. Supported work on diagnostics, drugs, and vaccines and made operational the Green Light Committee for second-line drugs and the Global Drug Facility for technical aid for first-line drugs, but sustainable impacts will depend on adequate funding.
Networking and development of analytical tools for research and international advocacy, but its resources are insufficient to meet the ambitious objective of helping close the 10/90 gap.
Modest donor coordination. Development of materials on best practices in the microfinance sector. Uncertain benefits and impacts.
Improved country-level donor coordination. Advocate for IPM. Helped shape international norms for IPM and pesticides. Improved application of Bank safeguard 4.09, Guidebook, and pest management plans. Increased institutional and human resource capacity. Insufficient evidence of long-term impacts on farmers.
Established/strengthened partnerships (25 country-specific, 45 area, and 11 regional). Unclear policy linkages, financial sustainability, and impacts on IWRM.
Country studies generating some interest among policymakers. Increased donor coordination. Unclear impact of studies on operational strategies to benefit children.

(*Table continues on the following page.*)

Table 4.3 Programs Financing Investments Have More Known Benefits to Developing Countries (*continued*)

Activities	Programs	Beneficiaries
Building capacity at the country level	*info*Dev	Public and private organizations and their staff
	World Links	Secondary students, teachers, and education policymakers
	GDN	Developing country researchers and policymakers
	FSAP, FIRST	Financial institutions, donors

Known outcomes and impacts
Increased advocacy and capacity to utilize ICTs and to conduct socioeconomic research, but no demonstrated impact.
Increased student and teacher IT skills and interests and created networks, but unclear impact on capacity building.
Grants for high-quality, policy-relevant research and networking to develop capacity of researchers and institutions, but no evidence of application in policymaking.
New laws, regulations, and regulatory institutions. Making standards more operational and relevant, improving analytical tools, and donor coordination. While addressing fragilities of financial systems, uncertain impacts on averting financial crises.

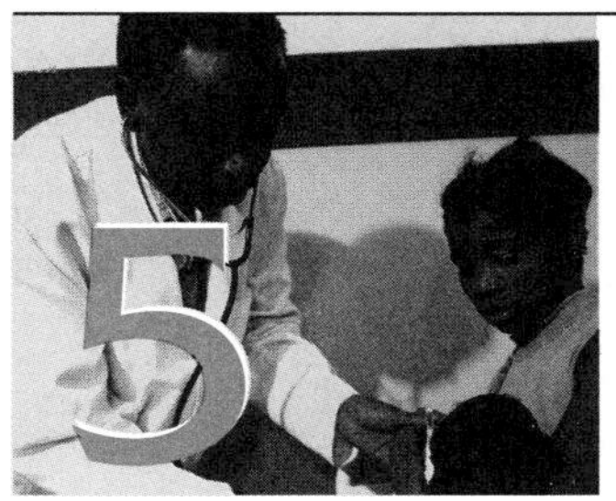

Governance, Management, Partnerships, and Participation

The governance of global partnerships is evolving and often ambiguous. The reviewed global partnerships do not clearly define who is a partner and who is a participant, and which ones have moved from shareholder- to stakeholder-style governance in the face of external challenges. Some have established executive committees to help with governance. The roles, responsibilities, and accountabilities of governors and managers tend to be weakly defined. The roles of the scientific and advisory committees are weak in several programs. Involving developing countries in program governance increases program relevance, ownership, and effectiveness, but facilitating their involvement remains a challenge. Their role too often seems ceremonial, to ensure legitimacy without addressing their concerns.

The Bank lacks an institutional strategy for partnering with developing countries or NGOs or for engaging in public-private partnerships. Donors and international agencies still largely govern the programs. Because they often enjoy permanent membership on the boards, donors and agencies are also primarily responsible for tracking program performance. This has raised issues of ownership and accountability in several programs.

Governance Functions, Principles, and Models

Governance can be defined as the structures, functions, processes, and organizational traditions that a board or other decisionmaking body uses to ensure that the mission of an organization or program is accomplished. Governance determines how power is exercised, how decisions are made, how stakeholders are included, and how decisionmakers are held accountable (DGF 2001). Governance can also be viewed as the set of rules and procedures that enable an organization to meet its objectives (Simpson 2002).

Five core functions of governance are:

- *Strategic direction*, usually exercised by the governing body
- *Oversight* of the unit responsible for day-to-day program management

- *Consultation* with other stakeholders, both formal and informal; one common formal method is through a technical, scientific, or professional advisory body
- *Risk management*, including reputational risks, fiduciary risks, conflict-of-interest risks, unfair-advantage risks, governance risks, and non-performance risks
- *Evaluation and audit*, which is often the least-developed governance function in many global programs.

The diversity of governance models makes assessing the effective conduct of core governance functions a challenge. How governance is practiced is rarely understood by simply looking at organizational charts. Personalities, the quality of relationships, and path-dependence all matter. There is no established, empirically tested method for evaluating global program governance. As summarized in table 2.3, the 26 programs have 9 different models of governance and management. The programs have adopted their particular governance models for reasons of history and of culture (box 5.1). Eight of the programs have delegated some governance functions to an executive body that meets more often than the governing body.

There is no established, empirically tested method for evaluating global program governance.

To assess governance outcomes, OED has adapted a set of four corporate governance principles developed by the OECD's Business Sector Advisory Group:[1]

- *Clear roles and responsibilities*—of the officers and bodies that govern and manage the program and of the mechanisms to modify and amend the governance and management of the program.
- *Transparency*—the program provides both shareholders and stakeholders with the information they need (such as decision-making responsibilities; accountabilities; and processes, accounting, audit, and material non-financial issues).
- *Fairness*—the program does not favor some immediate clients over others (such as Bank staff, participating agencies, or program secretariats, specific countries or their agencies, municipal agencies, local authorities, private service providers, NGOs, or community organizations).
- *Clear accountability*—for the exercise of power over resources to the program's stakeholders, including international organizations, donors, developing countries, the private sector, and NGOs.

It is often hard to determine who is a partner, who is a participant, and who exercises, or is believed to exercise, real influence.

It is difficult to determine who is a partner and who is a participant. The effectiveness of a partnership is a function of how clearly the partnership is defined at each level and how clearly the responsibilities and accountabilities are defined for each partner at each level and within their own organizations. But as noted in the Phase 1 report, it is often hard to determine who is a partner, who is a participant, and who exercises, or is believed to exercise, real influence (box 5.2) (World Bank 2002c). The review of the case study programs underlines this confusion. Global programs generally take a broad view of partnerships, and the actual influence of different partners on program direction is not always visible from a cursory view of the program organization. These partners encompass:

- The programmatic partners who are collectively responsible for the program, including the formal and informal co-sponsors, the financial contributors, and others involved in program governance
- The members of the organization
- Other program partners at the global level
- Financial partners not involved in governance
- Institutional partners, who are not program partners, with whom the program conducts joint or parallel activities at the global level
- Client countries
- Implementing partners of all types, including other international organizations, government agencies, and local NGOs.

Box 5.1 The Two Largest Programs Show the Roots of Diversity and Complexity

Through complex negotiations, GEF developed an independent, transparent, and equitably representative governing structure that involved industrial and developing countries, while pioneering procedures for a global financing mechanism for the environment. But the structure has design weaknesses. GEF evaluations have consistently noted the weak role of the Scientific and Technical Advisory Panel in strategy and investment operations, and the GEF Secretariat's unclear role and responsibility relative to the implementing agencies in accountability for *global* public goods outcomes. GEF's transformation from a pilot program to a restructured funding mechanism involved extensive negotiations. The Bank wanted the funds to be additional to IDA; industrial countries desired that GEF be housed in the Bank with the Bank as the trustee; and NGOs, U.N. agencies, and developing countries sought GEF's independence from the Bank and greater voice for developing countries. All got some of what they wanted.

The Bank is the trustee for GEF funds provided by donors through periodic replenishments. GEF's Council, composed of 14 industrial, 16 developing, and 2 transition countries, is responsible for policy, programming, strategies, oversight, and allocation of GEF funds among the focal areas. The evaluation function now reports to the Council. GEF is supported by a secretariat housed in the Bank, three main implementing agencies (the World Bank, UNDP, and UNEP), and the Scientific and Technical Advisory Panel. Other executing agencies include regional development banks and other U.N. agencies. NGOs have observer status at Council meetings, and they and the private sector participate in the implementation of GEF-funded programs designed, appraised, and overseen by each of the three main implementing agencies (who compete for a share of GEF business). GEF is a financial mechanism for the U.N. Convention on Biological Diversity, the U.N. Framework Convention on Climate Change, the Stockholm Convention on Persistent Organic Pollutants, the U.N. Convention on Desertification, and supporting activities under the Ozone Protocol, a number of International Waters Conventions, and the conventions on POPs and desertification. As the number and roles of the executing agencies have expanded, competition has increased.

The CGIAR has prided itself on its informal organizational structure. Initially, its large pool of unrestricted funds addressed focused objectives shared by a small number of like-minded donors. But that informal organization has posed major collective-action challenges as the number of donors, members, and research centers has expanded and the research agenda has grown. Funding has recently declined and become more restricted. The Bank has played a highly visible role as the founder and the largest donor, with increased responsibility over time for *system-level management* of the 15 international research centers, which are autonomous legal entities with their own governing boards. Although conceived as science-driven, in order to mobilize donor resources the CGIAR is chaired by the Bank, a financial institution with little internal scientific capacity. The CGIAR Secretariat is housed in the Bank, and its director reports to a World Bank vice president who chairs the system of 62 members, consisting of countries, international agencies, donors, multilateral and regional banks, and private foundations. Following a major financial crisis, the influence of the Bank and the donors in setting research priorities and allocating resources increased relative to the once-powerful scientific advisory committee. Roles and responsibilities for system-level performance became increasingly cumbersome and ambiguous among the Bank, donors, centers, and the technical advisory committee. CGIAR faces a changing external environment, scientifically, socioeconomically, and environmentally. In response, in 2000 the CGIAR launched an "evolutionary" change management process, established an Executive Council to expedite decisionmaking between annual general meetings, founded a Science Council, launched Challenge Programs to attract additional funding, and established a system office. It is now drafting a charter to clarify roles, responsibilities, and accountabilities for system-level performance. The centers are consolidating their activities. These reforms are encouraging, and funding has increased in response, but it is too soon to know their effects.

Governance styles are evolving from shareholder to stakeholder models. Effective governance requires both *efficiency* in the allocation of resources and *legitimacy* in the exercise of authority. Both theory and practice support the view that a shareholder model of corporate governance promotes efficiency and that a stakeholder model, while increasing legitimacy, may face collective action problems when the number of participants is large and the cost of organizing diverse interests to pursue a common goal is high relative to the expected benefit (box 5.3). Despite efficiency concerns, stakeholder models are increasingly being

Box 5.2 What Are Partnerships? Who Are Members and Partners?

- *Partnership:* An agreement between two or more parties to work together for a common purpose, with the parties committing resources (financial, technical, personnel, or reputational) to agreed objectives, to be implemented in accordance with the terms of the agreement.
- *Member:* Those who in some sense "own" the program and who have joint rights and responsibilities for the program.
- *Partner:* Members who are entitled to participate in the governance of the program, either directly or through a representative governance structure.
- *Participant:* Intermediaries who help to implement the program, generally at the country level, and who are not partners or contributors to the core program.
- *Beneficiaries:* The ultimate beneficiaries of the program at the national or local level.

adopted to improve relevance, ownership, fairness, and accountability (Etzioni 2001).

Most programs now include stakeholders beyond the traditional donors on their governing or executive bodies (table 5.1). A major change since CGIAR's financial crisis in the mid-1990s was the CGIAR chairman's effort, during and after the "renewal," to increase the membership and ownership of developing countries. A major change in some of the trust fund programs housed in the Bank, such as ESMAP and WSP, which became "global" programs after a financial crisis, was to give increased voice to donors and legitimacy and support to programs by establishing more formal governing boards.

Six programs—the Post-conflict Fund, FSAP, *info*Dev, PPIAF, FIRST, and UCW—have not adopted the stakeholder model.[2] Sixteen programs now include developing countries on their governing or executive bodies, 14 include civil society organizations, and 5 include the private sector. However, stakeholder and shareholder influence is not always balanced. Board membership does not translate into equal voice and influence for all stakeholders. By the same token, observer status can sometimes accord considerable influence on decisions to powerful stakeholders.

Fewer than a third rely on executive bodies for conducting business. Eight of the programs have

Box 5.3 Shareholder and Stakeholder Models

In a *shareholder model,* membership on the governing and executive bodies is limited to organizations that sponsor or pay for the program—in the case of global programs, typically international/regional organizations such as the United Nations and the World Bank, bilateral donors, and private foundations. In the *stakeholder model,* membership is extended to other groups, such as developing countries, NGOs, and the private sector, who are potentially affected by the program and who therefore have a stake in its effective functioning. This means involvement not just in implementing program activities, but also in defining the program's strategic direction.

The Bank has moved toward a stakeholder model—for example, in the country-owned Poverty Reduction Strategy Papers, by inviting broad stakeholder participation in the formulation of PRSPs. The Bank's Board has also begun to give more attention to the voice of developing and transition countries in the international financial architecture, including that of the international financial institutions. For example, the Bank has given a more direct voice in IDA replenishment consultations to IDA recipient countries, and worked with IDA executive directors and their domestic constituencies to bring in recipient perspectives.

Table 5.1 Most Programs Now Involve Stakeholders beyond Donors on Their Governing and Executive Bodies[a]

Governance model	International/regional organizations, bilateral donors, and foundations only	Plus developing countries only	Plus civil society organizations only[b]	Plus developing countries and civil society organizations	Commercial private sector representatives
	Shareholder model	Stakeholder model			
Line management within the Bank	PostConFund, FSAP				
Secretariat inside the Bank	*info*Dev, PPIAF	GEF, WSP, ESMAP	CGAP	Cities Alliance	ProCarbFund
Shared secretariat between Bank and external organization	FIRST				CGIAR[c]
Secretariat inside external organization	UCW	TDR, IF	CEPF, GIF	Stop TB	RBM, GAVI
Independent external entity		MLF	GDN	GWP, Global Forum, UNAIDS	World Links
Number of programs	6	6	4	5	5

a. Not including observers on governing and executive bodies.

b. Broadly defined to include NGOs, umbrella organizations, professional and trade associations, and the like that are independent of the state or government and do not have a commercial, for-profit motive.

c. The private sector is represented on the Executive Committee, but not on the Consultative Group.

had executive bodies that exercise some governance functions in between the annual meetings of the governing body (table H.12). Some others were forming such committees in response to external evaluations. In six of the eight, this has been done to improve efficiency and mitigate the collective action problems spawned by growth. In four of these six cases—GEF, MLF, Cities Alliance, and IF—the executive body is a representative subset of the governing body, with each membership group having representatives on the executive body. CGIAR's Executive Council includes a private sector and an NGO member who are not contributing members of the organization and do not represent any body. CGAP's Executive Committee of the Consultative Group of Member Donors was restructured in 2003 to create a nine-member Executive Committee, with four members appointed by donor constituencies, four members from the microfinance industry appointed by a vote of the Council of Governors, and a permanent World Bank seat.[3]

In two of the eight cases—CEPF and FIRST—the programs have established executive bodies specifically for accountability reasons. Membership of the executive committee mirrors that of the governing body; all five members of CEPF and all six members of FIRST are represented on both bodies. The Bank's representatives on the governing bodies are at a high level—the World Bank president and the ESSD vice president in the case of CEPF, and a managing director as a rotating chair in the case of FIRST—and its representatives on the executive bodies are lower-level operational staff who report to the high-level representatives on the governing body. There is an assumption in both of these cases, with which OED does not necessarily agree, that because the Bank chairs these programs and because the Bank has both developing and industrial countries on its own Board, the views of developing countries are being heard.

The Post-conflict Fund is the only global program reviewed that does not have any partners (other than the World Bank) at the governance level. While the Fund is in this regard similar to some other Bank-managed programs that are supported by multidonor trust funds, the Bank classified it as a global program in April 2000 because it receives DGF funding. While the Bank's six approval criteria for Bank involvement in partnership initiatives beyond the country level call (by implication) for a partnership in governance and financing, the DGF eligibility criteria for grant support are vague with regard to what constitutes a "partnership"—only that the program and its activities should promote and reinforce partnerships. The Post-conflict Fund argues that its partnerships at the activity level meet the DGF criterion. The issue of the Bank's partnership at the global level related to conflict is complex, however. While global peace and security is a global public good, the Bank has not classified peace and security as one of its global public-goods priorities. To complement the Bank's current country-by-country approach to conflict, U.N. partners have suggested a global partnership program to foster learning on the policy and operational issues of moving from relief to reconstruction and development, in the context of a long-term collaboration between the Bank and U.N. agencies. As far as this suggestion relates to the Post-conflict Fund, management has made the case that involving U.N. agencies in the governance of the Fund would create a potential conflict of interest, since U.N. agencies are the largest recipients of PostCon-Fund grants.

Clarity of Roles and Responsibilities

Roles, Responsibilities, and Accountabilities in Program Governance and Management Tend to Be Unclear, Resulting in Weak Program Accountability for Results

A GEF example highlights how many factors can affect accountability for outcomes. The Convention on Biodiversity, which was negotiated between industrial and developing countries, is one of GEF's four focal areas. Yet it is ambiguous on what biodiversity has global value, who should determine it, and how it should be determined. Thus definitions of the very things for which the GEF would be held accountable are vague. Organizational ambiguities compound the problem. The chief executive officer reports to the GEF Council, but the Council's roles and responsibilities for portfolio composition and performance, as distinct from those of the implementing agencies, are uncertain. It is unclear whose responsibility it is to track and monitor incremental progress; the program's external evaluations have commented on this. Those evaluations mention the lack of information on global outcomes and how implementing agencies have been slow to incorporate GEF's global environmental concerns into their country development strategies. Without such integration, the evaluations assert, GEF-funded activities are less likely to produce sustainable outcomes or impacts (GEF 1998, 2002). Yet it is equally unclear if providing incremental costs for five to ten years is enough to ensure sustainable conservation. Who should ultimately be held accountable for mainstreaming GEF's global concerns into national strategies—the GEF Secretariat, the implementing agencies, or signatories to the various conventions and treaties? How should they be held accountable? Will doing so promote GEF's outcomes? These and other questions are actively debated in the GEF community.

The managers of in-house programs that do not have independent governance structures report both to the program's governing body and to their managers within the housing organization—a classic "two masters" problem. There is often a lack of precision concerning how accountable they are to each, and for what, or how conflicts between the two should be resolved.[4] When a senior manager of the housing organization also chairs the governing body, as happens in most Bank-housed programs, it creates the perception that the housing organization stifles other partners' views and reduces the program's independence.

When governance is weak, secretariats and housing organizations acquire considerable de facto power. Evaluations of TDR, Roll Back Malaria, and Stop TB, all housed in WHO, point out the different strengths of the programs' governance mechanisms and the correspondingly different roles WHO plays relative to the program secretariats and the governance boards. The WHO's different roles are reflected in varying outcomes.

Several evaluations have observed that global program boards do not use effective business practices and lack enough support to reasonably be held accountable. In the extreme case when a partnership becomes dysfunctional, board meetings are not held, agendas are not discussed with members before they are fixed, agendas are crowded, and board members have unequal information and ability to participate. Much can be done to professionalize the conduct, transparency, efficiency, and accountability of board meetings and board decisions. Internal audits of some of the Bank's in-house programs confirm that, despite being founder, co-sponsor, donor, and board member, the role of the Bank on the boards of these programs has been variable on ensuring fiduciary aspects of the programs.

Some external evaluations do not assess board governance or the secretariats,[5] and those that do vary in their thoroughness. Evaluations of UNAIDS, RBM, and Stop TB have had significant effects on the programs, both strategically and with respect to governance and management.[6] Evaluations of IF, UCW, and Stop TB all stressed the need for more businesslike conduct of board meetings and the need for transparency and openness, including agendas developed in consultation with board members, specialized subcommittees for specific issues, and timely issuance of the minutes of board meetings.[7] The agendas tend to be crowded, the issues complex, the relevant expertise of board members variable, and the time for substantive discussion limited. Complex substantive issues often get set aside or glossed over.[8] Sometimes board members lack background or qualifications in complex subject matter (such as legal issues or an organization's international status) or have been insufficiently briefed on options to help the board make complex organizational decisions.[9] Several boards have never reviewed detailed budgets or work programs or the determination of program managers' salaries.

There are few incentives for programs to devote time to board functions. The time and resources board members are given tend to be limited relative to the magnitude of their responsibility. The time of Bank officials who serve on boards is un- or underbudgeted, and their annual performance evaluations ignore their role in global programs.

The managers of in-house programs that do not have independent governance structures report both to the program's governing body and to their managers within the housing organization—a classic "two masters" problem.

Even when programs have an executive body, its terms of reference and how its seats should be filled are often left undefined. In CGIAR's case, it is not clear if the members of its executive council represent their constituents or themselves. The council's function remains ambiguous: does it make decisions or just expedite de-cisions made at CGIAR's annual meetings?

Roles of Scientific/Technical Advisory Committees Need Strengthening

Many programs face analytical challenges. Hence, scientific advisory committees are supposed to help decide their strategies. Such committees can protect the programs' professional integrity and weigh the risks of alternative approaches. Most programs have such advisory bodies in their formal governance structures. Others have delegated this responsibility to formal and informal working groups.

Technical bodies can bring cutting-edge research and other knowledge from industrial to developing countries. They can share best practices on standards, norms, and values for conducting research or applying results and can establish peer review processes. But the quality of these advisory bodies varies consider-

Technical bodies can bring cutting-edge research and other knowledge from industrial to developing countries.

ably among programs. The MLF's decisionmaking process has been underscored by regular scientific and technical assessments. The program relies on both a standing subsidiary body, the Technical Economic Assessment Panel (TEAP) housed in UNEP, and the Bank's Ozone Operations Resource Group (OORG) to help it keep pace with the latest research and development of alternative technologies. Developing countries have relied on the resulting scientific assessments to formulate country programs and their phase-out schedules. At the same time, the gradual decline of CGIAR's Technical Advisory Committee (TAC) in its governance has gone hand-in-hand with the decline of strategic research, the rise in restricted funding, and the change to a matching-grant formula for the allocation of the Bank's resources.[10] These developments have allowed donor preferences to decouple resource allocation from TAC's medium- and longer-term priority setting. CGIAR recently appointed a new, independent science council. It is too early to know how effective this council will be in improving science quality or allocating resources back toward strategic research. A third program, the GEF, features a Scientific and Advisory Technical Panel that has limited itself to providing technical advice if and when requested by the GEF Secretariat.

In the health sector, TDR, GAVI, and the Stop TB Partnerships enjoy strong technical inputs. TDR's Scientific and Technical Advisory Committee has encouraged the program to maintain its relevance to the needs of its developing-country clients. Like CGIAR, it now faces challenges to maintaining its scientific excellence.[11] The GAVI board has a specialized agency that is responsible for the program's research and technical aspects. Some of its functions are performed by the U.S. Centers for Disease Control and Prevention. GAVI also has a working group to implement the board's decisions and task forces to address specific issues of concern to the board.[12] Some staff commented to OED that GAVI has also benefited from the long operational experience that partners such as WHO and UNICEF have in immunization.

Partnering with Developing Countries, Civil Society, and the Private Sector

The Active Participation of Developing Countries in Governance Increases Program Relevance, Ownership, and Development Effectiveness, but Involving Them Remains a Challenge

Although they are intended to be the principal beneficiaries of the Bank's global programs, developing countries do not always have influence over the content of global program strategies.

First, the programs' governing bodies typically meet too infrequently to give useful input to the programs. Many executive bodies have several permanent members supplemented by rotating members. In interviews, developing-country members of global programs indicated that they have limited support structures back home and do not have clear terms of reference for their exercise of board functions or training on their independent responsibilities and accountabilities.[13] By the time a board member has learned to be effective, it is often time to be rotated out.

Second, it is rarely clear whether the board members are supposed to represent their own views, the views of their governments, the views of their regions, or the views of their constituents. Such expectations are often implicit. Board members have few resources with which to solicit inputs from their regions. The most knowledgeable and informed persons may not be invited to sit on the governing bodies.

Third, many boards require member organizations to make financial contributions to the program. Such requirements can signify the ownership and commitment of board members to the sustainability of the program, but they can also bar entry to developing countries. In the case of FIRST, to maintain efficiency and cohesion in program governance, a large middle-income developing country that was willing to make the contribution was not invited to the board.[14] Some programs waive or reduce this requirement for developing countries.[15] Unless special efforts are made to engage developing countries, the unequal relationship between donors and recipients continues, reducing relevance, ownership, and development effectiveness.

Developing-country participation in GEF and MLF drove those two programs to deliver at least some national benefits, while focusing on producing global benefits. Although most of IF's diagnostic studies are said to be leading to a pipeline of trade-facilitation operations for future financing, its 2003 external evaluation indicates that the program lacks developing-country ownership. Such countries largely see IF as run by and for its six international-agency partners. Moreover, as indicated in chapter 3, the program does not and cannot address the issues that matter most to developing countries: agricultural trade and OECD-country agricultural subsidies. It is similarly unclear why UCW does not have qualified nationals from developing countries on its steering committee. OED interviews related to the UCW program in Morocco found that national stakeholders helped improve the relevance of the global program's country-level studies when they were asked to inform the studies' terms of reference. However, key stakeholders felt that they were consulted only after the country terms of reference had largely been drafted.[16] The Bank's country staff in some Regions were similarly uninvolved in the program's country-level work, even though the involvement and contribution of Bank operational staff in the MNA Region and, to some extent, South Asia has been considerable. Yet because research related to child work and labor has been funded by the same set of donors through other programs in the MNA Region, it is difficult to distinguish between the effects of global programs and other trust-fund-financed Bank activities.

Obtaining informed and thoughtful input from developing countries is both important and difficult, not only because the donor-recipient relationship is so unequal, but also because programs should benefit from involving *appropriate, relevant,* and *well-informed* stakeholders. This point was stressed by developing-country members and by other board members and professionals from industrial countries, who are not closely associated with international agencies and the principal financiers.

Obtaining informed and thoughtful input from developing countries is both important and difficult, not only because the donor-recipient relationship is so unequal, but also because programs should benefit from involving appropriate, relevant, and well-informed stakeholders.

Bank Partnerships with NGOs Could Benefit from an Institutional Strategy

International NGOs have shaped the global agenda and individual programs, sometimes directly but often indirectly. Constructive Bank engagement with NGOs that have relevant developing-country knowledge and experience advances the cause of poverty alleviation and sustainable development. NGOs have been ahead of international organizations such as the Bank and WHO in their activism on several fronts discussed in this review. They have pushed for affordable access to drugs; raised awareness about child labor; and fought for health and environmental standards relating to pesticide use, ozone depletion, and climate change. Activism in these areas has energized support in industrial countries and has empowered civil society to be more active in solving problems in their own countries. However, global interventionist approaches, when unaccompanied by empowerment or support of national organizations, raise issues of legitimacy and may not be the most appropriate or sustainable solutions from a development perspective. Appropriately supported local actors can devise more effective solutions that are attuned to developing countries.

NGOs have been ahead of international organizations such as the Bank and WHO in their activism on several fronts.

In the health sector, international NGOs filled a void by spearheading a global campaign to make existing drugs for HIV/AIDS, multi-drug-resistant tuberculosis, and other diseases affordable to the populations of developing countries. Through lobbying and court cases, NGOs took up the issues of preferential pricing for drugs and drug donations to developing countries. They confronted the research-based international pharmaceutical industry by advising developing countries of the potential to exercise their rights under international trade and intellectual property rights (IPR) agreements (such as the parallel importation of essential medicines, and invoking the trade-related intellectual property rights [TRIPS] provisions related to compulsory licensing). While the Bank and WHO were slow to take a position on these issues, with declining process and increased affordability, they have come to support wider access to drugs. Yet financial sustainability remains a major challenge.[17]

In the environment sector, NGOs have helped shape the agenda. They have been strong supporters of the Montreal Protocol, the Kyoto Protocol, and other Agenda 21 conventions now being implemented by the GEF. At the same time, some NGOs have opposed international carbon trading on the grounds that it detracts from efforts to encourage countries such as the United States to decrease their carbon and other greenhouse-gas emissions. Some NGOs also fear that the promotion of monoculture tree planting could lead to deforestation in developing countries.

NGOs have informed both the Bank's cosponsorship of the Global Integrated Pest Management Facility and the Bank's own pesticide and pest-management policies. Six years after OP 4.09 was issued in its revised form, there appears to be no Bankwide consensus on the development orientation of this policy. Moreover, evidence is lacking on the contribution of the policy's approach toward sustainably increasing farmers' yields and incomes while contributing to increased environment and health benefits through reduced pesticide use.

The reputational and other risks that a Bank-supported global program faces can be large if the program is implemented by an NGO that does not apply the Bank's safeguards and practices. Therefore, aside from operational collaboration, Bank oversight of CEPF has focused on ensuring the application of Bank safeguards through indirect controls, along with fiduciary management and reporting for increased emphasis on monitoring and evaluation.

Each of these issues is complex and requires analysis of short- and long-run winners and losers. The Bank's current approach to NGO partnerships is ad hoc, rather than strategic.

Public-Private Partnerships Present Opportunities and Risks, and Call for Harmonized Approaches within and among International Organizations

Many stakeholders remain skeptical about the motives of private corporations that engage in partnerships with international organizations,[18] even when their efforts have demonstrated public-goods benefits, as in the case of the Onchocerciasis program. Merck's experience with pharmaco-philanthropy (through the Ivermectin donation program) has helped poor West Africans with river blindness and burnished its corporate image. Where similar partnerships have not developed, as in the case of the schistosomiasis drug Praziquantel, potential health gains in developing countries have not been realized. Although public-private collaboration occurred during the development phase of Praziquantel, a partnership for its donation and distribution did not emerge, substantially limiting the number of people in developing countries who could benefit from the drug. Hence the importance of articulating goals of a partnership and regularly reporting on them as the partnership evolves. Partnerships require clearly defined public health goals, as well as a strategic plan for addressing the problem. The success of the partnership depends in part on the availability of technological alternatives, and in part on the collaborative efforts of several partners.[19]

The complexity of public-private partnerships in global programs has increased as the importance of IPR regimes has grown. Thanks to the advancement of international discussion on universal access to affordable, reliable drugs and vaccines, there is now potential for public-private partnerships to bring new products to a large, untapped market in developing countries. The same applies to patented varieties of crops (Lele 2003).

Five programs—the Prototype Carbon Fund, CGIAR, RBM, GAVI, and World Links—include representatives of the private sector on their governing or executive bodies. To develop appropriate policies in this regard, it is necessary to distinguish private sector entities with and without a *direct* commercial interest, as that interest has implications for conflicts of interest. In the cases of RBM and GAVI, pharmaceutical conglomerates or vaccine manufacturers with direct actual or potential interest in the markets for products and services serve on the governing bodies. GAVI illustrates some of the costs, benefits, and risks. GAVI promoted new vaccines to improve child health, reduce demands on delivery systems, and stimulate demand. The long-term financial viability of different vaccine regimens for developing countries became evident as they acquired some experience with both new and old vaccines.[20] Some developing countries indicated that they would be unable to finance immunization programs after GAVI is phased out. GAVI may eventually benefit from the Bank's leading the effort on sustainable financing.

When private sector representation brings in significant amounts of new money to the program, as it does in the Prototype Carbon Fund, that representation presents different accountability challenges. Because the fund is housed in the Bank, it answers to two constituencies: the Bank and the private sector participants who "own" the fund. The program faces diverging interests and expectations between investors and the Bank's developing-country clients in project selection and price setting. OED concluded that continuing Bank involvement is important, however, because the program demonstrates a potential win-win for both investors and developing countries and because it builds the capacity for international carbon trading in developing countries—a global public good. The Prototype Carbon Fund provides an example of why a Bank Board–approved global-program strategy for carbon trading activities would be desirable.

There is now potential for public-private partnerships to bring new products to a large, untapped market in developing countries. The same applies to patented varieties of crops.

Most of the private funding for global programs is through private, non-profit foundations with a humanitarian interest, such as the Gates (GAVI), Rockefeller (CGIAR), Ford (CGIAR and CGAP), and MacArthur (CEPF) foundations. Some such foundations serve on the governing bodies of their respective programs. Many programs, including MLF, GEF, and the six infrastructure and private sector development programs, interact with the private sector in their activities.

The Bank and other partners have begun to explore private sector partners in designing and implementing global programs, but have not yet explored the full implications of public-private partnerships. International organizations' policies on public-private partnerships are generally still being worked out, and are neither coherent within the Bank nor across partnering organizations.[21] Within the Bank, policy varies by sector. The private sector sits on the governing boards of the restructured RBM and GAVI. While the six infrastructure and private sector development programs housed in the Bank work with private sector service providers at the country level, they generally do not accept contributions from or welcome private companies on their governing bodies, precisely because of the potential conflicts of interest. TDR also works with the private sector at the activity level. But there is considerable variation in the clarity, consistency, and transparency with which programs provide information on public-private partnerships.[22] Balancing public and

International organizations' policies on public-private partnerships are generally still being worked out, and are neither coherent within the Bank nor across partnering organizations.

private interests in the agricultural sector has just begun, with CGIAR becoming more active in public-private partnerships at the system level.[23]

WHO guidelines on partnership with commercial enterprises posit the following basic criteria: (a) alignment with WHO's strategy (the relationship should contribute to improving public health); (b) relationships established on the basis of an exchange of clear, written agreements indicating the contribution (financial or otherwise) of each party to the relationship; and (c) public health gains commensurate with the time and expense involved in establishing and maintaining the relationship.

Partners acknowledge that they face similar legal, ethical, and reputational risks and would benefit from collaborating with the Bank on consistent, coherent guidelines for public-private partnerships. Sharing such guidelines and experience would allow the adoption of a common code of conduct on private sector partnerships and their monitoring across the various U.N. organizations and international and regional banks. This would harmonize many of the procedures across agencies, increase accountability, and accelerate progress on achieving the Millennium Development Goals.

Donors and International Organizations Retain an Overwhelming Share of Governance Responsibility

The Bank and other international organizations still exercise the major degree of formal and informal influence over the programs' strategic direction and continue to bear a disproportionate share of responsibility for oversight, consultation, risk management, and evaluation. This reality needs to be explicitly acknowledged, with clear designation of responsibility and accountability for performance vested in the programs' governing structures, as they would be in the private sector.

As already pointed out, the Bank continues to chair all but two of the programs housed within it. This, together with a high proportion of Bank financing in some cases, reduces the incentives for shared program governance and puts an ambiguous share of responsibility, accountability, and risk on the Bank. It also gives rise to real or potential conflicts of interest that limit the Bank's capacity to look at the programs objectively. The same problems exist in lesser form in programs that are not housed in the Bank, but for which the Bank gives most funds.

Senior Bank managers continue to be excessively involved in the day-to-day management of some programs. The arrangements for overseeing in-house secretariats and the Bank's participation remain fraught with real or potential conflicts of interest and permit considerable free-riding by other donors (for example, in CGAP). As such, the Bank cannot provide the disinterested leadership needed for the far-reaching reforms that some programs need. It is problematic for the Bank chair of an in-house program to press for reforms while simultaneously campaigning for continued funding. Having such a chairperson compromises the Bank's ability to press for reforms and increases the Bank's exposure and risks.

These conflicts of interest also distort the Bank's allocation of money among programs. The efforts by network vice presidents to keep DGF resources within their networks counter the program's objective of funding the programs that add the most value to achieving the Bank's institutional mission. The newly established GPP council should mediate inter-network resource allocation based on Bank-level priorities, the quality of proposals, and the quality of implementation.

Other conflicts of interests are organizational, in the sense that they arise from the design of the Bank's relationships with the global programs that it supports (Davis and Stark 2001, p. 220). These include staffing issues, differential treatment of programs, and inadequate oversight of programs to which current or former Bank staff migrate and, in turn, promote the programs. All have the potential to damage the Bank's reputation. Both the Board and management must address these issues, particularly for those programs in which the Bank has the most strategic, fiduciary, and reputational exposure, namely for the programs housed inside the Bank and for those established by the Bank and then spun off.

Overall Assessment and Lessons

A key finding of this chapter is that there are now enough cross-program experiences featuring different governance and management models that the Bank, in collaboration with its partners, can begin to determine good practices for the design and implementation of global programs. Its aim should be to generate global public goods that advance the Bank's mission.

To this end, OED rated the performance of each program (high, substantial, modest, or negligible) in relation to the OECD principles of corporate governance introduced at the beginning of this chapter (figure 5.1). Information across programs varies, and this is the first time that such an exercise has been tried. Hence, this should be seen more as a reflection of general tendencies and as a guide for future evaluations. Nevertheless, comparative application of the principles provides some useful insights.

GEF receives high marks for *transparency* in governance. The functions of the GEF Council are transparent, and GEF program discussions and decisions are available on the Internet. However, disseminating information at the country level is still a challenge, compounded by a confusion of different agencies' roles and their uneven capacity to plan and implement GEF programs. GEF's Second Overall Performance Study noted that posting information on the Internet is insufficient for full disclosure or complete transparency. UNAIDS is strong on transparency at the global level, but faces problems similar to GEF's at the country level. Both OED's and the external evaluations noted a lack of transparency in some decisions made at GDN. Its Memorandum of Understanding with the World Bank had not been seen by the Board members OED interviewed. GIF was rated negligible, since none of the program's governing documents, including those on governance or management decisions, minutes of meetings, financial statements, and evaluations, is available on its Web site. Moreover, GIF does not produce semiannual or annual reports that are circulated beyond its donors. To be fair, though, GIF has a relatively small administrative budget and operates with a skeleton staff.

Overseeing in-house secretariats and the Bank's participation remain fraught with real or potential conflicts of interest and permit considerable free-riding by other donors.

TDR has clear roles and responsibilities in its Memorandum of Understanding, which details the composition, function, and procedural operations for the governing body, secretariat, and Scientific and Technical Advisory Committee. This oldest of all global health programs faces a dynamic environment like CGIAR's and has a budget one-eighth the size, yet it has confronted fundamental issues about its scope, strategic objectives, role in global research, funding and partnership strategies, method of work, governance, and management.

Similarly, the charters of PPIAF, Cities Alliance, and FIRST clearly lay out the functions of their governing bodies, management units, and advisory committees, and seem to be working well in practice. IF received an assessment of modest since the roles of its member partners and governing bodies are not clear. While IF does define the roles of its Steering Committee and its Inter-Agency Working Group, it does not clearly define the roles of international organizations, bilateral donors and least-developed countries. This reduces the likelihood that the program's objectives will be incorporated in PRSPs and that governments and donors will support follow-up activities. UCW has an implicit division of labor among ILO, UNICEF, and the Bank based on their different institutional mandates, but no memorandum of understanding or formal division of responsibility among the three partners. Working relationships at the governance level have been interrupted, although country-level interaction has been relatively more effective.

There are now enough cross-program experiences to begin to determine good practices for the design and implementation of global programs.

ESMAP, PPIAF, and the Cities Alliance were

Figure 5.1 Overall OED Assessment of Governance and Management

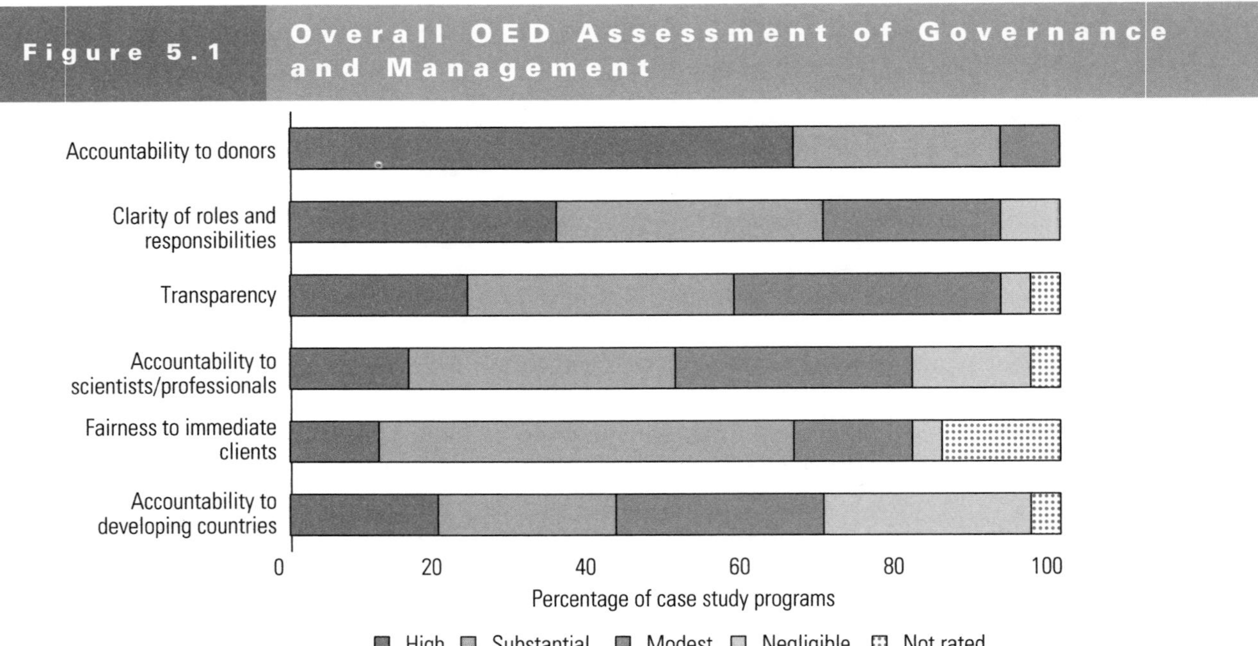

rated high with respect to *fairness to immediate clients*, since their competitive grant programs are open, transparent and accessible to potential developing-country clients. MLF's fairness to its immediate clients was assessed as substantial since it gives priority to projects with low costs per kilogram of ozone-depleting substances phased out. The project-by-project approach employed during the fund's first decade helped the implementing agencies to harvest all of the low-hanging fruit—in larger enterprises in low-cost countries that are large-volume consumers of ozone-depleting substances. WSP was rated modest, since the program gives little information on how it chooses its focus countries or its activities in each country. While selection criteria exist, it is not evident how these are applied. CEPF received a modest rating because, though consistent with the legal agreement the Bank signed with the program, a large share of the grants has gone to Conservation International, where the program is housed. Program staff project a change in future funding ratios as regionally based funding mechanisms, which target smaller civil-society groups, develop and as the program begins implementation in regions where Conservation International has not previously worked.[24]

Programs comprised mostly of international/regional organizations, bilateral agencies, and foundations are mainly *accountable* to donors. Although the programs that include developing countries have some accountability to them, this chapter's discussion has shown the possibility and the importance of increasing that accountability. The same point applies to the private sector and NGOs. The programs with well-functioning and effective scientific and technical advisory committees have helped programs to deliver outstanding results, but there is still scope for improvement in this area, too.

Global Programs Need Global Strategy

Global programs provide goods and services either directly (in-kind) or through research, technical assistance, and investment grants. From the Bank's point of view, their financing comes from four principal sources: donor trust funds, DGF grants, the Bank's administrative budget, and parallel donor financing of program activities.

The case study programs have a variety of funding mechanisms:

- *A triennial replenishment process* similar to that of the International Development Association (IDA) exists for two programs, GEF and MLF. The Bank is the trustee for the GEF, and UNEP is the trustee for MLF (table H.13).
- *Annual donor pledges and contributions* to trust funds, typically but not always administered by the organization that houses each program, provide support to all other programs in accordance with each donor's annual budget cycle.
- *The Bank's Development Grant Facility (DGF)* is the principal source of the Bank's financial contributions to global programs.
- *The Bank's administrative budget* has fully supported one program, FSAP (in coordination with the IMF). It partially supports four other programs—WSP, ESMAP, *info*Dev, and IF—mostly from trust fund fees and internal cross-support; this money is only for the Bank's in-kind contributions (such as staff time and travel) to these programs.
- *No financial support* is provided from the World Bank to four environmental programs: GEF, MLF, Prototype Carbon Fund, and GWP. The Bank receives administrative fees for implementing selected GEF and MLF activities and for managing the Prototype Carbon Fund (table 2.6).

In aggregate, there is no evidence, based on the cases reviewed, that global programs have added significant amounts of new money to official development assistance, with two exceptions: funds from private sources for the Prototype Carbon Fund and funds from the Bill and Melinda Gates Foundation for health.[1] It has been hard to show that GEF and MLF resources have come on top of other development assistance. The growth of global programs appears to have come mostly at the cost of country-level assistance.[2]

Although the Bank is the largest manager of donor trust funds, the Bank does not have an overarching strategy for financing global programs. Its existing criteria and processes do not add up to a strategy, and they are not rigorously applied. The

Although the Bank is the largest manager of donor trust funds, it does not have an overarching strategy for financing global programs.

following three subsections review weaknesses or inconsistencies in current strategies (1) to mobilize public resources for long-term global public-goods programs of benefit to the poor, (2) to foster a more flexible, rational, and informed approach to funding "venture capital" programs in which the DGF provides only initial financial support, and (3) to rationalize the roles and uses of Bank-administered trust funds for Bank-housed programs.

Funding Models of Global Programs That Combine DGF, Trust Funds, and Bank Budget Need Greater Clarity

OED's Phase 1 report identified three funding models for global programs that have evolved from earlier funding arrangements (OED 2002c, p. 39):

- *Long-term development model:* Funding is provided for long periods to support the program's development objectives. Implicit in this is a close relationship between the donors' funding and the program's overall strategy.
- *Foundation model:* Funding is intended to be catalytic, to expand or trigger support for promising economic and social innovations. Donors maintain an arm's-length relationship with the program.
- *Venture capital model:* Time-bound involvement in the "business" being funded brings benefits to the program's donors, through activities such as mentoring, monitoring, corporate governance, and recruitment of management.

Disconnects between program objectives and their funding arrangements create problems in at least 10 programs (table 6.1). Among the environment and agriculture programs, CGIAR, GEF, and MLF all address long-term development issues and provide some assurance of long-term funding, but CGIAR relies on annual donor contributions for its long-term research program, and its Bank funding consumes DGF funds that could be used for other worthy global initiatives, such as a global health-research network. CEPF's funding may have been justified as a venture-capital model, but its placement in Window 1 as a long-term development program crowds out other high-priority investments.

Among the health programs, TDR addresses the poor's long-term health-research needs, but the DGF cannot provide funding on the scale needed. RBM and Stop TB address long-

Table 6.1 Disconnects Between Program Objectives and Their Funding Arrangements Create Problems

Network/ sector	Long-term development model: Financing investments to produce GPGs	Long-term development model: Other	Foundation model	Venture capital model
Environment & agriculture	**CGIAR,** GEF, MLF, **CEPF**		GWP	ProCarbFund, GIF
Health	**TDR**	UNAIDS, Global Forum, RBM, Stop TB, GAVI		
Infrastructure & private sector development		WSP, ESMAP, **CGAP, *info*Dev**		PPIAF, **Cities Alliance**
Other		**PostConFund,** FSAP, **GDN**	**UCW**	**IF,** FIRST, World Links

Note: Programs are classified according to their current funding arrangements. The DGF implicitly views Window 1 programs as "long-term development" programs and Window 2 programs as "foundation" or "venture capital" programs. Programs in boldface show a disconnect between their actual objectives and their funding arrangements.

term development issues. DGF made the right decision to move RBM and Stop TB from Window 2 to Window 1. By previously assigning them to Window 2, the DGF Council had implicitly regarded them as operating on a venture-capital model.

Among the infrastructure and private sector development programs, CGAP and *info*Dev are justifiable as venture capital programs, while the Cities Alliance addresses long-term urban development issues. Having placed CGAP and *info*Dev in Window 1, and Cities Alliance in Window 2, the DGF Council has implicitly classified them as the opposite.

Among the other programs, DGF is unable to fund several programs on the scale they need. The DGF Council put GDN in Window 1 as a long-term development program. Having spun off the program in a venture-capital mode, though, the Bank had no exit strategy to ensure GDN's development as a soundly financed, independent identity. Nor has the GDN board established clear roles and responsibilities for itself, its secretariat, and the Bank or fostered the development of an identity and governance structure separate from the Bank. UCW and IF address long-term development issues. By putting them in Window 2, the DGF Council has implied that they are foundation and venture-capital models, respectively.

In many cases, funding drives programs. This is especially evident when donors give restricted rather than core funding, as in the case of CGIAR. Some lower-priority programs also crowd out other high-return, long-term investments in global public goods. The Bank could use its convening power to mobilize substantially more public resources for programs, such as a much-needed global health research network for the diseases of the poor or a mechanism for producing drugs at prices affordable to developing countries. The procedure should be to identify potential benefits to the poor that require global collective action and long-term funding, but that are un- or underfunded, rather than substituting for, or competing with, existing aid instruments. Without such an approach, global programs impinge on limited country capacity without bringing new funding (except as an extension of Bank activity) or new ideas.

In many cases, funding drives programs when donors give restricted rather than core funding, as in the case of CGIAR.

The share of the Bank's income allocated to grant making is too small to support large-scale investments in global public goods on its own. DGF funding should be used to stimulate the establishment of key programs, such as a global health-research network. Meanwhile, other donors should take on a greater burden and role in other DGF-supported programs. The Bank's health sector partners have emphasized the importance of long-term investment in public-health research. They stress the importance of the Bank allocating 2 to 5 percent of its health-sector lending to health research.[3] This would set an example for other donors and governments to contribute toward the much-needed financing of national health-research systems, as a complement to global health research.

The Bank's involvement in programs with important goals but little independently verified impact, such as CEPF and *info*Dev, has also diverted Bank resources and attention from higher-priority, more demonstrably effective programs. In some cases, such as CGAP and GDN, the Bank's willingness to provide most of the initial funding hampered the mobilization of funding from others. In the case of CGAP, the Bank made its initial $30 million available before other member donors had rounded up their expected $70 million. Had the Bank waited for its partners, other donors might have developed stronger ownership of CGAP.

Inconsistent Application of DGF Funding Rules Causes Confusion and Poses Reputational Risks

The Bank has not applied the eight criteria for DGF grant support consistently (box 6.1). Most noticeable has been the differ-

DGF funding should be used to stimulate the establishment of key programs, such as a global health-research network. Other donors should take on a greater burden and role in other DGF-supported programs.

DGF decisions to support particular programs represent important signals to current and prospective donors and clients concerning the Bank's strategy and priorities with regard to global programs.

ent application of these criteria between those programs that started before and after the DGF was established, with little indication of when the grandfathered programs will be expected to comply with the criteria. DGF decisions to support particular programs represent important signals to current and prospective donors and clients concerning the Bank's strategy and priorities with regard to global programs. How the eight criteria for DGF grant support for global programs are adhered to is thus important for the Bank's credibility, since these criteria are well known to the Bank's partners who seek DGF support. That the rules seem to be applied differently to different programs and that DGF decisions seem to be more the result of lobbying and negotiation send a message that is potentially damaging to the Bank's reputation.

Particularly for the programs grandfathered into the DGF, the criterion that "grants should not generally exceed 15 percent of expected

Box 6.1 The DGF Has Had Difficulty Applying Its Selectivity Criteria to the Bank's Global Programs

- *Subsidiarity:* Some in-house programs have activities similar to the Bank's country operations, such as economic and sector work and technical assistance (PPIAF and the Cities Alliance) and country-level investments (the Post-conflict Fund). Other in-house programs (CGAP and *info*Dev) have significantly scaled back their grant-making activities. All are justified on grounds of their global knowledge creation and dissemination activities. The incremental value added by the partnership, beyond what the Bank could do through partnerships at the country level, needs to be determined.
- *Comparative advantage:* As the only multisectoral development-finance institution with global reach, the Bank has a strong advantage at the global and country levels relative to its often more specialized partners. Its comparative advantage should be in linking the global-level activities of global programs with developing countries' own needs and priorities. Yet such links are generally weak within and among networks.
- *Multicountry benefits:* All the case studies are multicountry programs. They are engaged in activities with apparent economies of scale and scope, such as global knowledge creation and dissemination, capacity building, and donor coordination, but many seem to operate on a country-by-country basis and do not seem to have been "required" to develop cross-country and cross-regional networks.
- *Leverage:* The 15 percent rule has not been enforced, neither for some programs that preceded the DGF's formation in 1998 (CGAP, *info*Dev, Post-conflict Fund and World Links) nor for programs that started afterward (GDN, CEPF). Enforcing compliance has been hampered by incomplete information on program budgets and inadequate definitions of what constitutes "program funding."
- *Managerial competence:* When the CEPF, GDN, and World Links were established, and when GDN and World Links were moved outside the Bank, there was no exploration to see whether other providers could have served the same objectives more cost-effectively.
- *Arm's-length relationship:* Except in the case of CGAP, there has been no independent oversight of in-house programs. For both in-house and externally managed programs, there have been few budget allocations for oversight and no standard terms of reference outlining the responsibilities and accountabilities for Bank staff serving on the programs' governing bodies.
- *Disengagement strategy:* Disengagement has been poorly articulated and managed in three cases (GWP, GDN, and World Links). Some Window 1 programs (such as CGAP and *info*Dev), which predate the DGF, appear to enjoy "squatters' rights" compared to Window 2 programs (such as PPIAF and Cities Alliance), which started later. The DGF has had some external reviews, but it lacks the means to make informed decisions about moving programs between Windows 1 and 2.
- *Promoting partnerships:* The criterion is too vague. It does not say what kind (programmatic or institutional) or level (global or country) of partnership is expected. The term "partnership" has become all-encompassing. It even includes parties who are implementing program activities under contracts.

funding over the life of Bank funding to a given program, or over the rolling three-year plan period, whichever is shorter," has not been met. Eight of the 18 case study programs that received DGF grants in FY04 violated this criterion (table 6.2).[4] For three programs—the Post-conflict Fund,[5] CGAP, and GDN—the Bank's contribution has greatly exceeded the DGF criterion since 1998.

On a related matter, the Bank recently clarified its rules on the use of DGF grants and administrative budget for the program activities and secretariat costs of in-house and externally managed programs (Annex B, table B.1). These rules require all DGF grants to in-house programs "to flow to entities outside the Bank for funding costs of externally managed activities," and to restrict the use of the Bank's administrative budget to funding in-house secretariat costs. Trust funds may be used to fund either program activities or secretariat costs. This clarification is a welcome development, but it still leaves some unanswered questions, both short term and long term.

In the short term, can a proportion of the DGF grants (typically around 10 percent) still be used to fund the in-house secretariat costs of CGIAR and the Post-conflict Fund, or will these now have to come from a combination of the Bank's administrative budget and donor trust funds?[6] Can PPIAF and Cities Alliance still use some of their DGF grant to pay Regional operational staff to supervise grants to external entities? Will CGAP and *info*Dev have to discontinue using DGF funding for their in-kind technical assistance and global knowledge activities—in effect scaling back these activities to the amounts available from the Bank's administrative budget and donor trust funds? Will these rules be applied equally to the pre-1998 and post-1998 programs?[7] Will there be a phase-in period for the new rules for adversely affected programs?

In the long term, this means that vice-presidential units can once again allocate Bank budget for the secretariat costs of non-DGF in-house programs like WSP and ESMAP, and even, one presumes, for DGF-supported programs. This

Table 6.2 Eight of 18 DGF-Supported Programs Violate DGF's 15 Percent Guideline in FY04, and Windows 1 and 2 Need to Be Revisited[a]

World Bank share (%)	Window 1	Window 2: Considered for more than 3 years of support during grant allocation process for FY05	Window 2: Other (exit year in parentheses)	Non-DGF
Greater than 50	Post-conflict Fund, CGAP, GDN			
25–50	CEPF, Global Forum for Health Research		World Links (FY06)	FSAP
15–25	*info*Dev		IF (FY04)	
10–15	CGIAR	RBM		
1–10	TDR, UNAIDS, GAVI	Cities Alliance, PPIAF, Stop TB	FIRST (FY05), UCW (FY06)[b]	ESMAP, WSP, GIF
Less than 1				GEF, MF, GWP,[c] Prototype Carbon Fund

a. Based on FY04/CY03 data.

b. UCW received DGF funding as a Window 2 program for the first time in FY04.

c. The Global Water Partnership exited DGF funding in FY02.

may create some perverse incentives; for example, to locate inside the Bank those programs that do not successfully compete for DGF funds. The use of the Bank's administrative budget for global programs needs to be monitored carefully and assessed for development effectiveness.

Bank-Administered Trust Funds for Global Programs Could Be Deployed More Strategically

Several global programs, such as WSP and ESMAP, began with support from Bank-administered donor trust funds and only subsequently established formal collaborative processes to give donors an increased share in program governance and to mobilize additional trust funds. Indeed, global programs are often referred to as "programmatic trust funds" within the Bank. Such approaches have certainly mobilized more resources, as indicated by the proliferation of Bank-administered trust funds. Yet this strategy raises several issues.

The overlap between Bank operations and global program activities confuses borrowers. Where programs do studies or provide technical assistance similar to the Bank's economic and sector work, it is unclear whether the program adds value beyond the trust fund resources. Are the transaction costs of such partnerships commensurate with the benefits to the Bank's development objectives? Also, while some programs bring resources into the Bank, others such as CGAP receive most of their resources from the Bank.[8]

The Bank's global strategy would benefit from a procedure to distinguish between activities that are clearly adding value to the Bank's operations and those that substitute for, or compete with, them.

The lack of synergy between trust fund–related Bank activities and trust fund–supported global program activities is also an issue. For example, the Bank's trade and capacity building work in the Development Economics Vice Presidency (DEC) is supported by trust funds, and DEC and the Poverty Reduction and Environmental Management Vice Presidency (PREM) are actively involved in IF. DEC also does its own work on thematic issues, such as trade prospects for commodity-dependent countries or impacts of food safety-related non-tariff barriers on the poor. IF works on similar themes in some countries. There seems to be little synergy among these activities, even though the Bank has advocated OECD trade reforms since the Doha round.

Proliferation of trust fund activity means program managers have insufficient experience and support for fiduciary management. The Bank's Internal Audit Department has identified the problem of different donor reporting requirements and insufficient Bank support, particularly to the small programs, for reporting and fiduciary management. Relating expenditures to activities is thus a challenge, particularly since the programs' expenditures do not always coincide with the Bank's accounting when DGF, trust fund and Bank budget resources are commingled. The Bank's global strategy would benefit from a procedure to distinguish between activities that are clearly adding value to the Bank's operations and those that substitute for, or compete with, them.

Trust fund–financed staff and expenditures do not maximize institutional effectiveness. Bank budget constraints have resulted in the use of trust fund–financed staff to do activities that normally would be done by Bank staff. Shortages of travel funds have also encouraged the use of trust fund–financed consultants on the working groups of global program partnerships to do what would normally be Bank-staff work. When a busy senior Bank manager, who serves on the board of an external global program, is supported by trust fund–financed consultants who have no institutional Bank perspective, there is a risk that the Bank's concerns will not be represented in the program.

World Bank Performance in Global Programs

This chapter assesses the Bank's performance as a partner in individual global programs and draws additional lessons from the case studies for the Bank's strategic and programmatic management of its global portfolio.

Performance is assessed using four criteria:

- **Comparative advantage:** Whether the Bank is employing its comparative advantages in the programs (endorsed by the Development Committee in September 2000)[1]
- **Global-country links**: Whether the global program has operational links, where appropriate, to the Bank's country work (one of the six approval criteria established by Bank Management in April 2000)
- **Oversight:** Whether the Bank exercises independent oversight of its involvement in the program, as appropriate, for in-house and externally managed programs
- **Exit strategy:** Whether the Bank is facilitating flexible and transparent disengagement strategies, as appropriate (established by the DGF Council in October 1998).

The Bank's performance suffers from some systemic weaknesses. The Bank employs its comparative advantage at the country level less well and less often than it does at the global level, particularly as the premier *multisectoral* development finance institution with policy analysis capacity and lending ability *at the country level*. The Bank's matrix management system does not work well to link its global program activities to the Bank's Regional and country operations, the priorities of developing countries, or the Poverty Reduction Strategy process. Both the Bank and its partners have overlooked the internal budgetary and staffing implications of global programs. There are almost no resources for the network anchors and Regional staff to operationalize global knowledge and approaches at the country level. There are also no terms of reference for Bank staff serving on the governing bodies of global programs. In only two cases have budgetary resources been allocated for independent oversight. In only one case has there been independent oversight of in-house programs. Exits from DGF financing (in the case of GWP) and from Bank financing (in the case of GDN and World Links) were poorly conceived and managed.

The Bank employs its comparative advantage at the country level less well and less often than it does at the global level.

Comparative Advantage

The Bank's Strategic Directions Paper for fiscal 2002–04 described the Bank's comparative advantage at the global level as its (1) global mandate and reach, (2) convening power and (3) ability to mobilize financial resources; and at the country level as its (4) multisectoral capacity, (5) expertise in country- and sector-level analysis, and (6) in-depth country knowledge. This review confirms the findings of the Phase 1 report that the Bank uses its country comparative advantages better than its global ones, particularly for programs chaired by and/or housed in the Bank.

Other donors view the Bank's leadership role, its financial contributions, its operational support, and its fiduciary oversight as a seal of approval, giving them confidence to invest in a program. The Bank is sought as a partner for externally managed programs less for its financial contributions than for its activities as the largest lender and policy advisor to developing countries and for its potential to mobilize specialized knowledge of international organizations, donors, and the professional community to add value to the activities of client countries. Consider for example the Bank's role as a co-sponsor of UNAIDS, to which it contributes $4 million annually (UNAIDS receives $95 million in total annually). The Bank's greatest value to UNAIDS is as the largest lender (more than $18 billion between 1992 and 2002) to the health sector in developing countries. The Bank's value also lies in its potential to complement investments in communicable disease programs (being promoted by global programs) with support for health-system capacity building (box 7.1).

These examples show that the Bank's comparative advantage and global responsibilities go well beyond its roles in individual programs. The Bank has a responsibility to work with its global partners (including particularly the permanent members of the programs' governing boards) to raise the standards of priority setting, coordination, governance, management, and evaluation in global programs. These include links to country operations.

Synergies between and among activities at the global and country levels are crucial for the Bank's developing-country clients.

Global-Country Links

Synergies between and among activities at the global and country levels are crucial for the Bank's developing-country clients, both to ensure development impacts and to ensure that the clients' views are heard at the global level. The links needed in various sectors at the country level, and even among countries within global programs, tend to be very different. They depend on whether the programs try to address country-level or global-level constraints; bring in new financial resources for investment (such as MLF, GEF, or GAVI), new knowledge about approaches (as in Stop TB), or technical assistance at the country level (as in WSP); or promote an approach with implications for domestic priorities and resource allocation (UNAIDS). A direct link may be unnecessary, at least at first, where the global program can achieve its goals without country-level support *from the Bank*, as for example researching drugs or vaccines. But where complementary investments are needed—for example, in surveillance or in epidemiological research at the country level—where country capacity is insufficient, and where economies of scale matter, the Bank needs to attend to the links between its global and country activities.

Ensuring the appropriate synergy between global programs and Bank operations requires a clear global strategy in which a better matrix management is a necessary, but not a sufficient, condition for global priorities and strategies to emerge from the bottom up. To develop such a strategy, the Bank must address five issues:

- Integrating global opportunities and concerns into sector strategies—distinguishing between the need for investments in global public goods and complementary national goods
- Testing global program goals in country operations
- Providing complementary investments and helping countries benefit from global pro-

Box 7.1 The Effectiveness of Bank Cosponsorship as a Governance Tool Is Underexplored

The Bank's cosponsorship of seven programs—CGIAR, TDR, ESMAP, UNAIDS, Stop TB, GIF, and GWP—is a good reflection of the deployment of its global mandate and reach, convening power, and capacity to mobilize resources. The Bank has "cosponsored" programs, usually with specialized U.N. organizations. Cosponsorship provides an imprimatur of legitimacy for programs that are not based on formal international conventions.

The CGIAR was the first such program, with the CGIAR Secretariat based in the Bank and the Technical Advisory Committee Secretariat based in the FAO. The co-sponsorship with FAO was intended to increase the CGIAR's legitimacy in developing countries at a time when they had little voice. FAO's technical input was also considered necessary. UNAIDS was similarly formed with 6 co-sponsors (now 9, and likely 10 with the inclusion of UNHCR) to develop a U.N. systemwide coordinated response to HIV/AIDS, because individual agencies had not responded rapidly enough to the crisis, either individually or collectively.

The roles, responsibilities, and functions of co-sponsors vary among programs and have evolved over time. Traditionally, they have been assigned a mix of governance and management responsibilities—for example, for the selection of key office-holders, management and oversight of secretariats, mobilization and management of trust funds, management of technical advisory committees, and evaluation. Some cosponsors have had more staying power than others. There is a growing ambiguity in the functions of the co-sponsors in relation to donors and other partners (for example, the diminishing role of cosponsors in the older programs such as CGIAR, TDR, and GIF), compared with the strong role of co-sponsors in relation to the governance structures (such as the Program Coordinating Board of UNAIDS). These roles have been debated as the governance structures themselves have evolved, and competition for influence among agencies and partners has been considerable. Experience has raised issues about the role of co-sponsors in relation to the governance structures in giving strategic direction to the program. The issues are sharpened in cases where the co-sponsors also have implementing responsibilities that others think they have not fulfilled.

This review only found clear terms of reference for cosponsors in UNAIDS. Even in this case, the external evaluation raised questions about the roles of the Programme Coordinating Board in relation to the co-sponsors. In other programs, the Bank's responsibilities as a cosponsor are unclear or unarticulated, have evolved over time and, even in the case of DGF-supported programs, were unknown to the DGF secretariat or the Bank's legal department.

Within the Bank, the sector boards are responsible for conducting and monitoring co-sponsorships. Institutional cultures and resources vary considerably between the Bank and the U.N. agencies. Though the Bank is the largest trustee of trust funds, its networks often lack the budgetary and staff resources to meet their cosponsor duties. The U.N. agencies have similar issues. The sector boards and anchors are often understaffed and overcommitted to partnerships. They lack the experience to address dysfunctions involving themselves or the other partners. The Bank needs to work with its partners to clarify these roles and to determine its strategic role in partnerships. The GPP Council should support the networks in these efforts.

grams by linking global programs more effectively to the PRSP and CAS processes

- Ensuring coherence *among* various global program goals at the global and country levels
- Linking overarching resource mobilization strategies and global strategy with trust funds and the subsidiarity principle.

Integrating global issues into the Bank's sector strategies. For sector strategies to better link country realities with global programs, they need to confront the business-planning implications of different industrial- and developing-country priorities in the existing strategies. This would help the Bank to explore gaps at the global level, distinguish them from gaps at the country level, and draw the implications for sector strategies on both levels. Global programs too often try to achieve country-level objectives that others have seemingly ignored. This has happened with CGIAR, because of the lack of national-level investments in agricultural research; with GAVI's child-immunization programs, due to insufficient donor investments in immunization; and elsewhere. At the same time, many global-level issues on trade, aid, finance, and intellectual property, which developing countries and the Bank's country and Regional operations cannot address on their own, receive less attention. In addition, global program activity is intensifying

The goals of different global programs sometimes conflict.

at the country level, duplicating effort and tying up Bank resources better used in direct country work.

Testing individual global-program goals in country operations and establishing a feedback loop in continued program funding. Only when the Bank begins to use its comparative advantage, by testing and documenting the feasibility of global-program goals at the country level, will it be able to advance the global debate. On-the-ground knowledge will improve global programs' focus. Currently it is unclear, given the limited evidence, how much real value, beyond extra funds, global programs bring to country operations. The few notable exceptions include increased awareness of UNAIDS and the approaches of Stop TB. If each global program had to demonstrate in its DGF applications how it helped or would help a specific country and had to report results in the following years, the incentive to integrate the global-program portfolio into country operations would be established. As it is, task managers do not provide this information consistently because the DGF does not expect it.

Providing complementary investments and helping countries benefit from global programs. Complementary investments in agricultural research at the national level, along with investments at the global level, have helped some large developing countries to graduate from IDA. For programs without complementary investments, there is a risk that global programs are just wishful thinking. In China, the Stop TB program worked closely with the health task manager to help bring in grant funds to make Bank investments in tuberculosis treatment and prevention attractive to the government. On the other hand, following the excellent support the Integrated Framework received from Cambodia and discussion of its country case study at the consultative group meeting, the responsibility for mobilizing the much-needed follow-up investments has rested largely with the country. WHO has emphasized the importance of investment in surveillance and epidemiological research, but few of the Bank's health sector programs have included much investment in research or monitoring. The Bank's recent efforts to develop long-overdue investments in agricultural research in Africa are an encouraging sign.

The Bank's multisectoral presence and global reach can help improve coherence among these goals and the needs of developing countries.

Ensuring coherence among various global-program goals at the global and country levels. The goals of different global programs sometimes conflict—for example, the Global IPM Facility's goal to reduce the use of pesticides, IF's to increase agricultural exports, and UCW's to reduce child labor. The Bank's multisectoral presence and global reach can help improve coherence among these goals and the needs of developing countries. This calls for stronger links between the global agenda, economic and sector work, and the PRSPs and CASs.

Linking overarching resource-mobilization strategies and global strategy through trust funds and subsidiarity. In place of the current proliferation of global programs, some of the $7.1 billion in trust funds that the Bank is mobilizing could be used to establish a few long-term global public-goods programs that are big enough to reflect developing-country needs or priorities, and thus to make a difference.[2] For example, long-term investments in health research, on a scale similar to that of CGIAR in agriculture, are needed to mobilize the best science at the global level to address diseases of the poor. Clarity is needed about which activities are done through global programs, because they would add more value than if the Bank were acting alone through its country and Regional operations. While some overlap in activities will still probably occur, confusion among the Bank's clients arises more from the overlap in responsibilities and accountabilities of the programs and the Bank's regular operations—particularly when the programs provide additional (sometimes including budgetary) resources for technical assistance, training, or studies.

Linking global programs to country operations has budget implications for networks and Regions. For network anchor and Regional staff to operationalize the content of global programs, they need money.

Oversight

OED views the Bank's oversight of global program management as analogous to its supervision of borrower implementation of Bank-financed projects. The OPCS "Guidelines to Staff on Project Supervision" define and distinguish supervision from implementation and provide two reasons for supervision, which also apply to global programs:

- "To ensure that financing is used only for the purposes intended, with due regard to efficiency and economy"
- "[To see] that the projects [the Bank] supports achieve their development objectives."

Management also indicated, in its March 2003 update to the Board on the management of global programs and partnerships, that it would strengthen oversight to ensure that global programs (1) provide global public goods, (2) support international advocacy, (3) are coordinated multicountry programs and/or (4) mobilize substantial incremental resources.

Overall, despite management's emphasis on oversight as well as selectivity in its presentations to the Board between April 2000 and March 2003, OED finds independent oversight to be among the weakest aspects, if not the weakest aspect, of the Bank's management of its global-program portfolio. First, the Bank needs a global strategy that addresses global public policies that hurt developing countries' prospects for poverty-reducing growth and that fosters stronger links between global programs and country operations. Without this, increased oversight could just mean micro-management. Second, the Bank needs to apply the routine, Bankwide procedures of quality assurance, internal audits, risk assessment and risk management to its global program activities. Independent oversight and controls of this nature are particularly important in the early stages of each program.

OED finds independent oversight to be among the weakest aspects, if not the weakest aspect, of the Bank's management of its global-program portfolio.

Exercising independent oversight is more straightforward in principle for the 12 programs that the Bank neither chairs nor manages than for the 12 programs that it chairs, co-chairs or manages (table 7.1). Even in the former case, independent oversight requires clear terms of reference and budgetary allocations for those Bank staff/managers who serve on the boards. In interviews, OED noted considerable confusion among those serving on the boards about their functions. Many indicated that they would welcome clear terms of reference, training on board-member functions, and periodic meetings among board members to share experiences and learn from one another. OED was unable to assess precisely where the budgetary constraints lie. Network leaders emphasized the importance of the Bank allocating enough budgetary resources to networks and Regions to fund oversight and the linking of global programs to Bank operations. Others felt that the lack of budgetary resources was less of a problem than the low priority the networks and Regions give these tasks.

Exercising Bank oversight is particularly important for programs that the Bank has founded and spun off, such as GWP, World Links, and GDN. The Bank has a responsibility to ensure that these programs get a good start, establish their own identity, and begin to add value from their new external and independent perspective. This review found an understandable desire on the part of partners to establish a broader intellectual space, where new perspectives and approaches from outside the Bank can be brought to bear in spun-off programs. Yet weak strategies, governance, and financing plague all three programs, together with little or no independent Bank oversight.[3]

Of the 12 programs that the Bank chairs or houses, line management provides independent oversight for two programs managed inside the Bank: the Post-conflict Fund and FSAP. Only

Table 7.1 Bank Oversight of Case Study Programs, by Governance Model

Governance model	Lack of independent oversight [a]	Potential for independent oversight: Housed in the Bank	Potential for independent oversight: Externally managed [b]	Not applicable [c]
Line management within the Bank		PostConFund, FSAP [d]		
Secretariat inside the Bank	ProCarbFund, WSP, ESMAP, *info*Dev, PPIAF, Cities Alliance	CGAP [e]		GEF
Shared secretariat between Bank and external organization	FIRST	CGIAR [f]		
Secretariat inside external organization	CEPF [g]		GIF, RBM, Stop TB, GAVI, TDR, UCW, IF	
Independent external entity			GWP, Global Forum, UNAIDS, GDN, World Links	MLF
Number of programs	8	4	12	2

a. The Bank's representative on the governing (and executive) bodies is inside the vice presidency responsible for managing the program, which poses potential conflicts of interest.

b. These programs are located outside the Bank, the Bank does not chair the governing body, and the Bank's representative is a member of the governing body.

c. The Bank is an implementing agency for GEF and MLF; it does not have responsibility for overall direction and oversight. The Bank attends the meeting of the governing and executive bodies as an observer, and is responsible for that part of each program that is being implemented by the Bank. Individual GEF and MLF operations are appraised by the Bank, much like its own investment operations.

d. There is no governing body or arm's-length secretariat for the Post-conflict Fund and FSAP, and oversight is exercised within the management chain of the Bank. Regional operational staff outside the ESSD vice presidency are members of the Post-conflict Fund Steering Committee. Both Bank and IMF staff are members of the Financial Sector Liaison Committee, which coordinates FSAP activities.

e. The Bank's representative on the CG and Executive Committee is located in FSE and therefore outside the INF vice presidency, which is responsible for chairing the CG and managing the Secretariat.

f. Pursuant to OED's meta-evaluation, the Bank's Chief Economist will now exercise oversight of CGIAR. The financing and terms of reference are still being put in place.

g. In the case of CEPF, although the Bank's representative on the CEPF working group is located in the LCR Region, he reports to the Environment Director in the ESSD vice presidency for the purposes of this program. The Bank's President chairs the CEPF Donor Council, and the Environment Department provides the financial resources for oversight.

2 of the other 10 programs, CGAP and CGIAR, have the potential for independent oversight. For CGAP, the Bank's representative on the Council of Governors and the Executive Committee is located in the Financial Sector Vice Presidency, and therefore outside the management chain of the Infrastructure vice presidency responsible for CGAP's implementation. For the CGIAR, the Bank's Committee on Development Effectiveness (CODE) supported OED's recommendation in the CGIAR meta-evaluation to separate oversight and management functions within the Bank. Management has since given oversight responsibility to the Chief Economist.

Six of the remaining eight programs—WSP, ESMAP, *info*Dev, PPIAF, Cities Alliance, and FIRST—are housed in the Bank and the Bank's representative on the governing body reports to the vice president (or managing director in the case of FIRST[4]) who chairs the governing body. As OED pointed out in the CGIAR meta-evaluation, this creates potential for conflicts of interests.

In the case of the Prototype Carbon Fund, housed in the ESSD vice presidency, the Bank manager who heads the Fund Management Unit (the secretariat) also chairs the Fund Management Committee, which reports to the Participants Committee of public and private sector contributors. While there is some independent oversight on the Fund Management Committee (which is composed of Bank staff from various network and Regional vice presidencies), there is no independent oversight from the Bank on the crucial Participants Committee, because the Bank is not a member of the committee. In view of the various conflict-of-interest issues, one option might be for a Bank manager outside the ESSD vice presidency to sit on the Participants Committee (as in CGAP and CGIAR). For such external oversight to work well, however, the Bank should develop a Board-approved strategy before it involves itself further in the development of carbon markets. Without an overall Bank Group carbon finance strategy (including delineation of the Bank's and the IFC's roles, an issue currently under discussion), the external overseer would have no standard against which to compare performance.

For CEPF, which is housed in Conservation International, the World Bank president chairs the Donor Council (governing body), and the program's executive director, a Conservation International staff member, heads the secretariat and chairs the Working Group (executive body). The Environment Department has designated a staff member located in the Latin America and Caribbean Region to serve on the Working Group and exercise fiduciary oversight and allocated budget accordingly. While this oversight has served the program well so far, having even a senior staff member oversee a program chaired by the Bank's senior management can compromise the independence of such oversight.

What should oversight entail? In its global programs, the Bank should "exercise a degree of oversight consistent with the major roles that it plays in the program" (OED 2003b, p. 29). For example, in the case of CGIAR, where the Bank has been the "guardian" of the program and gives donors continuing confidence to invest in the program, independent oversight should not be limited to the Bank's financial contribution. Oversight should also encompass the Bank's stewardship of the program; the allocation rules for the Bank's contribution (which have important signaling effects for other donors); the progress in implementation, including mobilizing funding; and reporting this progress to the Bank's Board.

Who should exercise oversight? Oversight should involve someone experienced, with the appropriate level of seniority and demonstrated professional qualities and, in the case of in-house programs, from outside the implementing management chain.[5] He or she should provide an independent assessment of the program's performance to his or her own vice president and to the GPP Council. The Bank should develop standard terms of references outlining responsibilities and accountabilities, institute training for Bank staff serving on governing bodies of global programs, and routinely review whether oversight is performed satisfactorily (based on the terms of reference). The selection process should be transparent, and accountability should be well-defined.

How much might oversight cost? The budgetary resources allocated for oversight should be commensurate with the tasks and may change over time. The OPCS Project Supervision Guidelines (BP 1305) state that:

- Bank managers "should ensure that sufficient supervision resources are provided for each project, taking into account the nature, complexity, and size of the operation."
- "Good supervision responds flexibly and decisively to the changing environment and needs of a project. Therefore supervision requirements...change over the life of the project because project priorities and circumstances change."

Presently, FSE allocates $30,000 out of its own administrative budget for supervision of CGAP, a $14 million program, half of the funds for which come from the DGF. ESSD/ENV allocates $100,000 a year for supervision of CEPF, a $24 million program, $4 million of which comes from the DGF (although the Bank is also exercising supervision on behalf of the GEF and Japan).

Exit Strategy

This review distinguishes exit strategies from three perspectives: (1) the program declares "mission accomplished" and closes; (2) the program continues, but the Bank withdraws from all aspects of its participation; (3) the program continues and the Bank remains engaged, though the degree of engagement declines over time. Among the case study programs, the Prototype Carbon Fund, funded completely by the private sector, is the only program with a defined exit strategy from the first point of view. It was established as a pilot program and is scheduled to end by 2012 (Annex H, table H.13).[6]

There are no examples of the second perspective and three examples of the third. In the case of GWP, although the Bank co-founded the program in 1997, housed the secretariat for the first few years, facilitated its move to Stockholm in 2000, and terminated its DGF support in FY03, the Bank remains engaged as a co-sponsor and member of the Steering Committee (although the Bank's engagement at the operational level has been minimal). In the cases of World Links and GDN, the Bank founded both programs, housed their secretariats inside the Bank, and then spun them off as independent legal entities, while continuing to provide DGF support.

In-house secretariats pose problems, including potential conflicts of interest, excessive dependence on the Bank, and heightened expectations of continuing Bank support.

The latter three are the types of exits that have been most discussed within the Bank since the DGF established its arm's-length and exit-strategy criteria in 1998. The DGF issued guidelines for the arm's-length criterion in June 2000 and instituted the "two-window" approach, beginning with the FY02 DGF budget allocation, to facilitate the orderly exit of those programs—called Window 2—that did not qualify for long-term funding. OED's 1998 process review (OED 2002a) concluded, and the CGIAR meta-evaluation has subsequently confirmed, that in-house secretariats pose problems, including potential conflicts of interest, excessive dependence on the Bank, and heightened expectations of continuing Bank support. Donors say they prefer to house certain programs in the Bank to ensure ready access to the Bank's technical expertise and country operations. In reality, housing programs in the Bank has other, unstated advantages, related to the Bank's substantial infrastructure, recruitment, staffing, procurement and disbursement procedures, visa and travel facilities, and the tax-free status of an international organization.

Many programs, once created, are easily perpetuated. Some, like WSP, ESMAP, and CGAP, have reinvented themselves to pursue their objectives in different ways or even to pursue different objectives. This experience gives strong caution to the "venture capital" approach to public sector financing. While the public sector will need to continue to finance public-goods activities, the Bank's grant resources are limited and need continually to be reallocated to address new global issues as they arise. Encouraging in-house programs to move outside the Bank and facilitating an orderly exit from DGF support are seen as ways of reducing the programs' dependency on the Bank and letting them "sink or swim," depending on how much support they can garner from other donors.

While spinning off programs is a good idea, the Bank has not managed spin-offs well, particularly in terms of oversight. The financing strategies for GDN and World Links were poorly worked out.[7] World Links' governance structure is inappropriate for mobilizing long-term funding from the private sector, particularly for overhead costs and for regions such as Africa. The Bank's abrupt withdrawal in 2004 might reduce some of its matching-grant funding. GDN has had a weak governance structure, weak business management, weak Bank oversight, and, paradoxically, a perception of too close an identification with the Bank, because of its overwhelming financial dependence on the Bank. While some observers have criticized the Bank for not ensuring that the programs it has created establish independent identities and exhibit sound growth, there remains a strong sentiment on the GDN board that the Bank should fund this program over the long haul. How GDN's move to international organization status would affect its funding and governance arrangements remains unclear. GDN management believes that funding prospects will be no worse and probably better with IO status than under the alternative status of a not-for-profit organization incorporated in India. GDN management has also indicated that it will undertake the move to IO status only if the final version of the program's charter preserves GDN's independence as a research network. Bank membership on the GDN board would require endorsement of the Bank's Board—before this, a number of risks and uncertainties need to be resolved.[8]

The Bank has managed exit from DGF grant support better. But the DGF's two-window approach, while a useful stopgap, does not fully address program exit. Window 1 contains some programs (CGIAR, TDR, UNAIDS, CGAP, *info*Dev and the Post-conflict Fund) that were "grandfathered" when the Special Grants Facility was transformed into the DGF in 1998, as well as some new programs (GDN and CEPF) that started afterward. The grandfathered programs, particularly the CGIAR, claim a large share of DGF support, while internal mechanisms to independently monitor systemic reforms are still being put in place. At the same time, competition for DGF resources has increased, and some areas (such as health-research support for the poor, where returns to Bank investment may be higher) remain grossly underfunded.

Some Window 2 programs (RBM, Stop TB, PPIAF, and Cities Alliance) seem deserving of longer-term support either because they are being restructured or because they appear well run and could add considerable value to the Bank's long-term development objectives.[9] On the other hand, some Window 1 programs (*info*Dev and CEPF) hold less promise of long-term sustainable impacts and have potential alternative sources of financing. The DGF has no process for independent appraisal of existing programs. It therefore has no means to make informed decisions about promoting programs from Window 2 to Window 1 or relegating Window 1 programs to Window 2 (as a first step toward financial exit, if they fail to turn themselves around). The DGF's three-year rule for Window 2 programs is too rigid. It needs to be more flexible and to eliminate programs that either are not performing or are marginal to the Bank's mission. The Bank needs to improve the criteria and procedures for the DGF's Window 2 to foster a more flexible, rational, and informed approach to funding "venture capital" programs.[10]

Programs not receiving DGF support require similar scrutiny and an exit option. For example, the Bank's involvement in GIF calls for an independent assessment and redefinition of the objectives, governance, and management. The Bank should also rationalize its support for GWP and the various other donor-supported water initiatives, including the CGIAR Challenge Program on Water and Food, to help establish a cohesive set of global programs that will help the Bank reenter and add value through its lending to the water sector.

Findings and Recommendations

The findings and recommendations of this report build on three previous OED reports on the Bank's involvement in global programs—the 1998 process review of the Bank's grant programs, the 2002 Phase 1 report, and the 2003 CGIAR meta-evaluation—and on case studies of 25 other global programs. The report draws on extensive consultations internally and with partners. This cumulative approach has enabled OED to comprehensively assess the Bank's evolving approach to global programs, including the application of existing criteria and processes for selectivity, grant support, governance, management, and evaluation.

This final chapter summarizes the crosscutting lessons for selectivity, design, implementation, governance, management, financing, and evaluation of individual global programs; assesses the case studies' performance on the criteria endorsed by the Development Committee in September 2000 for the Bank's involvement in global programs; and recommends further actions that the Bank should take to improve the strategic and programmatic management of its portfolio of global programs.

OED Findings

Selectivity

"Letting a thousand flowers bloom" and experimenting with many new programs has helped the Bank to understand the diversity and complexity of global challenges in general and the intricacy of global-country links in particular. This has informed the formulation and the refinement of the Bank's selectivity criteria.

Global public-goods programs meet most criteria. While largely supply-driven, most Bank-supported global public-goods programs (MLF, GEF, ProCarbFund and CEPF, CGIAR, TDR, UNAIDS, Stop TB, Roll Back Malaria, Global Forum for Health Research, and GAVI's Global Research Funding) largely *meet the four Development Committee criteria for selectivity*. Most global programs also *largely meet* the approval and eligibility criteria for Bank involvement. CGIAR does not meet the arm's-length criterion; the Bank did not involve developing-country stakeholders in CEPF's establishment or its global-level governance;

Consensus is often driven by constituencies in donor countries and the staff of international agencies.

the Bank did not do a thorough analysis of the expected level of Bank resources required for the health programs, or of how to implement and manage this new commitment. These are exceptions to the general rule, however.

The corporate advocacy programs meet the Development Committee selectivity criteria. This is largely because the criteria are broad and difficult to apply precisely. For example, the first criterion—"an international consensus that global action is required," which all programs claim as their raison d'être—provides no basis for selectivity because the concept of international consensus is amorphous and loosely applied. The case studies illustrate that the consensus is often driven by constituencies in donor countries and the staff of international agencies. At the same time, few of the networks demand links to country operations, one of the most important criteria, before approval, nor do they track them during implementation.

The Bank deploys its comparative advantages more at the global level than at the country level. Financial and reputational risks and budgetary and staffing implications are rarely sufficiently assessed. The international consensus on the existence of a problem is usually strong; consensus on what collective action is required is often weak. Many global programs are implicitly (sometimes explicitly) established to promote consensus, to "harmonize" donor approaches to specific problems, to delineate donor comparative advantages in addressing those problems, and to give the donors specialized knowledge to use on the problems. Capacity building in the recipient countries is secondary in such projects.

Including developing-country voices at the concept stage enhances program ownership, makes the organizational design more effective, and increases program impacts.

Evidence is lacking that the programs are exploiting economies of scale and scope in such activities as knowledge creation and dissemination, capacity building, technical assistance, and donor coordination. It is also not clear whether the knowledge they disseminate is sufficiently evidence-based, quality-tested, and contextual to add value to what the Bank's client countries themselves do, need, or want or what the Bank can achieve working through country-level partnerships. Performance indicators to assess changed donor or international agency behavior do not exist. Performance indicators, when they exist at all, are focused on the behavior of developing countries. OED was able to identify only a few program-specific indicators of changed Bank and donor practices, procedures, and actions in response to the advocacy of global programs. In the case of corporate advocacy programs, the needs of the Bank's client countries should be the prime consideration for Bank involvement.

The voices of developing countries, or even those of the Bank's operational Regions, are inadequately represented in the international consensus. The case studies of corporate advocacy programs show that including developing-country voices at the concept stage enhances program ownership, makes the organizational design more effective, and increases program impacts. Based on the evidence OED has provided so far, management has acknowledged the need to strengthen the role of developing countries and the Bank's operational Regions in global programs.

Value Added to the Bank's Development Objectives

Evidence on value added to the Bank's development objectives varies, but is increasing. Some programs lack clearly defined objectives, and others have many unstated objectives; this makes it hard to judge what value they have added. It is hard to assess many young programs that have not had time to demonstrate impacts. However, evaluations are increasing, in part prompted by the DGF, and are beginning to affect program design and implementation. When programs do not meet all three requirements for effective evaluation—clear, shared, and measurable objectives; appropriate methodology; and measurable evidence—their global impacts remain unclear.

Programs delivering global public goods often add value. Global public-goods programs (CGIAR, TDR, MLF, parts of GEF, and even some new global-health programs) rate well in their impacts on reducing poverty or on focusing on the policy, institutional, infrastructural, or technological constraints developing countries face in achieving sustainable economic growth. Adding value on the ground in client countries is typically a joint product of global and country-level activities. For example, CGIAR, like TDR, has demonstrated impressive poverty-reducing impacts in part because the Bank, donors and some governments made complementary investments at the country level. However, as country-level investments have shrunk, donors have tried to compensate by encouraging CGIAR to move downstream. They have offered restricted funding tied to research programs that demonstrate immediate impacts, to push CGIAR toward more national- and local-level applied and adaptive work. Management agrees that the activities of several CGIAR research centers now resemble those that regular Bank instruments would support through country-level investments.

Programs close to the Bank currently add more value. Not surprisingly, the programs for which the Bank is an implementing agency are more closely linked with Bank operations. This is in part because the Bank is better at absorbing and using information and findings produced internally or nearby. The Bank needs to devise ways to increase its links to programs more distant from it. Keeping the governance of global programs at arm's length from the Bank and maintaining clear accountability for program performance offer the greatest potential for bringing new information and fresh perspectives to Bank operations.

Global programs have revealed major gaps in investment. Evidence indicates that investments in health research have substantial poverty-reducing impacts. The current global policy and aid environment has huge *investment gaps at the global level* in the provision of global health research, as well as *gaps in complementary investments at the country level*. Health research, like agricultural research, is a long-term activity unlikely to be addressed by the private sector on the scale needed.

Global programs have also revealed gaps in global public policy. Several global programs highlight the existence of global public-policy gaps—often involving industrial-country policies in trade, aid, finance and intellectual-property rights—that affect developing countries. Few programs regard it as within their mandate to address these policy gaps. If changing the international ground rules is the objective of the programs and if advocacy is the means to achieve it, then the programs should be assessed on their ability to deliver changed policies or a changed global environment from the perspective of the poor.

Governance, Management, and Financing

Governance is weak in several programs. While pure shareholder models of program governance are being replaced by stakeholder models, programs are still struggling to balance legitimacy and accountability for results with efficiency in achieving them. The permanent members of the programs' governing bodies, who tend typically to be the major international organizations and donors, have greater de facto responsibility, relative to the rotating members, to ensure that programs are successful. But such responsibility and accountability are rarely clearly articulated. Lack of effective governance and management must be addressed if the Bank's financial support is to continue.

Lack of effective governance and management must be addressed if the Bank's financial support is to continue.

Management arrangements can alter perceived and actual responsibilities. When the Bank or another international organization chairs programs that they house, this reduces the responsibility for shared governance. When programs are housed in the Bank or in another international organization, the program manager often reports both to the programs' governing body and to a line manager in the housing organization. This situation often places responsibility for both management and oversight in the same management chain, which in turn creates real or perceived conflicts of interest in monitoring performance.

Global programs have increased overall aid very little. At the aggregate level, the global programs reviewed have added little new money to official development assistance. Exceptions include funds from private sources for the Prototype Carbon Fund, from the Gates Foundation for health, and small amounts from pharmaceutical companies through new public-private partnerships for drug and vaccine development. Given the opportunity cost of ODA funds, the Bank's involvement in programs with important goals but little demonstrated value needs reconsideration. In some cases, too close an association with the Bank has hampered mobilization of other funds for these programs. It is time to move from "letting a thousand flowers bloom" to assessing which programs deserve continuing Bank support and which do not.

World Bank Performance

Bank performance in global programs is better at the global than at the country level. As a partner in global programs, the Bank has managed programs and mobilized resources better at the global level than at the country level. Other partners view the Bank's leadership role, its financial clout, its access to policymakers, its operational support, and its fiduciary oversight as a seal of approval, giving them confidence to invest in global programs, both in-house and externally managed. Even at the global level, though, the Bank's performance can be improved, particularly with respect to strategy, independent oversight, and global-country linkages.

The Bank still needs to strengthen its appraisal of new programs and to make its selectivity, oversight, evaluation, and exit strategies more transparent and results-based.

The recent reforms are promising. The establishment of the Global Programs and Partnership Council, together with the GPP Group, is a positive development. In line with the Phase 1 report's recommendation, the GPP Council could help oversee the development of the Bank's global strategy, anticipate changes in the global environment, and help set priorities and funding strategies. It can move global programs from the current network perspective to a Bankwide perspective and establish Bankwide standards for global programming and performance. The Bank still needs to strengthen its appraisal of new programs and to make its selectivity, oversight, evaluation, and exit strategies more transparent and results-based. Finally, assessment and oversight of complex global partnerships requires expert knowledge and *input*, not only from the program managers who promote them but also from other partners, developing countries, and experts in the field.

Independent oversight is needed. The Bank needs to institute independent oversight of all its programs—in the case of in-house programs, by senior managers outside the line management of the vice presidency handling the program. Oversight of both externally managed and in-house programs needs to be guided by clear terms of reference, have the necessary budget, and have accountability for performance. Independent oversight is particularly important early on to ensure that programs get off to a good start. Bank management also needs to institute routine procedures of quality assurance, internal audits, risk assessment, and risk management.

Exit strategies of programs are not working well. The Bank's record in managing the separation of in-house programs from the Bank needs improvement. For example, the mechanical, hands-off, three-year rule for DGF Window 2 programs has not facilitated orderly financial exits. More attention needs to be paid to strengthening governance and sustainable financing of programs being spun off.

The Bank's strategy for global programs is poorly defined. The Bank has lacked, but clearly needs, a global strategy that is developed in conjunction with its key partners and draws on the capacity that exists in its central vice presidencies, network anchors, and Regions to do so. The strategy needs to address the coherence, or lack thereof, between global expectations (particularly in the donor community) and the needs of developing countries. At its center, the global strategy needs a clear focus on sustainable, poverty-reducing growth in the Bank's client countries; on global policy issues that prevent such growth; and on mobilizing incremental, unrestricted funding to address global issues that are high-priority for developing countries. Such a strategy will not simply emerge from improved selectivity or oversight of individual global programs; it must be worked out. Furthermore, strengthening oversight in the absence of an overall strategy risks micro-managing the global program portfolio.

Overall Performance of the Case Study Programs

Taken together, how are the programs performing, and what lessons do they offer for adding value to the Bank's mission? Assessing the overall performance of the 26 global programs against the four Development Committee criteria[1] (figure 8.1) confirms this chapter's findings:

- The programs rate highest with respect to international consensus. But international consensus is an amorphous concept that, by itself, provides little basis for selectivity.
- The Bank's presence catalyzes non-Bank resources for global programs, and the Bank employs its comparative advantage better at the global level than at the country level.
- The programs rate lowest with respect to adding value to the Bank's development objectives and employing the Bank's comparative advantage at the country level. These support the previous findings that the programs are weak on results-based management and evaluation and that the Bank is weak on country links.

The strategy needs to address the coherence, or lack thereof, between global expectations and the needs of developing countries.

These lessons need to be applied to ensure more effective consultative processes involving specialized U.N. agencies, key donors, client countries and other stakeholders (civil society and private sector) to determine developing countries' needs and priorities and to establish a global strategy, global program selectivity, and global-country links. Adjustments are also needed to improve the Bank's internal management to ensure greater program selectivity, effective program management, and the use of operational country capacity.

It is time to adapt and apply to global programs many of the tools and processes that the Bank has developed for its country operations. OED consultations within the Bank and with external partners indicate that the budget and staff required to link partnership-based global programs with country needs are much greater than originally expected. This partly explains the often weak links between global programs and country activities. Furthermore, deciding to support a global program needs to be based on an assessment of the entire program life cycle, from concept, design, and appraisal to implementation, evaluation, and exit. The Bank needs to support those programs that can add value to its poverty alleviation mission by enhancing the quality and effectiveness of its own operations and the activities of its clients.

The budget and staff required to link partnership-based global programs with country needs are much greater than originally expected.

Figure 8.1 Overall OED Assessment of Current Consistency of Case Study Programs with the Development Committee Criteria

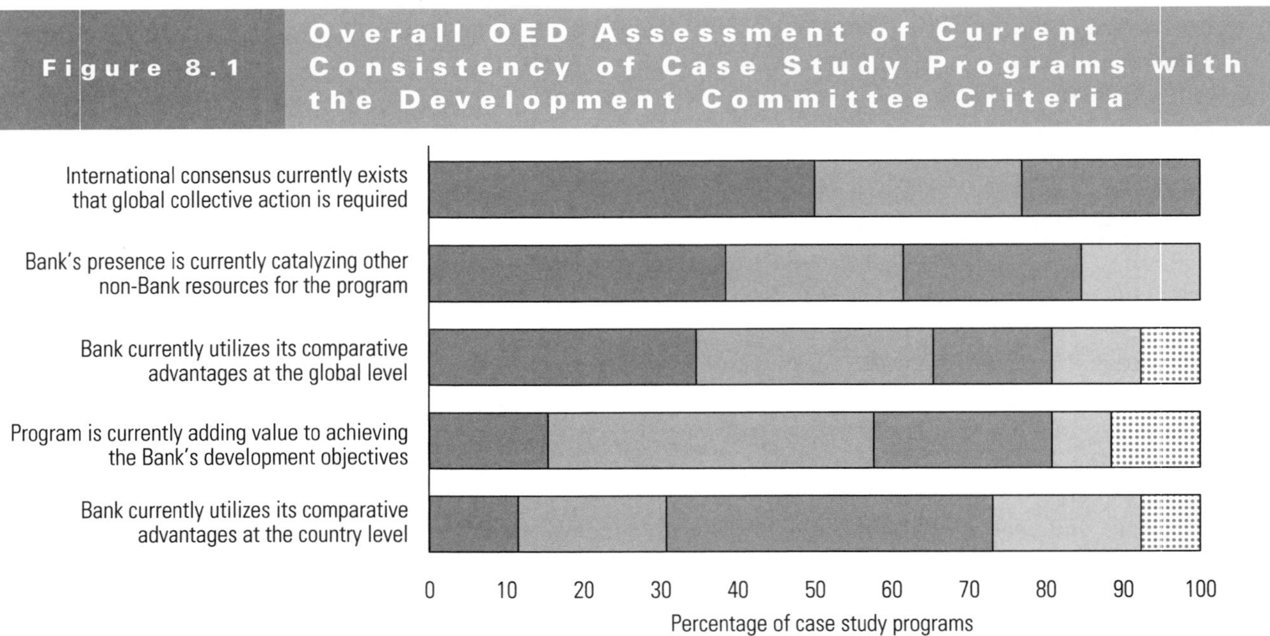

OED Recommendations

Strategic Framework for the Bank's Involvement in Global Programs

1. In consultation with U.N. agencies, donors, developing countries, and other partners, management should develop a global strategy for the Bank's involvement in global programs, approved by the Board and periodically updated, that:
   - Exploits the Bank's comparative advantage as a multisectoral development financing institution with a global reach and strong capacity in policy analysis
   - Gives greater prominence to alleviating poverty and to addressing global public policies that limit developing countries' prospects for rapid, sustainable, poverty-reducing growth
   - Fosters stronger links between global programs and the Bank's Regional and country operations in prioritizing its global programming activities
   - Ensures that global programs add value beyond what the Bank can accomplish through partnerships at the country level.

Linking Financing to Priorities

2. Management should develop a financing plan for high-priority programs, particularly for those providing genuine global public goods, whether in the form of global policies, new products, technologies, knowledge, or practices that benefit the poor. This requires:
   - Identifying underfunded long-term global public-goods programs that benefit the poor—such as a global health research and product development network for diseases that disproportionately affect the poor—and using the Bank's convening power to mobilize additional resources for them
   - Improving the criteria and procedures relating to the DGF's Window 2 to create a more rational and informed approach to funding "venture capital" programs, in which the DGF only provides initial support

- Developing a policy on the use of trust funds in the context of the overall strategy for global programs.

Selectivity and Oversight of the Global Program Portfolio

3. Management should establish approval, oversight, evaluation and exit/reauthorization criteria and procedures for Bank-supported global programs that will help them to add value to the Bank's mission. This includes:
   - Streamlining and clarifying the eligibility and approval criteria for Bank selectivity and grant support and instituting a two-stage approval process for global programs at the concept and appraisal stages
   - Sharpening and more rigorously applying the subsidiarity criterion for approval and grant support
   - Separating Bank oversight from the implementing management and, for Bank staff serving on the governing bodies of global programs, clarifying their roles, responsibilities, and accountabilities through standard terms of reference and training
   - Allocating money for oversight and money that the network anchor and Regional staff can use to operationalize global programs in the Bank's Regional operations
   - Instituting clear, well-planned, and well-executed reauthorization/exit processes, and ensuring that programs that the Bank spins off have an independent identity, accountability for results, and a good chance of succeeding.

Governance and Management of Individual Programs

4. Management should work with its global partners to develop and apply universally accepted standards of good governance, management, results-orientation, and evaluation to all Bank-supported global programs. These include:
   - Legal status and/or written charters, as appropriate
   - Transparent selection criteria and processes for board chairs and board members; clarifying their roles, responsibilities, accountabilities, and constituencies; and giving them authority to direct and oversee the program, its policies, and its budget
   - Voice of the Bank's client countries on the governing bodies of global programs for better balance between industrial and developing countries
   - Guidelines on conflicts of interests, on the roles of NGOs and the private sector in governing bodies, and on the roles and quality of advisory boards
   - Designation of evaluation and auditing as functions of the governing body, not the program management, with results that should routinely be made available to program financiers and other stakeholders.

Evaluation

5. OED should include global programs in its standard evaluation and reporting processes. This includes:
   - Working with the Bank's global partners to develop international standards for the evaluation of global programs
   - Reviewing selected program-level evaluations conducted by Bank-supported global programs (both internally and externally managed), much as OED reviews other self-evaluations at the project and country levels.

ANNEXES

ANNEX A: PREVIOUS OED RECOMMENDATIONS IN RELATION TO GLOBAL PROGRAMS

1998 Review

In 1998 OED reviewed the grant process (see OED 2002a) to inform the Bank's Executive Board's discussion of funding for grant programs in FY99 and beyond, under the auspices of the Special Grants Program (SGP) and its successor, the Development Grants Facility (DGF). The review focused on three things: the relevance of the Bank's grant-making programs to its overall strategy and developmental role; the quality of grant-program management; and grant programs' development effectiveness. As the largest and oldest of the Bank's grant programs, the Consultative Group on International Agricultural Research (CGIAR) figured significantly in this review.

OED recommended that the World Bank's grant programs be governed by three guiding principles: subsidiarity, maintaining an arm's-length relationship, and following an exit strategy.

Subsidiarity

The Bank should give grants in situations where lending is inappropriate and where there is no other source of funds, *to ensure that grants do not compete with the Bank's other instruments*. IDA 13 enables grant funding for specific country or Regional activities among the poorest countries. Still, DGF grant funding is more limited relative to IDA funding and should be used for activities for which countries are unlikely or unwilling to borrow or receive grants—activities that have benefits with strong spillovers across national borders, activities that require long-term investments before results can materialize, or those with large-scale economies in production, and hence activities that individual small countries will not be willing or able to undertake.

Arm's-length Relationship

The Bank should maintain an arm's-length relationship with grant recipients, because of the potential for conflicts of interest when the grantor is closely related to the grantee. A de facto dependency arises when the Bank is called upon to handle fund-raising, fiduciary, and administrative responsibilities in collaboration with its grantees.

Exit Strategy

The Bank needs exit strategies, because of the risk of dependency when grants continue over long periods. Grant programs without such strategies potentially undermine the grantee's independence, reduce the sustainability of program benefits, and impede revisions of the grant portfolio to reflect new programmatic priorities.

Phase 1 Report

Organization

Management should strengthen the strategic planning and oversight of global programs and partnerships. This will make priority setting more rigorous, improve management, and strengthen corporate leadership on global issues. While the networks would continue to have primary responsibility for task management and partner relations, management should establish a central vice-presidential unit to:

- Set standards, oversee programming and budgeting, assure quality, and report annually to senior management and the Board on implementation.
- Ensure that risk-management policies are defined by the appropriate unit and oversee net-

work implementation of risk management, including, as appropriate, reporting to the Board.

- Provide intellectual leadership, monitor and anticipate changes and emerging opportunities in the global environment, and draw partnership implications for the Bank.
- Identify constraints in the global policy environment on improving development outcomes for the Bank's clients.

Strategy

Management should articulate a strategy for Bank involvement in global programs that defines objectives, oversight responsibilities, and the Bank's comparative advantage. The strategy would explain how global programs should be distinguished from institutional partnerships, how they contribute to the Bank's mission, how strongly they should focus on providing global public goods, and what specific forms of partnership they should involve. The central vice-presidential unit (VPU) should:

- Develop and monitor performance indicators to ensure that networks and Regions link global programs, country assistance strategies, and sector strategies.
- Prepare annual reports for the Board based on information provided by the networks.
- Develop clear and transparent criteria and guidelines for resource allocation; budgeting, accounting, and auditing practices; and information systems for global programs.

Selectivity

The central VPU should establish and monitor global-program standards for the networks. Such standards would cover matters such as verifiable objectives, dedicated Bank resources, appropriate organizational and funding arrangements, and some form of cost-benefit or other ex ante criteria for Bankwide prioritization and quality assurance. The central VPU should:

- *For programs above a threshold size (which are likely to provide global public goods)*: help set up identification, preparation, appraisal, Board-approval, oversight, and evaluation processes.
- *For new, small, merit-goods programs that are not presented to the Board*: help improve approval, monitoring, and auditing in the DGF. Management could introduce independent reviews that are external to the programs—similar to those used by the World Bank Research Committee—for allocating small DGF grants.
- Help adapt the standards and procedures developed for innovative lending operations, such as the Learning and Innovation Loans and Adaptable Program Loans, to global programs.

Program Implementation

Management should clarify the responsibilities and accountabilities of the Board, Regions, networks, and task managers, and give each the resources they need to fulfill the Bank's commitments with its partners. This will require:

- For all programs:
  - Ensure the independence of the DGF's three-year evaluation process by extending the practice to all programs—including ongoing programs, regardless of whether funding comes from the Bank budget, the DGF, or Bank-managed trust funds—as a prerequisite for continuing support.
  - Include global programs in OED's standard evaluation and reporting processes, thus ensuring routine reporting to the Board of the findings of independent evaluations and management decisions about continuing program support.
- For programs under implementation:
  - Introduce a more systematic approach for task-manager monitoring of program performance and provision of audit reports.
  - Introduce independent panels similar to those used by the Bank's Quality Assurance Group to review quality of the ongoing portfolio.
  - Expand DGF audits to cover all programs receiving medium- to long-term Bank support (Window 1).
  - Introduce quality assurance and enhancement standards and clear network accountabilities.

The CGIAR Meta-Evaluation

Focusing the World Bank's Responsibilities

The Bank is a convener and donor to CGIAR and a lender to developing countries. Consequently, it has responsibilities for CGIAR's corporate governance. It should exercise a degree of oversight consistent with its major role. This will require:

- A concerted, high-level effort, much as when CGIAR was established, to fundamentally reform CGIAR's organizational structure, finance, and management—particularly to encourage donors to reverse their trend toward restricted funding and to establish targets for an increased share of unrestricted funding
- Separating oversight and management functions within the Bank to resolve the conflicts of interest faced by the Environmentally and Socially Sustainable Development (ESSD) vice president, the Agriculural and Rural Development (ARD) director, the Research Advisor, and the CGIAR director
- Independent triennial appraisals of CGIAR, with Board approval as the basis of continuing Bank support
- Abandoning the matching-grant model
- Regular reporting to the Board on the impact of Bank resource allocation on the system's incentive structure.

Such changes should ensure that the Bank's resources are allocated strategically, in support of global and regional public goods that improve agricultural productivity and reduce poverty, based on long-term priorities articulated by the science council. The Bank itself must see that a strong, qualified, independent science council is established and vested with the resources to establish systemwide priorities, policies, and strategies and to report to the membership on CGIAR's progress toward fulfilling them.

Reforming the CGIAR

CGIAR's strategic priorities should give more prominence to basic plant breeding and germplasm improvement and to research on productivity and sustainable use of natural resources for the benefit of developing countries. This will require the following:

- Postponing approval of new challenge programs pending the installation of the new science council, an assessment of system-level priorities, and a thorough review of the design and approval process of the two challenge programs already approved
- Increasing funding for conventional germplasm enhancement and plant- and animal-breeding research, in which the CGIAR possesses a comparative advantage
- Conducting an independent review of natural resource management, policy, and social-science research from a global and regional public-goods perspective to help address country- and regional-level issues constraining productivity and the sustainable use of natural resources
- Devolving that portion of the CGIAR's applied and adaptive natural resource management research program that does not involve public-goods research to national and regional agencies, supported by substantially larger funding for national and regional agricultural research from developing-country governments and donors
- Developing systemwide strategies and policies that facilitate businesslike partnerships with national agricultural research systems (NARS), agricultural research institutions, NGOs, and the private sector
- Strengthening the management and use of intellectual property and genetic resources
- Using new scientific areas like biotechnology and bioinformatics to complement conventional research
- Enhancing collaborative research as a means of building capacity and training
- Engaging developing country NARS to provide similar services to smaller and weaker NARS.

CGIAR governance should be reconfigured to promote greater efficiency, tougher priority-setting, and scientific excellence without sacrificing legitimacy and ownership. This will require:

- Adopting a written charter that delineates the roles, responsibilities, and accountabilities of the various officers and bodies that govern the system, and a mechanism to further reform system governance

- Analyzing the advantages and disadvantages of establishing all or part of CGIAR as a separate legal entity attuned to deal with today's realities on partnerships
- Making executive committee (ExCo) members more fully representative and accountable to the CGIAR membership
- Having donors share in the costs of the CGIAR secretariat, the science council and its secretariat, and other central bodies in the CGIAR system
- Increasing system efficiency in generating global and regional public goods through appropriate consolidation, decentralization, streamlining, and absorption of marginally effective centers, based on a management review of center organization, programs, and scientific quality
- Creating a body that reports to ExCo and has responsibility for annual system-level audits, triennial or quintennial external reviews in consultation with the science council, and transparency in reporting the system's expenditures, all to ensure the strategic public-goods nature of CGIAR research.

ANNEX B: PROGRESS IN IMPLEMENTING THE PHASE 1 RECOMMENDATIONS RELATING TO STRATEGIC AND PROGRAMMATIC MANAGEMENT

OED has made three sets of recommendations with respect to the Bank's grant and global programs (Annex A). The Phase 1 report assessed the progress made in implementing the recommendations of OED's 1998 process review of the Bank's grant programs (box B.1) (OED 2002c, pp. 39–48). This annex assesses progress in implementing the recommendations of the Phase 1 report and the CGIAR meta-evaluation.

Bank management has systematically reviewed, assessed, and implemented the report's recommendations in all four areas—organization, strategy, selectivity, and program implementation. Following the June 2002 CODE meeting, management established a review group led by the Operations Policy and Country Services vice presidency (OPCS) to study the report's recommendations in depth. That group issued its report in October 2002. Following discussions of the review group's report, which seconded most of OED's recommendations, senior management presented its conclusions and proposed courses of action to the Board in March 2003. Management then set up a second GPP Working Group on Implementation, also led by OPCS, which issued its report in July 2003. At that time, responsibility for implementing the new strategic and programmatic framework for global programs formally shifted from OPCS to the Concessional Financing and Partnerships (CFP) vice presidency.

Organization

Management has established a management committee, the Global Programs and Partnerships (GPP) Council. The Council's terms of reference are (1) to set the Bank's vision and priorities for engagement in GPPs, (2) to review VPU portfolios and the Bank's institutional partnerships, and (3) to set and oversee criteria for selection and evaluation of GPPs, including governance structures, risk management, exit strategies, and best practices. Management has also established the GPP Group in the CFP vice presidency to support the GPP Council. Its roles are to be an anchor for coordination and analysis

Box B.1 The DGF Made Substantial Improvements in Its Processes after OED's 1998 Process Review

In October 1998 the Bank adopted subsidiarity, arm's-length relationship, and exit strategy as three of its eight eligibility criteria for DGF grants.

In June 2000 the DGF issued guidelines for in-house secretariats to comply with the arm's-length criterion.

In June 2000 the DGF began regular evaluations, on a three-to-five-year cycle, for each program receiving more than $300,000 annually.

In June 2000 the DGF instituted the "two-window" approach, to commence with the FY02 DGF budget allocation, to facilitate orderly exit from programs that did not qualify for long-term funding.

The Phase 1 report also recommended that the DGF introduce an independent external review process for the allocation of grants to small programs that are not presented to the Board for approval, and that it ensure the independence of global program evaluations. The Phase 1 report promised further findings based on the 26 case studies.

across the Bank and to support network and regional teams involved in GPPs.

OED's phase 1 report had also recommended that, while the networks would continue to have the primary responsibility for task management and partner relations with respect to global programs, a central VPU (such as the GPP Council and Group now established) should:

- Oversee programming and budgeting for global programs.
- Perform quality assurance.
- Report annually to the Board on program implementation.
- Oversee network implementation of risk-management processes.
- Provide intellectual leadership, routinely monitor and anticipate changes and emerging opportunities in the global environment, and draw partnership implications for the Bank.
- Identify constraints in the global policy environment on improving development outcomes for the Bank's clients.

The GPP Council and Group are still works in progress, but their terms of reference do not include the authority to perform the above functions or to see that they are carried out by other Bank units reporting to the GPP Council. There is no indication of whether, when, or how the Council will gain such authority.

Strategy

OED's phase 1 report recommendations have supported several management initiatives with respect to global programs:

- Global programs are being explicitly incorporated into the business planning of network anchors, DEC, and the World Bank Institute (WBI).
- The tracking of spending on global programs is being improved by more uniform use of business processes and product lines related to global programs. Yet since VPUs use noncomparable approaches, it is still impossible to aggregate the Bank's budgetary expenditures, DGF grants, and trust fund expenditures on global programs.
- Rules for the use of Bank budget and grants for support of global programs have been clarified. For in-house programs, Bank budget can only be used for in-house secretariat costs. DGF grants must flow to externally managed activities in entities outside the Bank. Progress still needs to be made on applying these resources (table B.1).

The GPP Group has also begun some network-specific portfolio reviews.

The phase 1 report also recommended that the Bank articulate a global strategy that uses the Bank's comparative advantage. The present report reaffirms the need for a strategy that helps integrate global programs into the treatment of public policies that affect poverty and links global program activities to the Bank's regional and country operations, to the priorities of developing countries, and to the poverty reduction strategy process. Neither the steps the Bank has taken thus far nor the current criteria for Bank involvement in global programs can substitute for a global strategy.

Selectivity

In FY03, the DGF council instituted an ex ante review process, by reputable peers outside the Bank, for new global programs seeking DGF funding in FY04. Sector boards also played a more active role in reviewing applications in FY03 than they had in past. For the first time, several sector boards provided detailed written comments about program issues and concerns on the PATS forms. This demonstrated more careful scrutiny of proposals and improved program quality at entry. The quality of proposals reaching the DGF Council has increased noticeably over the past two years.

However, the Bank's 22 eligibility and approval criteria and 10 priorities are too numerous and inconsistent to ensure selectivity or quality at entry. The phase 1 report's recommendations—that management should (1) institute transparent identification, preparation, appraisal, Board approval, oversight, and evaluation processes for programs above a certain size and (2) help adapt the standards and procedures developed for innovative lending op-

Table B.1 Rules for Source of Funding for Global Programs and Partnerships

Governance	All key decisions on program execution are made by the Bank.	All key decisions are made jointly by the Bank and its partners.	All key decisions are made by an entity external to the Bank.
Source of funding	Primary source of funding is Bank administrative budget. Trust funds and reimbursements may be used, but do not affect the Bank's role as decisionmaker.	• Use of Bank budget is restricted to funding of in-house secretariat costs. • Trust-fund resources may fund both program costs and in-house secretariat costs. • DGF grants must flow to entities outside the Bank for funding costs of externally managed activities.	DGF is the only source of Bank funding. (World Bank administrative budget [BB] funding must not be used, because Bank is not accountable for outputs.)
Accountability	• Program outputs and outcomes should be approved as part of the budget process. • Program outputs and outcomes should be specified in the Unit Compact.	Where funding is from the Bank budget, program outputs and outcomes should be approved as part of budget process and specified in the Unit Compact as "partnership outputs."	Planning and monitoring of results handled as part of DGF budget process.

erations to global programs—have not yet been implemented. The Bank needs to clarify its criteria, enforce their application more strictly, analyze program budgets more thoroughly, and appraise program objectives and partners more carefully before entering into or continuing partnerships.

Program Design and Implementation

OED's Phase 1 report has also improved the monitoring and evaluation of DGF-supported programs. There is a deeper appreciation for the role that evaluation can play in enhancing the quality and focus of global programs—as a means both to understand where improvements in program performance can be made and to demonstrate program worth, thereby providing justification for continued funding. This has led to increased frequency of program-level evaluations, improved terms of reference, greater independence, and better conduct of evaluations. Evaluation and audit are increasingly viewed as functions of the governing body, not of the program management.

The second GPP Working Group on Implementation (led by OPCS from February to July 2003) analyzed existing GPPs with a view to developing standardized governance models for global programs. Based on this work, the GPP Group is giving global program teams early-stage advice on governance, management, and financing. This demonstrates increasing recognition of the concerns, raised by OED and others, about the balance between learning and control, about the balance between oversight and accountability in partnership, and about potential conflicts of interest, especially with respect to in-house secretariats. However, as demonstrated in chapter 5 of the main report, plenty of work remains to be done.

ANNEX C: EVALUATION FRAMEWORK FOR PHASE 2 REPORT AND 26 CASE STUDIES

The Phase 2 report and the case studies follow a common outline and address 20 evaluation questions (table C.1) that derive from OED's standard evaluation criteria (table C.2), the 14 eligibility and approval criteria for global programs (table C.3), and the 8 eligibility criteria for DGF grant support (table C.4).

The sheer number of these criteria, some of which overlap, can be daunting even to an evaluator. The OED evaluation team thus reorganized these criteria into four evaluation issues, which correspond to the four major sections of each report (table C.1):

- The overarching global relevance of the program
- Outcomes and impacts of the program and their sustainability
- Governance, management, and financing of the program
- The World Bank's performance as a partner in the program.

While program sponsorship by major international organizations may enhance the program's legitimacy in the Bank's client countries, it ensures neither developing-country ownership nor development effectiveness. "Relevance" and ownership by the Bank's client countries are more assured if those countries demand the program. On the other hand, some supply-led programs may acquire ownership over time by demonstrating substantial impacts, as in the case of the Internet. Assessing relevance is the most challenging task in global programs, since global and country resources, comparative advantages, benefit, costs, and priorities do not always coincide. Indeed, the divergence of benefits and costs between the global and country levels is often the fundamental reason why global public goods must be provided in the first place. Evaluating the relevance of global action to the Bank's client countries is nonetheless important, because the global *development* agenda is becoming crowded while finances have stagnated; selectivity has become more important.

For the global programs that have been operating for some time, efficacy can be assessed not only in terms of program outcomes but also in terms of impacts in developing countries. Outcomes and impacts in turn depend on the clarity and evaluability of each program's objectives, the quality of the monitoring and evaluation of results, and, where appropriate, the effectiveness of global program activities' links to the country level.

Since global programs are partnerships, efficiency must include some assessment of whether the benefits from the partnership, net of its costs, are superior to what the partners could achieve by acting alone. The institutional development impact and the sustainability of the program itself (as opposed to that of the outcomes and impacts of the program's activities) are also addressed in this section of each report.

Finally, these evaluations focus on whether the Bank uses its comparative advantage in its partnerships. The Bank is variously convener, trustee, and donor to global programs, and lender to developing countries. The Bank's financial support to global programs—including oversight and liaison activities and links to the Bank's Regional operations—comes from a combination of the its net income (for DGF grants), its administrative budget, and Bank-administered trust funds. In the case of the Global Environmental Facility (GEF), the Bank is a trustee; in the case of the Global Fund to Fight AIDS, Tuberculosis, and Malaria (GFATM), it is a "limited" trustee. The Bank is also an implementing agency for GEF and MLF. Thus, assessing Bank performance includes the use of the Bank's convening power, the Bank's trusteeship, Bank financing and implementation of global programs, and, where appropriate and necessary, links to country operations. Bank oversight of this entire set of activities is an important aspect of the Bank's strategic and programmatic management of its portfolio of global programs.

The first column in table C.1 indicates how the 4 sections and 20 evaluation questions addressed in the Phase 2 report and case studies relate to the 8 evaluation issues that the Bank's Executive Board raised in the various Board discussions of global programs during the design of OED's global evaluation:[1]

- Selectivity
- Monitoring and evaluation
- Governance and management
- Partnerships and participation
- Financing
- Risks and risk management
- Links to country operations.

The third column in table C.1 indicates how the 4 sections and 20 evaluation questions relate to OED's standard evaluation criteria for investment projects (table C.2), the 14 criteria endorsed by the Development Committee and established by Bank management for approving the Bank's involvement in global programs (table C.3), and the 8 criteria for grant support from the Development Grant Facility (table C.4).

The 14 eligibility and approval criteria for the Bank's involvement in global programs have

Table C.1 Key Evaluation Issues and Questions

Evaluation issues	Evaluation questions	Reference
Section I. Overarching global relevance of the program		
1. Selectivity	1. **Relevance.** To what extent are the programs: • Addressing global challenges and concerns in the sector • Consistent with client countries' current development priorities • Consistent with the Bank's mission, corporate priorities, and sector and country assistance strategies?	A modification of OED's relevance criterion (table C.2) for the purpose of global programs. The third bullet also relates to managing director (MD) approval criterion #1 regarding a "clear linkage to the Bank's core institutional objectives" (table C.3).
	2. **International consensus**. To what extent did the programs arise out of an international consensus, formal or informal: • Concerning the main global challenges and concerns in the sector • That global collective action is required to address these challenges and concerns?	Development Committee (DC) criterion #1 (table C.3).
	3. **MD eligibility criteria**. To what extent are the programs: • Providing global and regional public goods • Supporting international advocacy to improve policies at the national level • Producing and delivering cross-country lessons of relevance to client countries • Mobilizing substantial incremental resources?	The four bullets correspond to the four MD eligibility criteria (table C.3).
	4. **Subsidiarity**. To what extent do the activities of the programs complement, substitute for, or compete with regular Bank instruments?	DGF eligibility criterion #1 (table C.4).

Table C.1 Key Evaluation Issues and Questions (*continued*)

Evaluation issues	Evaluation questions	Reference
Section II. Outcomes, impacts, and their sustainability		
2. Monitoring and evaluation	5. **Efficacy**. To what extent have the programs achieved, or are expected to achieve, their stated objectives, taking into account their relative importance?	OED's efficacy criterion (table C.2).
	6. **Value added**. To what extent are the programs adding value to: • What the Bank is doing in the sector to achieve its core mission • What developing and transition countries are doing in the sector in accordance with their own priorities?	The first bullet corresponds to Bank management criterion #1 (table C.3).
	7. **Monitoring and evaluation**. To what extent do the programs have effective monitoring and evaluation: • Clear program and component objectives verifiable by indicators • A structured set of quantitative or qualitative indicators • Systematic and regular processes for data collection and management • Independence of program-level evaluations • Effective feedback from monitoring and evaluation to program objectives, governance, management, and financing?	MD approval criterion #6 (table C.3), since effective communications with key stakeholders, including the Bank's Executive Directors, requires good monitoring and evaluation practices.
	8. **Sustainability of outcomes and impacts**. To what extent are the outcomes and impacts of the programs resilient to risk over time?	OED's sustainability criterion (table C.2).
Section III. Organization, management, and financing of the program		
3. Governance and management	9. **Efficiency**. To what extent have the programs achieved, or are expected to achieve: • Benefits more cost-effectively than providing the same service on a country-by-country basis • Benefits more cost-effectively than if the contributors to the program acted alone?	A modification of OED's efficacy criterion for the purpose of global programs (table C.2). The first bullet also relates to MD eligibility criterion #3 (table C.3) and DGF eligibility criterion #3 (table C.4).
	10. **Legitimacy**. To what extent is the authorizing environment for the programs effectively derived from those with a legitimate interest in the program (including donors, developing and transition countries, clients, and other stakeholders), taking into account their relative importance?	A modification of OED's evaluation criteria (table C.2) for the purpose of global programs.
	11. **Governance and management**. To what extent are the governance and management of the programs: • Transparent in providing information about the programs • Clear with respect to roles and responsibilities • Fair to immediate clients • Accountable to donors, developing and transition countries, scientists/professionals, and other stakeholders?	MD approval of criterion #5 (table C.3) and DGF eligibility criterion #5 (table C.4).
4. Partnerships and participation	12. **Partnerships and participation**. To what extent do developing- and transition-country partners, clients, and beneficiaries participate and exercise voice in the various aspects of the program's:	DGF eligibility criterion #8 (table C.4).

(*Table continues on the following page.*)

Table C.1 Key Evaluation Issues and Questions (*continued*)

Evaluation issues	Evaluation questions	Reference
	• Design • Governance • Implementation • Monitoring and evaluation?	
5. Financing	13. **Financing**. To what extent are the sources of funding for the programs affecting, positively or negatively: • The strategic focus of the program • The governance and management of the program • The sustainability of the program?	MD approval criterion #4 (table C.3). The third bullet also relates to OED's sustainability criterion (table C.2).
	14. **Bank action to catalyze**. To what extent has the Bank's presence as a partner in the programs catalyzed, or is catalyzing, non-Bank resources for the programs?	DC criterion #3 (table C.3) and DGF eligibility criterion #4 (table C.4).
	15. **Institutional development impact.** To what extent has the program established effective institutional arrangements to make efficient, equitable, and sustainable use of the collective financial, human, and other resources contributed to the program?	A modification of OED's institutional development impact criterion (table C.2) for the purpose of global programs.
6. Risks and risk management	16. **Risks and risk management**. To what extent have the risks associated with the programs been identified and managed?	MD approval criterion #3 (table C.3).
Section IV. World Bank's performance		
7. Links to country operations	17. **Comparative advantage**. To what extent is the Bank playing up to its comparative advantages in relation to other partners in the programs: • At the global level (global mandate and reach, convening power, mobilizing resources) • At the country level (multisector capacity, analytical expertise, country-level knowledge)?	DC criterion #3 (table C.3), MD approval criterion #2 (table C.3), and DGF eligibility criterion #2 (table C.4).
	18. **Links to country operations**. To what extent are there effective and complementary links, where needed, between global program activities and the Bank's country operations, to the mutual benefit of each?	MD approval criterion #1 (table C.3) regarding "linkages to the Bank's country operational work."
	19. **Oversight**. To what extent is the Bank exercising effective and independent oversight of its involvement in the programs, as appropriate, for in-house and externally managed programs, respectively?	This relates to DGF eligibility criterion #6 on "arm's-length relationship" (table C.4). Both questions 17 and 18 together relate to OED's Bank performance criterion (table C.2).
	20. **Disengagement strategy**. To what extent is the Bank facilitating effective, flexible, and transparent disengagement strategies, as appropriate?	DGF eligibility criterion #7 (table C.4).

evolved since April 2000, when Bank management first proposed a strategy to the Board for such involvement. They include the four *overarching* criteria endorsed by the Development Committee, as well as the four *eligibility* criteria and the six *approval* criteria presented by Bank management to the Board. Each global program must meet at least one of the eligibility criteria and all six of the approval criteria. The first two eligibility criteria relate directly to the Bank's global public-goods and corporate-advocacy priorities (table C.3). Although the six ap-

Table C.2 Standard OED Evaluation Criteria

Criterion	Standard definitions for lending operations	Possible ratings
Relevance	The extent to which the project's objectives are consistent (1) with the country's development priorities and (2) with Bank country and sector assistance strategies and corporate goals (expressed in Poverty Reduction Strategy Papers, Country Assistance Strategies, Sector Strategy Papers, Operational Policies).	High, substantial, modest, negligible.
Efficacy	The extent to which the project's objectives were achieved, or expected to be achieved, taking into account their relative importance.	High, substantial, modest, negligible.
Efficiency	The extent to which the project achieved, or is expected to achieve, a return higher than the opportunity cost of capital and benefits, at least cost compared with alternatives.	High, substantial, modest, negligible.
Legitimacy[a]	The extent to which the authority exercised by the program is effectively derived from those with a legitimate interest in the program (including donors, developing and transition countries, clients, and other stakeholders), taking into account their relative importance.	High, substantial, modest, negligible.
Institutional development impact	The extent to which a project improves the ability of a country or region to make more efficient, equitable and sustainable use of its human, financial, and natural resources through (a) better definition, stability, transparency, enforceability, and predictability of institutional arrangements and/or (b) better alignment of the mission and capacity of an organization with its mandate, which derives from these institutional arrangements. IDI includes both intended and unintended effects of a project.	High, substantial, modest, negligible.
Sustainability	The resilience to risk of net benefits flows over time.	Highly likely, likely, unlikely, highly unlikely.
Outcome	The extent to which the project's major relevant objectives were achieved, or are expected to be achieved, efficiently.	Highly satisfactory, satisfactory, moderately satisfactory, moderately unsatisfactory, unsatisfactory, highly unsatisfactory.
Bank performance	The extent to which services provided by the Bank ensured quality at entry and supported implementation through appropriate supervision (including ensuring adequate transition arrangements for regular operation of the project).	Highly satisfactory, satisfactory, unsatisfactory, highly unsatisfactory.
Borrower performance	The extent to which the borrower assumed ownership and responsibility to ensure quality of preparation and implementation and complied with covenants and agreements, toward the achievement of development objectives and sustainability.	Highly satisfactory, satisfactory, unsatisfactory, highly unsatisfactory.

a. This represents an addition to OED's standard evaluation criteria in the case of global programs, since effective governance of global programs is concerned with the legitimacy of their exercise of authority, in addition to efficiency in the use of resources.

Table C.3 Selectivity and Oversight of Global Programs

Selectivity Criteria for Bank Involvement in Global Public Goods: Endorsed by Development Committee (September 2000)[a]

1. An emerging international consensus that global action is required
2. A clear value added to the Bank's development objectives
3. The need for Bank action to catalyze other resources and partnerships
4. A significant comparative advantage for the Bank.

Approval Criteria for Bank Involvement in Partnership Initiatives beyond the Country Level, Established by Bank Management (November 2000)[b]

1. A clear link to the Bank's core institutional objectives and, above all, to the Bank's country work
2. A strong case for Bank participation based on comparative advantage
3. A clear assessment of the financial and reputational risks to the Bank and how these will be managed
4. A thorough analysis of the expected level of Bank resources (both money and time) required and the contribution of other partners
5. A clear delineation of how the new commitment will be implemented, managed, and assessed
6. A clear plan for communicating with and involving key stakeholders and for informing and consulting the Executive Directors.

Global Public-Goods Priorities[c]

Communicable diseases
- HIV/AIDS, tuberculosis, malaria, and childhood communicable diseases, including the relevant link to education
- Vaccines and drug development for major communicable diseases in developing countries

Environmental commons
- Climate change
- Water
- Forests
- Biodiversity, ozone depletion, and land degradation
- Promoting agricultural research

Information and knowledge
- Redressing the digital divide and equipping countries with the capacity to access knowledge
- Understanding development and poverty reduction

Trade and integration
- Market access
- Intellectual property rights and standards

International financial architecture
- Development of international standards
- Financial stability (incl. sound public debt management)
- International accounting and legal framework

Strategic Focus for Oversight of Global Programs: Established by Bank Management (March 2003)

a. Provide global public goods

b. Support international advocacy for reform agendas that in a significant way address policy framework conditions relevant for developing countries

c. Are multicountry programs that crucially depend on highly coordinated approaches

d. Mobilize substantial incremental resources that can be used for development

Corporate Advocacy Priorities[c]

Empowerment, security, and social inclusion
- Gender mainstreaming
- Civic engagement and participation
- Social risk management (including disaster mitigation)

Investment climate
- Support to both urban and rural development
- Infrastructure services to support private sector development
- Regulatory reform and competition policy
- Financial sector reform

Public sector governance
- Rule of law (including anti-corruption
- Public administration and civil service reform (including public expenditure accountability)
- Access to, and administration of, justice (judicial reform)

Education
- Education for all, with emphasis on girls' education
- Building human capacity for the knowledge economy

Health
- Access to potable water, clean air, and sanitation
- Maternal and child health

a. From the Development Committee Communiqué issued on September 25, 2000. Both the Development Committee and Bank management envisaged global programs as being the principal instrument for Bank involvement in providing global public goods.

b. The Initiating Concept Memorandum in the Partnership Approval and Tracking System (PATS) was initially organized according to these six criteria.

c. These are the five corporate advocacy priorities and the five global public-goods priorities (and bulleted subcategories) from World Bank 2001b. Within the Partnership Approval and Tracking System (PATS), global programs are expected to identify, for tracking purposes, their alignment with at least one of these 10 corporate priorities.

proval criteria resemble the topics covered in a project concept or appraisal document for Bank lending operations, global programs need approval only at the concept stage (unlike lending operations, which also need approval at appraisal). New global programs need approval

Table C.4 Eligibility Criteria for Grant Support from the Development Grant Facility

1. Subsidiarity	The program contributes to furthering the Bank's development and resource mobilization objectives in fields basic to its operations, but it does not compete with, or substitute for, regular Bank instruments. Grants should address new or critical development problems and should be clearly distinguishable from the Bank's regular programs.
2. Comparative advantage	The Bank has a distinct comparative advantage in being associated with the program; it does not replicate the role of other donors. The relevant operational strengths of the Bank are in economic, policy, sector, and project analysis and management of development activities. In administering grants, the Bank has expertise in donor coordination, fundraising, and fund management.
3. Multicountry benefits	The program encompasses multicountry benefits or activities that it would not be efficient, practical, or appropriate to undertake at the country level. For example, informational economies of scale are important for research and technology work, and operations to control diseases or address environmental concerns (such as protect fragile ecosystems) might require a regional or global scope to be effective. In the case of grants directed to a single country, the program will encompass capacity-building activities where this is a significant part of the Country Assistance Strategy and cannot be supported by other Bank instruments or by other donors. This will include, in particular, programs funded under the Institutional Development Fund and programs related to initial post-conflict reconstruction efforts (e.g., in countries or territories emerging from internal strife or instability).
4. Leverage	The Bank's presence provides significant leverage for generating financial support from other donors. Bank involvement should provide assurance to other donors of program effectiveness, as well as sound financial management and administration. Grants should generally not exceed 15 percent of expected funding over the life of Bank funding to a given program or over the rolling 3-year plan period, whichever is shorter. Where grant programs belong to new areas of activities (involving, e.g., innovations, pilot projects, or seed capital), some flexibility is allowed for the Bank's financial leverage to build over time, and the target for the Bank grant not to exceed 15 percent of total expected funding will be pursued after allowing for an initial start-up phase (maximum 3 years).
5. Managerial competence	The grant is normally given to an institution with a record of achievement in the program area and financial probity. A new institution may have to be created where no suitable institution exists. The quality of the activities implemented by the recipient institution (existing or new) and the competence of its management are important considerations.
6. Arm's-length relationship	The management of the recipient institution is independent of the Bank Group. While quality and an arm's-length relationship with the Bank's regular programs are essential, the Bank may have a role in the governance of the institution through membership in its governing board or oversight committee. In cases of highly innovative or experimental programs, Bank involvement in supporting the recipient to execute the program will be allowed. This will provide the Bank with an opportunity to benefit from the learning experience and to build operational links to increase its capacity to deliver more efficient services to client countries.
7. Disengagement strategy	Programs are expected to have an explicit disengagement strategy. In the proposal, monitorable action steps should be outlined, indicating milestones and targets for disengagement. The Bank's withdrawal should cause minimal disruption to an ongoing program or activity.
8. Promoting partnerships	Programs and activities should promote and reinforce partnerships with key players in the development arena (for example, multilateral development banks, U.N. agencies, foundations, bilateral donors, professional associations, research institutions, private sector corporations, NGOs, and civil-society organizations).

Source: World Bank, Development Grant Facility documentation.

only from the managing director responsible for the network proposing the new program, not from the Board.

Program approval is logically separate from, and prior to, financing (whether from the DGF, trust funds, or other sources). The eight eligibility criteria for grant support from the DGF (table C.4) were established in 1998, although the processes of program approval, trust fund mobilization, and their relationship to the DGF have evolved considerably since then. Because each approval process and each set of criteria were developed independently, they are not always consistent with each other. Twenty of the 26 case studies and about two-thirds of the Bank's total portfolio of global programs have received DGF grants.

ANNEX D: SUGGESTED APPRAISAL TEMPLATE FOR GLOBAL PROGRAMS

Program aspect	Appraisal criteria
Global The activities of the program cut across more than one of the Bank's operational Regions.	1. Does the program cover more than one of the Bank's operational Regions? 2. Does the program demonstrate strong potential for development effectiveness and poverty alleviation, and hence relevance to developing countries? 3. Does the proposal demonstrate why the issue the program addresses requires public investments and action at the global level? 4. Does the proposal demonstrate the value added from the Bank's involvement? Does it articulate how the program fits with the Bank's mission, its global public-goods priorities, and its corporate-advocacy priorities? If the program does not meet these criteria, does the proposal explain why the program is still justified in addressing an important global issue? 5. Does the proposal either demonstrate the absence of alternative, cheaper sources of supply for addressing the issue or make a convincing case for why increased competition in supply entailing Bank involvement would be desirable? 6. Does the proposal provide a full accounting of the expected benefits of the program—including expected spillovers—to borrowers and donors, as well as to the private and public sectors? Does it explain how the realization of those benefits is being ensured in program design?
Partnership The program involves partners—who participate in the governance of the program—in addition to the World Bank.	1. Does the proposal demonstrate the value added by using a partnership? Could the Bank working alone accomplish the program goals? Does the proposal demonstrate that the benefits of the partnership outweigh the costs? 2. Does the proposal demonstrate how the program meets the Development Committee criteria for engaging in partnerships: • Evidence for an emerging international consensus that global action is required? Or if the program itself is intended to help develop international consensus where none currently exists? • Why Bank action is needed to catalyze other resources or if others can do it just as well? For example, is the Bank's convening power or potential linkage to country assistance critical in ensuring relevance of the global program and its eventual success? • The Bank's comparative advantage relative to other partners in relation to this program?[b] • The value added to the Bank's development objectives? 3. Does the proposal demonstrate why the Bank should address this issue as a global program, or regional program, rather than through an institutional partnership? [c] That is, does it have: • Clearly identified and deliverable new products or services • Shared objectives • Shared responsibility for governance • Shared resources? 4. Does the proposal demonstrate that all potential partners needed to ensure development effectiveness of the program were consulted, that the chosen partners are the most appropriate to achieve expeditious and cost-effective results and impact, and that the Bank's role is consistent with its comparative advantage? Are

Program aspect	Appraisal criteria
	other partners' roles, responsibilities, and accountabilities consistent with their comparative advantages and clearly spelled out?
Objectives Either formally or informally, the partners reach explicit agreements on objectives.	1. Does the proposal describe the process used to arrive at an agreement on objectives, including consultation with stakeholders? 2. Are the objectives of the program clearly defined and results-oriented, even if results are intermediate outcomes? 3. Do the objectives: • Give focus and direction to the program • Express a development purpose that is realistic, specific, and quantitatively or qualitatively measurable • Provide a basis for evaluating the performance of the program with specific and realistic schedules? Are there clear intermediate performance indicators, or is there a clear indication of how the program will develop such indicators?
Activities The program generates new products or services.	Are the program activities clustered into components that can deliver results on the stated objectives? Are the components clearly described, and are the objectives and components internally coherent? Examples: • For **global networking activities,** the proposal should demonstrate either current or proposed steps to ensure that developing countries receive the benefits of the program through ensuring access, building capacity, or other means. Similar steps should be evident for regional activities within the global program. • For **country-level technical assistance activities**, the proposal should articulate the steps needed to build capacity or involve borrowing countries in networking. It should also identify whether and how links to subsequent country assistance (including Bank lending) might bring this about. • For **country-level investments**, the proposal should argue the case for additionality or complementarity to current Bank lending operations. • For **new products and technologies**, such as collaborative research or analysis, the proposal should clearly demonstrate their global public goods nature and the absence of alternative sources of supply. It should justify international public involvement in the provision of these new products and technologies.
Governance and management Either formally or informally, the partners agree to establish a new organization or to vest an existing organization (including one of the Bank's own units or those of other international agencies) with a new and additional function.	1. What were the main scope and design options considered, and why were competing alternatives, such as regional programs, rejected? 2. Were relevant stakeholders consulted in the program design process? 3. Do relevant stakeholders have access to the program? What steps are being taken to ensure access? 4. Does the proposed authorizing environment for the program provide adequate balance between ensuring legitimacy in governance, relevance to developing countries, and efficiency in achieving results? 5. Do the governance and management structures include clear responsibilities among partners with respect to resources, risks, and decisionmaking? 6. Are there clear accountabilities for results, and clearly defined plans and target audiences (or stakeholders) for the activities of the program? 7. To what extent are developing countries (including transition countries) actively engaged in the governance of the program and in the design and management of program activities? 8. Does the program design ensure recruitment of high-quality advisory committees and clarify their accountability for ensuring scientific/professional excellence in approaches? 9. Are reporting arrangements of managers and advisors to specific levels clearly spelled out?
Financing The partners contribute dedicated resources to the program.	1. Where the Bank is providing DGF grants, do they comply with OP 8.45 for grant making and with the DGF criteria for subsidiarity, arm's length relationship, and exit strategy? [d] 2. Where the Bank is administering trust funds that support the program, do they comply with OP 14.40 for trust funds and address the five issues in the recent Trust Funds Review: • Alignment with the Bank's strategic priorities • Dependency risks

Program aspect	Appraisal criteria
	• Cost-effectiveness • Fiduciary risks • Reputational risks? 3. Where the Bank is providing resources for the program from its administrative budget (BB)—for program administration or program activities—is there a realistic assessment of BB needs, and is it a clearly appropriate use of BB resources? 4. Is the Bank's share of the overall resources dedicated to the program appropriate? [e] 5. Are regional- and central-unit BB needs spelled out? 6. Does the program have an exit strategy? Does it follow the foundation model, the venture capital model, or the long-term development assistance model? Is the model used clearly justified? Have steps been taken within the context of the model to ensure the long-term sustainability of the program? If the venture capital model is used, does it follow best practice on venture financing? Is the form of exit defined clearly (financial exit, participation exit, legal exit)? How well is the exit strategy planned?
Risks and risk management	This category cuts across the previous six, consistent with the way risks are treated in the Bank financing of projects. 1. Have the risks (applying to both the private sector and NGOs) been assessed at the outset? [f] • Reputational risks • Conflict-of-interest risks • Unfair-advantage risks • Governance risks 2. Are the risks associated with the program greater than the expected benefits? Have appropriate procedures been established to manage these risks during program implementation?
Monitoring and evaluation	1. Has a monitoring and independent evaluation system been established for the implementation phase of the program? Does it comply with OED standards for best practice? • Clear project and component objectives verifiable by indicators • A structured set of quantitative or qualitative indicators • Requirements for data collection and management • Institutional arrangements for capacity-building • Feedback from monitoring and evaluation to Bank management and the Board? 2. Is there adequate provision for routine Bank oversight of the program? 3. Is the Bank exercising adequate fiduciary responsibility for in-house secretariats and for the management of trust funds, with periodic centralized reporting of accounts and audits, which are routinely monitored for quality and completeness?
External review	Has the program been endorsed by independent external reviewers?

a. The *Strategic Directions Paper* (World Bank 2001b) mentions six comparative advantages: (1) global mandate and reach, (2) in-depth country-level knowledge, (3) multisector capacity, (4) convening power, (5) expertise in country and sector analysis, and (6) mobilizing financial resources. Others might include access to borrowing countries' policymakers and potential for country assistance.

b. "Institutional partnerships" typically involve information exchange and consultations with a variety of partners in order to improve the Bank's ability to conduct its traditional country- and regionally oriented business more effectively. These do not produce a new product or service and do not involve the establishment of a new organization or entity with separate governance and management structures.

c. These need to be assessed at the appropriate level. In some cases, the DGF is retailing grants to grantees, and in other cases, the DGF is wholesaling to global programs that are retailing to grantees.

d. This needs to be measured consistently across programs.

e. The following are the risks that are assessed in the private sector partnership assessment and approval process that is administered by PSI. See Annex K for a definition of each of these risks.

Source: Reproduced from the Phase 1 Report, Appendix 1, pp. 57–59.

ANNEX E: OED'S SUMMARY OF THE KNOWN OUTCOMES AND IMPACTS OF CASE STUDY GLOBAL PROGRAMS

Organized by the classifications used in table 2.2, with the start dates of each program in parentheses.

Financing Global-Level Investments to Deliver Global Public Goods for the Benefit of the Poor

***Programs:* Consultative Group for Agricultural Research (CGIAR) (1972), Special Program for Research and Training in Tropical Diseases (TDR) (1975), Parts of the Global Alliance for Vaccines and Immunization (GAVI) (1999)**

The older global programs in this category have seen high returns to their investments. There nonetheless is substantial underinvestment in the provision of global public goods and in the complementary national investments that are needed to increase developing-country accessibility to new products, information and technologies and to increase the speed and scale of sustainable poverty alleviation.

The high rates of return to *CGIAR*'s germplasm research and its impacts on food productivity, food prices, employment, and incomes were reported in OED's meta-evaluation. At least in large countries in Asia and Latin America, the poverty impacts have been sustainable and have supported broader development. CGIAR has developed an impressive global agricultural research system and a global network supported by nearly $400 million annually.

The $45 million annual expenditures of the *Special Program for Research and Training in Tropical Diseases* have helped mobilize global science to conduct research and promote technologies related to diseases of the poor. The external evaluation identified three important program outcomes: contributing to the development of new and improved tools for controlling several tropical diseases; leveraging support from other bodies to develop vaccines for malaria, leishmaniasis, and schistosomiasis; and using collaborative research to strengthen research capacity in developing countries. TDR's research publications are often cited in scientific journals, reflecting the high quality of its research. However, TDR is underfunded and overstretched, while the program's research mandate has expanded from 8 tropical diseases to 10, together with growing expectations among TDR's donors for faster results. Faced with this changing external environment, this oldest of global health programs confronts fundamental questions about its scope, strategic objectives, role in global research, funding, partnership strategies, methods of work, governance, and management. Underinvestment in research that would benefit the poor is far worse in health than in agriculture, despite the recent efforts of the Gates Foundation and some growth in the last decade in public-private partnerships to develop vaccines and drugs. Where complementary national investments have been made, such as India and Brazil's efforts in epidemiological and other applied and adaptive research, they have shown rich results. Yet the low level of investment in health research by the Bank and by developing countries has limited the country-level impacts of TDR's research.

Financing Country-Level Investments to Deliver Global Public Goods

***Programs:* Multilateral Fund for the Implementation of the Montreal Protocol (MLF) (1991), Global Environment Facility (GEF) (1991), Prototype Carbon Fund (2000), Critical Ecosystems Partnership Fund (CEPF) (2000)**

Some country-level investments in this category of global public goods have achieved major global impacts, but each raises issues about program design and incentives to deliver global results. The MLF and certain aspects of GEF have had some concrete impacts.

The *Multilateral Fund for the Implementation of the Montreal Protocol* has reduced consumption of ozone-depleting chemicals by more than 90 percent over the past decade (UNEP 2002). The Bank has played a crucial role in MLF activities. The Bank's MLF activities have reportedly eliminated a large share of the global targets of ozone-depleting chemicals, while using only 40 percent of the total international resources available, through an approach that has built institutional environmental capacity within the public and private sectors of its client countries. The fund's distinctive composition, governance, and management structure, characterized by a balanced representation of industrial and developing countries and consensus-style decision-making, has fostered an unprecedented model of international cooperation and has influenced the design of the GEF. At the same time, the fund's governance system, which includes both rotating and non-rotating membership, puts an inequitable burden on many small, developing countries. The MLF has had only one external evaluation (1995) in its 13-year existence, although a second review was begun in 2003.

The *Global Environment Facility*, in addition to significantly reducing ozone-depleting substances in transition countries, has had some success in promoting energy efficiency and renewable energy, improving management of standards in protected areas, and promoting and implementing global and regional agreements on fresh water and marine ecosystems. Yet it is difficult to determine whether GEF-funded activities in some focal areas, such as biodiversity conservation, have had sustainable global impacts. There have been some intermediate results, such as water-basin treaties ratified, water quality improved, and areas brought under protection. GEF's external evaluations note that the facility has faced numerous challenges: interpreting the conventions, ensuring high-quality investments, creating in-country understanding of GEF principles, addressing the socioeconomic and livelihood needs of the affected populations, defining incremental costs and benefits, and engaging the private sector. The evaluations have indicated that GEF's design does not clearly delineate the responsibilities and accountabilities of the program's monitoring and evaluation unit, nor those of GEF in relation to its implementing agencies. Although the more recent GEF portfolio (including the Bank-implemented portion) shows some learning from experience, the GEF Secretariat and the Bank have had different views about the speed with which the Bank is able to mainstream GEF's environmental objectives in the Bank's economic and sector work, policy dialogue, and lending.[1]

The *Prototype Carbon Fund*—the only public-private partnership to foster an international market in greenhouse-gas emissions reduction—is too new to evaluate. The program has many deals planned in all the Bank's Regions and is oversubscribed by private investors. Because it has to deliver internationally certifiable results, it has been highly attentive to project design and the means for measuring results. If the program succeeds, it will help the Bank add a new line of business, help investors in OECD countries to reduce emissions cheaply, provide a truly novel source of private sector investment to produce a public good, create employment, increase incomes, and potentially mitigate some of the risks of climate change. But, as a "mini-bank" within the Bank, the fund has to balance investor interests with those of the Bank's client countries. Therefore, the fund provides market information, training, and capacity-building—public goods that private investors would not necessarily provide. Any fund outcomes will be jeopardized if the Kyoto Protocol is not ratified, if the emissions reductions fail to materialize, or if emissions certificates turn out to be unmarketable.

The *Critical Ecosystems Partnership Fund* was established to conserve biodiversity in hotspots by "providing strategic assistance to nongovernmental and other private sector organizations for the protection of selected vital ecosystems." As of April 2004, the program had committed $41.8 million for 293 grants to various NGOs. Forty percent of the grant funds were allocated to Conservation International (CI) and

60 percent to external partners, including other international and national NGOs within civil society and, to a smaller extent, the private sector. The initial trend to favor CI in grant approval is changing, in part because of the establishment of re-granting funds at the hotspot level, to reach more grassroots grantees. The program focuses on areas within hotspots where CEPF funding can have the greatest incremental value. However, most hotspots are flush with other conservation activities. It may thus be difficult to attribute conservation success (or failure) directly to the program. The program does have a robust monitoring and evaluation system in place, with numerous checks and balances to ensure timely reporting and critical evaluations. While the program is relatively new, the findings from the two ecosystem-level evaluations completed thus far suggest that it has contributed to positive conservation outcomes. The Bank is committed to two more fiscal years of funding. It has not yet defined an exit strategy, nor has it committed to continued funding.

Financing Country-Level Investments to Deliver National Public Goods

***Programs:* Post-conflict Fund (1998), Global Alliance for Vaccines and Immunization (GAVI) (1999)**

Both programs in this category have provided additional resources to countries, but raise issues of subsidiarity; duplication of, or substitution for, Bank country operations; and, ultimately, sustainability.

The *Post-conflict Fund* was created in 1997 to improve and expand Bank instruments for dealing with post-conflict issues. The fund has given grants totaling over $66 million, mostly for small-scale reconstruction activities, to 34 countries or jurisdictions. The program's priority themes are conflict mitigation, internally displaced persons and refugees, rehabilitation of social sectors, start-up support for land-mine clearance, demobilization and reintegration of ex-combatants, economic recovery, governance, and capacity-building. The grants are awarded for socioeconomic analyses, watching briefs, transitional support strategies, and policy studies and forums. The program's external evaluation found that many of the fund's grants laid a base for follow-on financing. Yet the evaluation stressed the need to: (1) attract greater donor support, (2) become more active about funding projects, (3) improve implementation monitoring, and (4) strengthen knowledge generation and management. The evaluation was also cautious about drawing conclusions about the performance of individual activities. Individual project-level evaluations noted varied progress with respect to the sustainability of the funded activities. Apart from citing anecdotal evidence, the PCF has not tracked exactly how many of its funded activities managed to attract additional financing or proved sustainable. A review of project-level evaluations indicates that the grants may have greater success in positioning the Bank in a particular country than in ensuring sustainability of the particular projects' benefits. Since more than half of its funds have gone to eight of the most urgent conflict areas, the fund has served as a quick channel for addressing specific issues through targeted programs. While the program does what it was designed to do, issues have arisen with respect to the following DGF criteria: multicountry benefits, record of achievement and financial probity, disengagement strategy, and leverage. Since the fund was established before the DGF, it was grandfathered in. The DGF partnership criterion is vague and does not specify if partnerships are necessary at the governance or the activity level, making it difficult to ascertain a program's compliance with this criterion. The program meets this criterion at the activity level, but not at the governance level. A global partnership on conflict-affected countries with partners at the governance level might help the Bank, U.N. agencies, and other stakeholders to better respond to the transition from relief to rehabilitation and reconstruction and development.

As of March 2004, the *Global Alliance for Vaccines and Immunization*, supported by the Vaccine Fund and other donors, had committed grant funding of over US$1 billion to 69 countries for immunization services covering 6 childhood diseases (diphtheria, polio, tuberculosis, pertussis, measles, and tetanus).[2] The Vaccine Fund also finances the development of vaccines for rotavirus and pneumococcus. Each is a significant cause of mortality in developing countries.

The alliance initially largely promoted the use of new vaccines for yellow fever, Haemophilus influenza serotype b (Hib), and hepatitis-B. GAVI estimates that with its support, countries have cumulatively vaccinated 35.5 million children against hepatitis B; 6 million children against Hib; 2.7 million children against yellow fever; and 8 million more children have access to basic vaccines. The long-term sustainability of the GAVI approach was premised on easy, affordable access to patented drugs. In particular, GAVI relied heavily on new, patented multivalent vaccines, which cost more per use but require fewer uses than older types, in the hope that such vaccines would put less logistical stress on developing countries' health-delivery systems. GAVI also hoped that this approach would increase demand for, and supply of, the new vaccines. However, some African countries have indicated that they lack the resources to buy and deliver multivalent vaccines without GAVI's support. Some stakeholders argue that GAVI could have drawn more on the experience of its partners, such as UNICEF and the World Bank. Developing and producing vaccines has taken longer than expected, their supply has been neither timely nor reliable, and prices have remained high.

GAVI has begun to buy vaccines from multiple sources through competitive bidding. It has also helped governments to improve planning, implementing, and monitoring capacity to deliver immunization services, including staffing, delivery, supervision, and reporting systems; the establishment of baselines and data quality audits; and overall aid coordination. GAVI's approach has brought to the forefront the issue of the availability of new vaccines at affordable prices. Donors have not yet delivered the money they pledged to match the Gates Foundation's contribution, limiting GAVI's ability to meet its declared objective.[3] Learning from a combination of its own experience, board-commissioned studies, and experts in the field, GAVI has considerably changed its strategy to address long-term supply, demand, and financial sustainability. Once it became evident how long it would take to stimulate demand, production, and the market for vaccines in developing countries and how vaccine choice would affect the long-term financial viability of these markets, GAVI's board began exploring other choices with regard to program interventions. The program has also offered to pilot the International Financing Facility (IFF) initiative.

Financing Country-Level Technical Assistance to Promote Policy and Institutional Reforms, Public or Private Investments

***Programs:* Water and Sanitation Program (WSP) (1978), Energy Sector Management Assistance Program (ESMAP) (1982), Integrated Framework for Trade-Related Technical Assistance (IF) (1997), Public-Private Infrastructure Advisory Facility (PPIAF) (1999), Cities Alliance (1999)**

The programs in this category offer examples of evolving or unshared objectives and raise subsidiarity issues. The impacts of the two older programs, WSP and ESMAP, have not been independently assessed.[4] Both monitoring and evaluation are improving as programs adopt results-based management and evaluation systems.

The *Water and Sanitation Program* was founded in 1978. The program provides free, in-kind technical assistance to developing-country governments and agencies. Its objectives have evolved considerably, from the development of appropriate small-scale technology in the 1980s to applying and implementing the Dublin-Rio principles in the 1990s,[5] to the current focus on improving policies and institutions for water and sanitation and on capacity-building to stimulate public and private investments in water supply and sanitation. The partnership's principal added value appears to be its extensive field presence: 76 of its 82 staff are located in 16 focal countries. Its third (1999) evaluation concluded that the partnership had provided professional contributions to the sector in the countries where it is active, depending on the scope and duration of its involvement and the response by different countries. However, there is no systematic evidence that its ultimate beneficiaries—poor people in developing countries—enjoy increased access to safe and affordable water and sanitation services as a result of the program. Only in FY04 did WSP's business plan incorporate a systematic effort, including project sheets and outcome indicators, to monitor progress and evaluate the final outcome of program activities. WSP's impact on public and private investments, including Bank lending in support of such investments, is not clear. The second (1996) evaluation found little recognition of the WSP in the Bank's operational documents, although the WSP had been associated, up until that time, with more than $2 billion of Bank-funded projects. The 1996 evaluation also found systematic learning and exchange of information to be the weakest part of the WSP. The fourth program-level evaluation, now under way, also addresses these issues.

The *Energy Sector Management Assistance Program* was founded in 1983, following the second OPEC oil crisis, to assist developing countries that were facing the dual burden of higher energy costs and increased debt-service requirements. It provides Bank-executed technical assistance and policy advice on sustainable-energy development to developing and transition countries. In the 1980s, it focused almost exclusively on energy sector assessments. Today, following two evaluations in 1990 and 2000 and a restructuring in 1999, it focuses on studies, advisory services, and pilot projects, either upstream—where there is a potential for policy formulation and strategy development—or downstream—where it concentrates on evaluation and disseminating best practices. The 2000 evaluation found that the professional quality of ESMAP activities is generally high. The 2003 Report of ESMAP's Technical Advisory Group (TAG) concluded that ESMAP provides valuable services to donors, the Bank, and probably to client countries, though TAG could not confirm the last. While the 2000 evaluation gives examples of ESMAP's impacts on Bank operations, there is no systematic tracking of ESMAP's impacts on public and private investments in the energy sector, including those supported by Bank lending, nor on the ultimate beneficiaries—those unserved or underserved—in terms of increased access to more reliable, efficient, and affordable energy services. ESMAP's FY02-04 business plan incorporated for the first time a set of indicators to monitor the outputs and outcomes of its activities.

The *Integrated Framework for Trade-Related Technical Assistance* helps least-developed countries do diagnostic studies to inform those countries' trade-oriented development strategies. The program originally aimed to help countries meet their WTO commitments, but lack of ownership for this limited objective led to a new focus on diagnostic studies. A recent independent evaluation concludes that IF's revamping in 2002 and its efforts to mainstream trade into country development plans have sharpened its focus. The evaluation also found that the revamping failed to give the program results-based management processes, resulting in variable results across countries. The link with the PRSPs is beginning to improve: specific donors now "adopt" countries to help mobilize investments, and trade-facilitation lending operations are in the Bank's lending pipeline.[6] While links to Bank operations have improved, interviews revealed continued dissonance among partners regarding IF objectives, as well as continued divergence in countries and agencies' expectations of IF's proper role. While donors emphasize IF's partnership-enhancement value, developing countries stress the importance of increased market access abroad and more investment financing to remove export constraints at home. Now that the diagnostic studies have been done, countries are increasingly asking for funds to carry out the trade assistance identified therein. A greater share of IF expenditures is now being funneled to Window 2-financed capacity-building, with a cap of $1 million per country, as bridging finance.

An OED review of several IF country studies suggests that, while quality has improved, the studies could be more focused and operational toward promoting investment and facilitating policy and institutional reform. Another issue is the unwillingness of OECD countries to provide additional investment finance to overcome domestic export constraints or to remove some barriers to market access, such as restrictive agricultural trade policies and food-safety regulations. Although OED interviews indicate greater understanding and acceptance of the developmental aspects of the trade agenda, it is difficult to establish if such consensus building in donor countries and agencies is a lasting and attributable contribution of the program. Moreover, it is too early to know the program's impacts on ultimate beneficiaries through increased trade and enhanced development outcomes.

The *Public-Private Infrastructure Advisory Facility*, founded in 1999, arose out of the 1994 World Development Report on *Infrastructure for Development* and the Bank's Infrastructure Action Program (which was endorsed by the Development Committee in 1997). This multisector program provides free, Bank-executed technical assistance to facilitate private-sector involvement in infrastructure services. In its first three years, PPIAF funded the drafting of 25 sets of laws and regulations; facilitated the design of 30 public-private infrastructure transactions, such as management contracts, leases, auctions of telecom licenses, privatizations, and concessions; made recommendations leading to the implementation of 14 different sector-reform strategies in 11 countries; funded the creation or strengthening of 20 regulatory institutions; and funded training courses, primarily in regulation, attended by more than 1,500 participants. PPIAF has demonstrated that it is possible to set up an effective monitoring and evaluation system for a technical-assistance program. It has the most advanced monitoring and evaluation processes of the six programs in this group. Its Technical Advisory Panel (TAP) is involved in ex post, on-site reviews of many PPIAF activities. The 2003 TAP report concluded that three features of PPIAF have established it as a niche player in promoting private sector participation:

- High-quality, effective products
- Ability to identify and disseminate global good practices and to document experiences from unsuccessful projects
- Ability to customize global practices to specific countries.

It is too early to assess the impacts of PPIAF activities on its ultimate beneficiaries. Building consensus for policy reform and building implementation capacity both take a long time before impacts appear.

The *Cities Alliance*, also started in 1999, arose out of the Habitat II Conference and the Istanbul Declaration on Human Settlements in June 1996. This multisector program provides free Bank-executed, partner-executed, and recipient-executed technical assistance to support the development of suitable legal, regulatory, policy, and implementation practices in client countries. It focuses on two goals: "cities without slums" and better strategies for city development. The first program-level evaluation of the Cities Alliance, undertaken in 2002, used a results-based framework and is one of the best evaluations of Bank-supported global programs. It assessed the relevance, efficacy, and efficiency of the Cities Alliance during its first three years against the four stated objectives, the three strategies, and the six guiding principles laid out in its charter and followed a results chain (inputs => outputs => outcomes => impacts) as far as practicable given the short life of the alliance. The evaluation concluded that the alliance performed strongly in its first three years by:

- Raising awareness of the rapid urbanization of the developing world
- Leveraging donor commitments and collaboration on urban development
- Increasing the pooling and dissemination of lessons of experience
- Increasing the promise of significant action against urban poverty in the future.

Partial results indicate that more than $4 billion of investments are linked to Alliance-funded activities. Approximately $1.5 billion are already committed, and $2.5 billion are in various stages of preparation or appraisal. More than $2.3 billion are from World Bank loans and credits. As for PPIAF, it is too early to assess impacts on the ultimate beneficiaries—the urban poor and poor cities in developing and transition countries.

Common Approaches to Mitigating Communicable Diseases and Promoting Research on the Diseases of the Poor

***Programs:* Joint United Nations Program on HIV/AIDS (UNAIDS) (1996), Global Forum for Health Research (1998), Roll Back Malaria (RBM) (1998), Stop TB (1999)**

Programs in this category have raised awareness and persuaded donors to invest in communicable-disease control, but face challenges in achieving results on the ground.

The *Joint United Nations Program on HIV/AIDS* was established to develop stronger political commitment in U.N. member countries to address the causes and consequences of the epidemic and to develop a coherent U.N. response. Following an evaluation of its first five years and faced with changes in various countries' HIV/AIDS burdens, new actors and increased global financing for HIV/AIDS, UNAIDS has been wrestling with issues of its strategic direction and functions, including particularly its role in improving action on the ground. It monitors country-level HIV/AIDS strategies and programs. It gathers, analyzes, and disseminates information on the epidemic and responses to it and promotes harmonization of monitoring and evaluation efforts. UNAIDS also assesses country and global HIV/AIDS resource needs and flows and the information that various agencies use to devise strategies and policies. At the country level, UNAIDS theme groups support national policies, identify and disseminate best practices, and support implementation, monitoring, and evaluation. UNAIDS sees its added value as creating awareness, mobilizing political commitment, fostering global coordination, and promoting a three-pronged approach to coordination at the country level.

A recent evaluation of UNAIDS concluded that the program had made progress in developing national strategic plans, many with monitorable indicators and multisector responses, in consultation with persons living with HIV/AIDS, civil society, the private sector, and the donor community. Results have included improved donor coordination and cooperation and plans for developing national capacity, especially in the health system. That HIV/AIDS awareness has improved is indisputable; UNAIDS has helped make that happen. Yet attributing success to UNAIDS is difficult, given the number of actors involved. Coordination is stronger at the global level than at the country level.[7] There has been limited research on the effectiveness of HIV/AIDS interventions. The evaluation observed that UNAIDS must strike a new balance between its advocacy role and its functions in information provision, capacity-building, and technical support, particularly at the country level. UNAIDS is addressing each of these areas. It is working more with its principal co-sponsors, IFAD, the regional banks, civil society, and the private sector; it is providing country-level funding for training, policy planning, technical support, and institutional development; and it has signed new mutual-support agreements with GFATM and WHO. Yet the ongoing human and social fallout from the epidemic has only increased demands on UNAIDS to show results on the ground.

On both humanitarian and development grounds, UNAIDS has promoted a two-pronged strategy: increased focus on prevention and broad access to treatment with anti-retroviral drugs (ARVs). The issues of treatment and care are complex and controversial. The Bank, through its multicountry AIDS (MAP) projects, has increased its lending and focus on HIV/AIDS, in part because of the advocacy of and support from UNAIDS. The Bank's Sub-Saharan Africa region was at the forefront in providing financing and retrofitting other projects in other sectors to finance ARVs.[8] But the magnitude of support that national health systems need to apply the multisector approach is daunting. The consensus on increased access to drugs is premised on increased resource mobilization to offset the costs. Despite donors' recently increased HIV/AIDS commitments and the dramatic decline in drug prices, there is a chasm between the available money and delivery capacity and what is needed. The Bank's MAP projects grapple with many of these issues.

The *Global Forum for Health Research* was evaluated in 2001. The impact of the forum's five core activities was assessed: the annual forum meetings, analytic work, funding research initiatives, communications, and monitoring. The evaluation found that the annual forum meetings, in which 700 participated (300 as paying participants), while useful for networking, need to be more focused. The number of topics should be reduced and prioritized, and at least 50 percent more developing-country participants should be invited. The forum's analytical work was seen as having significant impact. The evaluation considered the range of analytical work impressive, but questioned its quality, given the paucity of in-house capacity. It noted the need for a clear link between research and the annual meetings, and suggested the need for impact assessment of the analytical work (e.g. tools for developing health research priorities to assist policymakers in making health sector allocations). The forum has developed an alliance of health systems and policy research and fostered several research initiatives by bringing in new public and private sector partners and mobilizing new sources of money. The evaluation noted a need for transparency in the forum's selection of research initiatives, as well as in its budget and disengagement processes. Its communication activities entail a network of more than 9,000 partners (both institutions and individuals) that exchange health research information. Over 10,000 copies of the forum's 10/90 annual report are printed and distributed, and the forum's Web site received more than 40,000 hits per month in 2003. The forum monitors and evaluates research-related materials. As with other new programs, the lack of formal criteria to assess initiatives' progress and the sheer time and resources needed to achieve that progress seemed to have been an issue. The forum's impact on resource allocations could not be assessed for lack of data. The forum has a new work program and a strategy to respond to these findings.

Roll Back Malaria was established to generate political support and provide training to support malaria control. RBM's external independent evaluation was one of the strongest in its coverage of issues and its recognition of the importance of partners' roles. It contrasted the program's initial, ambitious goal of reducing the malaria burden by 50 percent by 2010 with the program's absence of clear, monitorable, and realistic objectives. The evaluation found confusion about individual partners' responsibilities, slow progress in achieving country buy-in, insufficient political mobilization, mixed-quality technical advice, and a lack of country strategies to achieve the program's goals. The evaluation also noted that the partnership's loose initial governance structure introduced inefficiencies in decisionmaking and contributed to a lack of accountability within the partnership.

Since this evaluation, a major restructuring of RBM has taken place. The program now has a clearer strategy and a focus on selected countries. The program has also put in place a stronger governance structure, with clearer roles, responsibilities, and accountabilities among the board, secretariat, working groups, and regions, and with more focused participation of "beneficiary countries" in governance. The restructuring is too recent to assess its impact. Yet the Roll Back Malaria program nonetheless has some important accomplishments in advocacy, resource mobilization, and consensus-building on malaria-control activities at the global level, including ensuring its inclusion in the Global Fund for AIDS, Tuberculosis, and Malaria. The program is also better integrated into the Bank's health sector lending than the self-standing HIV projects. The link of RBM with the Bank's operational work has been variable, but is improving. Yet there remain daunting internal issues for the Bank, which needs to allocate money for the network anchors and regions to link RBM programs to one another and to the Bank's lending operations. It also needs to test and monitor the effectiveness of program messages in various countries and adjust its global advocacy accordingly.[9]

Stop TB was established to ensure effective diagnosis, treatment, and cure of patients; to stop TB transmission; to reduce the inequitable toll of TB; and to foster development of new preventive, diagnostic, and therapeutic tools and strategies (such as the directly observed therapy short course, or DOTS, used to interrupt TB transmission). It identifies emerging threats, such as TB/HIV links and multidrug resistant tuberculosis (MDR-TB), and develops technical guidelines and tools, including monitoring of program implementation at the country level, technical support, capacity building, and training. Stop TB operates the Global TB Drug Facility, which finances drug procurement and provides procurement services with financing from other sources (including the World Bank). This financing mechanism is meant to enable safe and efficient drug supply to countries facing supply constraints and to learn about increasing drug access at competitive prices. There is broader consensus on Stop TB's DOTS approach than there is on malaria prevention. DOTS strategy is promoted in all Bank-funded health programs.

In response to the independent external evaluation completed in December 2003, Stop TB is refining its governance and business practices and building further country partnerships. The evaluation found that Stop TB is relevant in the global health scene and that its strategic objectives are clear and well defined and in line with the United Nations' Millennium Goals targets and indicators. The evaluation also concluded that Stop TB has scored some major achievements in its three years, including building and sustaining a broad network of partners, broadening support for the partnership, and securing political commitment to a detailed Global Plan to Stop TB. Furthermore, the Stop TB Partnership has made significant progress against TB, even in difficult environments. The evaluation also praised Stop TB's work in the Green Light Committee for second-line TB drugs and the continued efforts of the Stop TB Global Drug Facility for its grant-making, procurement, partner mobilization, and technical assistance. At the same time, the evaluation observed that monitoring of coverage is nearly nonexistent and that the drug facility, instituted to help developing countries buy drugs at competitive prices, is grossly underfunded at the global level. At the country level, internal delivery capacity and the timely availability of supplies remain challenges. An important finding of the evaluation was that changes in donor priorities and the establishment of new financing mechanisms, such as the Global Fund, have intensified competition for already limited resources. Consequently, the evaluation suggested the need for better financial planning and more country-based, business-oriented strategies. The realism of the targets will depend on the availability of funding. The links between Bank operations and Stop TB are strong in China, India, and some Eastern European countries, but variable overall.[10]

Advocacy to Promote Approaches to Addressing Global Concerns at the Country Level

***Programs:* Consultative Group to Assist the Poorest CGAP (1995), Global Integrated Pest Management Facility (GIF) (1996), Global Forum for Health Research (1997), Global Water Partnership (GWP) (1997), FSAP (1999), Understanding Children's Work (UCW) (2000)**

Nearly all the programs in this category face changing or unclear objectives, lack of Bank or country involvement, and lack of evidence of impacts (on either donors or countries). The programs address specific development issues of global concern—the sustainable management of microfinance institutions, integrated pest management, public-private NGO partnerships in health, integrated water management, financial sector management, and child work.

The *Consultative Group to Assist the Poorest* was created to provide $100 million in microfinance, to increase the poorest households' access to economic activity. Joint or parallel financing with other donors was posited, with the Bank contributing $30 million. The objective then changed to improving the Bank's and other donors' internal capacity to deliver microfinance, and to the dissemination of best practices to microfinance institutions. At the same time, the emphasis changed from the poorest to the poor. The 2002 external evaluation found that CGAP's achievements in donor coordination were "modest and minimal." While CGAP has produced a great deal of material on best practice, there is little independent evidence of benefit to, or impact on, member donors or microfinance institutions. There is also no evidence of expanded microfinance provision by the CGAP consortium of donors, since CGAP has not tracked this. Another initially expected added value was the leveraging of Bank resources ($30 million) toward an additional $70 million from other donors. Yet over eight years of operation, about two-thirds ($65.3 million) of the $96 million CGAP has received has come from the Bank, more than twice the level (in percentage and absolute terms) that was agreed at the program's inception. The other 27 member donors have contributed less than half of the $70 million expected. Under Phase II of CGAP's operations, member donors contributed more to the provision of microfinance services individually than they did via the CGAP partnership

Despite its extremely limited budget (the second-smallest among the programs reviewed), the *Global Integrated Pest Management Facility* has produced a range of outcomes. It has increased global advocacy for integrated pest management. At the country level, it has promoted aid coordination by facilitating assistance to governments requesting IPM support (several pilot projects have led to follow-on financing of pesticide projects). In one notable case, Kyrgyzstan, the program promoted demonstrable national ownership of the principles (beyond technical ones) that underlie IPM for cotton and other crops. Facility staff have contributed to the growing body of international pesticide regulations and norms (CODEX). They have assisted the FAO Plant Protection Service and, through seconded staff, assisted the World Bank with the development of the Integrated Safeguard Policy Datasheet, a draft pest management guidebook, pest management plans, and training. However, the facility's guidelines, encapsulated in its Program Document and agreed upon by its co-sponsors in 1996, were weak in assigning criteria to assess impact (beyond outputs like increased farmer participation and outcomes like reduced pesticide use). The facility has recognized the need to adjust to developing-country needs in areas related to food safety and international trade (considering the recent activation of the Rotterdam and Stockholm conventions). Appropriate impact indicators for this work could include reductions in pesticide management costs as a proportion of total crop production costs and reductions in EU rejection of produce for reasons of excessive pesticide residues.

The most useful contribution of *Understanding Children's Work* has been the compilation of country-by-country information in studies of children's work. Some of these have generated enthusiasm for the issues among policymakers. However, the external evaluation observes that the collaborative process has had an "informative" rather than "formative" character and that little progress has been made in developing a common typology or in operationalizing key concepts like "child work," "child labor," and "worst forms of child labor." The use of general objectives rather than "specific, measurable, achievable, and time-bound" ones also opens the door to varied interpretations. The program has not sought to enhance its appeal beyond the countries where studies have been done, has not drawn on the experience of the more successful countries in reducing child labor, and has not sufficiently involved civil-society groups who can help set societal norms for the tolerance of child labor. Increased interagency collaboration has been a hallmark of this program (especially considering the historical inattention given to child labor in development research). But differences in viewpoints across co-sponsoring agencies have disrupted the program's original working relationships. A new co-sponsorship arrangement is being investigated. Meanwhile, closer involvement of Bank operational staff and developing-country policymakers is needed to give the program the more operational bent necessary to tackle the problem of child labor.

The *Global Water Partnership* is a global network of water partnerships focused on implementation of integrated water resources management (IWRM), a comprehensive and multisector approach to water issues. Thus far, it has established or sponsored 11 regional partnerships, 25 country-level partnerships, and 45 area water partnerships. A key rationale behind GWP is the assumption that water partnerships can save money by improving resource mobilization and increasing efficiencies in distribution, delivery, and use. Although a founder and early financial supporter, the Bank withdrew Development Grant Facility financial support for GWP in 2002. This has left the program's water partnerships facing the formidable challenge of ensuring their own financial sustainability. Given the lack of evidence of consistent performance and cost savings across partnerships, it is unclear whether most of them will manage on their own.

Although designed as an implementation mechanism for IWRM, GWP has focused more on advocacy than on on-the-ground activities, raising the issue of overlap with the World Water Council. A persistent problem for GWP has been its lack of quantitative performance indicators to show the impact of the program and its partnerships on water-use efficiency, equity, quality, and sustainability.

Country-Level Capacity Building

Programs: **Information for Development Program (*info*Dev) (1995), World Links for Development (World Links) (1998), Global Development Network (GDN) (1999), Financial Sector Assessment Program (FSAP) (1999), Financial Sector Reform and Strengthening Initiative (FIRST) (2002)**

These five capacity-building programs raise issues of their objectives and strategies, Bank oversight, and exit strategies. They have not yet demonstrated impacts beyond the direct beneficiaries of their activities.

The *Information for Development* program was founded in 1995, based on the realization that poor countries and poor communities were not just resource-poor but also information-poor, lacking access to information and knowledge that could improve lives. Until February 2003, its main activity was to make small capacity-building grants (up to $250,000) to help recipients design, test, and apply innovative uses of information and communication technology (ICT) at the country level. Its two program-level evaluations in 1998 and 2002 are among the weakest evaluations of global programs. The evaluations were not independent (since the evaluators reported to *info*Dev management), had no evaluation framework, did not follow a results-based framework, and did not assess achievements against stated objectives. The 2002 evaluation concluded that *info*Dev's advocacy of access to ICT as a global public good has been its biggest success. At the same time, the program's capacity-building grants were found to have had little impact beyond the direct beneficiaries, and *info*Dev has made little effort to distill lessons from these grants; until now, the main source of information and exchange has been its Web site. The 2001 report of its Technical Advisory Panel found that *info*Dev spent a great deal of its resources screening project proposals, and very little on supervision or monitoring after these were approved. The 2002 evaluation also pointed out that *info*Dev now operates in a crowded field, with many alternative sources of information. It concluded that *info*Dev must reinvent itself and "focus on its knowledge activities in order to capitalize on its initial success and stay ahead of the growing pack of ICT for development programs." Although *info*Dev is a Bank-dominated partnership, it appears to add very little value to the Bank. It has funded country-level activities through developed-country NGOs without the knowledge of the Bank's country directors. While *info*Dev has hosted workshops, symposia, and conferences advocating the importance of ICTs in developing countries, it has not worked closely with national policymakers to design policies to increase connectivity. Responding to the 2002 evaluation, *info*Dev management has begun restructuring programs and priorities, mainstreaming ICT in the core operational work of donors, and identifying strategies for scaling up the impact of ICT on core development goals (including the Millennium Development Goals).

World Links for Development, a global learning network linking students and teachers around the world, is designed to offer a set of education technology-related services ranging from basic school connectivity solutions to international tele-collaborative projects for teachers' professional development. The primary value it adds is though its training program to help teachers and students apply ICTs to teaching and learning. The program has been extended to more than 30 countries in all regions, creating networks of teachers and students. OED team visits to a number of countries in Asia found that the training provided by World Links is of high quality, but needs to be tailored to specific needs of client countries. Where private sector investment is less attractive, as in most of Sub-Saharan Africa, the program has helped leverage financing from donors, but those donors are increasingly requiring a match for their funds. Hence the loss to the program from the Bank's planned financial disengagement is much greater than the Bank's own financial share in the program. It will be a challenge for World Links to sustain itself when DGF support dries up in FY04 and the World Bank Institute also withdraws its support.

The lack of computers, hardware/software support, and Internet access continue to be major challenges. The external evaluation, commissioned by, and reported to, the program's management, found that student participation improves computer and other skills. Also, a gender-impact study of participating students in Africa commissioned by the program management found that girls have benefited more in academic results and communication skills. An independent external evaluation of the program would assist in understanding how the program could help the application of ICTs to achieve the Education for All goals, given the program's potential for scaling up and replicating successful projects. Given this program's multisector links, the Bank can employ its comparative advantage by lending to client countries for building the appropriate ICT infrastructure, including the related hardware, software, and communication solutions support, while the program improves the effectiveness of the Bank's lending. The Bank also can assist in tailoring the program content.

The *Global Development Network* has considerable potential as a tool for fostering high-quality, policy-relevant economic and social science research in developing and transition countries. Its aim is to support the generation and sharing of knowledge for development; strengthen the capacity of research and policy institutions in developing countries and transition economies to do high-quality, policy-relevant research; and bridge the gap between the development of ideas and their implementation. Conceived as a network of networks, GDN provides money for research grants to regional research networks, which are then allocated through regional competitions. Initially set up by senior managers in the Bank's Development Economics Vice Presidency and the World Bank Institute, GDN has continued to receive the Bank's strong backing, even after moving out of the Bank and incorporating as an NGO in 2001. With assured Bank funding for five years, creating some networks and bringing some established networks on board, the program has gotten started relatively quickly. Researchers value GDN's support for global research and give high ratings to its annual global development conferences. But the largely North-South conferences account for 20 percent of GDN's budget, with high opportunity cost of resources for funding research, and South-South cooperation. In the first few years GDN was seen primarily as an economic research network, an approach the World Bank, IMF, and the African Economic Research Council favor. But in response to stakeholder criticism and potential funders, GDN has moved to broaden its disciplinary scope, gaining greater acceptability among social scientists. Although its governance structure was built using a participatory approach, GDN is closely associated with the Bank and its costs have been high, albeit declining over time. The Bank provided scant oversight of the program, notwithstanding its major role in the GDN's establishment, potentially exposing the Bank to reputational risks. These risks are compounded by the fact that 8 of the 18 GDN board members are nominated by the same regional networks that participate in allocative decisions related to their regions, potentially posing a conflict of interest on the governing board. Besides, the board lacked key information on GDN's finances, including overhead and administrative costs, at the time of the evaluation.

GDN's external evaluation viewed GDN as facing three strategic weaknesses: 1. disagreement among important stakeholders on GDN mission and objectives; 2. weaknesses in program governance; 3. poor prospects for the long-term financial sustainability of the program, and the need to reexamine the decisions to locate GDN in India and to adopt an international organization (IO) status. It recommended reduced frequency of conferences, increased competition among regions for fund allocation, and the appointment of independent consultants with requisite skills to assess the GDN relocation decision and to determine whether the legal status of GDN as an international organization is in the best long-term interest of the network. GDN has not accepted all these recommendations. It is too early to assess its long-term impact. With its upcoming change in institutional status and relocation to New Delhi, India, GDN is attempting to establish its own independent identity, which would depend in part on its reduced financial dependence and an arm's-length relationship with the World Bank.

The *Financial Sector Assessment Program*, conceived in the aftermath of the Asian financial crisis, was intended to contribute to a global public good by diagnosing the strengths and fragilities of member countries' financial systems, ensuring better availability of data on those systems, and providing timely treatment of weaknesses to make countries less vulnerable to external shocks. OED interviews suggest that there is strong demand and commitment to the program in the executive boards of the IMF and the Bank among both part 1 and part 2 countries. The assessments conducted by the Bank's Quality Assurance Group have generally given it good marks. The program managers indicate that the program and its interaction with international standard-setting bodies have made financial standards more operational and relevant for developing countries. The program's assessments are backed by a range of analytical and assessment tools, and thus the assessments have helped improve the tools themselves. However, a number of tensions have emerged between the number of countries demanding the diagnostic work and the speed with which countries can be diagnosed. The comprehensiveness and the costs of studies have also been issues relative to the need for focus. Furthermore, FSAP faces the challenge of reaching a balance between coverage of "significant" countries (those that are a potential source of financial contagion) and small countries that nonetheless would benefit from the program. Within each country, the attention to the private and public sector components of the national financial system is also an issue. There is clarity on paper about the procedures for cooperation and the division of labor between the Bank and the IMF among the global programs OED has reviewed. But there is a general concern that the program serves the needs of the IMF more than those of the Bank, with greater focus on macroeconomic stability and less on generating investment funds and improving their allocation, including how developing countries, and particularly small countries, could better access international capital markets. The Bank expects to address the concern about small-country coverage in the future.

The *Financial Sector Reform and Strengthening Initiative* was originally intended to follow up on the findings of FSAP's diagnostic studies. This link is now less clear. It provides Bank- or partner-executed technical assistance to improve regulatory frameworks, institutional reforms, and domestic capacity in financial sector management. The scale at which the program provides these services could not be achieved either by the Bank or the IMF out of administrative budgets alone. The high overhead costs of operating two secretariats (one in Washington and another in London) are symptomatic of the lack of an agreed strategy among the major donor partners. Similarly, there is little balance of the public and private sector technical assistance skills that developing countries need and that partners bring. Fund and Bank staff, whose inputs are funded by donor trust funds, bring public sector expertise, while DGF contributions go to London to finance private sector expertise. FIRST's shareholder model does not benefit from the perspectives of developing countries and is too new for its impacts to be assessed.

ANNEX F: SOURCE MATERIAL

The World Bank's Approach To Global Programs: Phase 2 Report Case Studies	Author(s)
The CGIAR at 31: An Independent Meta-Evaluation of the Consultative Group on International Agricultural Research	Team Leader: Uma Lele
The Global Environment Facility (GEF)	Uma Lele, Saeed Rana, Lauren Kelly, & Kirsten Spainhower
The Multilateral Fund for the Implementation of the Montreal Protocol	Lauren Kelly
The Prototype Carbon Fund	Lauren Kelly & Jeffrey Jordan
The Critical Ecosystems Partnership Fund (CEPF)	Kirsten Spainhower
The Global Integrated Pest Management Facility (GIF)	Lauren Kelly
Global Water Partnership (GWP): An Independent Case Study	Saeed Rana & Lauren Kelly
Global Health Programs, Millennium Development Goals, and the World Bank's Role • Special Program for Research and Training in Tropical Diseases (TDR) • Global Forum for Health Research • UNAIDS (Joint United Nations Program on HIV/AIDS) • Roll Back Malaria (RBM) • Stop TB • Global Alliance for Vaccines and Immunization (GAVI)	Uma Lele, Naveen Sarna, Ramesh Govindaraj, & Yianni Konstantopoulos
Consultative Group for Assistance to the Poor (CGAP)	Edward Bresnyan
Global Infrastructure Programs: A Network Synthesis Report on Six Global Programs in Infrastructure and Private Sector Development • Water and Sanitation Program (WSP) • Energy Sector Management Assistance Program (ESMAP) • Consultative Group to Assist the Poorest (CGAP) • The Information for Development Program (*info*Dev) • Public-Private Infrastructure Advisory Facility (PPIAF) • Cities Alliance	Christopher Gerrard
The Post-conflict Fund: A Case Study	Caroline Bahnson & Jozefina Cutura
Understanding Children's Work (UCW) Program	Manmohan Agarwal & Lauren Kelly
Integrated Framework for Trade-Related Technical Assistance (IF): An Independent Case Study	Manmohan Agarwal

(*Table continues on the following page.*)

The World Bank's Approach To Global Programs: Phase 2 Report Case Studies	Author(s)
Financial Sector Assessment Program (FSAP) and Financial Sector Reform and Strengthening Initiative (FIRST)	Manmohan Agarwal
The Global Development Network (GDN): An Independent Mini Review	Naveen Sarna & Yianni Konstantopoulos
World Links: A Mini Review	Naveen Sarna & Yianni Konstantopoulos
Thematic Working Papers	
The CGIAR at 31: An Independent Meta-Evaluation of the Consultative Group on International Agricultural Research	Team leader: Uma Lele
Natural Resources Management Research in CGIAR: A Meta-Evaluation	Christopher B. Barrett
The CGIAR in Africa: Past, Present, and Future	Carl K. Eicher & Mandivamba Rukuni
Global Public Goods from the CGIAR: Impact Assessment	Bruce Gardner
Review of Biotechnology, Genetic Resource and Intellectual Property Rights Programs	William Lesser
CGIAR Effectiveness – A NARS Perspective from India	Dr. J. C. Kaytal & Dr. Mruthyunjaya
Brazil Country Paper for the CGIAR Meta-Evaluation	Jamil Macedo, Marcio C. M. Porto, Elisio Contini, & Antonio F. D. Avila
International Agriculture Research and the Role of the Private Sector	David J. Spielman

ANNEX G: PEOPLE CONSULTED

Cities Alliance Case Study			
Anwar Ravat, Chief Administrative Officer, Infrastructure Network Core Services; Nigel Twose, Manager, Investment Climate Department			
Damyanova, Victoria	Head, Foreign Investment Projects	Sofia Municipality	Bulgaria
Djorinski, P.	Chairman of Municipal Council Budget Commission	Sofia Municipality	Bulgaria
Kehaiova, Ekaterina	Mayor	Sofia Municipality	Bulgaria
Mihaylovitch, Ludmil	Chief Coordinator, Sofproject	Sofia Municipality	Bulgaria
Nikolov, Ventseslav	Deputy Mayor	Sofia Municipality	Bulgaria
Reffailova, Georgette	Expert, Urban Development	Sofia Municipality	Bulgaria
Terziev, Peter	Director Sofproject	Sofia Municipality	Bulgaria
Yanov, Stoyan	Chief Architect	Sofia Municipality	Bulgaria
Minis, Hal	Program Director	USAID - Local Government Initiative	Bulgaria
Mutter, Michael	Sr. Architectural and Urban Planning Adviser	DFID	United Kingdom
Barbalov, Doncho	Energy & Infrastructure Officer	The World Bank	Bulgaria
de Bruyn Kops, Oscar	Country Manager	The World Bank	Bulgaria
Kondova,Galia	Research Assistant	The World Bank	Bulgaria
Hildebrand, Mark	Program Manager	The World Bank	Washington, D.C.
Milroy, Kevin	Operations Officer	The World Bank	Washington, D.C.
Consultative Group on International Agricultural Research (CGIAR) Case Study			
For a complete list of people consulted, please refer to *The CGIAR at 31: An Independent Meta-Evaluation of the Consultative Group on International Agricultural Research.*			
Consultative Group to Assist the Poor (CGAP) Case Study			
Anwar Ravat, Chief Administrative Officer, Infrastructure Network Core Services; Nigel Twose, Manager, Investment Climate Department			
Balkenhol, Bernd	Director, Social Finance Program	ILO	Germany
Galusek, Grzegorz	Executive Director	Microfinance Center	Poland
Matul, Michal	Researcher	Microfinance Center	Poland
Szostek, Agata	Training Programme Director	Microfinance Center	Poland
Stanton, David	Chief Enterprise Development Officer	DFID	United Kingdom
Pojarski, Peter	Operations Office, ECSHD	The World Bank	Bulgaria
Barbalov, Doncho	Energy & Infrastructure Officer	The World Bank	Bulgaria
de Bruyn Kops, Oscar	Country Manager	The World Bank	Bulgaria
Kondova, Galia	Research Assistant	The World Bank	Bulgaria
Kourtev, Georgi	Communications Associate	The World Bank	Bulgaria
Cook, Tamara	Operations Analyst	The World Bank	Washington, D.C.
Cuevas, Carlos	Lead Financial Economist	The World Bank	Washington, D.C.

Littlefield, Elizabeth	Director	The World Bank	Washington, D.C.
Rosenberg, Richard	Adviser	The World Bank	Washington, D.C.
Sananikone, Ousa	Sr. Private Sector Development Spec.	The World Bank	Washington, D.C.
Critical Ecosystems Partnership Fund (CEPF) Case Study			
Kevin Cleaver, Sector Director, Agriculture & Rural Development Department; Kristalina Georgieva, Country Director, Russian Federation; Sushma Ganguly, Sector Manager, Agriculture & Rural Development Department			
Thomas, Vinod	Country Director	The World Bank	Brazil
Steer, Andrew	Country Director	The World Bank	Indonesia
Dean, Lisa	Director of Financial Management, CEPF	Conservation International	Washington, D.C.
Martin, Roberto	Sr. Director for Portfolio Management, CEPF	Conservation International	Washington, D.C.
Ocker, Donnell	Sr. Director for Program Management, CEPF	Conservation International	Washington, D.C.
Seligmann, Peter	CEO	Conservation International	Washington, D.C.
Thomsen, Jorgen	Executive Director CEPF	Conservation International	Washington, D.C.
Brylski, Phillip	Country Sector Coordinator	The World Bank	Washington, D.C
Canby, Kerstin	Consultant	The World Bank	Washington, D.C.
Carroll, Michael	Sr. Natural Resource Management Spec.	The World Bank	Washington, D.C.
Cassells, David	Sr. Environmental Specialist	The World Bank	Washington, D.C.
Castro, Gonzalo	Lead Environmental Specialist	The World Bank	Washington, D.C.
Douglas, James	Lead Operations Officer	The World Bank	Washington, D.C.
Georgieva, Kristalina	Country Director	The World Bank	Washington, D.C.
Jansen, Malcolm	Sr. Environmental Specialist	The World Bank	Washington, D.C.
Kiss, Agnes	Lead Ecologist	The World Bank	Washington, D.C.
Lintner, Stephen	Sr. Adviser	The World Bank	Washington, D.C.
MacKinnon, Kathleen	Sr. Biodiversity Specialist	The World Bank	Washington, D.C.
Peter, Christian	Forestry Specialist	The World Bank	Washington, D.C.
Ramirez, Jeanette	Operations Analyst	The World Bank	Washington, D.C.
Shen, Susan	Lead Ecologist	The World Bank	Washington, D.C.
Spears, John	Consultant	The World Bank	Washington, D.C.
Van Nieuwkoop, Martien	Lead Operations Officer	The World Bank	Washington, D.C.
Warner, Chris	Sr. Environmental Spec.	The World Bank	Washington, D.C.
Whitten, Anthony	Sr. Biodiversity Specialist	The World Bank	Washington, D.C.
Energy Sector Management Assistance Program (ESMAP) Case Study			
Anwar Ravat, Chief Administrative Officer, Infrastructure Network Core Services; Nigel Twose, Manager, Investment Climate Department			
Christov, Christo	Executive Director (consultant)	Energy Institute	Bulgaria
Drumev, Drumi	Chairman	State Energy Efficiency Agency	Bulgaria
Ivanov, Teodor	Chief Expert, Air Protection Department	Ministry of Environment & Water	Bulgaria
Konstantinoff, Metodi	Deputy Chairman	State Energy Efficiency Agency	Bulgaria
Kavachev, Milko	Minister	Ministry of Energy & Resources	Bulgaria
Petrov, Julian	Chief Secretary	State Energy Efficiency Agency	Bulgaria

Duda, Miroslaw	Acting Director	Energy Regulatory Authority	Poland
Zaleski, Boguslaw	Director, Foreign Cooperation & European Integration Office	Energy Regulatory Authority	Poland
Jaskolski, Tomasz	Director, Development & Production	Polish Oil & Gas Company	Poland
Nowak, Kazimierz	Director, Development & Investment Division	Polish Oil & Gas Company	Poland
Piwowarski, Andrzej	Sr. Advisor for Natural Gas Industry & European Union Accession	Polish Oil & Gas Company	Poland
Rokosz, Wieslaw	Deputy Director, Development & Production	Polish Oil & Gas Company	Poland
Staniewski, Jerzy	Vice President	Polish Oil & Gas Company	Poland
Altas, Burhan	Head of Planning & Financing Department	Ministry of Energy & National Resources	Turkey
Altas, Macide	Planning Expert, Research, Planning & Coordination Board	Ministry of Energy & National Resources	Turkey
Beba, Ali	Consultant	R&R Scientific & Technical Services	Turkey
Cakmak, Osman	Deputy Undersecretary	Ministry of Environment	Turkey
Kulakoglu, Aysen	Head of Department	Undersecretariat of the Treasury	Turkey
Ozalp, Camay	Senior Associate	Undersecretariat of the Treasury	Turkey
Barbalov, Doncho	Energy & Infrastructure Officer	The World Bank	Bulgaria
de Bruyn Kops, Oscar	Country Manager	The World Bank	Bulgaria
Kondova, Galia	Research Assistant	The World Bank	Bulgaria
Kourtev, Georgi	Communications Associate	The World Bank	Bulgaria
Carter, Michael	Country Director	The World Bank	Poland
Hall, Christopher	Chief, Warsaw Office & Sr. Portfolio Manager	The World Bank	Poland
Wojciechowicz, Jacek	External Affairs Officer	The World Bank	Poland
Ozdora, Gurhan	Sr. Operations Officer	The World Bank	Turkey
Feinstein, Charles	Lead Energy Specialist	The World Bank	Washington, D.C.
Lallement, Dominique	Adviser	The World Bank	Washington, D.C.
Saeed, Kazim	Operations Coordinator	The World Bank	Washington, D.C.
Global Development Network (GDN) Case Study			
Gwynne, Beris	GDN Governing Board Member	The Foundation for Development Cooperation	Australia
Makdisi, Samir	GDN Governing Board Member	American University of Beirut	Beirut
Hanousek, Jan	Director	CERG-EI	Czech Republic
Filer, Randall	President	CERG-EI	Czech Republic
Fiske, Ellen	Administrative Director	CERG-EI	Czech Republic
Jetton, Michael	Development & Public Relations Office	CERG-EI	Czech Republic
Jurajda, Stepan	Assistant Professor	CERG-EI	Czech Republic
Kocenda, Evzen	Associate Professor	CERG-EI	Czech Republic
Lizal, Lubomir	GDN Grant Recipient	CERG-EI	Czech Republic
Kmenta, Jan	GDN Governing Board Member	Charles University	Czech Republic
Hiemenz, Ulrich	GDN Governing Board Member	Organisation for Economic Co-operation & Development	France

Gerlach, Frederick	GDN Evaluator		
Muth, H. Peter	GDN Evaluator		
Agarwal, Bina	GDN Governing Board Member	Institute for Economic Growth	India
Ahluwalia, Isher	GDN Governing Board Member	International Food Policy Research Institute	India
Patel, Sujata	GDN Governing Board Member	University of Pune	India
Ray, Subhorota	Fellow	Indian Council for Research in International Economic Relations	India
Virmani, Arvind	Executive Secretary	SANEI	India
Killick, Tony	Board Member	AERC	Kenya
Lyakurwa, William	Executive Secretary	AERC	Kenya
Petsieau, Caroline	Board Chair	AERC	Kenya
King, Vita	Grant Recipient	Euro Faculty	Latvia
Hernandez, Carolina	Director	Institute for Strategic & Development Studies	Philippines
Lamberte, Mario	President	Philippine Institute for Development Studies	Philippines
Cukrowski, Jacek	Sr. Export	CASE Foundation	Poland
Jakubiak, Malgorzata	Grant recipient	CASE Foundation	Poland
Wojciechowicz, Grazyna	Managing Director	CASE Foundation	Poland
Wozniak, Przemek	Grant Recipient	CASE Foundation	Poland
Bezbaruah, Supriti	Administrator	ISEAS	Singapore
Yue, Chia Siow	Director & Regional Coordinator	ISEAS	Singapore
Jayawardena, Lal	GDN Governing Board Member	SSASL	Sri Lanka
Jittrapanun, Thawatchai	Head, Faculty of Economics	Chualongkorn University	Thailand
Jivastantikarn, Nirund	President	Yonok College	Thailand
Sussangkarn, Chalongphob	GDN Governing Board Member	Thailand Development Research Institute	Thailand
Mintchev, Vesselin	Secretary for Economic Affairs	Office of the President	Turkey
Stone, Diane	GDN Governing Board Member	University of Warwick	United Kingdom
Cooper, Richard	Joint Deputy Chair, GDN Governing Board	Harvard University	United States
McMahon, Gary	Principal Economist	Global Development Network	United States
Squire, Lyn	Director	Global Development Network	United States
Kaul, Inge	GDN Governing Board Member	UNDP	United States
Mooke, Joyce	Vice President	The Rockefeller Foundation	United States
Schultz, Paul	Professor	Yale University	United States
Khan, Mohsin	Director	IMF Institute	Washington, D.C.
Carter, Michael	Country Director	The World Bank	Poland
Hall, Christopher	Chief, Warsaw Office & Sr. Portfolio Manager	The World Bank	Poland
Wojciechowicz, Jacek	External Affairs Officer	The World Bank	Poland
Bourguignon, Francois	Sr. Vice President & Chief Economist	The World Bank	Washington, D.C.

Collier, Paul	Sr. Adviser	The World Bank	Washington, D.C.
Diwan, Ishac	Country Director	The World Bank	Washington, D.C.
Duvall, Thomas	Chief Counsel	The World Bank	Washington, D.C.
Garcia-Thoumi, Ines	Chief Admin. Officer	The World Bank	Washington, D.C.
Gelb, Alan	Chief Economist	The World Bank	Washington, D.C.
Gwin, Catherine	Lead Evaluation Officer	The World Bank	Washington, D.C.
Hubbard, Paul	Manager	The World Bank	Washington, D.C.
Kirby-Zaki, Jane	Sr. Program Officer	The World Bank	Washington, D.C.
Leautier, Frannie	Vice President	The World Bank	Washington, D.C.
Nankani, Gobind	Vice President	The World Bank	Washington, D.C.
Ndulu, Benno	Research Manager	The World Bank	Washington, D.C.
Perry, Guillermo	GDN Governing Board Member	The World Bank	Washington, D.C.
Ramphele, Mamphela	Managing Director	The World Bank	Washington, D.C.
Stern, Nick	Former Staff	The World Bank	Washington, D.C.
Stumpf, Andrea	Sr. Counsel	The World Bank	Washington, D.C.
Wangwe, Samuel	Former Staff	The World Bank	Washington, D.C.
Winters, L. Alan	Director, Development Research Group	The World Bank	Washington, D.C.
Global Environment Facility (GEF) Case Study			
Kevin Cleaver, Sector Director, Agriculture & Rural Development Department; Kristalina Georgieva, Country Director, Russian Federation; Sushma Ganguly, Sector Manager, Agriculture & Rural Development Department			
Hagerman, Ellen	CIDA		Canada
Carabias, Julia	Chair, STAP	GEF	Mexico
Prouvost, Amedee	Director & CFO	MIGA	Washington, D.C.
Shepardson, Karin	Sr. Regional Coordinator	The World Bank	Croatia
Ahmed, Kuslum	Lead Environmental Specialist	The World Bank	Washington, D.C.
Aryal, Dinesh	Operations Analyst	The World Bank	Washington, D.C.
Broadfield, Robin	Sr. Regional Coordinator	The World Bank	Washington, D.C.
Castro, Gonzalo	Lead Environmental Specialist	The World Bank	Washington, D.C.
Crepin, Christophe	Program Manager	The World Bank	Washington, D.C.
El Ashry, Mohammed	Former Staff	The World Bank	Washington, D.C.
Georgieva, Kristalina	Country Director	The World Bank	Washington, D.C.
Good, Len	CEO & Chairman	The World Bank	Washington, D.C.
Harstad, Jarle	Lead Monitoring & Evaluation Officer	The World Bank	Washington, D.C.
Khanna, Rohit	Sr. Operations Officer	The World Bank	Washington, D.C.
King, Kenneth	Manager	The World Bank	Washington, D.C.
Kumar, Kanta	Sr. Environmental Specialist	The World Bank	Washington, D.C.
MacKinnon, Kathleen	Sr. Biodiversity Specialist	The World Bank	Washington, D.C.
Shen, Susan	Lead Ecologist	The World Bank	Washington, D.C.
Wedderburn, Samuel	Sr. Operations Officer	The World Bank	Washington, D.C.
Vidaeus, Lars	Consultant	The World Bank	Washington, D.C.
Volonte, Claudio	Sr. Monitoring & Evaluation Specialist	The World Bank	Washington, D.C.
Zazueta, Aaron	Sr. Monitoring & Evaluation Specialist	The World Bank	Washington, DC

Global Health Programs (HNP) Case Study			
Jacques Baudoy, Sector Director, Health, Nutrition, and Population; Robert Hecht, Sector Manager, Health, Nutrition and Population; James Christopher Lovelace, Senior Manager, Kyrgyz Republic Country Office			
Gaere, Elizabeth	Representative	DFID	Accra
Adjei, Sam	Director of Medical Services	MOH	Accra
Melville, George	Country Representative	WHO	Accra
Alemseged, Eskendir	Civil Engineer	African Development Bank	Addis Ababa
Namakando, George	Principal Macroeconomist	African Development Bank	Addis Ababa
Shaaeldin, Elfaith	Resident Representative	African Development Bank	Addis Ababa
Alem, A.	Health Worker	City Hospital	Addis Ababa
Tekle, Ms.	Senior Nurse Supervisor	City Hospital	Addis Ababa
Tekalegne, Agonafer	Head	CRDA (National NGO umbrella organization)	Addis Ababa
Herzig, Peter	Health Project Advisor	GTZ	Addis Ababa
Labahn, Thomas	Director	GTZ	Addis Ababa
Seidel, Bjorn	Deputy Director	GTZ	Addis Ababa
Azene, Girma	Head of Planning	MOH	Addis Ababa
Seifu, Yohannes	Head, Health Services and Training	MOH	Addis Ababa
Wit, Klaas	First Secretary, Economic	Netherlands Embassy	Addis Ababa
Broek, Antonius	Deputy Resident Representative	UNDP	Addis Ababa
Nyambi, S.	Resident Representative for UNDP	UNDP	Addis Ababa
Sheth, Mahandra	Representative	UNICEF	Addis Ababa
Jancloes, Michel	Executive Director	WHO	Addis Ababa
Oedi	Sr. Health Officer	WHO	Addis Ababa
Gebreselassie, O.	Senior Health Specialist	The World Bank Office	Addis Ababa
Singh, Surjit	Resident Representative	The World Bank Office	Addis Ababa
Plasai, Valaikanya	Faculty and Malaria Expert, College of Public Health	Chulalongkorn University	Bangkok
Chareonsuk, Sompong	Country Program Advisor	UNAIDS	Bangkok
Melgaard, Bjorn	WHO Representative	WHO	Bangkok
Laruelle, Jacques	Belgian Ministry of International Cooperation	DGC	Belgium
Gaseitsiwe, D.M.	Director of Economic Affairs	Ministry of Finance and Development Planning, Government of Botswana	Botswana
Molomo, Batho	Director of Strategic and Contingency Planning	Ministry of Finance and Development Planning, Government of Botswana	Botswana
Hutt, Janine	Program Advisor	CIDA	Canada
Rockhold, Pia	Technical Advisor on Health	MOFA (Danida)	Denmark
Rantona, Koketso	Executive Director	Community Solutions	Gabarone
Agizew, Tefera	PMO	Epidemiology Unit	Gabarone
Koosimile, Boitshwarelo	Technical Assistant (TB)	Epidemiology Unit	Gabarone
Moakofni, Kentse	Senior Nursing Officer, Malaria	Epidemiology Unit	Gabarone
Mwansa, R.A.	PHS I	Epidemiology Unit	Gabarone
Phindela, Thandie	Principal Health Officer, Malaria	Epidemiology Unit	Gabarone
Khan, Banu	National AIDS Coordinator	NACA	Gabarone

Mandevu, Rose	Chief Health Officer, AIDS/STD Unit	National AIDS Control Program, MOH	Gabarone
Percy, Fiona	AusAID Advisor	National AIDS Coordinating Agency	Gabarone
Rahman, Mafizur	STI Program Coordinator and Head	National STI Referral Training & Research Center, MOH	Gabarone
Jere, Ackim	Project Manager, Statistics Training	SADC	Gabarone
Odirile, Elliott	Statistician	SADC	Gabarone
Saint-Victor, Rosalind	Country Program Adviser	UNAIDS	Gabarone
Kamau, Macharia	Resident Representative	UNDP	Gabarone
Kalilani, Jean	WHO Representative	WHO	Gabarone
Alnwick, David	Program Manager, RBM	WHO	Geneva
Aitken, Denis	Assistant Director-General	WHO	Geneva
Arnold, Virginia	Task Manager for the Global Drug Facility	Stop TB	Geneva
Asamoa-Baah, Anarfi	Assistant Director-General for Communicable Diseases	WHO	Geneva
Bebhehani, Kazem	Assistant Director-General for External Relations and Governing Bodies	WHO	Geneva
Bellah, Ahmed	TDR Scientific Officer	WHO	Geneva
Binh Khanh, Nguyen	Planning Officer, Budget and Management Reform	WHO	Geneva
Blanc, Leopold	WHO Coordinator for the Stop TB Department	WHO	Geneva
Blas, Erik	Program Manager	WHO	Geneva
Brundtland, Gro Harlem	Director General	WHO	Geneva
Carael, Michel	Chief, Evaluation Program Development & Coordination	UNAIDS	Geneva
Clark, John Paul	Roll Back Malaria Project	WHO	Geneva
Coll-Seck, Awa	Executive Secretary	Roll Back Malaria	Geneva
Currat, Louis	Executive Secretary	Global Forum for Health Research	Geneva
Defrancisco, Andres	Deputy Executive Director	Global Forum for Health Research	Geneva
Dragger, Nick	Director, Reproductive Health & Research	WHO	Geneva
Espinal, Marcos	Executive Secretary	Stop TB Partnership	Geneva
Godal, Tore	Executive Director	GAVI	Geneva
Guindon, Emmanuel	Economist (Tobacco), Non-Communicable Diseases	WHO	Geneva
Hayward, David	Head, Finance and Administration	Global Forum for Health Research	Geneva
Heitkamp, Petra	Principal Officer	Stop TB Partnership	Geneva
Herbert, Brad	Associate	Global Fund for ATM	Geneva
Hetschel, Chris	CEO	MMV	Geneva
Heymann, David	Executive Director, Communicable Diseases	WHO	Geneva
Janovsky, Katja	Director, Strategies for Cooperation and Partnership	WHO	Geneva
Karam, Marc	Communicable Disease Control Cluster Representative	WHO	Geneva
Kumaresan, Jacob	Executive Secretary, Stop TB	WHO	Geneva
Kuruneri, Patience	Senior Advisor	Roll Back Malaria	Geneva
Lee, J. W.	Director General	WHO	Geneva

Matlin, Stephen	Executive Director	Global Forum for Health Research	Geneva
Mertens, Theirry	Director, the Mediterranean Center for the Reduction of Vulnerability	WHO	Geneva
Morel, Carlos	Director, TDR	WHO	Geneva
Nabarro, David	Executive Director	GAVI	Geneva
Nafo-Traore, Fatoumata	Executive Secretary	Roll Back Malaria	Geneva
Pang, Tikki	Director, Evidence for Policy Unit	WHO	Geneva
Piot, Peter	Executive Director	UNAIDS	Geneva
Pradhan, Namita	Senior Policy Analyst, Office of the Director General	WHO	Geneva
Prost, Andre	External Relations Dept.	WHO	Geneva
Rabeneck, Sonya	Technical Secretary	WHO	Geneva
Raviglione, Mario	Coordinator, TB Strategy & Operations	WHO	Geneva
Saxena, Abha	Consultant, Evidence for Policy Unit	WHO	Geneva
Schapira, Allan	Coordinator, Policy and Strategy Team	Roll Back Malaria	Geneva
Sherry, Jim	Program Manager	UNAIDS	Geneva
Smith, Ian	Director General	WHO	Geneva
Souteyrand, Yves	Officer at the HIV/AIDS Department	WHO	Geneva
Stensen, Bo	Principal Officer	GAVI	Geneva
Suzuki, Yasuhiro	Executive Director, Health Technology and Medicines	WHO	Geneva
Tanvir, Mehreen	Consultant, TDR	WHO	Geneva
Thapa, Deepak	Internal Oversight Svc	WHO	Geneva
Tillfors, Lars	External Relations	WHO	Geneva
Van Look, Paul	Director, Reproductive Health & Research	WHO	Geneva
Venugopal, P.V.	Director, International Operations	MMV	Geneva
Widdus, Roy	Project Manager	Global Forum for Health Research	Geneva
Korte, Rolf	Director of the Health and Education Department	GTZ	Germany
A. Tung	Chairman	Nationals AIDS Committee	Hanoi
Zessler, Laurent	Country Program Advisor	UNAIDS	Hanoi
Ryan, Jordan	Resident Representative	UNDP	Hanoi
Brudon, Pascale	WHO Representative	WHO	Hanoi
Nguyen, Mai Thi	Health Specialist	The World Bank Office	Hanoi
Rees, Helen	Director, RHRU	Baragawanath Hospital	Johannesburg
Pick, William	Head, School of Public Health	Witwatersrand University	Johannesburg
Price, Max	Dean, Medical School	Witwatersrand University	Johannesburg
Schneider, Helen	Director, Center for Health Policy	Witwatersrand University	Johannesburg
Asquitu, Joanne	Evaluation Officer	DFID	London
Mittal, Onkar	Health and Population Department	DFID	London
Sabey, Steven	Health and Population Department	DFID	London
Bennett,Steve	Infectious Disease Epidemiology Unit	London School of Hygiene & Tropical Medicine	London
Brugha, Ruairi	Health Policy Unit	London School of Hygiene & Tropical Medicine	London

Cleland, John	Head, DFID-funded Safe Passages to Adulthood	London School of Hygiene & Tropical Medicine	London
Godfrey-Faussett, Peter	Head, DFID-funded TB Program	London School of Hygiene & Tropical Medicine	London
Haines, Andy	Dean	London School of Hygiene & Tropical Medicine	London
Hayes, Richard	Professor, Epidemiology & International Health	London School of Hygiene & Tropical Medicine	London
Meek, Sylvia	Malaria Consortium	London School of Hygiene & Tropical Medicine	London
Mills, Anne	Professor, International Health Policy	London School of Hygiene & Tropical Medicine	London
Timaeus, Ian	Center for Population Studies	London School of Hygiene & Tropical Medicine	London
Walt, Gill	Professor, International Health Policy	London School of Hygiene & Tropical Medicine	London
Zaba, Basia	Center for Population Studies	London School of Hygiene & Tropical Medicine	London
Hemmer, Robert	National Service of Infectious Diseases	MAE	Luxembourg
Palmer, Kevin	Regional Adviser in Vector-borne and Parasitic Diseases	WHO, WPRO	Manila
Schapira, Allan	Regional Adviser in Malaria	WHO, WPRO	Manila
Postma, Sjoerd	Representative	DANIDA	New Delhi
Martineau, Tim	Senior Health Adviser	DFID	New Delhi
Nair, Dinesh	Health Adviser	DFID	New Delhi
Bulusu, Saraswati	National Program Officer	Global Micronutrient Initiative	New Delhi
Sankar, Rajan	National Program Officer	Global Micronutrient Initiative	New Delhi
Schaetzel, Thomas	Regional Coordinator and Senior Program Specialist	Global Micronutrient Initiative	New Delhi
Gupta, Deepak	Joint Secretary, MOHFW	Government of India	New Delhi
Khatri, G.R.	Deputy Director General (TB)	Government of India	New Delhi
Malhotra, S.	Asst. Commissioner (CH)	Government of India	New Delhi
Garg, Subhash Chandra	Director of the Bank Fund	Government of India, Ministry of Finance	New Delhi
Kelkar, Vijay	Minister	Government of India, Ministry of Finance	New Delhi
Saxena, N.C.	Principal Officer	Government of India, Ministry of Finance	New Delhi
Arora, V.K.	Director	LRS Institute of TB and Allied Diseases	New Delhi
Nagpaul, Dr.	President	TB Association of India	New Delhi
Bhatnagar, P.C.	Senior Coordinator, Community Health and Development	VHAI	New Delhi
Roy, Taposh	Director, Health	VHAI	New Delhi
Shiva, Meera	Chairman	VHAI	New Delhi

Heywood, Peter	Lead Health Specialist	The World Bank Office	New Delhi
Ramana, G.N.V.	Senior Health Specialist	The World Bank Office	New Delhi
Singh, Suneeta	Senior Public Health Specialist	The World Bank Office	New Delhi
Sudahakar, K.	Senior Health Specialist	The World Bank Office	New Delhi
Moock, Joyce Lewinger	Associate Vice President	Rockefeller Foundation	New York
Yacoob, May	Director of Monitoring, Evaluation and Knowledge Management	UN Foundation	New York
Barbour, Paul	Economic Adviser	DFID	Pretoria
Balfour, Thuthula	Director	SADC Health Sector Coordinating Unit	Pretoria
Ijsselmuiden, Carel	Director	School of Health Systems, University of Pretoria	Pretoria
Russell, Michele	Regional HIV/AIDS Program Coordinator, S. Africa	USAID	Pretoria
Shasha, Welile	WHO Liaison Officer	WHO	Pretoria
Martin, Gayle	Health Specialist	The World Bank Office	Pretoria
Omar, Fayez	Country Director	The World Bank Office	Pretoria
Sackey, James	Economist	The World Bank Office	Pretoria
Borkar, M.B.	Executive Director	Serum Institute of India	Pune
Dhere, R.M.	Director	Serum Institute of India	Pune
Dodwadkar, S.M.	Director	Serum Institute of India	Pune
Jadhav, S.S.	Executive Director	Serum Institute of India	Pune
Carlsson, Barbro	Chief Coordinator	SIDA/SAREC	Sweden
Svensson, Par	Principal Officer	SIDA/SAREC	Sweden
Berger, Martine	Special Adviser	SDC	Switzerland
Meyers, Richard	Senior Operations Officer	HD Sector Unit, EAPHD, The World Bank	Washington, D.C.
Habayeb, Salim	Lead Public Health Specialist	SASHD, The World Bank	Washington, D.C.
Ehmer, Paul G.	Deputy Officer	USAID	Washington, D.C.
Barat, Lawrence	Technical Specialist	The World Bank	Washington, D.C.
Batson, Amie	Sr. Health Specialist	The World Bank	Washington, D.C.
Chow, Jack	Assistant Director-General of WHO for HIV/AIDS, Tuberculosis, and Malaria	U.S. State Department	Washington, D.C.
Hoben, Christopher	Former Operations Advisor	The World Bank	Washington, D.C.
Nassim, Janet	Senior Operations Officer	The World Bank	Washington, D.C.
Nawaz, Tawhid	Lead Operations Officer	The World Bank	Washington, D.C.
Pannenborg, Ok	Senior Health Advisor	The World Bank	Washington, D.C.
Ritzen, Jo	Vice President	The World Bank	Washington, D.C.
Saxenian, Helen	Lead Economist	The World Bank	Washington, D.C.
Stout, Susan	Lead Monitoring and Evaluation Specialist	The World Bank	Washington, D.C.
Tannan, Nandita	Operations Analyst	The World Bank	Washington, D.C.
Tzannatos, Zafiris	Advisor	The World Bank	Washington, D.C.
Upadhyay, Jagadish P.	Lead Project Officer	The World Bank	Washington, D.C.
Weil, Diana	Sr. Public Health Specialist	The World Bank	Washington, D.C.
Zewdie, Debrework	Program Director	The World Bank	Washington, D.C.
Carty, Lisa	Manager	Gates Foundation	Washington, D.C.

Marsten, Hilary	Research Analyst	Gates Foundation	Washington, D.C.
Carter, Michael	Country Director	The World Bank	Washington, D.C.
Liese, Bernhard	Senior Health Advisor	The World Bank	Washington, D.C.
Walker, Christopher	Lead Specialist	The World Bank	Washington, D.C.
Global Integrated Pest Management (IPM) Case Study			
Kevin Cleaver, Sector Director, Agriculture & Rural Development Department; Kristalina Georgieva, Country Director, Russian Federation; Sushma Ganguly, Sector Manager, Agriculture & Rural Development Department			
Fleischer, Gerd	Pesticide Policy Project	University of Hannover	Germany
Waibel, Hermann	Institute of Horticultural Economics	University of Hannover	Germany
Aiazzi, Tulia		FAO	Italy
Kato, Masa	Chief, Evaluation Service	FAO	Italy
Kenmore, Peter	Coordinator	FAO	Italy
Settle, William		FAO	Italy
Stemerding, Pieter		FAO	Italy
Van der Wulp, Harry		FAO	Italy
Holdernews, Mark		CABI Bioscience	United Kingdom
Voss, Janny		CABI Bioscience	United Kingdom
Dinham, Barbara	Director	PAN-UK	United Kingdom
Eisha-litman, Marcia		PAN-UK	United Kingdom
Gopalan, Hiremagalur		UNEP	
Willis, Jim		UNEP	
Badiane, Ousmane	Lead Rural Development Specialist	The World Bank	Washington, D.C.
Di Leva, Charles	Chief Counsel	The World Bank	Washington, D.C.
Feder, Gershon	Research Manager	The World Bank	Washington, D.C.
Forno, Doug	Former Staff	The World Bank	Washington, D.C.
Freestone, David	Chief Counsel	The World Bank	Washington, D.C.
Ganguly, Sushma	Sector Manager	The World Bank	Washington, D.C.
Gautam, Madhur	Sr. Economist	The World Bank	Washington, D.C.
Granier, Laurent	Sr. Environmental Specialist	The World Bank	Washington, D.C.
Khokhar, M.	Former Staff	The World Bank	Washington, D.C.
Kiss, Agnes	Lead Ecologist	The World Bank	Washington, D.C.
Lagnaoui, Aziz	Sr. Pest Management Specialist	The World Bank	Washington, D.C.
Lintner, Stephen	Sr. Adviser	The World Bank	Washington, D.C.
McMahon, Matthew	Lead Agriculturalist	The World Bank	Washington, D.C.
Nawaz, Tawhid	Lead Implementation Specialist	The World Bank	Washington, D.C.
Nelson, Ridley	Consultant	The World Bank	Washington, D.C.
Pehu, Eija	Adviser	The World Bank	Washington, D.C.
Saifullah, Malik	Former Staff	The World Bank	Washington, D.C.
Schillhorn-Van Veen, Tjaart	Consultant	The World Bank	Washington, D.C.
Sennhauser, Ethel	Sr. Rural Development Specialist	The World Bank	Washington, D.C.
Shen, Susan	Lead Ecologist	The World Bank	Washington, D.C.
Wilson, John	Lead Economist	The World Bank	Washington, D.C.

Global Water Partnership (GWP) Case Study			
Kevin Cleaver, Sector Director, Agriculture & Rural Development Department; Kristalina Georgieva, Country Director, Russian Federation; Sushma Ganguly, Sector Manager, Agriculture & Rural Development Department			
Astorga, Yamileth	Representative	Global Water Partnership	Costa Rica
Ballestero, Maureen	Coordinator	Global Water Partnership	Costa Rica
Reyes, Virginia	Technical Official	Global Water Partnership	Costa Rica
Zimmer, Daniel	President	World Water Council	France
Bertilsson, Per	Deputy Executive Secretary	Global Water Partnership	Sweden
Gabbrielli, Emilio	Executive Secretary	Global Water Partnership	Sweden
Lenahan, James		Global Water Partnership	Sweden
Mohtadullah, Khalid		Global Water Partnership	Sweden
Rogers, Peter	Member, Technical Committee	Global Water Partnership	Sweden
Meinzen-Dick, Ruth		IFPRI	Washington, D.C.
Ahmad, Masood	Lead Water Resources Specialist	The World Bank	Washington, D.C.
Barghouti, Shawki	Adviser	The World Bank	Washington, D.C.
Briscoe, John	Sr. Water Adviser	The World Bank	Washington, D.C.
Cleaver, Kevin	Sector Director	The World Bank	Washington, D.C.
Darghouth, Salah	Adviser	The World Bank	Washington, D.C.
Eguchi, Yoko	Partnership Coordinator	The World Bank	Washington, D.C.
Grey, David	Sr. Water Adviser	The World Bank	Washington, D.C.
Iyer, Parameswaran	Sr. Water & Sanitation Spec.	The World Bank	Washington, D.C.
Kemper, Karin	Sr. Water Resources Management Specialist	The World Bank	Washington, D.C.
Pitman, George Keith	Sr. Evaluation Officer	The World Bank	Washington, D.C.
Sadoff, Claudia	Lead Economist	The World Bank	Washington, D.C.
Stottman, Walter	Manager	The World Bank	Washington, D.C.
Financial Sector Assessment Program (FSAP) Case Study			
Behounek, Jiri	Banking Department	Ministry of Finance	Czech Republic
Birdman, Vojtech	Office of State Supervision in Insurance & Pension Funds	Ministry of Finance	Czech Republic
Kinstva, Pavla	International Organizations Department	Ministry of Finance	Czech Republic
Loula, Dimiitrij	Acting Deputy Director General, International Organizations Department	Ministry of Finance	Czech Republic
Novotna, Marta	Banking Department	Ministry of Finance	Czech Republic
Svoboda, Petr	Office of State Supervision in Finance and Pension Funds	Ministry of Finance	Czech Republic
Dedek, Oldrich	Vice Governor	Czech National Bank	Czech Republic
Fencl, Ivan	Director, Payment Systems	Czech National Bank	Czech Republic
Frait, Jan	Member of Bank Board	Czech National Bank	Czech Republic
Racocha, Pavel	Member of Bank Board	Czech National Bank	Czech Republic
Krcmar, Zdenek	Justice of the Supreme Court	Czech Republic	Czech Republic
Seifert, Filip	Assistant of Minister	Ministry of Justice	Czech Republic
Jezek, Tomas	Member of the Presidium	Czech Securities Commission	Czech Republic
Valujevs, Guntis	Head, Foreign Relations Department	Bank of Latvia	Latvia
Cerps, Uldis	Chairman	Financial and Capital Markets Commission	Latvia
Senderwoicz, Krzysztof	Deputy Director, Payment Systems Department	National Bank of Poland	Poland

Wyczanski, Pawel	Deputy Director, Research Department	National Bank of Poland	Poland
Knowles, Julie	Resource Management Officer	The World Bank	Washington, D.C.
Promisel, Larry	Sr. Adviser	The World Bank	Washington, D.C.
Tapiero, Dafna	Program Coordinator	The World Bank	Washington, D.C.
Waxman, Margery	Program Director/Sr. Adviser	The World Bank	Washington, D.C.
Financial Sector Reform and Strengthening Initiative (FIRST) Case Study			
Knowles, Julie	Resource Management Officer	The World Bank	Washington, D.C.
Promisel, Larry	Sr. Adviser	The World Bank	Washington, D.C.
Tapiero, Dafna	Program Coordinator	The World Bank	Washington, D.C.
Waxman, Margery	Program Director/Sr. Adviser	The World Bank	Washington, D.C.
Information for Development Program (*info*Dev) Case Study			
Badinsky, Nikolay	Technical Director	ARC Fund	Bulgaria
Dinkova, Dinka	Program Director	ARC Fund	Bulgaria
Shentov, Ognian	President	Centre for the Study of Democracy	Bulgaria
Barbalov, Doncho	Energy & Infrastructure Officer	The World Bank	Bulgaria
de Bruyn Kops, Oscar	Country Manager	The World Bank	Bulgaria
Kondova, Galia	Research Assistant	The World Bank	Bulgaria
Kourtev, Georgi	Communications Associate	The World Bank	Bulgaria
Czerniejewski, Borys	Director, International Liaison Office	Infovide	Poland
Fuolewicz, Piotr	Adviser to the Board	Infovide	Poland
Stokalski, Borys	President	Infovide	Poland
Carter, Michael	Country Director	The World Bank	Poland
Hall, Christopher	Chief, Warsaw Office & Sr. Portfolio Manager	The World Bank	Poland
Wojciechowicz, Jacek	External Affairs Officer	The World Bank	Poland
Biochenko, Elmira	Deputy Head, Pediatric Oncology	Children's Hospital No. 1	Russia
Korenev, Pavel	Medical Director	Children's Hospital No. 1	Russia
Petrova, Eleonora	Head, Pediatric Oncology	Children's Hospital No. 1	Russia
Popov, Sergei	Chief, Pathology Department	Children's Hospital No. 1	Russia
Blom, Anders		Eurofacts Oy, Finland	Russia
Lopota, Vitaly	Director & Chief Designer	State Scientific Centre of Russia	Russia
Spasski, Boris	Head, Marketing & International Contacts Department	State Scientific Centre of Russia	Russia
Zaborovski, Vladimir	Deputy Director	State Scientific Centre of Russia	Russia
Ivanova, Elena	Chief Expert	St. Petersburg Administration	Russia
Naumenko, Serguei	Chief, External Affairs Committee	St. Petersburg Administration	Russia
Frolova, Elena	St. Petersburg Rep.	Restropovich Foundation	Russia
Bretaudeau, Henri	Consultant	The World Bank	Washington, D.C.
Chaudhry, Vivek	Program Administrator	The World Bank	Washington, D.C.
Dubow, Jacqueline	Program Coordinator	The World Bank	Washington, D.C.
Lanvin, Bruno	Adviser	The World Bank	Washington, D.C.

Integrated Framework for Trade-Related Technical Assistance (IF) Case Study			
Belisle, J. Denis	Executive Director	ITC	Geneva
Geoffroy, Francesco	Sr. Trade Promotion Officer	ITC	Geneva
Fortin, Carlos	Officer in Charge	UNCTAD	Geneva
Hamdani, Khalil	Chief, Investment Policies & Capacity Building	UNCTAD	Geneva
Prestigiacomo, Astrid	Associate Expert	UNCTAD	Geneva
Namfua, Marcel	Sr. Trade Policy Adviser	UNCTAD	Geneva
Sahami-Malmberg, Massi	Economic Affairs Officer	UNCTAD	Geneva
Tortora, Manuela	Coordinator, Commercial Diplomacy Programme	UNCTAD	Geneva
Chapelier, Georges	Director, Governance and Management Division	UNDP	Geneva
Quoidbach, Vinciane	Jr. Professional Officer	UNDP	Geneva
Antonakakis, Panos	Development Division	WTO	Geneva
Blank, Annet	Head LDC Unit	WTO	Geneva
Mchumo, Zainab	Legal Affairs Officer	WTO	Geneva
Osakwe, Chiedu	Director, Technical Cooperation Division	WTO	Geneva
Oshikawa, Maika	Economics Affairs Officer	WTO	Geneva
Phongsa, Phouvieng	Technical Staff Member	WTO	Geneva
Werner, Peter	Information & Media Relations	WTO	Geneva
Mohammed, Nadir	Country Manager	The World Bank	Albania
Von Amsberg, Joachim	Country Director	The World Bank	Manila
Benhua, Wei	ED	IMF	Washington, D.C.
Calika, Nur	Economist	IMF	Washington, D.C.
Chauffour, Jean-Pierre	WTO Representative	IMF	Washington, D.C.
Junguito, Roberto	ED	IMF	Washington, D.C.
Kelkar, Vijay	Former ED	IMF	Washington, D.C.
Marquez, Mary	Policy Development & Review Department	IMF	Washington, D.C.
Wijnholds, J. de Beaufort	ED	IMF	Washington, D.C.
Rustomjee, Cyrus	ED	IMF	Washington, D.C.
Aksoy, Attaman	Consultant	The World Bank	Washington, D.C.
Benjamin, Nancy	Sr. Country Economist	The World Bank	Washington, D.C.
Bhattacharya, Amar	Sr. Adviser	The World Bank	Washington, D.C.
Bhattasali, Deepak	Lead Economist	The World Bank	Washington, D.C.
Braga, Carlos	Sr. Adviser	The World Bank	Washington, D.C.
Dadush, Uri	Director	The World Bank	Washington, D.C.
Dhar, Sanjay	Lead Economist	The World Bank	Washington, D.C.
Finger, Joseph Michael	Consultant	The World Bank	Washington, D.C.
Haddad, Mona	Sr. Economist	The World Bank	Washington, D.C.
Hinkle, Lawrence	Lead Technical Specialist	The World Bank	Washington, D.C.
Hoekman, Bernard	Research Manager	The World Bank	Washington, D.C.
Kraus, Christiane	Economist	The World Bank	Washington, D.C.
Martin, William	Lead Economist	The World Bank	Washington, D.C.
Nabi, Ijaz	Sector Manager	The World Bank	Washington, D.C.
Nehru, Vikram	Director	The World Bank	Washington, D.C.
Ody, Anthony	Sr. Adviser	The World Bank	Washington, D.C.
Panzer, John	Sector Manager	The World Bank	Washington, D.C.

Peuker, Axel	Manager	The World Bank	Washington, D.C.
Samen, Salomon	Sr. Economist	The World Bank	Washington, D.C.
Saponara, Miguel	Consultant	The World Bank	Washington, D.C.
Solleveld, Leendert	Adviser	The World Bank	Washington, D.C.
Song, Su Yong	Sr. Economist	The World Bank	Washington, D.C.
Stern, Nicholas	Former Staff	The World Bank	Washington, D.C.
Thirriot, Claire	Sr. Economist	The World Bank	Washington, D.C.
Tsikata, Yvonne	Lead Evaluation Officer	The World Bank	Washington, D.C.
Yagci, Fahrettin	Lead Economist	The World Bank	Washington, D.C.
Mohammed, Nadir	Sr. Country Economist	The World Bank	Yemen
Multilateral Fund for the Implementation of the Montreal Protocol (MLF) Case Study			
Kevin Cleaver, Sector Director, Agriculture & Rural Development Department; Kristalina Georgieva, Country Director, Russian Federation; Sushma Ganguly, Sector Manager, Agriculture & Rural Development Department			
Grof, Tamas		UNIDO	Austria
Hakizimana, Gabriel		Ministry of Land & Environment	Burundi
Hagerman, Ellen		CIDA	Canada
El-Arini, Omar		MLF Secretariat	Canada
Eussner, Ansgar		MLF Secretariat	Canada
Nolan, Maria	Chief Officer	MLF Secretariat	
Reed, Andrew		MLF Secretariat	Canada
Chandrasekhar, Usha			India
Shende, Rajendra	Chief	UNEP DTIE's Energy & Ozone Action Unit	India
Inomata, Tadanori			Japan
Prapasawat, Anat		Industrial Finance Corporation	Thailand
Ataman, Senol		Technology Development Foundation	Turkey
Horwitz, Paul	International Advisor	EPA	United States
Strickland, Mia		Environmental Investigation Agency	Washington, D.C.
Carvalho, Suely		UNDP	United States
Chan, Helen	Sr. Operations Officer	The World Bank	Washington, D.C.
Di Leva, Charles	Lead Counsel	The World Bank	Washington, D.C.
Foley, Mary-Ellen	Research Analyst	The World Bank	
Fostvedt, Nils	Sr. Adviser	The World Bank	Washington, D.C.
Freestone, David	Chief Counsel	The World Bank	Washington, D.C.
Gorman, Steve	Lead Environmental Specialist	The World Bank	Washington, D.C.
Liebenthal, Andres	Country Sector Coordinator	The World Bank	Washington, D.C.
Manibog, Fernando	Lead Evaluation Officer	The World Bank	Washington, D.C.
Newcombe, Kenneth	Sr. Manager	The World Bank	Washington, D.C.
Pedersen, Erik	Sr. Environmental Engineer	The World Bank	Washington, D.C.
Prasad, Neeraj	Sr. Operations Officer	The World Bank	Washington, D.C.
Rahill, Bilal	Lead Environmental Specialist	The World Bank	Washington, D.C.

Siles, Sandra	Team Assistant	The World Bank	Washington, D.C.
Terraza, Horacio	Environmental Specialist	The World Bank	Washington, D.C.
Tlyaie, Laura	Sector Manager	The World Bank	Washington, D.C.
Post-conflict Fund Case Study			
Cartier, Paul	Attaché Development Cooperation	Embassy of Belgium	Belgium
Severe, Stefano	Representative	UNHCR	Burundi
Lambrette, Bernarnd	Program Officer	UNHCR	Burundi
Royer, Arnaud	Reintegration Officer	UNHCR	Burundi
Nahimana, Marie-Goreth	Project Officer	UNHCR	Burundi
Bijojote, Salvatore	General Director	Ministry of Reinstallation and Resettlement of Returnees	Burundi
Kankindi, Jacqueline	Project Coordinator	Muyinga Ministry of Social Action	Burundi
Lazare, Karekezi	Governor	Muyinga	Burundi
Nzayanga, Gratien	Advisor to the Governor	Ruyigi	Burundi
Manirakiza, Deogratias	Provincial Health Director	Ruyigi	Burundi
Ntamahangarizo, Dieudonne	Communal Administrator	Ruyigi	Burundi
Civye, Bernard	Provincial Education Director	Action Aid Ruyigi	Burundi
Lubbers, Ruud	High Commissioner for Refugees	UNHCR	Geneva
Doherty, Kolude	Special Adviser of the High Commissioner	UNHCR	Geneva
Crisp, Jeff	Senior Policy Research Officer	UNHCR	Geneva
Bartsch, Dominik	Senior Policy Research Officer	UNHCR	Geneva
Harild, Niels	Reintegration and Local Settlement Section	UNHCR	Geneva
Delgermaa, Arslandbaatar	Associate Economist	UNHCR	Geneva
Date-Bah, Eugenia	Director, InFocus Program	ILO	Geneva
Krishnamurty, J.	Sr. Economist	ILO	Geneva
Specht, Irma	Reintegration Specialist	ILO	Geneva
Pavlovska, Kristina	Assistant Head of Department	Ministry of Finance	Macedonia
Smileviski, Balsko		Agency for Sports and Youth	Macedonia
Burvi, Renata		Agency for Sports and Youth	Macedonia
Lazarevska, Spomenka	Program Coordinator	Open Society Institute	Macedonia
Kreshova, Xhane	President	Forum of Albanian Women	Macedonia
Strackova, Martha		Babylon Center in Veles	Macedonia
Stojanovska, Biljana		Babylon Center in Stip	Macedonia
Broughton, Sally	Media Officer	IOM	Macedonia
Misic, Elana	Project Officer	UNICEF	Macedonia
Tall, William	Field Coordinator	UNHCR	Macedonia
Biondi, Aldo	Correspondent	ECHO	Macedonia
Steeghs, Gerard	Acting Director, UN and IFI's Department	Ministry of Foreign Affairs	Netherlands
Cemerska, Rajna	Operations Officer	The World Bank	Macedonia
Bannon, Ian	Manager, Conflict Prevention	The World Bank	Washington, D.C.
Campeau, Lisa	Consultant	The World Bank	Washington, D.C.

Collier, Paul	Sr. Adviser	The World Bank	Washington, D.C.
Eriksson, John	Consultant	The World Bank	Washington, D.C.
Gilbert, Roy	Lead Evaluation Officer	The World Bank	Washington, D.C.
Holtzman, Steve	Lead Social Development Specialist	The World Bank	Washington, D.C.
Hubbard, Paul	Manager	The World Bank	Washington, D.C.
Jorgensen, Steen	Sector Director	The World Bank	Washington, D.C.
Kafka, Barbara	Senior Manager	The World Bank	Washington, D.C.
Kantabaze, Pamphile	Sr. Operations Officer	The World Bank	Washington, D.C.
Keller, Barbry	Operations Analyst	The World Bank	Washington, D.C.
Kuroda, Kazhuide	Sr. Knowledge Management Officer	The World Bank	Washington, D.C.
Lopes, Ana Paula	Knowledge Monitoring Specialist	The World Bank	Washington, D.C.
Meesook, Oey	Former Staff	The World Bank	Washington, D.C.
Miovic, Peter	Consultant	The World Bank	Washington, D.C.
Purcell, Randall	Sr. Partnership Specialist	The World Bank	Washington, D.C.
Scott, Colin	Sr. Social Development Specialist	The World Bank	Washington, D.C.
Sfeir-Younis, Alfredo	Sr. Adviser	The World Bank	Washington, D.C.
Tassoni Estense, Natalia	Operations Analyst	The World Bank	Washington, D.C.
Prototype Carbon Fund Case Study			
Kevin Cleaver, Sector Director, Agriculture & Rural Development Department; Kristalina Georgieva, Country Director, Russian Federation; Sushma Ganguly, Sector Manager, Agriculture & Rural Development Department			
Bianchi, Ana	Host Country Representative		Argentina
Stephens, Jean-Claude	Head of European & Industrial Affairs	Electrabel	Belgium
Searle, Juan Pedro	Host Country Representative		Chile
Manso, Paulo	Host Country Representative		Costa Rica
Pretel, Jan	Host Country Representative		Czechoslovakia
Ayala, Mauricio	Host Country Representative		El Salvador
Katagiri, Makoto	Consultant	Mitsubishi International Corp.	Japan
Koenuma, Akihiko		JBIC	Japan
Nishimura, Ikuo		TEPCO	Japan
Akumu, Grace		Climate Network	Kenya
De Jonge, Lex		Ministry of Environment	Netherlands
Rathe, Liv		Norsk Hydro/Hydro Electric	Norway
Gonzales, Alberto	Host Country Representative		Peru
Bjork, Ole		Ministry of Industry, Employment & Communications	Sweden
Apuuli, Bwango	Host Country Representative		Uganda
Nicholson, Charles		British Petroleum	United Kingdom
Santos, Luis	Host Country Representative		Uruguay
Wong, Grace		Conservation International	Washington, D.C.
Newcombe, Kenneth	Sr. Manager	The World Bank	Washington, D.C.
Heister, Johannes	Sr. Environmental Economist	The World Bank	Washington, D.C.
Bishop, Veronique	Sr. Financial Specialist	The World Bank	Washington, D.C.
Sinha, Chandra	Sr. Environmental Specialist	The World Bank	Washington, D.C.

Lecocq, Franck	Consultant	The World Bank	Washington, D.C.
Clarke, Denis	Chief Investment Officer	The World Bank	Washington, D.C.
Freestone, David	Chief Counsel	The World Bank	Washington, D.C.
Busz, Henk	Sector Manager	The World Bank	Washington, D.C.
Strek, Charlotte	Sr. Counsel	The World Bank	Washington, D.C.
Smyth, Sophie	Sr. Counsel	The World Bank	Washington, D.C.
Duvall, Thomas	Sr. Counsel	The World Bank	Washington, D.C.
Searle, Juan	Consultant	The World Bank	Washington, D.C.
Prasad, Neeraj	Sr. Operations Officer	The World Bank	Washington, D.C.
Public Private Partnership Infrastructure Advisory Facility (PPIAF) Case Study			
Anwar Ravat, Chief Administrative Officer, Infrastructure Network Core Services; Nigel Twose, Manager, Investment Climate Department			
Vasilev, Grigor	Director of Public Works	Ministry of Regional Development & Public Works	Bulgaria
Tomeva, Vania	Manager, Corporate Finance	KPMG	Bulgaria
Vatralova, Albena	Country Representative	Halcrow Group, Ltd.	Bulgaria
Buse, Dina	Head, Foreign Assistance Coordination Unit	Ministry of Economy	Latvia
Feldmane, Ieva		Public Utilities Commission	Latvia
Korna, Karina		Public Utilities Commission	Latvia
Preimate, Ilga	Deputy State Secretary	Ministry of Economy	Latvia
Steinbuka, Inna		Public Utilities Commission	Latvia
Vabale, Inese		Public Utilities Commission	Latvia
Grawe, Roger	Country Director	The World Bank	Poland
Hall, Christopher	Chief, Warsaw Office & Sr. Portfolio Manager	The World Bank	Poland
Wojciechowicz, Jacek	External Affairs Officer	The World Bank	Poland
Akinci, Cahit	International Relations and EU Coordination	Energy Market Regulatory Authority	Turkey
Aydin, Ahmet	Natural Gas Working Group	Energy Market Regulatory Authority	Turkey
Erenel, Murat	Electricity Working Group	Energy Market Regulatory Authority	Turkey
Gunay, Yusuf	President	Energy Market Regulatory Authority	Turkey
Harmanci, Mehmet	Natural Gas Working Group	Energy Market Regulatory Authority	Turkey
Ozkog, Hasan	Natural Gas Working Group	Energy Market Regulatory Authority	Turkey
Ulgen, Seckin	Electricity Working Group	Energy Market Regulatory Authority	Turkey
Pike, Tery		DFID	United Kingdom
Barbalov, Doncho	Energy & Infrastructure Officer	The World Bank	Bulgaria
de Bruyn Kops, Oscar	Country Manager	The World Bank	Bulgaria
Kondova, Galia	Research Assistant	The World Bank	Bulgaria
Kourtev, Georgi	Communications Associate	The World Bank	Bulgaria
Muir, Russel	Lead Economist	The World Bank	Washington, D.C.

Nunez-Ollero, Cynthia	Sr. Private Sector Development Spec.	The World Bank	Washington, D.C.
Schwartz, Jordan	Sr. Infrastructure Spec.	The World Bank	Washington, D.C.
Understanding Children's Work (UCW) Case Study			
Rosati, Furio	Project Coordinator	UCW	Florence
Hagemann, Frank	Sr. Policy Analyst	IPEC	Geneva
Roselaers, Frans	Director	IPEC	Geneva
Wichmand, Peter	Sr. Evaluation Officer	IPEC	Geneva
Adnane, Abdelaziz	Head, Social Sector Division	Ministry of Economy	Morocco
Bouazzaoui, M.	Director	Ministry of Education	Morocco
Benchekroun, Sabah	Deputy Secretary	Ministry of Economic Affairs	Morocco
Baddou, Yasmine	Deputy Secretary	Ministry of Labor	Morocco
Ayoub, Maie	Representative	UNICEF	Morocco
Berrada, Rajae	Representative	Child Protection Program	Morocco
Benchekroun, Malak	Program Administrator	IPEC	Morocco
Tadili, Mohamed	Director of Labor	Labor Ministry	Morocco
Belhaj, Ferid	Country Manager	The World Bank	Morocco
Allison, Christine	Lead Human Development Specialist	The World Bank	Washington, D.C.
Baudouy, Jacques	Sector Director	The World Bank	Washington, D.C.
Carvalho, Soniya	Lead Evaluation Officer	The World Bank	Washington, D.C.
Dar, Amit	Sr. Economist	The World Bank	Washington, D.C.
Fallon, Peter	Former Staff	The World Bank	Washington, D.C.
Fares, Jean	Economist	The World Bank	Washington, D.C.
Harding, David	Sr. Education Specialist	The World Bank	Washington, D.C.
Holzmann, Robert	Sector Director	The World Bank	Washington, D.C.
Kim, Bonna	Former Staff	The World Bank	Washington, D.C.
Solleveld, Leendert	Adviser	The World Bank	Washington, D.C.
Tzannatos, Zafiris	Adviser	The World Bank	Washington, D.C.
Water and Sanitation Program (WSP) Case Study			
Anwar Ravat, Chief Administrative Officer, Infrastructure Network Core Services; Nigel Twose, Manager, Investment Climate Department			
Evans, Barbara	Consultant	The World Bank	Washington, D.C.
Iyer, Parameswaran	Sr. Water & Sanitation Specialist	The World Bank	Washington, D.C.
Stottman, Walter	Manager	The World Bank	Washington, D.C.
World Links Case Study			
Bhaskar, T.M. Vijay	Commissioner for Public Instruction	State Govt. of Karnataka	India
Chauhan, Pamela	Teacher		India
Gill, Balgindar	Teacher		India
Hemareddy, N.	Principal		India
Hiremath, Dayanand			India
Jha, M.M.	Joint Secretary	Ministry of Education	India
Kapoor, Poornima	Head Teacher		India
Karadi, R.S.	Principal	Govt. Boys Jr. College	India
Krishnappa, Meera	Trainer	World Links	India
Modle, Shanker	Headmaster	Govt. High School for Girls	India
Mukerjee, Rauni	Computer Trainer		India
Satyamurthy	Deputy Director	State Government of	

		Karnataka	India
Sharma, Deepika	Sr. Manager, Pedagogy	Schoolnet India, Ltd.	India
Srinivasan, Renu	Trainer		India
Villas, Ravi	Sr. Research Officer	State Government of Karnataka	India
Pascual, Patricia	Director for Research & Policy Advocacy	Digital Philippines	Philippines
Tinio, Victoria	Director for E-Learning	Foundation for Information Technology	Philippines
Bay, Ester	Manager	Nanyan Polytechnic	Singapore
Fong, David	Manager	Nanyan Polytechnic	Singapore
Yong, Danils	Director, International Program	Nanyan Polytechnic	Singapore
Clark, Prema	Sr. Education Economist	The World Bank	India
Carlson, Samuel	Sr. Human Development Economist	The World Bank	Washington, D.C.
Hawkins, Robert	Sr. Operations Officer	The World Bank	Washington, D.C.
Leautier, Frannie	Vice President	The World Bank	Washington, D.C.
Drissel, Marie	Director, Finance & Human Resources	World Links	Washington, D.C.
Hoyer, Hans	Executive Director	World Links	
Kante, Cheick	Chief Operating Officer	World Links	
Additional World Bank & IMF Staff Consulted			
World Bank Executive Directors and Staff			
Agha, Tanwir	ED	The World Bank	Washington, D.C.
Alyahya, Yaya	ED	The World Bank	Washington, D.C.
Brookins, Carole	ED	The World Bank	Washington, D..C
Guadagni, Alieto	ED	The World Bank	Washington, D.C.
Kasekende, Louis	ED	The World Bank	Washington, D.C.
Vasudev, Chander	ED	The World Bank	Washington, D.C.
Alzetta, Gino	Alternate ED	The World Bank	Washington, D.C.
Alvarex, Jaime	Adviser to ED	The World Bank	Washington, D.C.
Olsson, Jonathan	Adviser to ED	The World Bank	Washington, D.C.
Waslander, Jacob	Sr. Adviser to ED	The World Bank	Washington, D.C.
IMF Executive Directors			
Chambrier, Alexander	ED	IMF	Washington, D.C.
Benhua, Wei	ED	IMF	Washington, D.C.
Kelkar, Vijay	Former ED	IMF	Washington, D.C.
Junguito, Roberto	ED	IMF	Washington, D.C.
Rustomjee, Cyrus	ED	IMF	Washington, D.C.
Wijnholds, J. de Beaufort	ED	IMF	Washington, D.C.
World Bank Managing Directors			
Goldstein, Jeffrey	MD	The World Bank	Washington, D.C.
Ramphele, Mamphela	MD	The World Bank	Washington, D.C.
Zhang, Shengman	MD	The World Bank	Washington, D.C.
Sandstrom, Sven	Former MD	The World Bank	Washington, D.C.
Sood, Anil	Special Adviser	The World Bank	Washington, D.C.
World Bank Senior VPs			
Bourguignon, Francois	Sr. VP	The World Bank	Washington, D.C.

Sarbib, Jean Louis	Sr. VP	The World Bank	Washington, D.C.
Stern, Nicolas	Former Sr. VP	The World Bank	Washington, D.C.
World Bank VPs			
Adams, James	Vice President	The World Bank	Washington, D.C.
Goldin, Ian	Vice President	The World Bank	Washington, D.C.
Johnson, Ian	Vice President	The World Bank	Washington, D.C.
Kusakabe, Motoo	Former VP	The World Bank	Washington, D.C.
Lamb, Geoffrey	Vice President	The World Bank	Washington, D.C.
Leautier, Frannie	Vice President	The World Bank	Washington, D.C.
Ritzen, Jozef	Former VP	The World Bank	Washington, D.C.
Shafik, Nemat	Vice President	The World Bank	Washington, D.C.
Nankani, Gobind	Regional Vice President	The World Bank	Washington, D.C.
Garg, Prem	Director, QAG	The World Bank	Washington, D.C.
World Bank Country Directors			
Carter, Michael	Country Director	The World Bank	New Delhi
Grawe, Roger	Country Director	The World Bank	Warsaw
Karlsson, Mats	Country Director	The World Bank	Accra
Lim, Edward	Former Country Director	The World Bank	New Delhi
Steer, Andrew	Country Director	The World Bank	Jakarta
Thomas, Vinod	Country Director	The World Bank	Brasilia
Von Amsberg, Joachim	Country Director	The World Bank	Manila
Wallich, Christine	Country Director	The World Bank	Dhaka
Global Programs and Partnerships & Development Grant Facility Staff			
Hubbard, Paul	Manager	The World Bank	Washington, D.C.
Kirby-Zakim, Jane	Sr. Program Officer	The World Bank	Washington, D.C.
Drewnowski, Sophia	Sr. Partnership Specialist	The World Bank	Washington, D.C.
Lu, Judy	Research Analyst	The World Bank	Washington, D.C.
Purcell, Randall	Sr. Partnership Specialist	The World Bank	Washington, D.C.
Sharma, Anju	Operations Officer	The World Bank	Washington, D.C.
Trust Fund Quality Assurance & Compliance Staff			
Zulfiqar, Arif	Director	The World Bank	Washington, D.C.
Hill, Dale	Head, TFO	The World Bank	Washington, D.C.
Cadario, Paul	Sr. Manager, TQC	The World Bank	Washington, D.C.
Corbin, Diana	Operations Officer	The World Bank	Washington, D.C.
Harper, Caroline	Lead Operations Officer	The World Bank	Washington, D.C.
Operations Evaluation Department Staff			
Ainsworth, Martha	Lead Evaluation Officer	The World Bank	Washington, D.C.
Chu, Lily	Lead Evaluation Officer	The World Bank	Washington, D.C.
Effron, Laurie	Lead Evaluation Officer	The World Bank	Washington, D.C.
Eriksson, John	Lead Evaluation Officer	The World Bank	Washington, D.C.
Galenson, Alice	Consultant	The World Bank	Washington, D.C.
Gilbert, Roy	Lead Evaluation Officer	The World Bank	Washington, D.C.
Grasson, Patrick	Adviser	The World Bank	Washington, D.C.
Gwin, Catherine	Lead Evaluation Officer	The World Bank	Washington, D.C.
Manibog, Fernando	Lead Evaluation Officer	The World Bank	Washington, D.C.

Nelson, Ridley	Consultant	The World Bank	Washington, D.C.
Pitman, Keith	Sr. Evaluation Officer	The World Bank	Washington, D.C.
Tsikata, Yvonne	Lead Evaluation Officer	The World Bank	Washington, D.C.
World Bank External Relations Staff			
Ingram, Joseph	Special Representative	The World Bank	Geneva
Zarcone, Fabrizio	Research Analyst	The World Bank	Geneva
Taylor, Isabelle	Executive Assistant	The World Bank	Geneva
Bolard, Sophie	Consultant	The World Bank	Geneva
Agerskov, Anders	Sr. Policy Adviser	The World Bank	Washington, D.C.
World Bank Legal and Operations Staff			
Duvall, Thomas	Chief Counsel	The World Bank	Washington, D.C.
Hartmann, Arna	Former Staff	The World Bank	Washington, D.C.
Jonas, Olga	Economic Adviser	The World Bank	Washington, D.C.
Mikitin, Kathleen	Sr. Auditor	The World Bank	Washington, D.C.
Smyth, Sophie	Sr. Counsel	The World Bank	Washington, D.C.
Streck, Charlotte	Sr. Counsel	The World Bank	Washington, D.C.
Stumpf, Andrea	Sr. Counsel	The World Bank	Washington, D.C.
Todd, John	Consultant	The World Bank	Washington, D.C.
Tuluy, Hasan	Director	The World Bank	Washington, D.C.
Underwood, John	Director	The World Bank	Washington, D.C.

ANNEX H: CASE STUDY SUMMARY INFORMATION

Table H.1 Phase 2 Case Study Programs at a Glance

Program	Operational start date[a]	Independent legal entity	Housed in World Bank	Corporate priorities[b] Major category
Environment & Agriculture				
1. Consultative Group on International Agricultural Research	1972	No[c]	Shared with FAO	Environmental commons
2. Global Environment Facility	1991	No[d]	No	Environmental commons
3. Multilateral Fund for the Implementation of the Montreal Protocol	1991	Yes	No	Environmental commons
4. Prototype Carbon Fund	2000	No	Yes	Environmental commons
5. Critical Ecosystem Partnership Fund	2000	No	No	Environmental commons
6. Global Water Partnership	1997	Yes	No	Environmental commons
7. Global Integrated Pest Management Facility	1996	No	No	Environmental commons
Health				
8. Special Program for Research and Training in Tropical Diseases (TDR)	Dec. 1975	No	No	Communicable diseases
9. Global Forum for Health Research	Jan. 1997	Yes	No	Communicable diseases
10. UNAIDS (Joint United Nations Program on HIV/AIDS)	Jan. 1996	Yes	No	Communicable diseases
11. Roll Back Malaria	Nov. 1998	No	No	Communicable diseases
12. Stop TB	July 1999	No	No	Communicable diseases
13. Global Alliance for Vaccines and Immunization[l]	Oct. 1999	No	No	Communicable diseases
Infrastructure				
14. Water and Sanitation Program	March 1978	No	Yes	Health
15. Energy Sector Management Assistance Program	Jan. 1982	No	Yes	Investment climate
16. Consultative Group to Assist the Poorest	Aug. 1995	No	Yes	Investment climate
17. The Information for Development Program (*info*Dev)	Sept. 1995	No	Yes	Information & knowledge
18. Public-Private Infrastructure Advisory Facility	Dec. 1999	No	Yes	Investment climate
19. Cities Alliance	Dec. 1999	No	Yes	Investment climate
Social Development & Protection				
20. Post-conflict Fund	1998	No	Yes	Empowerment, security and social inclusion
21. Understanding Children's Work	2000	No	No	Empowerment, security and social inclusion

Corporate priorities[b] / Subcategory	FY04/CY03 Program expenditures ($million)	DGF status	FY05 DGF grant ($million)	Bank trust fund	FY04 (CY03) TF contributions ($million)	Country-level TA	Retailing grants
Promoting agricultural research	395.0	Window 1	50.0	Yes	110.0	Yes	No
Biodiversity, climate change, international waters, ozone depletion, land degradation & persistent organic pollutants	387.53[e]	non-DGF	–	Yes	136.05	Yes	Yes
Biodiversity, ozone depletion & land degradation	158.6[f]	non-DGF	–	Yes	–	No	Yes
Climate change	6.5[g]	non-DGF	–	Yes	23.18	Yes	Yes
Biodiversity, ozone depletion & land degradation	20.19	Window 1	4.00	No	–	Yes	Yes
Water	10.3	Exited FY02	–	No	–	Yes	No
Biodiversity, ozone depletion & land degradation	1.33	non-DGF	–	No	–	Yes	Yes
HIV/AIDS, TB, malaria & childhood diseases	47.5[h]	Window 1	2.00	Yes	0.00[i]	Yes	Yes
Vaccines & drug development	3.07	Window 1		No	–	No	Yes
HIV/AIDS, TB, malaria & childhood diseases	95.0[j]	Window 1	4.00	No	–	Yes	No
HIV/AIDS, TB, malaria & childhood diseases	11.4	Window 2, moving to Window 1	1.00	No	–	Yes	No
HIV/AIDS, TB, malaria & childhood diseases	20.8[k]	Window 2, moving to Window 1	0.70	Yes	–	Yes	Yes
Vaccines & drug development	124.1[m]	Window 1	1.50	No	–	Yes	Yes
Access to potable water, clean air & sanitation by poor people	13.6	non-DGF	–	Yes	12,12	Yes	No
Infrastructure services to support private sector development	7.58	non-DGF	–	Yes	8.97	Yes	Yes
Financial sector reform	12.67	Window 1	5.52	Yes	6.27	Yes	Yes
Redressing the digital divide	6.07	Window 1	2.50	Yes	n.a.	Yes	Yes
Regulatory reform & competition policy	15.61	Window 2	2.00	Yes	17.15	Yes	Yes
Support to both urban & rural development	13.25	Window 2	1.70	Yes	13.67	Yes	Yes
Social risk management	10.6	Window 1	8.00	Yes	0.30	Yes	Yes
Social risk management	0.56	Window 2	.10	No	–	No	No

(*Table continues on the following page.*)

Table H.1 Phase 2 Case Study Programs at a Glance (*continued*)

Program	Operational start date[a]	Independent legal entity	Housed in World Bank	Corporate priorities[b] Major category
Trade & Finance				
22. Integrated Framework	1997	No	No	Trade & integration
23. Financial Sector Assessment Program	May 1999	No	Shared with IMF	International financial architecture
24. Financial Sector Reform & Strengthening	July 2002	No	Shared with DFID	International financial architecture
Information & Knowledge				
25. Global Development Network	Dec. 1999	Yes	No	Information & knowledge
26. World Links for Development	1998	Yes	No	Education

a. Refers to the Bank's fiscal year (July to June) unless otherwise specified.

b. As indicated on the Partnership Approval and Tracking System (PATS) form. This refers to the five Global Public Good Priorities and the five Corporate Advocacy Priorities that were established in the Strategic Directions Paper for FY02-04, March 28, 2001.

c. While the CGIAR System as a whole is not an independent legal entity, the 16 international agricultural research centers are legal entities.

d. While the GEF is physically housed in a World Bank building, it has its own management structure that is independent of the Bank's management.

e. Includes GEF administrative expenses, fees to implementing agencies and investment grants to recipient countries.

f. Includes MLF secretariat expenses, fees to implementing agencies and investment grants to recipient countries.

g. Includes administrative expenses plus capital grants (emissions reductions) of $295,000 in FY02 and $918,000 in FY03.

h. $95.2 million for 2002 and 2003.

i. Bank-administered trust fund established in FY03.

j. $190.0 million for 2002 and 2003.

k. Includes $5.6 million disbursed by the Global Drug Facility in 2002 and $15.6 million in 2003.

l. The Vaccine Fund is an independent legal entity – a 501 (29) non-profit corporation under US law.

m. Includes $14.5 million expensed by GAVI and $109.6 million disbursed by the Vaccine Fund.

n. Based on a World Bank share of 45 percent. Precise IMF expenditures on FSAP are not known.

o. The FY03 application was deferred to FY04 and the uncommitted FY02 balance was carried over to FY03.

Corporate priorities[b] / Subcategory	FY04/CY03 Program expenditures ($million)	DGF status	FY05 DGF grant ($million)	Bank trust fund	FY04 (CY03) TF contributions ($million)	Country level TA	Retailing grants
Market access	2.71	Window 2	-	No	–	Yes	No
Financial stability	10.46[n]	non-DGF	–	No	–	Yes	No
Financial stability	4.64	Window 2	0.60[o]	Yes	13.0	Yes	Yes
Understanding development & poverty reduction	8.67	Window 1	4.00	Yes	,5	Yes	Yes
Building human capacity for the knowledge economy	6.5	Window 2	1.52	Yes	0.00	Yes	No

Table H.2 Goals and Development Objectives of Case Study Programs

	Mission/goal
Environment & Agriculture	
1. Consultative Group on International Agricultural Research	To contribute to food security and poverty eradication in developing countries through research, partnership, capacity building and policy support, promoting sustainable agricultural development based on the environmentally sound management of natural resources. To achieve sustainable food security and reduce poverty in developing countries through scientific research and research-related activities in the fields of agriculture, forestry, fisheries, policy and environment.
2. Global Environment Facility	To assist the developing countries in meeting their obligation of global environment protection, particularly in relation to the various international conventions (e.g., the Convention on Biological Diversity, the United Nations Framework Convention on Climate Change, and Convention to Combat Desertification), and other treaties and agreements to reach common goals (such as the Montreal Protocol of the Vienna Convention on Ozone Layer Depleting Substances) and a mosaic of regional and international water agreements.
3. Multilateral Fund for the Implementation of the Montreal Protocol	To provide a financial mechanism to assist developing countries in meeting the incremental costs of compliance with the Montreal Protocol on Substances that Deplete the Ozone Layer, delivered via grants or on a concessional basis.
4. Prototype Carbon Fund	To pioneer the market for project-based greenhouse-gas emission reductions within the framework of the Kyoto Protocol and to contribute to sustainable development.
5. Critical Ecosystem Partnership Fund	To prevent species extinction in biodiversity hotspots by advancing conservation of the Earth's biologically richest and most threatened areas.

Development objectives
To mobilize cutting-edge science to reduce hunger and poverty, improve human nutrition and health, and protect the environment. To conduct both strategic and applied research on the entire range of problems affecting agricultural productivity and to link these problems to broader concerns about poverty reduction, sustainable management of natural resources, protection of biodiversity, and rural development. To conduct research to improve the productivity of tropical agriculture, focusing on: • Higher-yielding food crops and more productive livestock, fish, and trees • Improved farming systems that are environmentally benign • Better policies • Enhanced scientific capacities in developing countries. To advocate science-based approaches to solving some of the world's most pressing developmental problems.
To establish a mechanism for international cooperation for the purpose of providing new and additional grant and concessional funding to meet the agreed incremental costs of measures to achieve agreed global benefits in the following focal areas: • Biodiversity • Climate change • Degradation of international waters • Ozone depletion • Persistent organic pollutants • Land degradation
To meet, on a grant or concessional basis as appropriate, and according to criteria to be decided upon by the Parties, the agreed incremental costs. To finance clearinghouse functions to: • Assist Parties operating under paragraph 1 of Article 5, through country-specific studies and other technical cooperation, to identify their needs for cooperation • Facilitate technical cooperation to meet these identified needs • Distribute, as provided for in Article 9 of the Protocol, information and relevant materials, and hold workshops, training sessions, and other related activities for the benefit of Parties that are developing countries • Facilitate and monitor other multilateral, regional, and bilateral cooperation available to Parties that are developing countries To finance the secretarial services of the Multilateral Fund and related support costs.
High-quality emission reductions – to show how project-based greenhouse gas emission reductions transactions can promote and contribute to sustainable development and lower the cost of compliance with the Kyoto Protocol. *Knowledge dissemination* – to provide the parties to the UNFCCC, the private sector, and other interested parties with an opportunity to "learn by doing" in the development of policies, rules, and business processes for the achievement of emission reductions under the Clean Development Mechanism and Joint Implementation. *Public-private partnership* – to demonstrate how the World Bank can work in partnership with the public and private sectors to mobilize new resources for its borrowing member countries while addressing global environmental problems through market-based mechanisms.
To provide strategic coordination and assistance in the form of grants to support in situ conservation. To address biodiversity loss in targeted areas within each hotspot by: • Gazetting additional protected areas • Improving the management of existing protected areas • Consolidating fragmented ecosystems through the creation of corridors.

(*Table continues on the following page.*)

Table H.2 Goals and Development Objectives of Case Study Programs (*continued*)

	Mission/goal
6. Global Water Partnership	To support countries in the sustainable development of their water resources.
7. Global Integrated Pest Management Facility	To assist interested governments and NGOs to initiate, develop, and expand Integrated Pest Management (IPM) programs that aim to reduce pesticide use and associated negative impact on health and environment, while increasing production and profits through improved crop and pest management.
Health, Nutrition, & Population	
8. Special Program for Research and Training in Tropical Diseases (TDR)	To help coordinate, support, and influence global efforts to combat a portfolio of major diseases that affect the poor and disadvantaged.
9. Global Forum for Health Research	The *vision* of the Global Forum is a world in which health research is recognized as a global public good and a critical input in health system development; where priority is given, at the global and national levels, to the study of those factors with the largest impact on people's health and to the effective delivery of research outcomes for the benefit of all people, particularly the poor.

Development objectives
To achieve global water security as a contribution to eliminating poverty, improving the well-being of mankind, and protecting natural resources. Toward achieving the above main objective: • To establish partnerships of beneficiaries and the stakeholders • To build strategic alliances for action • To promote good practice in integrated water resource management • To develop and facilitate actions at the various levels of water partnership (area, basin, country, regional, and global).
To create awareness and an enabling environment for IPM through: • Study tours to successful ongoing IPM programs • Exchange visits and briefings among policymakers, development agencies, and NGOs. To help in the development of pilot field programs by: • Identifying appropriate IPM expertise • Preparing IPM curriculum and operational guidelines • Enhancing national capabilities in IPM training and policy • Assisting donors and lending institutions • Facilitating government-potential donor contacts. To access other programs and information by: • Facilitating effects of investments in IPM (local/national) • Strengthening networking and collaboration (local/national/regional) • Scientific research and strategies. To establish technical and policy IPM linkages by: • Facilitating access and information exchange among farmers' groups, NGOs, governments, international development agencies, etc. • Studying national and donor policy reform • Assisting in finding new solutions to field and policy problems • Promoting demand-driven research • Carrying out and commissioning analytical studies • Analyzing pilot projects to improve the quality of IPM.
Research and Development • To improve existing, and develop new, approaches for preventing, diagnosing, treating, and controlling neglected infectious diseases • Readily integrating into the health services of countries where these diseases are endemic and focusing on the health problems of the poor. *Training and Strengthening* • To strengthen the capacity of countries where these diseases are endemic to undertake the research required for developing and implementing these new and improved disease control approaches.
• Contribute to the efforts to measure the 10/90 gap, monitor developments and disseminate pertinent information regarding this gap and its causes and consequences. • Support the development of priority-setting methodologies to identify research priority areas, including in sectors other than health which have a crucial role to play in the promotion of health. • Identify and debate critical, controversial and burning issues affecting the 10/90 gap in health research.

(*Table continues on the following page.*)

Table H.2 Goals and Development Objectives of Case Study Programs (*continued*)

	Mission/goal
	Its *central objective* is to help correct the 10/90 gap in health research and focus research efforts on the health problems of the poor, by bringing together key actors and creating a movement for analysis and debate on health research priorities, the allocation of resources, public-private partnerships, and access of all people to the outcomes of health research.
10. UNAIDS (Joint United Nations Program on HIV/AIDS)	As the main advocate for global action, UNAIDS leads, strengthens, and supports an expanded response to the epidemic. This response has four goals: • To prevent the spread of HIV • To provide care and support for those infected and affected by the disease • To reduce the vulnerability of individuals and communities to HIV/AIDS • To alleviate the socioeconomic and human impact of the epidemic.
11. Roll Back Malaria	To halve the world's malaria burden by 2010.
12. Stop TB	To increase access, security, and support to: • Ensure that every tuberculosis patient has access to treatment and a cure • Protect vulnerable populations from tuberculosis • Reduce the social and economic toll that tuberculosis exerts on families, communities, and nations.
13. Global Alliance for Vaccines and Immunization	The Global Alliance for Vaccines and Immunization is a public-private partnership committed to one goal: saving children's lives and people's health through the widespread use of vaccines. The GAVI partners created the Vaccine Fund to provide long-term financing to the world's poorest countries to strengthen health systems and introduce new and underused vaccines
Infrastructure & Private Sector Development	
14. Water and Sanitation Program	To alleviate poverty by helping the poor in developing countries gain sustained access to safe drinking water and sanitation. To work with partners in the field to seek innovative solutions to the obstacles faced by poor communities and to strive to be a valued source of advice in order to achieve widespread adoption of these solutions.

Development objectives
• Give special consideration to the health problems of the poor. • Ensure that gender analysis is consistently and systematically applied to all work on the 10/90 gap. • Be a platform for debate and synthesis review of efforts in the field of research capacity strengthening, paying special attention to the needs of the national health research systems. • Support concerted efforts and the development of networks/partnerships (between public sector, private commercial sector, and civil society organizations) in the priority sectors of health research, when appropriate and when the benefits of joint action are larger than the sum of individual actions.
The partnership aims to build stronger political commitment in all sectors of society, to promote a sense of urgency among the public and create a more supportive environment, while providing the political and strategic guidance to enhance the coherence and coordination of the global response to HIV/AIDS by providing: • Leadership and advocacy for effective action on the epidemic • Strategic information to guide efforts against AIDS worldwide • Tracking, monitoring, and evaluation of the epidemic and of responses to it • Civil society engagement and partnership development • Mobilization of resources to support an effective response.
Provision of an enabling environment (e.g., political commitment; development and implementation of appropriate recruitment and career policies; provision of facilities and resources; strengthened training institutions). Intensification of training and retraining of personnel. Technical support mechanisms (e.g., information, communication, and supply systems to support trained personnel, supervision, monitoring and evaluation).
To expand the current strategy—DOTS—so that all people with TB have access to effective diagnosis and treatment. To adapt this strategy to meet the emerging challenges of HIV and TB drug resistance. To improve existing tools by developing new diagnostics, new drugs, and a new vaccine. To strengthen the Global Partnership to Stop TB so that proven TB-control strategies are effectively applied.
To fulfill its mission of protecting children of all nations and of all socioeconomic levels against vaccine-preventable diseases, GAVI has established six strategies: • Improve access to sustainable immunization services • Expand the use of all existing safe and cost-effective vaccines, and promote delivery of other appropriate interventions at immunization contacts • Support the national and international accelerated disease control targets for vaccine-preventable diseases • Accelerate the development and introduction of new vaccines and technologies • Accelerate research and development efforts for vaccines needed primarily in developing countries. • Make immunization coverage a centerpiece in international development efforts.
To impact its direct clients (central governments, municipal agencies, local authorities, NGOs, community organizations, private service providers, and external support agencies) through the adoption of improved sector management policies and practices, and creation of more capacity to implement these policies and practices for poor people on the ground.

(*Table continues on the following page.*)

Table H.2 Goals and Development Objectives of Case Study Programs (*continued*)

	Mission/goal
15. Energy Sector Management Assistance Program	To promote the role of energy in poverty reduction and economic growth in an environmentally responsible manner. To contribute to the achievement of internationally agreed development goals in low-income, emerging, and transition economies.
16. Consultative Group to Assist the Poorest	To help build financial systems that work for the poor, providing large numbers of people with diverse financial services through a wide range of organizations.
17. The Information for Development Program (*info*Dev)	To promote innovative projects on the use of information and communication technology (ICT) for economic and social development, with a special emphasis on the needs of the poor in developing countries.
18. Public-Private Infrastructure Advisory Facility	To help eliminate poverty and achieve sustainable development in developing countries by facilitating private sector involvement in infrastructure. To help developing countries improve the quality of their infrastructure through private sector involvement.
19. Cities Alliance	To marshal the resources, experience, and knowledge of its partners to focus on two priorities for action: • *Cities Without Slums*, through citywide and nationwide upgrading of low-income settlements to improve the livelihoods of the urban poor • *City Development Strategies*, aimed at formulating a broad consensus on a vision and a set of priorities for city actions. To foster new tools, practical approaches, and knowledge sharing in these two areas, so as to create a new coherence of effort to help realize the rich promise of what well-managed cities can achieve.
Social Development & Protection	
20. Post-conflict Fund	To position the Bank, through constructive engagement, in such countries where normal instruments and budget provisions cannot apply.

Development objectives
As a global technical assistance agency: • To help build consensus and provide policy advice on sustainable energy development to governments of developing countries and economies in transition. • To contribute to the transfer of technology and knowledge in energy sector management and the delivery of modern energy services to the poor.
To support the development of financial systems that work for the poor, by improving the capacity of microfinance institutions to deliver flexible, high-quality financial services to the poor on a sustainable basis. The five strategic priorities for CGAP III (2003–08) are as follows: • Fostering a diversity of financial institutions that serve the poor; • Promoting a broader range of financial services available to the poor; • Improving the availability and the quality of information on the performance of microfinance providers; • Promoting a sound policy, legal and regulatory framework for microfinance; • Improving aid effectiveness in microfinance.
To help developing economies fully benefit from modern information systems. To encourage policies that increase connectivity, and especially that increase the access of the poor to ICT. To promote and facilitate strategies that exploit information technologies for poverty alleviation and sustainable development, including the preparation and implementation of activities at the sector, subsector and multisector levels. To build human capacity, consensus and networks of interest needed for the introduction and utilization of new ICT in developing countries. To pilot, demonstrate and learn from innovative applications of ICT. Through partnerships with governments, multilateral and bilateral donors, private sector corporations and associations, research institutions, and not-for-profit organizations, to coordinate the efforts of parties with relevant interest in fostering information-based services in emerging economies.
To complement and reinforce donor support to developing countries in the private infrastructure area, and to increase the volume and effectiveness of this support by: • Mobilizing and leveraging donor resources. • Exploiting the expertise and economies of scale and scope available from an integrated, multi-donor program. • Promoting the exchange of lessons of experience between sectors, regions and donors. • Facilitating coordination between bilateral and multilateral programs addressing the same concerns.
As a global partnership, the Cities Alliance aims: • To improve the quality of urban development cooperation and urban lending • To strengthen the impact of grant-funded urban development cooperation • To expand the level of resources reaching the urban poor, by increasing the coherence of effort of existing programs and sharpening the focus on scaling up successful approaches • To provide a structured vehicle for advancing collective know-how.
To provide investment grants that focus on the restoration of the lives and livelihoods of war-affected populations, with a premium on: • Innovation (new approaches to conflict work) • Partnership (donors and executing agencies)

(*Table continues on the following page.*)

Table H.2 Goals and Development Objectives of Case Study Programs (*continued*)

	Mission/goal
21. Understanding Children's Work	To help accelerate the elimination of child labor • In countries where progress in the fight against child labor has been relatively slow • In lagging areas in countries that are otherwise successful in reducing the prevalence o child labor.
Trade & Finance 22. Integrated Framework	To help least-developed countries integrate better into the multilateral trading system in order to enhance their ability to participate in and benefit from the system. To assist least-developed countries to improve their export performance in order to accelerate their economic growth and reduce poverty.
23. Financial Sector Assessment Program	To promote the soundness of financial systems in member countries in order to contribute to national and international financial stability and growth. To help build stronger and more diversified financial systems capable of absorbing increased shocks in order to reduce the likelihood of financial crises and mitigate their damage.
24. Financial Sector Reform & Strengthening	To help strengthen financial systems in low-income countries and middle-income countries so that the financial systems of such countries may make a strong and positive contributio to growth and poverty reduction.

Development objectives
• Leveraging resources (through a variety of funding arrangements). To provide other grants that have strategic positioning value for the Bank and its partners, including: • Watching briefs on countries in conflict • Early assessment, planning, and piloting of reconstruction activities • A small number of capacity-building and action research activities.
To develop a common analytical framework for understanding and studying child labor and assessing the impact of government policies in the area. To improve data collection, data analysis, and research on child labor. To enhance country capacity in child labor data collection and research. To improve impact assessments of child labor interventions. To strengthen and disseminate tools and methods for addressing child labor by: • Developing common methodologies for child labor data collection and analysis, including development of a data bank of statistics to facilitate analysis • Working with local participants to carry out intensive studies on child labor in selected countries, resulting in country-specific recommendations to address the problem • Conducting training programs to enhance local capabilities in data collection and analysis, policy analysis, and intervention assessment.
To provide technical assistance to help least-developed countries: • Meet their WTO requirements and ensure the compatibility of the countries' laws with WTO commitments. • Devise strategies to benefit from opportunities resulting from the Uruguay Round agreements, which had placed a heavy administrative burden on LDCs to ensure that their trade regimes conformed to agreements. • Analyze trade policies and problems facing the external sector. To strengthen, streamline, and improve the efficiency of trade-related technical assistance by reducing donor overlap, increasing synergies, and improving coordination among the six international agency partners. To enhance the coherence of advice provided on trade policy and increase its acceptability.
To identify the strengths and vulnerabilities of a country's financial system in order to reduce the potential for a financial crisis. To determine how key sources of financial risks are being managed. To help prioritize policy responses. To provide a foundation for financial sector technical assistance programs by ascertaining the financial sector's developmental and technical assistance needs. To emphasize prevention and mitigation, rather than crisis resolution. For the IMF and World Bank: • To optimize scarce expert resources, reduce duplication of efforts, and provide more uniform advice in financial sector work. • To cooperate more closely in assisting countries reduce the likelihood and/or severity of financial crises.
To facilitate systematic follow-up of FSAP and ROSC recommendations in response to country needs and provide support to eligible countries strengthening their financial systems and implementing standards and codes in advance of FSAPs or ROSCs, in both cases, by funding the provision of technical assistance to support policy implementation and dialogue in the areas of financial sector regulation, supervision and development, including, but not limited to: • Financial system reform • Financial sector legal, regulatory & supervisory frameworks

(*Table continues on the following page.*)

Table H.2 Goals and Development Objectives of Case Study Programs (*continued*)

	Mission/goal
Information & Knowledge	
25. Global Development Network	To work together to address the problems of national and regional development.
26. World Links for Development	To link secondary school students and teachers around the world via the internet, in order to improve educational opportunities, develop information technology skills, facilitate cultural understanding, and promote broad-based support for economic development.

Development objectives
• Banking systems • Capital markets • Payment systems • Corporate governance • Accounting and auditing • Insolvency regimes • Debt markets and management • Insurance/other collective investment schemes, including pensions • Market integrity and financial crime (anti-money laundering) • Financial systems diversification (development of non-bank financial institutions and new market instruments). To serve as an information exchange on the availability of financial and human resources to participate in projects and build an information base for countries and donors. To promote better coordination in the delivery of technical assistance and capacity building. To mobilize additional resources from the international community directed toward implementation of initiatives undertaken by FIRST. To support research on and the dissemination of information about best practices and useful tools in financial sector reform and development in low-income and middle-income countries. To work with international standard-setting bodies and other relevant partners to broaden the base of providers supporting countries' efforts to implement standards and codes in accordance with FSAP/ROSC recommendations and strengthen their financial systems.
To support multidisciplinary research in social sciences. To promote the generation of local knowledge in developing and transition countries. To produce policy-relevant knowledge on a global scale. To build research capacity to advance development and alleviate poverty. To facilitate knowledge sharing among researchers and policymakers. To disseminate development knowledge to the public and policymakers.
To establish sustainable, educational on-line communities for students and teachers around the world, in order to improve educational opportunities, facilitate cultural understanding across nations help develop skills needed for the knowledge-based global economy. To promote the application of information technology for economic and social development. To provide training of trainers and teachers for the purposes of integrating technology as a learning tool in the classroom. To contribute to initiatives that improve education, health, and employment and that reduce poverty in developing countries.

Table H.3 Governance and Management Arrangements of Case Study Programs

Classification Scheme

- **I. Line management within the Bank**
  - **A. Standard multidonor trust fund (Post-conflict Fund)**
  - **B. Programmatic trust fund**
  - **C. Carefully coordinated parallel partner activities (FSAP)**
- **II. Secretariat inside the Bank**
  - **A. Bank as lead partner (Prototype Carbon Fund, WSP, ESMAP, CGAP, *info*Dev, PPIAF, Cities Alliance)**
  - **B. Independent governance structure (GEF)**
- **III. Secretariat functions shared between the Bank and an external organization (CGIAR, FIRST)**
- **IV. Secretariat inside external organization**
  - **A. External organization as lead partner (CEPF, Global IPM Facility, RBM, Stop TB, UCW, IF)**
  - **B. Independent governance structure (GAVI, TD**
- **V. Independent external entity**
  - **A. Not a legal entity**
  - **B. Legal entity (MLF, Global Forum, GWP, UNAID**
  - **C. Legal entity with close identification with th Bank (GDN, World Links)**

Phase 2 Case Study Programs: Models of Governance and Management Arrangements

Program (and size)[a]	I. Bank line management			II. Internal secretariat		III. Shared secretariat
	A	B	C	A	B	
Environment & Agriculture						
1. Consultative Group on International Agricultural Research ($395 million)						X
2. Global Environment Facility ($387.53 million)					X	
3. Multilateral Fund for the Implementation of the Montreal Protocol ($158.6 million)						
4. Prototype Carbon Fund ($6.5 million)				X		

IV. External secretariat		V. Independent external entity			
A	B	A	B	C	Comments
					• World Bank is the legal entity[b] • Program does not have a written charter • CGIAR secretariat in Bank, Science Council secretariat in FAO, and 16 centers (14 in developing countries) • Staff are Bank, FAO and Center employees, respectively • No agreed annual replenishments • Bank policies apply to funds channeled through Bank
					• World Bank is the legal entity • Program is implementing international conventions • GEF Secretariat in Bank, but with an independent governing council to whom CEO reports • UNDP, UNEP and World Bank are implementing agencies • GEF staff are Bank employees • Bank personnel and procurement policies apply to funds channeled through the Bank, i.e., the secretariat and Bank-implemented GEF portfolio
			X		• MLF is the legal entity – an intergovernmental organization under Canadian law • Program is implementing an international convention • Secretariat in Montreal, cost-shared between UNEP and the Government of Canada • UNDP, UNEP, UNIDO and World Bank are implementing agencies • MLF staff are MLF employees • UNEP personnel and procurement policies apply
					• World Bank is the legal entity • Secretariat in Bank • Prototype Carbon Fund staff are Bank employees • Bank's personnel and procurement policies apply

(*Table continues on the following page.*)

Table H.3 Governance and Management Arrangements of Case Study Programs (*continued*)

Program (and size)[a]	I. Bank line management A	I. Bank line management B	I. Bank line management C	II. Internal secretariat A	II. Internal secretariat B	III. Shared secretariat
5. Critical Ecosystem Partnership Fund ($20.19 million)						
6. Global Water Partnership ($10.25 million)						
7. Global Integrated Pest Management Facility ($1.33 million)						
Health						
8. Special Program for Research and Training in Tropical Diseases (TDR) ($47.5 million)						
9. Global Forum for Health Research ($3.07 million)						
10. UNAIDS (Joint United Nations Program on HIV/AIDS) ($95.0 million)						
11. Roll Back Malaria ($11.4 million)						

IV. External secretariat		V. Independent external entity			
A	B	A	B	C	Comments
X					• Conservation International (CI) is the legal entity – an NGO under U.S. law. • Secretariat in CI (Washington, D.C.). • Bank safeguard and procurement policies apply. • CI's administrative management practices apply to management and disbursement of grants.
			X		• GWP is the legal entity—an intergovernmental organization under Swedish law. • Secretariat in Stockholm (not in SIDA)—initially located in World Bank. • GWP staff are GWP employees. • GWP personnel and procurement policies apply.
X					• FAO is the legal entity. • Program has a Program Document (signed by cosponsors). • Secretariat in FAO (Rome). • GIF staff are FAO employees. • FAO personnel and procurement policies apply.
	X				• Although WHO is the legal executing agency, TDR has an independent governance structure and external chair. • Program has a written MOU (first adopted in 1978, amended in 1988, changes proposed in 2003). • Secretariat in Geneva (moved physically out of WHO headquarters in Oct. 2002). Joint Coordinating Board (JCB) with 31 members is the top governing body. • Scientific and Technical Advisory Council (15–18 members) meets annually. • TDR staff are WHO employees; TDR Director appointed by the WHO Director-General. • WHO personnel and procurement policies apply.
			X		• Global Forum is the legal entity—an NGO under Swiss law. • Secretariat in Geneva. • GF staff are GF employees. • GF personnel and procurement policies apply.
			X		• UNAIDS is the legal entity—a U.N. specialized agency with its own governing body, created by U.N. ECOSOC resolution. • Program has a written charter. • Secretariat in Geneva. • UNAIDS staff are UNAIDS employees. • UNAIDS personnel and procurement policies apply.
X					• WHO is the legal entity. • Program has a written charter. • Secretariat in WHO.

(*Table continues on the following page.*)

Table H.3 Governance and Management Arrangements of Case Study Programs (*continued*)

Program (and size)[a]	I. Bank line management			II. Internal secretariat		III. Shared secretariat
	A	B	C	A	B	
12. Stop TB ($20.8 million)						
13. Global Alliance for Vaccines and Immunization ($124.1 million)						
Infrastructure						
14. Water and Sanitation Program ($12.4 million)				X		
15. Energy Sector Management Assistance Program ($7.58 million)				X		
16. Consultative Group to Assist the Poorest ($12.67 million)				X		
17. The Information for Development Program (*info*Dev) ($8.90 million)				X		
18. Public-Private Infrastructure Advisory Facility ($15.61 million)				X		

IV. External secretariat		V. Independent external entity			
A	**B**	**A**	**B**	**C**	**Comments**
					• RBM staff are WHO employees. • WHO personnel and procurement policies apply.
X					• WHO is the legal entity. • Program has a written charter. • Secretariat in WHO. • Stop TB staff are WHO employees. • WHO personnel and procurement policies apply.
	X				• Although UNICEF is the legal entity, GAVI has an independent governance structure and external chair. • Program has a written charter. • GAVI Secretariat housed in UNICEF. • GAVI staff are UNICEF employees. • UNICEF personnel and procurement policies apply. • The Vaccine Fund, the GAVI finance mechanism, is an independent charitable body under U.S. law with its own governance structure.
					• World Bank is the legal entity. • Program has a written charter. • Secretariat in World Bank. • WSP staff are Bank employees. • Bank personnel and procurement policies apply.
					• World Bank is the legal entity. • Secretariat in World Bank. • ESMAP staff are Bank employees. • Bank personnel and procurement policies apply.
					• World Bank is the legal entity. • Program has a written charter. • Secretariat in World Bank. • CGAP staff are Bank employees. • Bank personnel and procurement policies apply
					• World Bank is the legal entity. • Program has a written charter. • Secretariat in World Bank. • *info*Dev staff are Bank employees. • Bank personnel and procurement policies apply.
					• World Bank is the legal entity. • Program has a written charter. • Secretariat in World Bank. • PPIAF staff are Bank employees. • Bank personnel and procurement policies apply.

(*Table continues on the following page.*)

Table H.3 Governance and Management Arrangements of Case Study Programs (*continued*)

Program (and size)[a]	I. Bank line management			II. Internal secretariat		III. Shared secretariat
	A	B	C	A	B	
19. Cities Alliance ($13.25 million)				X		
Social Development & Protection						
20. Post-conflict Fund ($10.60 million)	X					
21. Understanding Children's Work ($0.56 million)						
Trade & Finance						
22. Integrated Framework ($2.71 million)						
23. Financial Sector Assessment Program ($10.46 million)			X			
24. Financial Sector Reform & Strengthening ($4.64 million)						X
Information & Knowledge						
25. Global Development Network ($18.67 million)						

IV. External secretariat		V. Independent external entity			
A	B	A	B	C	Comments
					• World Bank is the legal entity. • Program has a written charter. • Secretariat in World Bank. • Cities Alliance staff are Bank employees. • Bank personnel and procurement policies apply.
					• World Bank is the legal entity and the only partner at the governance level. • Program does not have a written charter. • Secretariat located in Bank. • Post-conflict Fund staff are Bank employees. • Bank personnel and procurement policies apply.
X					• UNICEF is the legal entity. • MOU has remained in draft form over the life of the program. • Secretariat located in Florence.
X					• WTO is the legal entity. • Secretariat located in WTO. • UNDP manages the trust fund and World Bank is the principal implementing agency. • IF staff are WTO employees.
					• World Bank and IMF are the legal entities. • Joint IMF-Bank program, coordinated through an Interagency Financial Sector Liaison Committee. • Staff are Bank and IMF employees. • Bank and IMF personnel and procurement policies apply.
					• Program has a written charter. • Management Unit is located in London and Coordination Unit is located in World Bank. • Staff are employees of their respective organizations. • Respective personnel and procurement policies apply.
				X	• GDN is the legal entity—an NGO under U.S. law. • Spun off from the World Bank. • Program has a written charter. • Secretariat presently located in Washington, D.C., but moving to New Delhi. • 11 regional research networks are implementing agencies for regional activities. • GDN staff are GDN employees. • GDN personnel and procurement policies apply.

(*Table continues on the following page.*)

Table H.3 Governance and Management Arrangements of Case Study Programs (*continued*)

Program (and size)[a]	I. Bank line management A	I. Bank line management B	I. Bank line management C	II. Internal secretariat A	II. Internal secretariat B	III. Shared secretariat
26. World Links for Development ($6.52 million)						

a. FY04 or Calendar Year 2003 expenditures in parentheses. For the following cases, updated audited data were not readily available so the previous fiscal or calendar year expenditures were used: Global Integrated Pest Management Facility, Water and Sanitation Program, The Information for Development Program, Integrated Framework for Trade-Related Technical Assistance.

b. While the World Bank is the legal entity at the system level, the 16 international agricultural research centers are their own independent legal entities.

IV. External secretariat		V. Independent external entity			
A	B	A	B	C	Comments
				X	• World Links is the legal entity—an NGO under U.S. law. • Spun off from the World Bank. • Program does not have a written charter. • Secretariat in Washington, D.C. • Staff are World Links employees. • Own personnel and procurement policies apply.

Table H.4 World Bank's Roles in Case Study Programs

Program	Founder or co-founder	Chair of governing body	Member of governing body	Housed in World Bank
Environment & Agriculture				
1. Consultative Group on International Agricultural Research	Yes	Yes	Yes	Shared with FA
2. Global Environment Facility	Yes	No	No	No[e]
3. Multilateral Fund for the Implementation of the Montreal Protocol	No	No	No	No
4. Prototype Carbon Fund	Yes	Yes	Yes	Yes
5. Critical Ecosystem Partnership Fund	Yes	Yes	Yes	No
6. Global Water Partnership	Yes	No	Yes	No
7. Global Integrated Pest Management Facility	Yes	No	Yes	No
Health				
8. Special Program for Research and Training in Tropical Diseases (TDR)	Yes	No	Yes	No
9. Global Forum for Health Research	No	No	Yes	No
10. UNAIDS (Joint United Nations Program on HIV/AIDS)	Yes	No	Yes	No
11. Roll Back Malaria	Yes	No	Yes	No
12. Stop TB	Yes	No	Yes	No
13. Global Alliance for Vaccines and Immunization	Yes	No	Yes	No
Infrastructure				
14. Water and Sanitation Program	Yes	Yes	Yes	Yes
15. Energy Sector Management Assistance Program	Yes	Yes	Yes	Yes
16. Consultative Group to Assist the Poorest	Yes	Yes	Yes	Yes
17. The Information for Development Program (*info*Dev)	Yes	Yes	Yes	Yes
18. Public-Private Infrastructure Advisory Facility	Yes	Yes	Yes	Yes
19. Cities Alliance	Yes	Yes	Yes	Yes
Social Development & Protection				
20. Post-conflict Fund	Yes	Yes	Yes	Yes
21. Understanding Children's Work	Yes	–	–	No
Trade & Finance				
22. Integrated Framework	Yes	No	Yes	No
23. Financial Sector Assessment Program	Yes	–	–	Shared with IM
24. Financial Sector Reform & Strengthening	Yes	Yes	Yes	Shared with DF
Information & Knowledge				
25. Global Development Network	Yes	No	Yes	No
26. World Links for Development	Yes	No	No	No

a. In the case of in-house programs, not including secretariat staff—only if the Bank's operational staff outside the secretariat are involved in supervision or implementation of program activities, typically on a cross-support basis.

b. Financial contributions to the program itself, not including Bank budgetary resources spent on oversight and liaison activities.

c. Involves responsibility for oversight and management of how the trust fund resources are utilized.

d. The World Bank takes the initiative to organize meetings and conferences in the sector on issues related to but outside the scope of the program in order to advocate change, reach consensus and/or mobilize resources with respect to emerging issues in the sector.

e. While the GEF is physically housed in a World Bank building, it has its own management structure that is independent of the Bank's management.

Implementing agency[a]	Funding[b]	TF trustee	TF manager[c]	Lender to the sector	Convener of initiatives in the sector[d]
No	DGF	Yes	No	Yes	Yes
Yes	No	Yes	No	Yes	Yes
Yes	No	Yes	Yes	Yes	No
Yes	No	Yes	Yes	Yes	Yes
No	DGF	No	No	Yes	Yes
No	No	No	No	Yes	Yes
No	BB	No	No	Yes	No
No	DGF	No	No	Yes	Yes
No	DGF	No	No	Yes	Yes
No	DGF	No	No	Yes	Yes
No	DGF	No	No	Yes	Yes
No	DGF	Yes	No	Yes	Yes
No	DGF	No	No	Yes	Yes
No	BB	Yes	Yes	Yes	Yes
Yes	BB	Yes	Yes	Yes	Yes
No	DGF	Yes	Yes	Yes	Yes
Yes	BB, DGF	Yes	Yes	Yes	Yes
Yes	BB, DGF	Yes	Yes	Yes	Yes
Yes	DGF	Yes	Yes	Yes	Yes
Yes	DGF	Yes	Yes	Yes	No
Yes	DGF	No	No	Yes	No
Yes	DGF	No	No	Yes	Yes
Yes	BB	No	No	Yes	Yes
Yes	DGF	Yes	Yes	Yes	Yes
No	DGF	Yes	No	No	Yes
No	DGF	Yes	No	Yes	Yes

Table H.5 Chairs, Program Managers, and Bank Oversight of Case Study Programs

Program	Location	Governing body (& executive body, if applicable)	Chair of governing body	Program management un
Environment & Agriculture				
1. Consultative Group on International Agricultural Research	World Bank	Consultative Group & Executive Council	Chair of both: Ian Johnson (World Bank)	Secretariat
2. Global Environment Facility	World Bank	Assembly & Council	Co-chairs of both: Len Good (CEO) & one rotating co-chair	Secretariat
3. Multilateral Fund for the Implementation of the Montreal Protocol	Montreal	Meeting of the Parties & Executive Committee	Rotating chairs, selected annually from members	Fund Secretariat
4. Prototype Carbon Fund	World Bank	Participants' committee & Fund Management Committee	Separate chairs: Jean-Claude Steffens & Ken Newcombe (World Bank)	Fund Managemen

rogram manager (and title)	World Bank program oversight[a]	Current Bank unit	FY03 budget allocation for oversight	Comments[b]
ncisco Reifschneider irector)	Kevin Cleaver[c] (Director)	ARD	Nil	• Bank's ESSD vice president chairs CG and ExCo. • Director heads Secretariat, and reports to CG Chair. • ARD director is CG and ExCo member, and reports to the ESSD vice president.
n Good (Chair and O) & Kenneth ng (Assistant CEO)	James Warren Evans (Sector Manager)	ENV	Not applicable	• Independent, full-time CEO and one GEF member co-chair Assembly and Council. • CEO heads Secretariat, and reports to GEF Assembly and Council. • Bank attends Assembly and Council meetings as observer. • The manager of the Bank's GEF coordination unit reports to the ENV Director. • BB allocation is for program coordination for the Bank as an implementing agency for the GEF.
nar El-Arini iief Officer)	Steve Gorman (Sr. Environmental Specialist)	ENV	Not applicable	• Member chair of Executive Committee for one-year term, rotating among Article 5 and non-Article 5 members. • Chief Officer heads secretariat, and reports to Executive Committee. • Bank attends Executive Committee meetings as observer. • The manager of the Bank's MLF coordination unit reports to the ENV Director. • BB allocation is for program coordination for the Bank as an implementing agency for the MLF.
n Newcombe enior Manager)	Ian Johnson	ENV		• Member chair of Participants' Committee for 1-year term, rotating among public and private sector participants. • Program manager chairs Fund Management Committee, heads secretariat and reports to ESSD vice president. • Prototype Carbon Fund trust funds pay for entire secretariat costs (including Bank staff salaries). • Fund Management Unit prepares projects for approval of Fund Management Committee and Participants' committee.

(*Table continues on the following page.*)

Table H.5 Chairs, Program Managers, and Bank Oversight of Case Study Programs (continued)

Program	Location	Governing body (& executive body, if applicable)	Chair of governing body	Program management uni
5. Critical Ecosystem Partnership Fund	Conservation International	Donor Council & Working Group	James Wolfensohn (World Bank) & Jorgen Thomsen (CI)	CEPF Unit
6. Global Water Partnership	Stockholm	Steering Committee	Margaret Catley-Carlson (Canada)	Secretariat
7. Global Integrated Pest Management Facility	FAO	Governing Group	Not applicable	Not applicable
Health				
8. Special Program for Research and Training in Tropical Diseases	WHO	Joint Coordinating Board	Dr. J. Lariviere (Canada) Vice Chair Professor N. K. Ganguly (India)	Secretariat
9. Global Forum for Health Research	Geneva	Foundation Council	Richard Feachem (GFATM)	Secretariat
10. UNAIDS (Joint United Nations Program on HIV/AIDS)	Geneva	Program Coordinating Board	Brian Chituwo (Zambia)	Secretariat

rogram manager (and title)	World Bank program oversight[a]	Current Bank unit	FY03 budget allocation for oversight	Comments[b]
gen Thomsen ecutive Director)	Michael Carroll (Sr. Natural Resource Management Specialist)	LCSER	$100,000	• Bank's President chairs Donor Council. • Program manager chairs Working Group, heads secretariat and reports to both Donor Council and CI Board. • Bank's overseer is member of Working Group and exercises management and fiduciary oversight. • BB allocation covers two supervision missions per year, and staff time to a series of bilateral meetings between the Bank and CI, Working Group Meetings, and the annual Donor Council meeting.
lio Gabbrielli ecutive Secretary)	John Briscoe	SASRD	Nil	• Independent, part-time chair of GWP Steering Committee for term of how many years? • Executive Secretary heads secretariat and reports to Steering Committee. • Bank is cosponsor and member of the Steering Committee, but no longer a donor.
er Kenmore ordinator)	Eija Pehu	ARD	Nil	• Who chairs Governing Group? • Coordinator heads secretariat and reports to FAO and/or Governing Group. • Bank's overseer is Governing Group member.
R. Ridley ecutive Director interim)	Ok Pannenborg (Sr. Adviser)	AFTHD	Approximately $500,000	• Member chair of JCB for three-year rotating term. • Executive Director heads secretariat; appointed by the Director-General of WHO; and reports to JCB • JCB meets annually • Bank's overseer is JCB member.
phen Matlin	Robert M. Hecht (Sector Manager)	HDNHE		• Independent, part-time chair of Foundation Council for 2-year term. • Executive Secretary heads secretariat and reports to Foundation Council. • Bank's overseer is Foundation Council member. • See TDR comment regarding oversight.
er Piot ecutive Director)	Debrework Zewdie (Program Director)	HDNGA		• Member chair of PCB for three-year rotating term. • Executive Director heads secretariat and reports to PCB. • Bank's overseer is PCB member. • See TDR comment regarding oversight.

(*Table continues on the following page.*)

Table H.5 Chairs, Program Managers, and Bank Oversight of Case Study Programs (*continued*)

Program	Location	Governing body (& executive body, if applicable)	Chair of governing body	Program management u
11. Roll Back Malaria	WHO	Steering Committee	George Amofah (Ghana)	Secretariat
12. Stop TB	WHO	Coordinating Board	Ernest Loevinsohn (Canada)	Secretariat
13. Global Alliance for Vaccines and Immunization	UNICEF	GAVI Board	Carol Bellamy (UNICEF)	Secretariat
Infrastructure				
14. Water and Sanitation Program	World Bank	Program Council	Nemat Shafik (World Bank)	Program Manage Team
15. Energy Sector Management Assistance Program	World Bank	Consultative Group	Nemat Shafik (World Bank)	Secretariat
16. Consultative Group to Assist the Poorest	World Bank	Council of Governors & Executive Committee	Separate chairs: Nemat Shafik (World Bank) & David Stanton (U.K.)	Operational Team

Program manager (and title)	World Bank program oversight[a]	Current Bank unit	FY03 budget allocation for oversight	Comments[b]
toumata Nafo-Traoré xecutive Director)	Ok Pannenborg (Sr. Adviser)	AFTHD		• Member chair of Steering Committee for two-year rotating term. • Executive Director heads secretariat and reports to WHO for administrative purposes and Steering Committee for operational purposes. • Bank's overseer is Steering Committee member. • See TDR comment regarding oversight.
arcos Espinal xecutive Director)	Diana Weil (Sr. Public Health Specialist)	ECCKG/HDNHE		• Member chair of Coordinating Board for two-year rotating term. • Executive Director heads secretariat and reports to WHO for administrative purposes and Coordinating Board for operational purposes. • Bank's overseer is Coordinating Board member. • See TDR comment regarding oversight.
re Godal xecutive Secretary)	Amie Batson (Sr. Health Specialist)	HDNHE		• Member chair of GAVI Board for two-year rotating term. • Executive Secretary heads secretariat and reports to GAVI Board. • Bank's overseer is GAVI Board member. • See TDR comment regarding oversight.
alter Stottman lanager)	Jamal Saghir (Director)	EWDDR		• Bank's INF vice president chairs Program Council. • Program manager heads secretariat and reports both to Program Council and EWD Director. • No independent oversight outside INF vice presidency.
ominique Lallement lanager)	Jamal Saghir (Director)	EWDDR		• Bank's INF vice president chairs Consultative Group. • Program manager heads secretariat and reports both to Program Council and EWD Director. • No independent oversight outside INF vice presidency.
izabeth Littlefield xecutive Director)	Carlos Cuevas (Lead Financial Economist	FSE/OPD		• Bank's INF vice president chairs Council of Governors. • Bilateral donor chairs Excom. • Executive director heads secretariat and reports both to CG and INF vice president.

(*Table continues on the following page.*)

Table H.5 Chairs, Program Managers, and Bank Oversight of Case Study Programs (*continued*)

Program	Location	Governing body (& executive body, if applicable)	Chair of governing body	Program management uni
17. The Information for Development Program (*info*Dev)	World Bank	Donors' Committee	Nemat Shafik (World Bank)	Secretariat
18. Public-Private Infrastructure Advisory Facility	World Bank	Program Council	Nemat Shafik (World Bank)	Program Managem Unit
19. Cities Alliance	World Bank	Consultative Group & Steering Committee	Co-chairs of both: Nemat Shafik (World Bank) & Anna Kajumulo Tibaijuka (UN-Habitat)	Secretariat
Social Development & Protection				
20. Post-conflict Fund	World Bank	Steering Committee	Steen Jorgenson (World Bank)	Secretariat
21. Understanding Children's Work	UNICEF (Florence)	Steering Committee	Not applicable	Secretariat
Trade & Finance				
22. Integrated Framework	WTO	Steering Committee & Working Group	Separate chairs: Hendrik Reé Iversen (Denmark) & Dr. Kipkokir Aly Azad Rana (WTO)	Secretariat

'rogram manager (and title)	World Bank program oversight[a]	Current Bank unit	FY03 budget allocation for oversight	Comments[b]
				• Bank's overseer is Excom member and CG member. That he is located in a different vice presidency from CGAP Chair enables some measure of independent oversight.
ıstafa Terrab anager)	Mohsen Khalil (Director)	CITDR		• Bank's INF vice president chairs Donors' Committee • Program manager heads secretariat and reports both to Donors' Committee and CIT Director. • No independent oversight outside INF vice presidency.
ɔti Shukla anager)				• Bank's INF vice president chairs Program Council. • Program manager heads secretariat and reports both to Program Council and INF vice president. • Who exercises oversight?
ırk Hildebrand anager)	Maryvonne Plessis-Fraissard (Director)	TUDDR		• World Bank and UN-Habitat co-chair both CG and Steering Committee. • Program manager heads secretariat and reports both to CG and to TUD Director. • No independent oversight outside INF vice presidency.
in Scott ɔgram Manager)	Ian Bannon (Manager)	SDV		• Bank's SDV Director chairs Steering Committee. • Program manager heads secretariat and reports to manager of Conflict Prevention and Reconstruction Team. • Bank staff members of Steering Committee provide some oversight from outside SDV Department.
io Rosati ɔject Coordinator)	Jean Fares (Economist)	HDNSP		• Who chairs Steering Committee? • Project Coordinator heads secretariat and reports to Steering Committee. • Bank's overseer is Steering Committee member.
ınet Blank	John Panzer (Sector Manager)	PRMTR		• Member chair of Steering Committee for X-year rotating term • WTO chairs Working Group. • Program manager heads secretariat and reports to Working Group and WTO? • Bank's overseer is Working Group member.

(*Table continues on the following page.*)

Table H.5 Chairs, Program Managers, and Bank Oversight of Case Study Programs (continued)

Program	Location	Governing body (& executive body, if applicable)	Chair of governing body	Program management un
23. Financial Sector Assessment Program	IMF and World Bank	Financial Sector Liaison Committee	Co-chairs: Larry Promisel (World Bank) & Thomas Balino (IMF)	
24. Financial Sector Reform & Strengthening	DFID and World Bank	Governing Council & Steering Committee	Separate chairs: Jeffrey Goldstein (World Bank) & Larry Promisel (World Bank)	Management Unit Coordination Unit
Information & Knowledge				
25. Global Development Network	Washington, D.C.	Governing Body	Richard Cooper (USA) & Akilagpa Sawyerr (Africa)	Secretariat
26. World Links for Development	Washington, D.C.	Governing Board	Co-chairs: Robert M. Chefitz (NJTC Venture Fund, USA) & Dina Dublon (JP Morgan Chase, USA)	Secretariat

a. Person who is immediately responsible for oversight of the program from the point of view of the World Bank, as distinct from the person who is managing the program.

b. Comment in particular on the degree of independence of the oversight, and give brief reasons for the assessment.

c. Bank management has recommended the Bank's Chief Economist.

rogram manager (and title)	World Bank program oversight[a]	Current Bank unit	FY03 budget allocation for oversight	Comments[b]
managers: ʒan Marcus ɔrld Bank) & rk O'Brien F)	Larry Promisel (Sr. Adviser)	FSEGP		• Bank and IMF co-chair Liaison Committee. • Co-managers report to their respective managers. • Some financial sector board oversight (changed from no independent oversight outside FSE vice presidency).
ɔert Stone ad) & 'na Tapiero ınager)	Larry Promisel (Sr. Adviser)	FSEGP		• Bank chairs both the Governing Council and Steering Committee. • Manager of Coordination Unit reports to both the Steering Committee and FSE Sr. Adviser. • No independent oversight outside of FSE vice presidency.
Squire	Guillermo Perry (Chief Economist, LAC)	LCRCE	Not applicable	• Member co-chairs of Governing Body. • Executive Director heads secretariat and reports to Governing Body. • Bank's overseer is member of Governing Body.
ɪs Hoyer	Sam Carlson (Sr. Human Development Specialist)	LCSHE	Not applicable	• Member co-chairs of Governing Board. • Executive Secretary heads secretariat and reports to Governing Board. • Bank's overseer is member of Governing Board.

Table H.6 Relationship of Case Study Programs to International Conventions/ Conferences/ Agreements

Program	Convention/agreement
Environment & Agriculture	
1. Consultative Group on International Agricultural Research (CGIAR)	U.N. Conference on Environment and Development (UNCED), Rio de Janeiro, 1992 World Summit on Sustainable Development, Johannesburg, 2002
2. Global Environment Facility (GEF)	Montreal Protocol, 1987 U.N. Conference on Environment and Development (UNCED), Rio de Janeiro, 1992 U.N. Framework Convention on Climate Change (UNFCCC), 1992 Convention on Conservation of Biological Diversity (CBD), 1992 U.N. Convention on Combating Desertification (CCD), 1994 Global Program of Action for the Protection of the Marine Environment from Land-based Activities (encompasses regional and bilateral conventions/agreements), and Washington Declaration, 1995 Stockholm Convention on Persistent Organic Pollutants, 2001 World Summit on Sustainable Development, Johannesburg, 2002
3. Multilateral Fund for the Implementation of the Montreal Protocol (MLF)	Vienna Convention for the Protection of the Ozone Layer, 1985. Montreal Protocol on Substances That Deplete the Ozone Layer, 1987.
4. Prototype Carbon Fund (ProCarbFund)	U.N. Framework Convention on Climate Change, 1992 Kyoto Protocol, 1997 Buenos Aires Plan of Action, 1998 Bonn Agreement, 2001 Marrakech Accords, 2001 World Summit on Sustainable Development, Johannesburg, 2002
5. Critical Ecosystem Partnership Fund (CEPF)	Convention on Conservation of Biological Diversity (CBD), 1992
6. Global Water Partnership (GWP)	Dublin Conference on Water and Environment, 1992. U.N. Conference on Environment and Development, Rio de Janeiro, 1992
7. Global Integrated Pest Management Facility (GIF)	Agenda 21 and the Convention on Conservation of Biological Diversity
Health	
8. Special Program for Research and Training in Tropical Diseases (TDR)	Chiang Mai Declaration, 2000
9. Global Forum for Health Research	
10. UNAIDS (Joint United Nations Program on HIV/AIDS)	U.N. Special Session on HIV/AIDS 2001
11. Roll Back Malaria (RBM)	Abuja Summit 2000 Okinawa Summit 2000
12. Stop TB	Amsterdam Declaration 2000
13. Global Alliance for Vaccines and Immunization (GAVI)	Dakar Declaration 2000.

Role[a]
The CGIAR responded to Rio 1992 by broadening its mission and has undertaken to help implement the goals adopted by the Johannesburg Summit.
GEF arose out of the 1992 U.N. Conference on the Environment and Development (UNCED). GEF is formally responsible for implementing the UNFCCC, CBD, CCD and Stockholm Convention.
The MLF is formally responsible for implementing the Montreal Protocol.
The Prototype Carbon Fund is facilitating implementation of the Kyoto Protocol. It is a prototype for project-based carbon-emissions trading under flexible mechanisms established by Convention.
The CEPF is facilitating the implementation of the CBD.
The GWP built on the Dublin-Rio principles agreed during these conferences.
The GIF is facilitating implementation of Agenda 21.
Strongly endorsed the TDR/WHO global strategy for prevention and control of dengue and dengue hemorrhagic fever.
–
The U.N. General Assembly adopted a Declaration of Commitment on HIV/AIDS and fully endorsed the UNAIDS program
Both Summits endorsed actions synonymous with those proposed by the RBM Partnership.
Formally recognized the efforts of the Stop TB Initiative and endorsed the program.
The Summit formally requested that the partners of the GAVI and the Vaccine Fund continue to assist countries in the mobilization of additional financial resources for health and immunization.

(*Table continues on the following page.*)

Table H.6 Relationship of Case Study Programs to International Conventions/ Conferences/ Agreements (*continued*)

Program	Convention/agreement
Infrastructure	
14. Water and Sanitation Program (WSP)	World Water Conference, Mar del Plata, Argentina, 1977 Dublin Conference on Water and Environment, 1992 U.N. Conference on Environment and Development, Rio de Janeiro, 1992
15. Energy Sector Management Assistance Program (ESMAP)	–
16. Consultative Group to Assist the Poorest (CGAP)	–
17. The Information for Development Program (*info*Dev)	Genoa Plan of Action to Address the Digital Divide, endorsed by G8 Heads of State, July 2001
18. Public-Private Infrastructure Advisory Facility (PPIAF)	–
19. Cities Alliance	Habitat II, Istanbul Declaration on Human Settlements, June 1996 Millennium Declaration 2000
Social Development & Protection	
20 Post-conflict Fund (PostConFund)	–
21. Understanding Children's Work (UCW)	Oslo Agenda for Action, adopted at the 1997 International Conference on Child Labor
Trade & Finance	
22. Integrated Framework for Trade-Related Technical Assistance (IF)	First WTO Ministerial Conference, Singapore, December 1996 WTO High-Level Meeting, October 1997 Doha Ministerial Declaration, November 2001
23. Financial Sector Assessment Program (FSAP)	International standards that have been established for banking supervision, payments system oversight, securities and insurance markets, accounting practices, corporate governance, and anti-money laundering, as well as data dissemination and monetary and fiscal policy transparency.
24. Financial Sector Reform and Strengthening (FIRST)	International standards that have been established for banking supervision, payments system oversight, securities and insurance markets, accounting practices, corporate governance, and anti-money laundering, as well as data dissemination and monetary and fiscal policy transparency.
Information & Knowledge	
25. Global Development Network (GDN)	–
26. World Links	–

a. Indicates whether the program (1) is formally responsible for implementing the Convention, (2) is facilitating implementation of the Convention, or (3) arose out of the Convention.

Role[a]
WSP arose out of the World Water Conference and the declaration of the 1980s as the "International Drinking Water and Sanitation Decade." WSP committed to implement the Dublin-Rio principles regarding policy and institutional reform and investments in the water sector.
–
–
*info*Dev served as Digital Opportunity Task Force secretariat that produced the Genoa Plan of Action.
–
Arose out of Habitat II. The Millennium Declaration endorsed the Cities Alliance's own target regarding improving the lives of slum dwellers.
–
The Agenda, which provides guidance to UCW, identified the need for more data and research on child labor and called for stronger cooperation among international agencies involved in addressing child labor.
The 1997 High-Level Meeting formally endorsed the IF initiative. The 2001 Doha Declaration explicitly identified IF as an important contribution to meeting LDC needs and encouraged its extension to all low income countries.
The program assesses country compliance with these standards and identifies vulnerabilities in domestic financial systems.
The program provides technical assistance to address weaknesses that have been identified in domestic financial systems in relation to these standards.
– –

Table H.7 Relationship of Case Study Programs to Millennium Development Goals

Goals	Targets	Direct relationship[a]	Less-direct relationship[b]
1. Eradicate extreme poverty and hunger	1. Halve, between 1990 and 2015, the proportion of people whose income is less than one dollar a day.		CGAP
	2. Halve, between 1990 and 2015, the proportion of people who suffer from hunger.	CGIAR	
2. Achieve universal primary education	3. Ensure that, by 2015, children everywhere, boys and girls alike, will be able to complete a full course of primary schooling.		UCW
3. Promote gender equality and empower women	4. Eliminate gender disparity in primary and secondary education, preferably by 2005, and in all levels of education no later than 2015.		
4. Reduce child mortality	5. Reduce by two-thirds, between 1990 and 2015, the under-five mortality rate.	GAVI	TDR, UNAIDS, RBM, Stop TB
5. Improve maternal health	6. Reduce by three-quarters, between 1990 and 2015, the maternal mortality ratio.		TDR, Global Forum, UNAIDS, RBM, Stop TB, GAVI
6. Combat HIV/AIDS, malaria and other diseases	7. Have halted and begun to reverse the spread of HIV/AIDS by 2015.	UNAIDS, GFATM[c]	
	8. Have halted and begun to reverse the incidence of malaria and other major diseases by 2015.	RBM, Stop TB, GFATM	TDR, Global Forum, GAVI
7. Ensure environmental sustainability	9. Integrate the principles of sustainable development into country policies and programs and reverse the losses of environmental resources.	GEF, MLF, ProCarbFund, ESMAP	CEPF, GWP, GIF
	10. Halve by 2015 the proportion of people without sustainable access to safe drinking water and sanitation.	WSP	GWP, PPIAF
	11. Have achieved, by 2020, a significant improvement in the lives of at least 100 million slum dwellers.	Cities Alliance	
8. Develop a global partnership for development	12. Further develop an open, rule-based, predictable, nondiscriminatory trading and financial system.		IF, FSAP, FIRST
	13. Address the special needs of the least-developed countries.	IF	PostConFund
	14. Address the special needs of landlocked countries and small-island developing states.		
	15. Deal comprehensively with the debt problems of developing countries through national and international measures in order to make debt sustainable in the long term.		

Table H.7 Relationship of Case Study Programs to Millennium Development Goals (*continued*)

Goals	Targets	Direct relationship[a]	Less-direct relationship[b]
	16. In cooperation with developing countries, develop and implement strategies for decent and productive work for youth.		
	17. In cooperation with pharmaceutical companies, provide access to affordable essential drugs in developing countries.		TDR, UNAIDS, RBM, Stop TB, GAVI, GFATM
	18. In cooperation with the private sector, make available the benefits of new technologies, especially information and communications.	*info*Dev	PPIAF, GDN, World Links

a. The stated objectives of these programs are directly related to specific MDG targets, although their outputs are only part of the ingredients needed to achieve the MDGs.

b. The objectives of these programs are also related to the achievement of the MDGs in the sense that the goods and services the programs provide are important ingredients needed to achieve particular MDG targets.

c. GFATM, not included in this review, is by far the largest effort to make resources available to developing countries for halting the spread of AIDS, TB, and malaria. Similarly, the International AIDS Vaccine Initiative is attempting to develop vaccines for HIV/AIDS.

Table H.8 OED Assessment of Programs' Actual Activities, Classified According to Bank Management's Four Strategic Foci and OED Subcategories

(See definitions of OED's subcategories at the end of the table. OED's assessments of high, substantial, modest, or negligible are internal to each program and therefore do not provide comparisons across programs, nor do these ratings represent assessments of the quality or efficacy of these program activities.)

Activities	High or substantial	Modest	Negligible
Providing global public goods			
• Implementing conventions, rules, or formal and informal standards and norms	GEF, MLF, ProCarbFund Stop TB FSAP, FIRST	CGIAR, CEPF, GWP, GIF CGAP	TDR, Global Forum, UNAIDS, RBM, GAVI WSP, ESMAP, *info*Dev, PPIAF, CA PostConFund, UCW, IF, GDN, World Links
• Financing R&D for new products and technologies	CGIAR TDR, GAVI	Global Forum, Stop TB	GEF, MLF, ProCarbFund, CEPF, GWP, GIF UNAIDS, RBM WSP, ESMAP, CGAP, *info*Dev, PPIAF, CA PostConFund, UCW, IF, FSAP, FIRST, GDN, World Links
• Financing country-level investments to deliver global public goods	GEF, MLF, ProCarbFund, CEPF	Stop TB PostConFund	CGIAR, GWP, GIF TDR, Global Forum, UNAIDS, RBM, GAVI WSP, ESMAP, CGAP, *info*Dev, PPIAF, CA UCW, IF, FSAP, FIRST, GDN, World Links
• Promoting common approaches to mitigating communicable diseases	UNAIDS, RBM, Stop TB		CGIAR, GEF, MLF, ProCarb Fund, CEPF, GWP, GIF TDR, Global Forum, GAVI WSP, ESMAP, CGAP, *info*Dev, PPIAF, CA PostConFund, UCW, IF, FSAP, FIRST, GDN, World Links
Supporting international advocacy for reform agendas to improve national-level policies			
• Advocacy	CGIAR, GEF, ProCarbFund, CEPF, GWP, GIF UNAIDS, Global Forum, RBM, Stop TB, GAVI WSP, ESMAP, CGAP, *info*Dev, PPIAF, CA PostConFund, FSAP, FIRST, IF, GDN, World Links	MLF TDR UCW	

Table H.8 OED Assessment of Programs' Actual Activities, Classified According to Bank Management's Four Strategic Foci and OED Subcategories (*continued*)

Activities	High or substantial	Modest	Negligible
• Supporting national-level policy, institutional & technical reforms	CGIAR, GEF, MLF UNAIDS, GAVI WSP, ESMAP, PPIAF, CA IF, FSAP, FIRST	ProCarbFund, CEPF, GWP, GIF Global Forum, RBM, Stop TB CGAP PostConFund, GDN, World Links	TDR *info*Dev UCW
• Financing country-level investments to deliver national public goods	GAVI PostConFund	UNAIDS, Stop TB	CGIAR, GEF, MLF, ProCarb Fund, CEPF, GWP, GIF TDR, Global Forum, RBM WSP, ESMAP, CGAP, *info*Dev, PPIAF, CA UCW, IF, FSAP, FIRST, GDN, World Links
Coordinated multicountry programs			
• Generation and dissemination of information and knowledge	CGIAR, GEF, ProCarbFund, GIF TDR, Global Forum, UNAIDS, RBM, Stop TB, GAVI WSP, ESMAP, CGAP, *info*Dev, PPIAF, CA PostConFund, UCW, IF, FSAP, FIRST, GDN, World Links	MLF, CEPF, GWP	
• Capacity building and training	CGIAR, GEF, MLF, ProCarbFund, CEPF, GIF TDR, UNAIDS, GAVI WSP, ESMAP, CGAP, *info*Dev, PPIAF, CA PostConFund, IF, FSAP, FIRST, GDN, World Links	GWP RBM, Stop TB	Global Forum UCW
• Improving donor coordination	CGIAR, GEF UNAIDS, Stop TB, GAVI CGAP, PPIAF, CA PostConFund, IF, FIRST	MLF, ProCarbFund, GIF RBM, Global Forum WSP, ESMAP FSAP	CEPF, GWP TDR *info*Dev UCW, GDN, World Links
Mobilizing substantial incremental resources			
• Directly	CGIAR, GEF, MLF, ProCarbFund GAVI	CEPF TDR, UNAIDS, Stop TB PPIAF, CA FIRST	GWP, GIF Global Forum, RBM WSP, ESMAP, CGAP, *info*Dev PostConFund, UCW, IF, FSAP, GDN, World Links
• Indirectly	Global Forum, UNAIDS, Stop TB	RBM WSP, ESMAP, PPIAF, CA	CGIAR, GEF, MLF, ProCarb Fund, CEPF, GWP, GIF TDR, GAVI

(*Table continues on the following page.*)

Table H.8 OED Assessment of Programs' Actual Activities, Classified According to Bank Management's Four Strategic Foci and OED Subcategories (*continued*)

Activities	High or substantial	Modest	Negligible
			CGAP, *info*Dev PostConFund, UCW, IF, FSAP, FIRST, GDN, World Links

Bank Management's Strategic Focus for Global Programs

Management noted that to enhance strategic focus, oversight will be strengthened to ensure that global programs comprise activities that: (a) provide global public goods; (b) support international advocacy for reform agendas that in significant ways address policy framework conditions relevant for developing countries; (c) are multicountry programs that crucially depend on highly coordinated approaches; and/or (d) mobilize substantial incremental resources that can be effectively used for development.

Definitions of OED Subcategories to More Sharply Define Program Activities

Rules are generally formal. *Standards* can be formal or informal, and binding or nonbinding, but *implementing standards* involves more than simply advocating an approach to development in a sector. In general, there should be some costs associated with noncompliance. Costs can come in many forms, including exposure to financial contagion, bad financial ratings by the IMF and other rating agencies, with consequent impacts on access to private finance; lack of access to OECD markets for failing to meet food safety standards, or even the consequences of failing to be seen as *progressive* in international circles.

New products and technologies are generally physical products or processes—the hardware as opposed to the software of development.

Financing country-level investments to deliver global public goods refers primarily to physical and institutional investments of the type found in Bank loans and credits (not the financing of studies) to deliver public goods such as conserving biodiversity of global value and reducing emissions of ozone-depleting substances and carbon dioxide, the benefits of which accrue globally.

Promoting common approaches to mitigating communicable diseases may involve a range of activities intended to develop approaches to containing communicable diseases with widespread application and to provide this specialized information and knowledge to developing countries.

Advocacy comprises proactive interaction with policymakers and decisionmakers concerning approaches to development in a sector, commonly in the context of global, regional, or country-level forums. Intended to create reform conditions in developing countries, as distinct from physical and institutional investments in public goods, this is more proactive than generating and disseminating information and knowledge.

Supporting national-level policy, institutional, and technical reforms is more directed to specific tasks than advocacy. This represents concrete involvement in specific and ongoing policy, institutional, and technical reform processes in a sector, from deciding on a reform strategy to implementation of new policies and regulations in a sector. It is more than just conducting studies.

Financing country-level investments refers primarily to physical and institutional investments of the type found in Bank loans and credits (not the financing of studies), the benefits of which accrue primarily at the national level.

Generation and dissemination of information and knowledge comprises two related activities. The first is gathering, analyzing and disseminating information on, for example, the evolving HIV/AIDS epidemic and responses to it, including epidemiological data collection and analysis, needs assessment, resource flows, and country readiness. The second is the systematic assembling and dissemination of knowledge (not merely information) with respect to best practices in a sector on a global basis.

Capacity building refers to building the capacity of human resources through proactive training (in courses or on-the-job), as well as collaborative work with the active involvement of developing country partners.

Improving donor coordination should be an active process, not just the side effect of other program activities. This may involve resolving thorny interagency issues that need addressing.

Mobilizing substantial incremental resources represents substantial resources (in absolute size) from diverse and novel sources that have been or appear to be sustainable over the long term. *Direct* resources are those that are mobilized for, and managed by, the program itself. *Indirect* resources are those that are mobilized as a result of the program's advocacy, but are managed and spent by others (such as the World Bank and bilateral donors) outside the framework of the global program itself.

Table H.9 Recent Sector Strategies and OED Sector Studies Relating to Case Study Programs[a]

Network/sector	Type of report	Date	Title	Principal author (if applicable)
Environmentally and Socially Sustainable Development				
Social Development	Bank sector strategy	December 2003	(DRAFT) Social Development In World Bank Operations: Results and Way Forward	
	OED sector study	June 1998	The World Bank's Experience with Post-conflict Reconstruction	Alcira Kreimer et al.
Water Resources	Bank sector strategy	February 2003	Water Resources Sector Strategy: Strategic Directions for World Bank Engagement	
	OED sector study	2002	Bridging Troubled Waters: Assessing the World Bank Water Resources Strategy	George Pitman
Forestry	Bank sector strategy	October 2002	A Revised Forest Strategy for the World Bank Group	
	OED sector study	October 2000	The World Bank Forest Strategy: Striking the Right Balance	Uma Lele et al.
Environment	Bank sector strategy	December 2001	Making Sustainable Commitments: An Environment Strategy for the World Bank.	
	OED sector study	January 2002	Promoting Environmental Sustainability in Development: An Evaluation of the World Bank's Performance	Andres Liebenthal
Rural Development	Bank sector strategy	October 2001	Reaching the Rural Poor: A Renewed Strategy for Rural Development	
	OED sector study	April 2002	Toward Sharpening the Focus on Rural Poverty: A Review of World Bank Experience	Ridley Nelson
	OED sector study	June 2000	Rural Development: From Vision to Action? (Phase II)	Chris Gerrard and John Heath
	OED sector study	June 1999	Rural Development: From Vision to Action?	John Heath
Indigenous Peoples	Operational policies/ Bank procedures	March 2001	(DRAFT) Indigenous Peoples: Operational Policies (DRAFT) Indigenous Peoples: Bank Procedures	
	OED sector study	April 2003	Implementation of Operational Directive 4.20 on Indigenous Peoples: An Evaluation of Results	Gita Gopal
Human Development Network				
Health, Nutrition, & Population	Bank sector strategy	September 1997	Health, Nutrition, and Population: Sector strategy	
		December 2003	The Millennium Development Goals for Health: Rising to the Challenges	
	Regional sector strategy	June 2000	The World Bank Strategy for Health, Nutrition and Population in the East Asia and Pacific Region	
	Regional sector strategy	September 1999	A Health Sector Strategy for the Europe and Central Asia Region	
	Regional sector strategy	No date	World Bank: Middle East and North Africa Region Strategy Paper	

(*Table continues on the following page.*)

Table H.9 Recent Sector Strategies and OED Sector Studies Relating to Case Study Programs[a] (*continued*)

Network/sector	Type of report	Date	Title	Principal author (if applicable)
	OED sector study	July 1999	Investing in Health Development Effectiveness in the Health, Nutrition, and Population Sector	Susan Stout
Social Protection	Bank sector strategy	September 2000	Social Protection Sector Strategy: From Safety Net to Springboard	
	OED sector study	May 2002	Social Funds: Assessing Effectiveness	Soniya Carvalho
Education	Bank sector strategy	July 1999	Education Sector Strategy	
Infrastructure and Private Sector Development				
Water & Sanitation	Bank business strategy	September 2003	Water Supply and Sanitation Business Strategy: Fiscal 2003–2007	
	OED sector study	September 2003	Efficient, Sustainable Service for All? An OED Evaluation of the World Bank's Assistance to Water Supply and Sanitation	Klas Ringskog
Private Sector Development	Bank sector strategy	April 2002	Private Sector Development Strategy – Directions for the World Bank Group	
Energy	Bank sector strategy	December 2001	The World Bank Group's Energy Program – Poverty Reduction, Sustainability, and Selectivity	
	OED/OEG/OEU sector study	October 2003	Power for Development: A Review of the World Bank Group's Experience with Private Participation in the Energy Sector	Rafael Dominguez, Fernando Manibog, and Stephan Wegner
	OED sector study	March 1998	The World Bank Environment Strategy for the Energy Sector: An OED Perspective	
Information & Communication Technologies	OED/OEG sector study	January 2001	Information Infrastructure: The World Bank Group's Experience. A Joint OED/OEG Review	Alain Barbu, Rafael Dominguez, and William Melody
	Bank sector strategy	2002	Information and Communication Technologies: A World Bank Group Strategy	
Urban	Bank sector strategy	September 2000	Cities in Transition: World Bank Urban and Local Government Strategy	
	OED sector study	June 2002	Improving the Lives of the Poor through Investment in Cities: An Update on the Performance of the World Bank's Urban Portfolio	Roy Gilbert
Financial Sector				
Finance	Bank sector strategy	March 2001	The World Bank Group Strategy for the Financial Sector	
	OED sector study	Forthcoming 2004	Financial Sector Reform	Laurie Effron

Table H.9 Recent Sector Strategies and OED Sector Studies Relating to Case Study Programs[a] (*continued*)

Network/sector	Type of report	Date	Title	Principal author (if applicable)
	OED sector study	June 1998	Financial Sector Reform: A Review of World Bank Assistance	Nicolas Mathieu
	OED sector study	1996	A Review of Bank Lending for Agricultural Credit and Rural Finance (1948–1992): A Follow-Up	
	OED sector study	1993	A Review of Bank Lending for Agricultural Credit and Rural Finance (1948–1992)	

a. Within each network, the sectors are sorted chronologically starting with the most recent sector strategy.

Table H.10 Most Recent Program-Level Evaluations of Case Study Programs

Program	Date	Commissioned by	Managed by	Reported to
Environment and Agriculture				
1. CGIAR	1998	CGIAR Chair	CGIAR Secretariat	Consultative Group
2. GEF	2002	GEF Secretariat	GEF Secretariat	GEF Council and Assembly
3. MLF	March 1995			
4. ProCarbFund				
5. CEPF	2003			
6. GWP	June 2003			
7. GIF	Feb. 2001			
Health				
8. TDR	October 1998	TDR Joint Coordinating Board (JCB)		TDR JCB
9. Global Forum	Dec. 2001	Global Forum Foundation Council		Foundation Council
10. UNAIDS	October 2002	UNAIDS Program Coordinating Board (PCB)		UNAIDS PCB
11. RBM	August 2002	U.K. DFID		DFID and the RBM Steering Committee
12. Stop TB	December 2003	Stop TB Partnership Coordinating Board		Coordinating Board
	April 2003	Stop TB Partnership Coordinating Board		Coordinating Board
13. GAVI	June 2002	GAVI Board		GAVI Board
Infrastructure				
14. WSP	May 1999	SIDA, NORAD, CIDA		
	June 1999	SDC		
	July 1999	DANIDA		
	Sept. 1999	DANIDA		
15. ESMAP	June 30, 2000	World Bank Energy, Mining, & Telecoms Sector Board	*info*Dev Secretariat	Energy, Mining, & Telecoms Sector Board
16. CGAP	April 4, 2002	Excom	CGAP Secretariat	Excom and CG

Conducted by	Title
Maurice Strong	The International Research Partnership for Food Security and Sustainable Development: Third System Review of the CGIAR
Christoffersen, Davidson, Donoso, Fargher, Hammond, Hooper, Matthew, and Seyani	The First Decade of the GEF: Second Overall Performance Study
COWIconsult	Study on the Financial Mechanism of the Montreal Protocol
	Mid-Term Evaluation
R. Hoare, Bert van Woersem, G. Brustzt, Doug Flint, and Juliet Pierce	External Review of GWP
Janice Jiggins et al.	The Mid-Term Review of the Global IPM Facility
H. Wigzell, F. K. Nkrumah, G. T. Castillo, J. Amor, W. P. Thalwitz, H. G. Boyer	Final Report: Third External Review of TDR
Fred Binka, Jan Holmgren, Nimala Murthy	Findings from the External Evaluation: A Report to the Foundation Council
Derek Poate (leading a four-person team)	Five-Year Evaluation of UNAIDS, Final Report
R. Feachem (leading a seven-person team)	Achieving Impact: Roll Back Malaria in the Next Phase
Karen Caines et al. Institute for Health Sector Development, London, U.K. McKinsey & Co.	Independent External Evaluation of the Global Stop TB Partnership Review of the Global Drug Facility[a]
Karen Caines, Hatib N'jie	Report of the External Review of the Functions and Interactions of the GAVI Working Group, Secretariat, and Board
Ake Nilsson (leading a five-person team) François Münger (leading a three-person team) Vagn Rehoj (leading a five-person team)	Review of Support to the World Bank-UNDP Water & Sanitation Program – South Asia External Evaluation of the Swiss Agency for Development and Cooperation contribution to the UNDP-World Bank Water and Sanitation Program and to the Pan-American Center for Sanitary Engineering and Environmental Sciences (CEPIS/PHO) Joint Assessment of the Regional Water and Sanitation Group for Eastern and Southern Africa (RWSG-ESA) Review of the Support for the UNDP-World Bank Regional Water and Sanitation Groups for South Asia and for West and Central Africa
Guy Caruso (leading a five-person team)	Donor-Funded Energy Programs: Final Report of the External Review
James W. Fox, Mark Havers, and Klaus Maurer	Evaluation and Strategic Review of the Consultative Group to Assist the Poorest (CGAP)

(*Table continues on the following page.*)

Table H.10 Most Recent Program-Level Evaluations of Case Study Programs (*continued*)

Program	Date	Commissioned by	Managed by	Reported to
17. *info*Dev	May 2002	*info*Dev	*info*Dev Secretariat	*info*Dev Management
18. PPIAF				
19. Cities Alliance	Sept. 2002	CA Consultative Group	CA Secretariat	Consultative Group
Social Development and Protection				
20. PostConFund	February 2002	PostConFund Steering Committee	PostConFund Secretariat	PostConFund Steering Comm
21. UCW	June 2003	UCW Steering Committee	UNICEF Evaluation Office	UCW Steering Committee
Trade & Finance				
22. IF	September 2003	IF Steering Committee	UNDP Evaluation Office	IF Steering Committee
23. FSAP				
24. FIRST				
Information & Knowledge				
25. GDN	March 2004			
26. World Links				

a. The McKinsey Review of the Global Drug Facility and GAVI's external review are not full program evaluations.

Conducted by	Title
Eduardo da Costa (coordinator), Ernest Wilson III, and Barbara Fillip	*info*Dev External Evaluation 2002: Final Report
Development Planning Unit, University College, London	Cities Alliance: An Assessment of the First Three Years
Development Alternatives Inc.	Covering New Ground: Evaluation of the Post-conflict Fund
Roland Rodts	Developing Strategies for Understanding Children's Work and Its Impact: Review Report
Capra International Inc. and Trade Facilitation Office, Canada	Evaluation of the Revamped Integrated Framework for Trade-related Technical Assistance to the Least Developed Countries: Final Report
Dr. H. Peter Muth Dr. Frederick H. Gerlach	Independent Evaluation of the Global Development Network

Table H.11 Global TM Statements of Beneficiaries and Benefits of Case Study Programs

Program	Intended beneficiaries (intermediate and ultimate)
Environment & Agriculture	
1. Consultative Group on International Agricultural Research	
2. Global Environment Facility	The intermediate beneficiaries are the Bank's client countries—particularly their sectors that depend heavily on natural resources and the integrity of ecosystems, as well as those responsible for energy, transport and urban development. The ultimate beneficiaries are the international community, given the global environmental objectives of the GEF.
3. Multilateral Fund for the Implementation of the Montreal Protocol	
4. Prototype Carbon Fund	
5. Critical Ecosystem Partnership Fund	The CEPF targets civil society, which includes nongovernmental organizations, community groups, academia, and private sector partners in the biodiversity conservation field as the immediate beneficiaries and recipients of grant monies. Grant recipients implement programs in line with strategic priorities established within each critical ecosystem. The ultimate beneficiaries are humankind at the local and global levels. Local benefits are derived from the conservation of local environmental services and the natural resources derived from an area rich in biodiversity. The global community benefits from the preservation of globally important ecosystems.
6. Global Water Partnership	The ultimate beneficiaries are the poor who lack access to water and water-related services. The intermediate beneficiaries are the stakeholders who, through the GWP, have a forum for interaction.
7. Global Integrated Pest Management Facility	Small resource-poor farmers (gender also explicitly mentioned). Extension systems, pesticide policy experts.
Health	
8. Special Program for Research and Training in Tropical Diseases (TDR)	The intended beneficiaries are the poor and disadvantaged populations affected by these diseases.
9. Global Forum for Health Research	The intended beneficiaries are the poor in developing countries, the governments and agencies enabled to provide more effective remedies, and the institutions whose capacity is reinforced by involvement in the research efforts.
10. UNAIDS (Joint United Nations Program on HIV/AIDS)	Intermediate: Those infected and affected by HIV/AIDS. Ultimate: The next generation in Africa (in its entirety) and potentially in other regions.
11. Roll Back Malaria	People suffering with malaria. Health systems burdened with malaria patients.

Principal benefits (intended and unintended)
The principal benefit that beneficiaries receive from the GEF is grant financing that complements a financing package that consists of loans/ credits and other resources. GEF is also the financial mechanism for three international conventions (on biodiversity, climate change, and persistent organic pollutants), and the financing it provides helps recipient countries fulfill their responsibilities under these conventions. The GEF resources enable the Bank to provide a more complete array of financing instruments to our clients, in response to the specific nature of interventions and project objectives. This package of financing is critical to supporting mainstreaming in our clients' sectoral development plans.
Despite scattered successes, providing modest-scale, narrowly targeted, and expeditious assistance for privately implemented biodiversity conservation has proven a significant challenge for international financial institutions, including the World Bank. The CEPF is a new strategy for project delivery that attempts to overcome typical obstacles and delay through a nontraditional set of working arrangements between the Bank and nongovernmental organizations. CEPF makes grants to the leading international, national, regional and local NGOs and other conservation-oriented stakeholders in the world's most critically threatened ecosystems in Bank client countries. It targets effective organizations in each ecosystem in order to strengthen their ability to alter the course of each eco-region's degradation.
The principal benefits received by the (intermediate) beneficiaries are the facilitating and networking functions of the program, particularly as it provides a neutral space for stakeholder interaction.
Small groups of farmers attend farmer field schools, learn the IPM methodology, and develop social cohesion; however, participants are few. There is some policy advice for subsidy policies to governments.
The ultimate benefit is poverty reduction, targeting the poorest of the poor, and promoting sustainable economic development. Beneficiaries enjoy a life without a disabling or disfiguring disease, restoring their human dignity.
At various levels, these comprise: products, information, development of prioritization methodology for use at country level, developing country involvement in international research efforts, and data on health research flows to guide decisionmakers. The October 2000 Global Forum prompted *The Lancet's* decision to form a commission to address the 10/90 gap in health research publication. The commission will look at practical ways in which the journal can encourage researchers from resource-poor countries to submit their work, and also to participate in its peer-review process—an obvious boost to research capacity building, and an outlet for developing-country researchers' voice in the research agenda.
Adequate funding, the creation of a favorable environment to execute culturally appropriate programs of their own design, better care and treat ment (for the infected), better support (for the affected), and averted HIV infection (for those not infected).
Increased prioritization of malaria—resulting in better trained staff, more cost-effective protocols, increased education on malaria, access to bed nets, access to effective antimalarials.

(*Table continues on the following page.*)

Table H.11 Global TM Statements of Beneficiaries and Benefits of Case Study Programs (*continued*)

Program	Intended beneficiaries (intermediate and ultimate)
12. Stop TB	• Low-income developing nations and middle-income countries with high TB burdens, as well as industrialized nations with TB risks. • Those working to control TB, develop new tools or related challenges (HIV/AIDS) (drug supply) in all nations. • TB patients and populations at risk—ultimate beneficiaries.
13. Global Alliance for Vaccines and Immunization	The ultimate beneficiaries of GAVI's efforts are the children, women, and men in the poorest 74 countries of the world. National governments also benefit from direct support for their immunization infrastructure. To date, 36 countries across all regions of the Global South are destined to receive vaccines and support for immunization services. Intermediate beneficiaries also include the partners—national governments, U.N. agencies, the World Bank, the private sector, bilateral governments, foundations, and others—who benefit from the enhanced collaboration that the GAVI umbrella/coordinating mechanism permits.
Infrastructure	
14. Water and Sanitation Program	The ultimate beneficiaries of our activities are poor people living in developing countries and lacking adequate access to safe and affordable water and sanitation services. Works through intermediate clients (governments and civil society) as illustrated in results framework.
15. Energy Sector Management Assistance Program	The intermediate beneficiaries come in many shapes and sizes: government policymakers and planners, utility officials, administrators in bilateral aid programs, consultants and consulting firms, academics, and World Bank staff. The ultimate beneficiaries are primarily poor energy consumers in developing countries who consume dirty energy inefficiently and spend up to 20% of their income on meeting their energy needs—if they have access to modern energy at all.
16. Consultative Group to Assist the Poorest	The ultimate beneficiaries of CGAP are the poor, including microentrepreneurs and very poor households, who lack access to formal credit and savings services. The vast majority of these ultimate beneficiaries are poor women. Local microfinance institutions that directly provide financial services to the poor at the community level are the intermediate beneficiaries. CGAP member donors and governments also benefit from activities aimed at improving donor microfinance practices and the policy environment for microfinance.
17. The Information for Development Program (*info*Dev)	People are the ultimate beneficiaries of *info*Dev activities. In the process, private and public organizations also benefit through an increase in their capacity to utilize ICT.
18. Public-Private Infrastructure Advisory Facility	The intended ultimate beneficiaries of PPIAF's activities are citizens of developing countries, particularly the poorest, who benefit from improved access to more reliable infrastructure services. Intermediate beneficiaries include recipient economies as a whole, with PPIAF technical assistance helping to increase the efficiency of key sectors, supporting private investment and freeing up public resources for other social purposes. The World Bank Group is also an intermediate beneficiary since PPIAF supports and complements the Bank's programs, including through better donor coordination.

Principal benefits (intended and unintended)
• Access to new resources (either directly from Stop TB or through partners participating in Stop TB). • Rapid sharing of news, best practices. • Recommendations or priority investments, assistance in development and implementation of strategic plans. • Political attention to problems. • Direct access to drugs.
The principal benefits that the ultimate beneficiaries receive are protection against killer diseases through vaccination, such as the routine 6 vaccines, and improved systems for immunizations. In addition, GAVI and the Vaccine Fund have made it possible for poor countries to protect their citizens against diseases for which newer and more expensive vaccines have been purchased, e.g., Hepatitis-B and Haemophilus influenzae type b (Hib). GAVI and the Vaccine Fund have also stimulated policy dialogue related to immunizations. Another GAVI benefit is that gaps—financial and technical—in relation to immunizations are being identified and addressed. A perhaps unintended benefit has been increased focus on health outcomes, as GAVI has adopted a performance-based (so-called "shares") approach. GAVI has also had the unintended effect of encouraging new and creative strategies that bring financing down to the community level. Thus, exploring new and creative financing schemes has been an important spinoff of the larger GAVI partnership.
Increased access to safe water and sanitation is the primary benefit. This is not achieved through direct investment and construction, but rather through support and development of suitable legal, regulatory, policy, and implementation practices in client countries. In addition, intermediate (and some ultimate) clients also gain access to an international body of experience on sector reform and development issues. This benefit flows both ways. Many clients have become strong advocates for sector reform and for new ideas, both in their own countries and in a wider international arena.
Primarily knowledge that helps define choices. The beneficiaries receive quality, unbiased, and relevant advice based on emerging global best practice in technical, economic, and institutional options to meet their energy needs while minimizing impacts on the natural/social environment and on public financial resources.
The principal intended benefit that the poor, the ultimate beneficiaries, receive from CGAP's activities is access to credit, savings and other financial services that are necessary to help them manage their daily lives. These financial services enable the poor to increase their income, build their businesses, reduce their economic vulnerability, and improve the well-being of their families in the process. Through this access to financial services, poor people, especially women, become more confident and assertive and have more control of their lives. They are better able to access public services and better able to negotiate and even confront the structures of patriarchy and inequity that traditionally have kept them poor.
Beneficiaries have increased access to critical information directly related to their well-being (education, health, government, environmental management, etc.). They also directly benefit from the project by increasing their capacity to use ICT tools. *info*Dev projects also have positive unintended consequences such as the development and dissemination of local cultural content.
PPIAF's interventions are directed to achieving the following benefits for client governments: • Improve the coverage, quality, and efficiency of water, power, transport, and telecom services, particularly to the poorest, with consequential benefits for the broader economy and the delivery of specific services, including health and education. • Reduce the fiscal and managerial burden on governments. • Expand the flow of private investment (including foreign direct investment).

(*Table continues on the following page.*)

Table H.11 Global TM Statements of Beneficiaries and Benefits of Case Study Programs (*continued*)

Program	Intended beneficiaries (intermediate and ultimate)
	Other participating donors also benefit through improved coordination of their programs and activities in this area, and by gaining access to global best practices in the design of such interventions. The private sector, both locally and internationally, benefits through expanded business opportunities.
19. Cities Alliance	The ultimate beneficiaries are: • The urban poor (particularly in the case of slum upgrading)—poor people living in slum settlements and typical lacking basic urban services and security of tenure • Poor cities (particularly in cases of city development) committed to implementing improved urban service delivery, economic development, and governance in a financially sustainability manner Intermediate clients (national/state governments, associations of local authorities and civil society) as illustrated in the results framework.
Social Development & Protection	
20. Post-conflict Fund	Conflict-affected communities and their governments and institutions.
21. Understanding Children's Work	The main beneficiaries of this program are countries where child labor is a major problem. Intermediate beneficiaries also include multilateral, bilateral, and national agencies working on the issue.
Trade & Finance	
22. Integrated Framework	Direct beneficiaries are those countries that participate.
23. Financial Sector Assessment Program	The ultimate beneficiaries of the FSAP are developing countries vulnerable to financial instability, and particularly their poor inhabitants, who are usually the hardest hit by financial crisis. In the intermediate term, the beneficiaries include all partners involved, particularly the World Bank, IMF, and other multilateral banks; bilateral agencies; and development organizations working on strengthening financial systems. The aim of the FSAP is to create a systematic mechanism for providing countries with the technical assistance support they need to build more robust financial systems.
24. Financial Sector Reform & Strengthening	Least developed countries in the first instance, but ultimately, all low-and middle-income countries, as the tools, strategies, experiences, and (eventually) funding become available and applicable to them. Also, the Bank itself is a beneficiary to the extent that the IF has prompted a much closer cooperation between various central units themselves (DECPG, PREMEP, DECRG) and among these and the operations.

Principal benefits (intended and unintended)
• PPIAF seeks to achieve these results in a way that helps: connect local policymakers with lessons of international best practices in a fast-moving area; build consensus for often politically sensitive reforms; and support local capacity building. Additional benefits flow because PPIAF has been designed to respond very quickly to urgent requests for assistance. Donor resources are also structured to reduce any potential suspicion of conflicting commercial or other interests. PPIAF also benefits participating donors by: • Mobilizing and leveraging resources • Exploiting the expertise and economies of scale and scope available from an integrated, multidonor work program • Promoting the exchange of lessons of experience among sectors, regions, and donors • Facilitating coordination between bilateral and multilateral programs addressing the same concerns.
In the case of the urban poor, increased access to safe water and sanitation and to security of tenure are the primary benefits. This is not achieved through direct investment and construction, but rather through support and development of suitable legal, regulatory, policy, and implementation practices in client countries. In the case of poor cities, benefits include improved urban governance and management, increased economic growth and employment, and sustained poverty reduction. Intermediate (and some ultimate) clients also gain access to an international body of experience on sector reform and development issues. This benefit flows both ways. Many clients have become strong advocates for sector reform and for new ideas, both in their own countries and in a wider international arena.
Rebuilding lives and livelihoods through critical activities such as demobilization, start-up support for land mine clearance, reintegration of IDPs and refugees, essential infrastructure rehabilitation, community development activities, reconciliation activities, etc.
It is essential to increase capacity building within countries, and this objective remains an integral part of the project. The UCW project aims to strengthen appropriate capacity for data analysis and use of information by helping identify and direct resources where they are most needed. Specific activities to support this goal include the development of the Training Packet on Child Labor, hosting the Field-Based Needs Assessment/Regional Workshop, supporting research through direct funding to local researchers, promoting inclusion of child labor panels on economic symposiums, and the UCW Working Paper series. By including researchers, field personnel of other agencies working on the issue, and others from developing countries in the listed activities, the UCW project will help develop a global network of experts, built on the principles of increased knowledge-sharing and effective use of limited resources.
Enhanced capacity of the financial sector to intermediate growth, and improved access to financial services—two goals intended for countries that participate in the FSAP—benefit the full spectrum of people living in those countries.
The benefits received include: improved coordination of donor activities (which will prevent duplication of efforts), better leveraging of resources, increased resources devoted to financial sector strengthening, greater diversity of technical capacity drawn from many resources, improved coordination of technical assistance delivery, and a simple, straightforward mechanism for accessing the resources to address vulnerabilities or target development opportunities.
Thorough analysis of the impediments to their integration into the world economy and how to tackle these and the poverty impact. Capacity building, technical assistance, greater voice in international forums. A more focused and better-coordinated approach by development agencies in their assistance strategy.

(*Table continues on the following page.*)

Table H.11 Global TM Statements of Beneficiaries and Benefits of Case Study Programs (*continued*)

Program	Intended beneficiaries (intermediate and ultimate)
Information & Knowledge	
25. Global Development Network	Intended beneficiaries of the program include developing-country researchers, who receive support to undertake their work; the broader development community, which gains access to this research; and policymakers, who can use both the research and the increased local pool of expertise.
26. World Links for Development	Intended direct beneficiaries are secondary students, teachers, pre-service teacher trainees, and education policymakers in World Links countries.

Principal benefits (intended and unintended)
Principal benefits include support for research undertaken in developing and transition countries, building networks with researchers in other countries, and access to expert commentators on their work. In addition, policymakers receive more locally produced research and a greater pool of research expertise to draw upon.
These individuals will receive improved and expanded educational opportunities and develop skills in effective use of information and communication technologies. In the medium to long term, employment prospects for participating youth are expected to be enhanced, and graduates will be able to help their countries compete in a global economy in the Information Age. It is also expected that the program will contribute to narrowing the in-country gap between the "information haves" in urban areas and the "information have-nots" in rural areas, as two-thirds of World Links schools are public schools located outside capital cities, a share that is expected to grow with DGF funding. Finally, in FY02, a new training initiative designed with FY01 DGF funds to disseminate lessons learned from three years of World Links Program experience will benefit senior-level policymakers in ministries of education, telecommunications, and finance.

Table H.12 OED Assessment of Monitoring and Evaluation of the Case Study Programs

	High	Substantial
Clear and coherent program objectives and strategies	5 MLF, ProCarbFund, Stop TB, GAVI, PPIAF	11 GEF, TDR, Global Forum, UNAIDS, RBM, ESMAP, CGAP, CA, FIRST, WSP, GDN
A structured set of quantitative or qualitative indicators	4 MLF, ProCarbFund, Stop TB, GAVI	8 CGIAR, TDR, UNAIDS, RBM, ESMAP, WSP, PPIAF, GDN
Systematic and regular processes for data collection and management	8 CGIAR, GEF, MLF, ProCarbFund, TDR, UNAIDS, GAVI, PPIAF	7 Global Forum, RBM, Stop TB, CA, GDN, World Links, UCW
Independence of program-level evaluations	5 TDR, UNAIDS, RBM, Stop TB, IF	7 CEPF, Global Forum, CGAP, ESMAP, CA, WSP, PostConFund
Effective feedback of evaluations on the strategic focus of the program	5 TDR, RBM, WSP, CA, IF	6 GEF, UNAIDS, Stop TB, ESMAP, CGAP, PostConFund
Effective feedback of evaluations on program-level organization, management, and financing	6 TDR, RBM, WSP, ESMAP, CA, IF	6 CGIAR, UNAIDS, Stop TB, CGAP, PostConFund

Note: The five criteria are based upon OED's standards of best practice as identified in OED's report, *Monitoring and Evaluation Plans in Staff Appraisal Reports Issued in Fiscal Year 1995* (OED 1995), pp. 23–24.

Modest	Negligible	Not enough information or too early to rate	No program-level evaluations yet
10 CGIAR, GWP, GIF, *info*Dev, IF, UCW, PostConFund, World Links, CEPF, FSAP			
4 Global Forum, CGAP, CA, World Links	9 GEF, CEPF, GIF, *info*Dev, PostConFund, FSAP, IF, GWP, UCW	1 FIRST	
8 CEPF, WSP, ESMAP, CGAP, *info*Dev, PostConFund, GDN, GIF, IF	1 GWP	2 FIRST, FSAP	
8 CGIAR, GEF, MLF, GWP, GIF, *info*Dev, UCW, GDN			6 ProCarbFund, GAVI, PPIAF, FSAP, FIRST, World Links
6 CGIAR, MLF, CEPF, GIF, *info*Dev, GDN	3 Global Forum, UCW, GWP		6 ProCarbFund, GAVI, PPIAF, FSAP, FIRST, World Links
5 GEF, MLF, CEPF, Global Forum, *info*Dev	2 GWP, GIF	1 GDN	6 ProCarbFund, GAVI, PPIAF, FSAP, FIRST, World Links

Table H.13 Phase 2 Case Study Programs: Members of the Governing and Executive Bodies

Program	International/regional organizations[a]	Industrial countries	Developing countries
Environment & Agriculture			
1. Consultative Group on International Agricultural Research (62 members)	AfDB, Arab Fund for Economic and Social Development, AsDB, FAO, IDB, IDRC, IFAD, OPEC Fund for International Development, UNEP, UNDP, World Bank	Australia, Austria, Belgium, Canada, Denmark, EU, Finland, France, Germany, Ireland, Israel, Italy, Japan, Luxembourg, Netherlands, New Zealand, Norway, Portugal, Spain, Sweden, Switzerland, U.K., U.S.,	Bangladesh, Brazil, China, Colombia, Côte d'Ivoire, Egypt, India, Indonesia, Iran, Kenya, Korea, Malaysia, Mexico, Morocc Nigeria, Pakistan, Peru, Philippines, Romania, Russia, South Africa, Syria, Thailand, Uga
Executive Council (21 members)	FAO, IFAD, World Bank	Denmark, Germany, Japan, Netherlands, U.S.	China, Colombia, South Africa, Syria, AARINENA
2. Global Environment Facility GEF Assembly (174 members and 3 implementing agencies)	UNDP, UNEP, World Bank (implementing agencies)	55 GEF member countries	129 GEF member countries
GEF Council (32 members)	UNDP, UNEP, World Bank (observers)	14 GEF member countries	18 GEF member countries
3. Multilateral Fund for the Implementation of the Montreal Protocol Meeting of the Parties (187 members and 4 implementing agencies)	UNIDO, UNDP, UNEP, World Bank (implementing agencies)	55 MLF member countries (non Article 5 countries)	129 MLF member countries (Article 5 countries)
Executive Committee (14 members and 7 observers)	UNIDO, UNDP, UNEP, World Bank (observers)	Austria, Belgium, Canada, France, Japan, Hungary, U.S. (Japan, U.S., and one EU member are permanent; others rotate)	Bolivia, Burundi, China El Salvador, India, Jordan, Mauritius, Saint Lucia (rotating members; India and China rotate among themselves)
4. Prototype Carbon Fund (23 participants—6 public sector and 17 private sector—and 27 host countries)	World Bank	Canada, Finland, Japan, Netherlands, Norway, Sweden	Brazil, Bulgaria, Chile, Colombia, Costa Rica, Czech Republic, Ecuador, Guatemala, Honduras, Hungary, India, Indonesia, Kenya, Latvia, Mauritius, Mexico, Moldova, Morocco, Nicaragua, Peru, Poland, Romania, South Africa, Thailand, Uganda, Uzbekistan, Vietnam

Foundations	Commercial private sector	Civil society organizations[b]	Others
Ford, Kellogg, Rockefeller, Syngenta	–	–	–
Rockefeller	Private Sector Committee Chair	NGO Committee Chair (temporarily vacant)	CDC Chair, CBC Chair, TAC/SC Chair, GFAR Chair
–	–	–	–
–	–	–	–
–	–	–	–
–	Industry representatives (observers)	NGOs (observers)	Treasurer (observer)
–	BP Amoco, Chubu Electric Power Company, Chugoku Electric Power Company, Deutsche Bank, Electrabel, Fortum OYJ, Gilde Strategic Situations BV, Gaz de France, Kyushu Electric Power Company, MIT Carbon Fund, Mitsubishi, Mitsui, Norsk Hydro ASA, RWE AktiengesellschaftShikoku, Statoil, Tohuku Electric Power Company, Tokyo Electric Power Company	–	–

(*Table continues on the following page.*)

Table H.13 Phase 2 Case Study Programs: Members of the Governing and Executive Bodies (*continued*)

Program	International/regional organizations[a]	Industrial countries	Developing countries
Participants' committee (7 members)	–	Four representatives	One observer
5. Critical Ecosystem Partnership Fund Donor Council (5 members)	GEF, World Bank	Japan	–
Working Group (5 members)	GEF, World Bank	Japan	–
6. Global Water Partnership (12 financial partners and 9 regional partnerships)	UNDP	Canada, Denmark, Finland, France, Germany, Luxembourg, Netherlands, Norway, Sweden, U.K.	Regional partnerships in Southern Africa, West Africa, China, Southeast Asia, Southern Asia, Central and Eastern Europe, the Mediterranean, South America and Central America.
Consulting Partners (10 members)	UNDP, World Bank, WMO, WSSCC (cosponsors)	France, Germany, Netherlands, Switzerland (financial partners)	–
Steering Committee (22 members)	UNDP, World Bank, WMO, WSSCC (cosponsors)	France, Germany, Netherlands, Switzerland (financial partners)	–
7. Global Integrated Pest Management Facility Governing Group (4 cosponsors, 3 donors, and 3 specialized technical partners)	FAO, UNEP, UNDP, World Bank (cosponsors)	Netherlands, Norway, Switzerland (donors)	–
Health			
8. Special Program for Research and Training in Tropical Diseases Joint Coordinating Board (30 members)	UNDP, World Bank, WHO, UNICEF (2003) (cosponsors)	Belgium, Canada, Denmark, Germany, Japan, Luxembourg, Netherlands, Norway, Portugal, Switzerland, Sweden, U.K., U.S.	Argentina, Armenia, Banglades Brazil, Burkina Faso, Cameroon, China, Cuba, India, Kuwait, Laos, Malaysia, Saudi Arabia, Thaila
9. Global Forum for Health Research Foundation Council (19 members currently out of maximum of 20)	GFATM, TDR, World Bank, WHO	Canada, Denmark, Netherlands, Norway, Sweden, Switzerland	India, National Institute of Medical Research (Tanzania Academy of Sciences (Russia)

Foundations	Commercial private sector	Civil society organizations[b]	Others
–	Three representatives	–	–
MacArthur	–	Conservation International	–
MacArthur	–	Conservation International	–
Ford	–	–	–
–	–	World Water Council (permanent observer)	Executive Secretary, Technical Committee Chair (ex officio)
–	–	World Water Council (permanent observer)	12 individuals, including the chair, from public agencies and NGOs in industrialized and developing countries
			Executive Secretary, Technical Committee Chair
CERES/Locustox Foundation	–	GTZ/University of Hannover, CABI Bioscience	–
–	–	–	–
Gates, Rockefeller	–	Asian-Pacific Research and Resource Center for Women, Center for Research and Advanced Studies, International Federation of Pharmaceutical Manufacturers Associations,	–

(*Table continues on the following page.*)

Table H.13 Phase 2 Case Study Programs: Members of the Governing and Executive Bodies (*continued*)

Program	International/regional organizations[a]	Industrial countries	Developing countries
10. UNAIDS (Joint United Nations Program on HIV/AIDS) Program Coordinating Board (35 members) (cosponsors)	ILO, UNDP, UNESCO, UNFPA, UNICEF, UNODC, World Bank, WFP, WHO	Canada, Denmark, Germany, Ireland, Japan, Portugal, Spain, Sweden	Bahamas, Brazil, Burundi, China, Côte d'Ivoire, Guatemal India, Kenya, Myanmar, Pakistan, Philippines, Romania Russian Federation, Tunisia, Zam
11. Roll Back Malaria Steering Committee (15 members currently, out of a maximum of 17)	UNICEF, World Bank, WHO (cosponsors)	Italy, Netherlands, U.S.	Ghana, D.R. Congo, India, Senegal, Zambia
12. Stop TB Coordinating Board (27 members)	UNICEF, World Bank, WHO (cosponsors)	Canada, Japan, Netherlands, U.K., U.S.	Brazil, India, Mexico, Nigeria, Pakistan, Philippines
13. Global Alliance for Vaccines and Immunization GAVI Board (16 members)	UNICEF, World Bank, WHO	Canada, Centers for Disease Control (USA), Institut Pasteur (France), U.K.	India, Mongolia, Mozambique Serum Institute of India
Infrastructure			
14. Water and Sanitation Program Program Council (19 members)	UNDP, World Bank	Australia, Austria, Belgium, Canada, Denmark, France, Germany, Italy, Luxembourg, Netherlands, Norway, Sweden, Switzerland, U.K.	One country-level member, representing the national advisory committees
15. Energy Sector Management Assistance Program Consultative Group (16 members)	UNDP, World Bank	Belgium, Canada, Denmark, Finland, France, Germany, Netherlands, Norway, Sweden, Switzerland, U.K	Two members at large from countries receiving ESMAP assistance
16. Consultative Group to Assist the Poorest Council of Governors (28 members)	AfDB, AsDB, EBRD, IDB, IFAD, ILO, UNCDF, UNDP, World Bank	Australia, Belgium, Canada, Denmark, EU, Finland, France, Germany, Italy, Japan, Luxembourg, Netherlands, Norway, Sweden, Switzerland, U.K., U.S.	–
Executive Committee (10 members)	AsDB, World Bank	Norway, U.K.	–

Foundations	Commercial private sector	Civil society organizations[b]	Others
		International Planned Parenthood Federation, International Women's Health Coalition	
dian Foundation for Drug Policy, Hong Kong AIDS Foundation	–	AAL HDN Organizacion de SIDA-Redla+ (Argentina), Abraco (Portugal), Faith, Hope and Love (Guatemala), Ghana HIV/AIDS Network	–
–	Bayer Pharmaceutical	Health and Nutrition International	Executive Secretary of RBM Secretariat, The Executive Director of the Global Fund for ATM
Soros	–	Six chairpersons of the working groups	Six regional representatives
Gates, UN Foundation, Vaccine Fund	Wyeth-Ayerst Global Pharmaceuticals	Sierra Leone Red Cross	–
–	–	One member from a strategic partner organization	One internationally recognized water supply and sanitation expert
UN Foundation	–	–	–
Argidius, Ford	–	–	–
Ford	–	World Council of Credit Unions	Four microfinance industry leaders

(*Table continues on the following page.*)

Table H.13 Phase 2 Case Study Programs: Members of the Governing and Executive Bodies (*continued*)

Program	International/regional organizations[a]	Industrial countries	Developing countries
17. The Information for Development Program (*info*Dev) Donors' Committee (18 members)	World Bank	Australia, Belgium, Canada, Denmark, EU, Finland, France, Germany, Ireland, Italy, Japan, Luxembourg, Netherlands, Sweden, Switzerland, U.K., U.S.	–
18. Public-Private Infrastructure Advisory Facility Program Council (12 members)	UNDP, AsDB, World Bank	Canada, France, Germany, Japan, Netherlands, Norway, Sweden, Switzerland, U.K.	–
19. Cities Alliance Consultative Group (18 members)	AsDB, UNEP, UN-Habitat, World Bank	Canada, France, Germany, Italy, Japan, Netherlands, Norway, Sweden, U.K., U.S.	Brazil
Steering Committee (5 members)	UN-Habitat, World Bank	Two representatives: Netherlands, U.K.	–
Social Development & Protection			
20. Post-conflict Fund (1 member)	World Bank	–	–
21. Understanding Children's Work Steering Committee (3 members and 6 donors)	ILO, UNICEF, World Bank	Canada, Finland, Netherlands, Norway, Sweden, U.K.	–
Trade & Finance			
22. Integrated Framework Steering Committee (70 members)	ITC, IMF, UNCTAD, UNDP, World Bank, WTO	Belgium, Canada, Denmark, EU, Finland, France, Ireland, Italy, Japan, Netherlands, Norway, Sweden, Switzerland, U.K., U.S.	49 least-developed countries
Interagency Working Group (10 members)	ITC, IMF, UNCTAD, UNDP, World Bank, WTO, OECD/DADC (observer)	Two donor representatives	Two LDC representatives
23. Financial Sector Assessment Program Liaison Committee (2 members)	IMF, World Bank	–	–
24. Financial Sector Reform & Strengthening Initiative Governing Council (6 members)	IMF, World Bank	Canada, Netherlands, Switzerland, U.K. Sweden (observer)	–

Foundations	Commercial private sector	Civil society organizations[b]	Others
–	–	–	
		–	
–	–	–	–
–	–	International Union of Local Authorities, Metropolis, World Federation of United Cities, World Association of Cities and Local Authorities Coordination	–
–	–	One representative	–
–	–	–	–
–	–	–	–
–	–	–	–
–	–	–	–
–	–	–	–
–	–	–	–

(*Table continues on the following page.*)

Table H.13 Phase 2 Case Study Programs: Members of the Governing and Executive Bodies (*continued*)

Program	International/regional organizations[a]	Industrial countries	Developing countries
Steering Committee (6 members)	IMF, World Bank	Canada, Netherlands, Switzerland, U.K. Sweden (observer)	–
Information & Knowledge			
25. Global Development Network Governing Body (18 members)	UNDP, World Bank	–	11 regional research networks of developing and transition economies
26. World Links for Development Governing Board (14 members)	World Bank	–	Senegal

a. Refers to international and regional public sector organizations only, including the World Bank.

b. Broadly defined to include NGOs, umbrella organizations, professional and trade associations, and the like that are independent of the state or governments and without a commercial, for-profit motive.

Foundations	Commercial private sector	Civil society organizations[b]	Others
–	–	–	–
–	–	International Economics Association, International Political Science Association, International Sociological Association	2 members-at-large (academia)
–	Accenture, DireqLearn, Goldman Sachs, J. P. Morgan Chase, NJTC Venture Fund, Schools Online, Talal Abu-Ghazaleh & Co	–	5 private entrepreneurs

Table H.14 Financing of Case Study Programs

Program	Program expenditures (US$ millions)		World Bank share (%)[a]		World Bank DGF allocation (US$ millions)		
	FY03 (CY02)	FY04 (CY03)	FY03	FY04	FY03	FY04	FY05
Environment & Agriculture							
1. CGIAR	380.0	395.0	14	13	50.0	50.0	50.0
2. GEF	447.2	387.53[d]	0.0	0.0	–	–	–
3. MLF	156.3	158.6[e]	0.0	0.0	–	–	–
4. Prototype Carbon Fund	5.01	6.5[f]	0.0	0.0	–	–	–
5. CEPF	21.79	20.19	27.6	35.0	4.00	4.00	4.00
6. GWP	7.75	10.3	5.3	0.0	0.40	–	–
7. GIF	1.3	n.a.	n.a.	0.0	–	–	–
Health							
8. TDR	47.8	47.4[g]	5.5	5.5	2.50	2.50	2.00
9. Global Forum for Health Research	2.47	3.07	25.9	33.3	0.70	1.00	6.78[h]
10. UNAIDS	95.0[i]	95.0	4.2	4.2	4.00	4.00	4.00
11. RBM	11.4	11.4	13.2	13.2	1.50	1.50	1.00
12. Stop TB	10.5	20.8[j]	15.4	15.4	0.70	0.70	0.70
13. GAVI	101.3	124.1[k]	1.5	1.2	1.50	1.50	1.50
Infrastructure							
14. WSP	12.4	13.6	6.1	10.9	–	–	–
15. ESMAP	6.01	7.58	12.6	7.0	–	–	–
16. CGAP	13.2	12.67	51	55.5	6.73	6.33	5.52
17. *info*Dev	8.90	6.07	21.9	n.a.	3.00	2.54	2.50
18. PPIAF	14.5	15.61	7.8	10.5	2.00	2.00	2.00
19. Cities Alliance	9.67	13.25	27.6	9.8	1.70	1.70	1.70
Social Development & Protection							
20. Post-conflict Fund	13.7	10.6	9.72	99.0	14.3[l]	9.22	8.00
21. UCW	0.39	0.56	0.0	6%	–	0.10	0.10
Trade & Finance							
22. IF[n]	2.71	n.a.	25.2	24.5	0.63	0.80	-
23. FSAP	10.51	10.46[p]	45	45	–	–	–

World Bank BB contribution[b] (US$ millions)		Trustee	Other donor contributions (US$ millions)		How program is funded[c]
03 (CY02)	FY04 (CY03)		FY03	FY04	
–	–	World Bank	307.1	331.0	Annual donor contributions, either directly to centers or channeled through Bank-administered trust funds
–	–	World Bank	673.44	805.46	Triennial donor replenishments
–	–	UNEP	142.4	142.1	Triennial donor replenishments Funds transferred from UNEP to Bank's ozone TF for Bank expenditures
–	–	World Bank	6.50	23.18	Public and private sector participant contributions
–	–	CI	10.5	7.35	Annual donor contributions
–	–	GWP	7.16	9.31	Annual donor contributions
n.a.	–	FAO	n.a.	1.3	Annual donor contributions
–	–	TDR	45.2	45.0	Annual donor contributions
–	–	Global Forum	2.0	2.3	Annual donor contributions
–	–	UNAIDS	91.0	91.0	Annual donor contributions
–	–	WHO	9.90	9.90	Annual donor contributions
–	–	WHO, World Bank	3.85	3.83	Annual donor contributions to WHO-administered trust funds Supplementary Bank-administered TF created in FY03 for specific activities
–	–	GAVI, Vaccine Fund	2.10	13.0	Annual donor contributions to these two trust funds
1.00	n.a.	World Bank	15.5	12.12	Annual donor contributions
1.03	0.55	World Bank	7.14	7.27	Annual donor contributions
–	–	World Bank	6.19	6.27	Annual donor contributions
0.76	.09	World Bank	10.98	n.a	Annual donor contributions
–	–	World Bank	23.5	17.15	Annual donor contributions
–	–	World Bank	15.6	13.67	Annual donor contributions
–	–	World Bank	0.27	0.33	Annual donor contributions
–	–	UNICEF	2.04[m]	1.5	Annual donor contributions
.76[o]	n.a.	UNDP, World Bank	2.77	4.30	Annual donor contributions to a UNDP-administered TF Funds transferred from UNDP to Bank-administered TF for Bank expenditures
4.71	4.73	–	5.8	5.73	World Bank and IMF administrative budgets

(*Table continues on the following page.*)

Table H.14	Financing of Case Study Programs (continued)						
	Program expenditures (US$ millions)		World Bank share (%)[a]		World Bank DGF allocation (US$ millions)		
Program	FY03 (CY02)	FY04 (CY03)	FY03	FY04	FY03	FY04	FY05
24. FIRST	.78	2.58	3.2	2.25	.50	0.40[q]	0.60
Information & Knowledge							
25. GDN	10.9	8.67	51.1	54.7	4.70	4.45[r]	4.00
26. World Links	3.96	6.52	28.6	21.4	1.52	1.51	–
Total							

a. Of total financial contributions to the program in each year.
b. BB contributions to the program itself, not including BB resources for oversight and liaison activities.
c. The process by which the program is financed.
d. Includes GEF administrative expenses, fees to implementing agencies, and investment grants to recipient countries.
e. Includes MLF secretariat expenses, fees to implementing agencies, and investment grants to recipient countries.
f. Includes administrative expenses plus capital grants (emissions reductions) of $295,000 in FY02 and $918,000 in FY03.
g. $95.2 million for the 2002/03 biennium.
h. Out of the total for Global Forum, $1.5 million goes to GAVI. Additionally, funding is channeled through the Global Forum umbrella to several other partnerships as well, including, for example, IAVI. OED was not able to obtain an updated breakdown of this distribution for FY05.
i. $190.0 million for the 2002/03 biennium.
j. Includes $5.6 million disbursed by the Global Fund facility in 2002 and $15.6 million in 2003.
k. Includes $14.5 million expended by GAVI and $109.6 million disbursed by the Vaccine Fund.
l. Includes a special $5 million allocation for East Timor.
m. Finland, Sweden, and Norway contributed $2.04 million in FY01 for the 2001-03 triennium.
n. Program expenditures include Bank's in-kind contributions.
o. In-kind contributions, not included in the official IF expenditures reported by UNDP, the administrator of the principal IF trust fund.
p. Based on a World Bank share of 45 percent. Precise IMF expenditures on FSAP are not known.
q. For FY02. The FY03 application was deferred to FY04 and the uncommitted FY02 balance was carried over to FY03.
r. For the core program only, not including the 1.18 m for the Education Research Component in GDN.
s. Does not include in-kind contribution of $45,115.00 for FY04.

World Bank BB contribution[b] (US$ millions)			Other donor contributions (US$ millions)		
03 (CY02)	FY04 (CY03)	Trustee	FY03	FY04	How program is funded[c]
–	–	World Bank	15.1	17.4	Annual donor contributions to Bank-administered trust funds
–	.40[s]	GDN	6.30	3.65	Annual donor contributions to GDN-administered trust funds
–	–	World Links	3.8	5.5	Annual donor contributions to World Links-administered trust funds

Table H.15 OED Assessment of Governance and Management of Case Study Programs

	High	Substantial
Transparency[a]	6 GEF, TDR, GAVI, PPIAF, CA, FSAP	9 MLF, ProCarbFund, CEPF, UNAIDS, Stop TB, ESMAP, CGAP, GDN, World Links
Clarity of roles and responsibilities[b]	9 ProCarbFund, TDR, RBM, Stop TB, GAVI, PPIAF, CA, FSAP, FIRST	9 GEF, MLF, CEPF, GWP, WSP, ESMAP, CGAP, PostConFund, World Links
Fairness to immediate client[c]	3 ESMAP, PPIAF, CA	14 CGIAR, GEF, MLF, ProCarbFund, GWP, TDR, UNAIDS, RBM, Stop TB, GAVI, UCW, IF, FSAP, GDN
Accountability to donors[d]	17 CGIAR, MLF, ProCarbFund, CEPF, TDR, Global Forum, UNAIDS, RBM, Stop TB, GAVI, ESMAP, CGAP, PPIAF, CA, FSAP, FIRST, World Links	7 GEF, GWP, GIF, WSP, *info*Dev, PostConFund, UCW
Accountability to developing countries	5 GEF, MLF, TDR, RBM, Stop TB	6 CGIAR, ProCarbFund, UNAIDS, WSP, CGAP, CA
Accountability to scientists/professionals	4 MLF, ProCarbFund, TDR, Stop TB	9 CGIAR, Global Forum, GAVI, ESMAP, CGAP, PPIAF, CA, FSAP, GDN

a. Transparency – the program provides both shareholders and stakeholders with the information they need in an open and transparent manner (such as accounting, audit, and nonfinancial but material issues).

b. Clarity of roles and responsibilities – of the various officers and bodies that govern and manage the program, as well as clear mechanisms to modify and amend the governance and management of the program in a dynamic context.

c. Fairness – the program does not favor some immediate clients over others (such as Bank staff, central governments and their agencies, municipal agencies, local authorities, private service providers, NGOs, and community organizations).

d. Accountability – of the program for the exercise of power over resources to each of the four groups of stakeholders listed here, "other stakeholders" being those not otherwise mentioned with a legitimate interest in the activities of the program (such as international NGOs).

Modest	Negligible	Not enough information or too early to rate
9 CGIAR, GWP, Global Forum, RBM, WSP, *info*Dev, PostConFund, IF, UCW	1 GIF	1 FIRST
6 CGIAR, Global Forum, UNAIDS, *info*Dev, IF, GDN	2 GIF, UCW	
4 GIF, WSP, CGAP, *info*Dev	1 CEPF	4 Global Forum, PostConFund, FIRST, World Links
2 IF, GDN		
7 GIF, Global Forum, GAVI, ESMAP, PPIAF, World Links, GDN	7 CEPF, GWP, *info*Dev, PostConFund, UCW, IF, FSAP	1 FIRST
8 GEF, CEPF, GWP, UNAIDS, RBM, WSP, *info*Dev, World Links	4 GIF, PostConFund, UCW, IF	1 FIRST

Table H.16 Stated Exit Strategies of Case Study Programs

Program	Regarding the program
Environment & Agriculture	
1. CGIAR	
2. Global Environment Facility	None.
3. Multilateral Fund for the Implementation of the Montreal Protocol	
4. Prototype Carbon Fund	As a pilot activity, the Prototype Carbon Fund does not endeavor to compete in the emission reductions market; it is restricted to $180 million and is scheduled to terminate in 2012.
5. Critical Ecosystem Partnership Fund	Initially, the closing date for the program was June 30, 2006, but the Financing Agreement for the Fund was amended on February 11, 2003, to extend the closing date of the program to June 30, 2010. The current partners are still trying to identify additional organizations to join the partnership and effectively extend the life of the program.
6. Global Water Partnership	
7. Global Integrated Pest Management Facility	Facility was initially established for a five-year period in 1997. No clear exit strategy is in place.
Health	
8. Special Program for Research and Training in Tropical Diseases (TDR)	Because of the time needed to develop new therapeutic agents and the specific epidemiological features of some diseases, the TDR has an open-ended time frame. However, through its internal review mechanism, the program "exits" from diseases once tools have become available. Examples include leprosy, onchocerciasis, and, to a large extent, schistosomiasis.
9. Global Forum for Health Research	The Global Forum for Health Research works to correct the 10/90 gap in health research. The 10/90 gap has also been highlighted by the Commission on Microeconomics & Health. The program is a long-term endeavor.
10. UNAIDS	HIV/AIDS will require a long-term commitment from the UNAIDS co-sponsors and partner organizations.
11. Roll Back Malaria	Sustaining program activities will be accomplished through increasing recognized credibility of the institution and of the activities, which will increasingly be supported by other financiers and beneficiary countries themselves.

Regarding the Bank's involvement in the program	Regarding DGF funding
	None given
	Not applicable
Last project completion reports are scheduled to be finalized in 2011.	Not applicable
	Not applicable
Currently, the Bank's involvement, as outlined in the Memorandum of Understanding, is effective until 30 days after delivery of a final report, which is due June 30, 2006, or a later date (because the Donor Council may determine that continuation of program beyond this time frame is necessary).	
	DGF support has been key in getting the GWP off the ground. There is an application for a fourth year of funding from the DGF. The Bank's resources are key in paying the costs of the Technical Committee and the Secretariat. FY02 is the final year of DGF funding.
Bank has exited financially, but continues to be a cosponsor.	Not applicable
The Bank has been involved with TDR since its inception, with a full understanding that combating the diseases that the program targets will take a long-term commitment.	Window 1
The Bank has been involved in the Global Forum since its inception, as a financial donor, catalyst of additional resources, and legitimizing force. Moreover, the Bank channels some of its funds through the Global Forum for use by other programs and organizations. Presently, there is no strategy for Bank disengagement from the program.	Window 1
The Bank has been involved in UNAIDS from the outset. It is a co-sponsor of the program and appears as a permanent member on the UNAID Program Coordinating Board. There is presently only a partial strategy for Bank disengagement from the program—based on partnership progress as monitored by the sector board.	Window 1
The Bank has been involved in RBM since the program's inception as a co-sponsor and appears as a permanent member on the RBM Governing Board. There is presently no stated disengagement strategy on behalf of the Bank regarding the program.	Request to move from Window 2 to Window 1[a]

(*Table continues on the following page.*)

Table H.16 Stated Exit Strategies of Case Study Programs (*continued*)

Program	Regarding the program
12. Stop TB	The Stop TB Initiative was launched as a two-year activity, 1999–2000. However, as its work program has evolved, its partners have agreed that it must continue to operate at least until 2005.
13. Global Alliance for Vaccines and Immunization	Childhood immunization is seen to be the most cost-effective health intervention. There exist 33 million annual unvaccinated children, and the program has strong financial support from the Gates Foundation and other international agencies, including UNICEF and the Bank, to not only immunize but also establish the basic infrastructure to carry out child immunization programs for the near future.
Infrastructure	
14. Water and Sanitation Program	There is no exit strategy. The program will operate as long as there are participating partners and available funding. Termination is not anticipated. All funding is ongoing. Some donors renew annually, and some make longer-term commitments.
15. Energy Sector Management Assistance Program	There is no exit strategy. The program will continue as long as there is a demand for it.
16. Consultative Group to Assist the Poorest	The present mandate of CGAP extends through FY08. The Council of Govern will conduct a review in FY06 in order to determine post-FY08 options for CG (disband, expand, or transform).
17. Information for Development Program (*info*Dev)	The program is expected to continue as long as new knowledge will have to be generated about ICT for development and poverty reduction.

Regarding the Bank's involvement in the program	Regarding DGF funding
The Bank has been involved in Stop TB since the program's inception and appears as a permanent member on the Stop TB Coordinating Board. There is no stated disengagement strategy on behalf of the Bank regarding the program.	Request to move from Window 2 to Window 1.[b]
The Bank has been involved in GAVI since the program's inception as a co-sponsor and permanent member on the GAVI Board. There is no stated disengagement strategy on behalf of the Bank.	Window 1
No changes in the Bank's role are anticipated.	Not applicable
INFVP does not have a strategy for Bank disengagement from ESMAP.	Not applicable
The two sponsoring vice presidencies, FSE and INF, have no strategy at the present time for completely disengaging the Bank from CGAP. However, they are supporting CGAP's current strategy of reducing its financial dependence on the Bank (amount requested from DGF is reduced by $400,000 every year).	CGAP is a Window 1 program. When CGAP was established, it was with the full expectation that the Bank would remain the majority funder because of CCAP's global mandate. Since CGAP's integration into the DGF, non-Bank member donors have contributed financially, and some have increased their funding commitments in order to meet the DGF's 15% funding criterion. This has resulted in an increase in ownership among other members and a more balanced treatment of all donors, even though the Bank remains CGAP's largest donor. CGAP's present strategy is to gradually reduce the share of DGF funding in its total budget by $400,000 annually, by seeking increased contributions from other member donors as well as new member donors. Accordingly, the DGF allocation declined from $7.5 million in FY01 to $7.13 million in FY02, to $6.73 million in FY03, and to $6.33 million in FY04.
In the light of the new ICT Strategy endorsed by the Bank's Executive Directors on September 6, 2001, there is an increasingly closer integration of *info*Dev activities with World Bank Group operations. Indeed, the experience of recent years has shown that in the fast-changing environment of ICT, a program like *info*Dev is uniquely placed to respond quickly to new opportunities and challenges. It is expected that an independent external review will be conducted in FY05 to assess the relevance of *info*Dev, its objectives, and the value of housing *info*Dev within the Bank. Based on the results of the external review, an exit strategy will be considered and activated, if deemed appropriate.	*info*Dev is a DGF Window 1 program. Following a modification of the strategy, focusing essentially on "flagship" activities and knowledge dissemination, support from the DGF, at the requested level, is expected at least through FY08 in order to ensure continuity in implementing the new strategy and provide other donors with sufficient assurance of the World Bank Group's commitment to the objectives and strategy of *info*Dev.

(*Table continues on the following page.*)

Table H.16 Stated Exit Strategies of Case Study Programs (*continued*)

Program	Regarding the program
18. Public-Private Infrastructure Advisory Facility	
19. Cities Alliance	Cities Without Slums Action Plan has a 20-year target. All funding is ongoing some donors renewing annually, some with longer-term commitments.
Social Protection & Development	
20. Post-conflict Fund	
21. Understanding Children's Work	Phase I was completed in August 2003. Phase II is scheduled to end January 2007.
Trade & Finance	
22. Integrated Framework	
23. Financial Sector Assessment Program	
24. FIRST	
Information & Knowledge	
25. Global Development Network	GDN's objectives are to support the generation and sharing of knowledge and also to support the capacity of research in developing countries. There is no stated exit strategy for the program, and it proposes to continue as long as there is a demand for it.

Regarding the Bank's involvement in the program	Regarding DGF funding
Based on informal discussions with existing and potential donors, it is our assessment that PPIAF could not credibly continue without World Bank financial and substantive participation. The Bank brings intellectual leadership, convening power, and much-needed independence to the commercially important topic of private participation in infrastructure. From the Bank's perspective, there is a view that PPIAF's work on the challenging issues facing private participation in infrastructure remains a high priority and that Window 1 funding is the only way to signal its commitment under the current rules.	PPIAF is a DGF Window 2 program. Current DGF funding is until end FY04. Other donors have made commitments for continued funding for at least 3 years. PPIAF recognizes the budget constraints faced by DGF at this time. While a medium-term commitment from the Bank is important, it is recommended that the Window 1 status for PPIAF should not be open-ended. It is suggested that a fixed-term commitment would be more appropriate, with an independent evaluation to consider exit from Window 1 at the end of that period. One option could be to have a period that runs in parallel with PPIAF's three-year life cycle.
The INF vice president has no plans to exit the partnership at any time in the foreseeable future. The VPU launched the partnership, as part of its renewed engagement with UN-HABITAT, and through VPU leadership has helped position the partnership to become a focal point for the Bank's interventions in urban development. The partnership's Cities Without Slums Action Plan (now established as MDG Target 11) sets impact targets to be achieved by 2020, leaving the partnership only 17 years to achieve the goals. The Bank's urban-sector strategy recognized that the challenges facing cities require coordinated and concerted efforts, beyond what any single development agency could provide alone.	Cities Alliance is a Window 2 program. Current DGF funding is through the end of FY04, all of which is for core funds. The program disengaged from DGF funding for financing the Cities Alliance Secretariat in FY03. All Secretariat costs are now covered by donor trust funds.
	All individual activities financed by the PostConFund have a specific grant period. The FY02 DGF application continues a 3-year strategy to maintain DGF support while the potential for donor support is tested.
	Expected that donors will eventually support the program independently. In three years (by FY04), trade policy reforms should have been mainstreamed in Bank work in LDCs.
	Not applicable.
	The proposed disengagement strategy is for the FSSF Governing Council, beginning July 2003, to evaluate two options for disengagement from DGF Window 2 funding: (1) bilateral donor funding of the entire budget or (2) DGF Window 1 funding.
The Global Development Network launched with the strong personal leadership of the president of the World Bank. Since then, the program has spun off from the Bank and is independent. However, the program still receives Bank funding, as the president of the Bank has assured the funding of GDN's administrative costs up to US$1.8 million per year through 2006. The Bank is also represented on the program's governance board.	Window 1

(*Table continues on the following page.*)

Table H.16 Stated Exit Strategies of Case Study Programs (*continued*)

Program	Regarding the program
26. World Links for Development	The World Links program started as a pilot initiative of the Bank, explicitly designed to have a 3-year lifespan in each country in which it operated. It was expected that, after 3 years, participating countries would be able to continue and expand activities on their own. Presently, the program has evolved into an independent legal organization and continues its work on a long-term basis with no disengagement strategy.

a. As a Window 2 program, Roll Back Malaria will soon hit the three-year limit for Window 2 programs and will have to exit from DGF funding in FY04 if current rules are applied rigidly. The program has requested extending DGF support to the RBM Malaria Partnership beyond FY04 until FY15 under Window 1. In its most recent annual report, DGF indicates that RBM is considered important for Bank's clients by the sector boards and networks because it is closely aligned with sector priorities and essential for sustaining Bank engagement. Thus, the sector board is expected to request longer-term DGF support starting in FY05.

b. As a Window 2 program, Stop TB will hit the three-year limit for Window 2 programs and will have to exit from DGF funding in FY04. It has been proposed that DGF financing continue at a level that enhances the Bank's active engagement with key agencies and demonstrates Bank commitment to overcoming obstacles to meeting the MDGs (#8). In its most recent annual report, DGF indicates that Stop TB is considered important for Bank's clients by the sector boards and networks because it is closely aligned with sector priorities and essential for sustaining Bank engagement.

Regarding the Bank's involvement in the program	Regarding DGF funding
World Links was a pilot initiative of the president of the World Bank. Since then, the program has spun off from the Bank and is independent. However, the program still receives Bank funding, and the Bank is represented on the program's governance board. A Memorandum of Understanding is proposed between the program and the World Bank Institute to delineate the roles and responsibilities relating to the activities of the program.	Window 2. Scheduled to exit in FY04.

Table H.17 OED Assessment of Current Level of Consistency of Case Study Programs with the Development Committee Criteria for the Bank's Engagement in Global Programs

	High	Substantial	Modest	Negligible	Too early to rate[a]
An international consensus currently exists that global collective action is required.	13 CGIAR, GEF, MLF, GWP, TDR, UNAIDS, RBM, Stop TB, GAVI, WSP, CA, PostConFund, FSAP	7 ProCarbFund, GIF, Global Forum, ESMAP, CGAP, *info*Dev, FIRST	6 CEPF, PPIAF, UCW, IF, GDN, World Links		
The program is currently known to be adding value to achieving the Bank's development objectives of poverty alleviation and sustainable development.	4 CGIAR, TDR, UNAIDS, GAVI	11 GEF, MLF, ProCarbFund, RBM, Stop TB, WSP, ESMAP, PPIAF, CA, PostConFund, FSAP	6 CEPF, GIF, Global Forum, CGAP, UCW, IF	2 GWP, *info*Dev	3 FIRST, GDN, World Links
The Bank's presence is currently catalyzing other non-Bank resources for the program.	10 CGIAR, GEF, ProCarbFund, CEPF, TDR, Global Forum, RBM, Stop TB, CA, FSAP	6 MLF, UNAIDS, WSP, ESMAP, PPIAF, FIRST	6 GAVI, CGAP, *info*Dev, IF, GDN, World Links	4 PostConFund, GWP, GIF, UCW	
The Bank is currently playing up to its comparative advantages at the global level.[a]	9 CGIAR, GEF, MLF, ProCarbFund, TDR, UNAIDS, ESMAP, PPIAF, CA	7 CEPF, RBM, Stop TB, GAVI, WSP, IF, World Links	5 Global Forum, CGAP, UCW, GDN, PostConFund	3 GWP, GIF, *info*Dev	2 FIRST, FSAP
The Bank is currently playing up to its comparative advantages at the country level.[b]	3 MLF, PPIAF, CA	6 GEF, ProCarbFund, PostConFund, UNAIDS, WSP, ESMAP	11 CGIAR, GIF, TDR, Global Forum, RBM, Stop TB, GAVI, UCW, IF, GDN, World Links	4 CEPF, GWP, CGAP, *info*Dev	2 FIRST, FSAP

a. Global mandate and reach, convening power, and mobilizing financial resources.

b. Multisector capacity, expertise in country and sector level analysis, in-depth country-level knowledge.

ANNEX I: MANAGEMENT RESPONSE

I. Introduction

Management welcomes this report, which has been read with great interest and stimulated constructive discussion throughout the Bank. This second phase of OED's major study of global programs reinforces the actions management put in train in response to OED's Phase 1 findings. Core findings of this Report continue to underscore the Bank's important global role, and the need for more systematic attention to the management of global programs. OED's recommendations pick up many of the same themes as the first report and focus on (i) strategic framework; (ii) linking financing to priorities; (iii) selectivity and oversight of the global program portfolio; (iv) governance and management of individual programs; and (v) OED's role in evaluation.[1]

II. Management Comments

Overall, management agrees with the direction of this report, which deepens core messages of the Phase 1 Report (OED 2002c), such as the need for strong and proactive management by the Bank of this important area of activity. Management has taken these Phase 1 recommendations on board, moving forward in a range of key areas. A Global Programs and Partnerships (GPP) Council has been established as the senior management committee overseeing the strategic direction and operational policies for Bank involvement in GPPs.[2] The Council develops the Bank's vision and priorities for its engagement in GPPs; reviews VPU portfolios and the Bank's institutional partnerships; and oversees criteria for selection and evaluation of GPPs, including governance structures, risk management, exit strategies, and best practice. A new GPP Group was established in mid-2003, led by a Director reporting to the Vice President, Concessional Finance and Global Partnerships. The GPP Group provides primary support for the GPP Council. It works closely with Trust Funds, LEG, SFR, and OPCS as well as a network of GPP liaisons in VPUs managing GPP portfolios, and provides advice to task teams in the Networks and Regions undertaking new partnership initiatives at the Regional or global level. The GPP Group is engaged in a substantial work program in developing business processes, portfolio management approaches, governance models, and good evaluation procedures for GPPs, and it manages the annual Development Grant Facility allocation process. A community of best practice on global programs and partnerships is developing across the Bank.

Lessons that are Consistent with the Phase 1 Report. Broadly speaking, OED's ambitious Phase 2 report is consistent with—and will in future inform—ongoing work on GPPs. The report emphasizes the importance of GPPs as development vehicles, and notes the Bank's global role and comparative advantage in this field. It reinforces the point that GPPs are now a significant business line for the Bank and strongly reinforces the Bank's existing work program on GPPs, in particular the need for a more systematic approach to managing the GPP portfolio, and the implementation of more rigorous selectivity and oversight of GPPs from birth to final evaluation. The report's recommendations follow the major areas of work we are undertaking to improve GPP processes and management, such as fostering more effective links between global programs and country programs, and instituting best practice approaches to the GPP lifespan—design, financing, governance, selectivity, approval, evaluation, exit/reauthorization, and portfolio assessment. Management's response to OED's recommendations is outlined in more detail in the Annex.

Assessment of Specific Programs. Moving from the big picture assessment to specific programs, however, management has found less consensus among operational units involved in managing global programs about the report's conclusions and categorizations. Moreover, the overall conclusions of the report do not reflect equally the situation of each individual global program, nor do they apply in all cases to the wider population of partnerships in which the Bank is involved. Management will carefully consider the relevance of the recommendations to global programs but will consider each case individually going forward.

Case Studies. Some program-specific differences of view relate to the process surrounding the background papers covering the 26 case studies underlying OED's Report. These studies have been discussed in draft among OED, Bank staff, and other partners, given the necessity of providing those being evaluated with the opportunity to provide further information or alternative analysis. Some differences in opinion among partner organizations are to be expected given the diversity and evolving nature of global programs. However, since individual programs are cited in support of broader conclusions, management notes that it will need to take account of the outcome of these important ongoing OED discussions with partners and program managers on the case studies as it follows up on the findings of the OED review.

Global Programs Versus Country Programs. One area where greater clarity would be helpful is the issue of determining which activities should be pursued via global programs versus through country programs. This difficult question is placed by OED sometimes in the context of strategic selectivity (global programs should support global public goods whose externalities cut across many countries) and sometimes as a program design and financing issue (GPPs should exhibit subsidiarity to country programs). Management agrees with OED that a more tailored perspective may be appropriate. Some global programs relate not to global public goods but are inherently multi-country programs that deliver country-level services that may be best organized at the sector or thematic level in order to benefit from cross-country knowledge sharing, specialized expertise, economies of scale, and targeted resource mobilization. The activities and objectives of a global program should be assessed for the benefit to developing countries and value in leading to poverty reduction, and different approaches to ensuring global to country linkages are possible.

Governance of Global Programs. The OED review brings out some of the difficulties with regard to the governance of global programs. On the one hand (in Chapter 5), OED findings suggest that global programs have governance structures independent from the Bank, to avoid the potential for even the perception of dual loyalties and to bring in new knowledge and perspectives. Yet (in Chapter 4) OED recommends stronger linkage of global programs to country programs and indicates that programs where Bank staff implement the global program activities often have better country operational linkages. Reviewers in the Bank found merit in both the arguments for independence and for Bank country team involvement, but also thought it was unrealistic to expect a governance structure to do both things well. OED recognized these tensions and pointed out that its findings present a challenge for the Bank. Management believes that decisions about governance arrangements should reflect best practice and sound principles—but be driven by the needs of specific programs, particularly in terms of their activities and objectives.

III. Conclusion

OED has provided valuable insights for strengthening the Bank's management of its involvement in global programs. Management broadly agrees with four key recommendations: that a strategic framework is needed for global programs; that financing for global programs should be allocated with due regard to priorities and value added for developing countries; selectivity and oversight of the Bank's global program portfolio should continue to be strengthened; and that individual program design should reflect good practice with respect to governance, management, results orientation, and evaluation. As noted earlier, the review has already fed into the work of the Bank on global programs.

OED Recommendation	Management Response
Strategic Framework **In consultation with U.N. partners, donors, developing countries, and other partners, management should develop a global strategy that is approved by the Board and periodically updated, and that:** • Exploits the Bank's comparative advantage as a multisectoral development financing institution with a global reach and strong capacity in policy analysis. • Gives greater prominence to alleviating poverty and to addressing global public policies that adversely affect developing countries' prospects for rapid, sustainable, poverty-reducing growth. • Fosters stronger linkages between global programs and the Bank's Regional and country operations and ensures that global programs add value beyond what the Bank can accomplish through partnerships at the country level alone.	Management agrees that the Bank's role in global programs must be based on a strong strategic framework. This must reflect the Bank's corporate strategic agenda as agreed with the Board and in the Development Committee, and consider the Bank's role in supporting country programs. The strategic framework will draw on OED's findings, a review of the Bank's ongoing portfolio of global and regional partnership programs, as well as discussions in international fora on global issues and priorities. The Bank will consult with key partners in this process. The strategic framework paper will be presented to the Board before the end of FY05.
Linking Financing to Priorities **Management should develop a financing plan for high-priority programs, particularly for those providing genuine global public goods of benefit to the poor. This requires:** • Identifying long-term global public goods programs of benefit to the poor that are currently under-funded, and using the Bank's convening power to mobilize additional resources for such programs, such as a global health research and product development network for the diseases of the poor. • Improving the current criteria and procedures relating to the DGF's Window 2 in order to foster a more rational and informed approach to funding "venture capital" programs in which the DGF provides initial but not long-term financial support. • Developing a policy on the roles and uses of trust funds in the context of the overall Board-approved global strategy and financing plan for global programs.	Management broadly accepts this recommendation and agrees that financing for global programs—which is often mobilized in a program-specific fashion—should be considered in a more systematic fashion by the Bank and its partners. The GPP Group will raise the issue of financing modalities and strategies with the GPP Council during FY05. Management believes that the first explanatory bullet on global public goods is primarily about selectivity and is the responsibility of the GPP Council. While global programs (as defined in the OED report) can often be useful delivery mechanisms for global public goods, important positive externalities are delivered by country programs as well. The Window 2 "venture capital" approach needs to be revisited. The GPP Group will sponsor a discussion within the GPP Council on the DGF criteria during FY05. With regard to trust funds, work is already under way on the Bank's trustee role and relevant financial management issues in global programs. As already discussed with

OED Recommendation	Management Response
	the Board, management believes that trust funds should be shifted over time into broader programmatic vehicles.
Selectivity and Oversight of the Global Program Portfolio **Management should establish approval, oversight, evaluation, and exit/reauthorization criteria and procedures for global programs so that Bank-supported global programs routinely demonstrate value added to the Bank's mission of sustainable poverty alleviation. This includes:** • Improving, streamlining, and clarifying the eligibility and approval criteria for Bank selectivity and grant support, and instituting a two-stage approval process for global programs at the concept and appraisal stages. • Sharpening and more rigorously applying the subsidiarity criterion for approval and grant support. • Separating Bank oversight from the management chain responsible for implementation of each global program; and for Bank staff serving on the governing bodies of global programs, clarifying their roles, responsibilities, and accountabilities by means of standard terms of reference and training. • Allocating Bank budgetary resources for oversight, and for Network anchor and Regional staff to access on a competitive basis to operationalize the content of global programs in the Bank's Regional operations. • Instituting clear, well-planned, and well-executed reauthorization/exit processes, and ensuring that programs that exit from the Bank have an independent identity, with accountability for results and a good chance of succeeding.	Management broadly accepts this general recommendation and is moving ahead on a number of areas. During FY04, management established a GPP Council as the senior management committee overseeing the strategic direction and operational policies for Bank involvement in GPPs. Its role is to develop the Bank's vision and priorities for its engagement in GPPs; review VPU portfolios and the Bank's institutional partnerships, and oversee criteria for selection and evaluation of GPPs, including governance structures, risk management, and exit strategies. A GPP Group was established in CFP to support the Council, and its work program includes developing business processes, portfolio management approaches, governance models, and good evaluation procedures for GPPs. GPPs will be integrated into the Bank's operational procedures and management information systems, including a two-stage review process involving an appraisal for new programs and exit/reauthorization processes for ongoing ones. The new system will go online during FY05. Management agrees that subsidiarity is an important principle; its implementation in global and country programs can be complex. Both management and OED have recognized that some global programs deliver country-level services. Multi-country programs may be best organized at the sector or thematic level in order to benefit from cross-country knowledge sharing, specialized expertise, economies of scale, and targeted resource mobilization, but will depend on close coordination with the Bank's country programs, particularly when the Bank is the implementing agency. Separation of Bank oversight from the management chain responsible for implementation depends critically on the nature of the program itself; in some cases this may improve governance, while in others, the Bank is effectively responsible for implementation, and clarity of management accountability should be maintained. An additional and growing issue is the Bank's role as trustee for global programs and the fiduciary responsibility of the Bank in such

OED Recommendation	Management Response
	cases. (This was not one of the topics covered in depth in the OED review.) With regard to principles governing the terms of reference for Bank staff serving on boards, management agrees, and the GPP Group, in coordination with LEG, will develop these during FY05.
Governance and Management of Individual Programs **Management should work with its global partners to develop and routinely apply to all Bank-supported global programs universally accepted standards of good governance, management, results-orientation, and evaluation. These include:** • Legal status and/or written charters as appropriate. • Transparent selection criteria and processes for board chairs and board members; clarifying their roles, responsibilities, accountabilities, and what constituencies they represent; and ensuring that they have the necessary authority to exercise strategic direction and oversight of the program, its policies, and its budgetary resources. • Effective voice of the Bank's client countries on the governing bodies of global programs to achieve better balance between developed and developing countries. • Guidelines on conflicts of interests, on the roles of NGOs and the private sector on governing bodies, and on the roles and quality of advisory boards. • Evaluation and audit designated as functions of the governing body not the management of the program, and routinely made available to program financiers and other stakeholders.	Management accepts this recommendation. The Bank is working to influence positively the quality of governance for global programs in which it is involved. Work is under way to develop standard governance models to strengthen transparency and provide more systematic approaches to GPPs. At the same time, management notes that, while core principles of good governance are essential to the design and management of global programs, the wide diversity of GPPs, the range of governance arrangements, the Bank's varied roles and level of responsibility for program implementation and other factors all require sensible, not mechanical, application of core governance principles program by program. The diversity of global programs and the weight and influence of other stakeholders means that, in many cases, the Bank can press for better standards of governance. As one of many stakeholders, however, and in support of increasing voice, the Bank alone cannot—and should not—dictate the governance approach.
Evaluation **OED should include global programs in its standard evaluation and reporting processes to the Board. This includes:** • Working with the Bank's global partners to develop international standards for the evaluation of global programs. • Reviewing selected program-level evaluations conducted by Bank-supported global programs (both internally and externally managed), much as OED reviews other self-evaluations at the project and country levels.	This recommendation is primarily directed at OED, although it has implications for the self-evaluation structure discussed above.

ANNEX J: CHAIRMAN'S SUMMARY: COMMITTEE ON DEVELOPMENT EFFECTIVENESS (CODE)

On September 20, 2004, the Committee on Development Effectiveness (CODE) met to discuss *Addressing the Challenges of Globalization—An Independent Evaluation of the World Bank's Approach to Global Programs—Phase 2 Report*.

OED Evaluation Findings. OED conducted the evaluation of global programs in two phases. *The World Bank's Approach to Global Programs: An Independent Evaluation - Phase 1* was discussed at a CODE meeting on June 12, 2002. A major global program case study, *The CGIAR at 31,* was discussed by CODE on April 23, 2003. In March 2003, management updated the Board about a number of organizational and procedural changes. The Phase 2 report, based on case studies of 26 global programs, has three distinguishing features. First, it looks across the global programs to compare and draw cross-cutting lessons with regard to the design, implementation, and evaluation of global programs. Second, it provides an overview of the 26 case studies. Third, it focuses specifically on the role of the Bank in the global program partnerships. OED's recommendations pick up many of the themes presented in the Part 1 Report and cover the following areas: (i) strategic framework; (ii) linking financing to priorities; (iii) selectivity and oversight of the global program portfolio; (iv) governance and management of individual programs; and (v) OED's role in evaluation.

Management Comments. Overall, management agrees with the direction of the report, and noted that many actions were put in train since the OED's Phase 1 report, such as the establishment of Global Programs and Partnership (GPP) Council and Group. Management understands that the ongoing work on GPP is consistent with the Phase 2 report, and agrees that (i) financing should be allocated with due regard to priorities and value added for developing countries; (ii) selectivity and oversight should continue to be strengthened; and (iii) that individual program design should reflect good practice with respect to governance, management, results orientation, and evaluation. Management committed to present a strategic direction paper on GPP which will report on the state and focusing of the portfolio, and on the strategic view defining the Bank's comparative advantage in this field.

Key Outcomes. Members broadly commended OED for a comprehensive and coherent report on an intrinsically challenging evaluation, and appreciated the pragmatic Draft Management Response (MR). There was broad agreement on the issues elicited by OED. In some areas there appears to be a difference of opinion between OED and management. With management's offer to come back to the Board with a strategic framework in the second half of FY05, speakers felt that the difference had narrowed. The discussion evolved around the following issues: (i) the need for a stronger strategic framework for the Bank's involvement in global programs; (ii) selectivity and oversight of the Global Program Portfolio; (iii) exit strategy; (iv) governance; and (v) evaluation. Among the specific issues raised during the Committee meeting were:

Global Strategy. Many speakers agreed with OED's recommendation that in consultation with U.N. agencies, donors, developing countries, and other partners, management should develop a global strategy that is approved by the

Board and periodically updated. These speakers also welcomed management's intention to prepare a paper on the strategic directions of the Bank's involvement in global programs. They stressed that the paper should be prepared in consultation with Stakeholders, including developing and developed country partners. They emphasized that the strategic framework paper should not result in another bureaucratic layer and that it should be very results-oriented. Management expressed its commitment to results orientation, and to do consultation with other partners at the program level and at the corporate level. A speaker said that in his view the Bank's comparative advantage is in financing and implementing measures for addressing global issues, rather than in defining the global agenda, which is better left to the UN. Another speaker noted that donor coordination is a Bank role. Management responded that the Bank's distinctive advantage for participation in global programs is its financial and technical capacity as well as country expertise and presence.

Selectivity of the GPP. Some speakers said that the Bank is involved in too many GPPs and may be spreading its resources too thinly and losing the focus on its main mission. They were joined by other speakers in stressing that a better process is needed to select new global programs, to justify the existing ones, and to merge overlapping programs in order to take advantage of economies of scale—i.e., integrating administrative structures. Management agreed with this observation, but indicated that some caution is needed because the Bank is just one of many partners and players in GPPs, sometimes a minor one. Speakers indicated that the four selectivity criteria endorsed by the Development Committee are a good starting point, with some aspects to be clarified. Establishing sound results-based frameworks and enhancing the monitoring of program quality and results with effective performance indicators would foster increased selectivity. Several members broadly supported the need for prioritization of programs, concentration on feasible regional and country initiatives that directly address the local needs, benefit the poor, and improve the investment climate. Other speakers said that the Bank should focus its interventions on global issues relevant to its core mandate and should keep the clients' needs at the forefront of its decisionmaking. It was also mentioned that global programs must be based on country ownership, be consistent with the country's priorities, and avoid being supply driven. A speaker noted that having case studies completed before the Phase 2 Report discussions would have been helpful.

Oversight of GPP. With respect to OED's recommendation that Bank oversight should be separated from the management chain responsible for implementation of a global program, the committee expressed a diversity of opinions. Several speakers acknowledged that some progress had been made to improve oversight, but more needed to be done, and therefore agreed with the recommendation. Others agreed with management that it is not always practical or beneficial to separate oversight from the management chain. The issue should be addressed on a case-by-case basis in their view. In this respect management noted that the Bank engages in several ways with its development partners, including through a multiplicity of governance structures of Global Programs, which include board and oversight structures. Several speakers suggested that the Board should play a more proactive role in overseeing the Bank's involvement in global programs, including reviewing the recommendations of the GPP Council.

Exit Strategy. Several speakers stressed the importance of a strategy that allows the Bank to exit global programs in a way that ensures sustainability and integration into country development programs. An accountability structure should also be in place. A few speakers noted that the DGF's "two-window" approach helped to improve program exit management. A speaker said that the GPP Council should have greater influence on the decision to continue or exit from global programs.

Governance of Programs. Several speakers agreed with OED's recommendation that the client countries should have an effective voice on the governing bodies of the global programs. They suggested that the Bank could help to address this challenge by promoting country ownership, encouraging the participation of civil society, improving overall transparency and accountability, and strengthening the demand orientation of global programs. Several speakers said that the GPP Council should take a more proactive role in establishing and promoting standards of good governance and management of all Bank-supported global programs. Speakers noted that the identification of financing plans requires a clear Bank internal governance system that defines the use of financing mechanisms (trust funds, global funds, Bank resources) and differentiation of windows (DGF, administrative budget, Bank-administered trust funds). Others cautioned that the convergence of funds to global programs should not create a crowding out of funds to other relevant poverty reduction initiatives. They also stressed that the activities of the global programs should not simply substitute what the Bank would provide through its normal operations.

Evaluation. Several speakers endorsed OED's suggestion that global programs should be included in its standard evaluation and reporting processes to the Board, but stressed that OED should be pragmatic and cost-conscious in this regard. A speaker stressed the importance of working with partners to develop a common framework for evaluating global programs to avoid overburdening countries with multiple evaluation requirements.

Next steps. The Draft MR will be revised based on the comments and suggestions raised during the discussion, including the linkage to the strategic paper that management has committed to present for Board discussion in a few months time. The OED Phase 2 report will be made publicly available after the CODE discussion together with management's response and a summary of the Chairman's report. The 21 case studies undertaken in parallel with the Phase 2 Report will be disclosed to the public after the disclosure of the Phase 2 Report. If members desired, one or more of these studies could be discussed either at CODE or at the CODE Subcommittee meeting.

Pietro Veglio
Acting Chairman

ENDNOTES

Foreword

1. The case studies that have been disclosed are in the OED Working Paper series at <http://www.worldbank.org/oed/gppp/>

Prologo

1. Los estudios de casos que se difundido se encuentran en la serie de Documentos de Trabajo del DEO en <http://www.worldbank.org/oed/gppp/>

Avant-propos

1. Les études de cas qui ont été publiées sont reprises dans la série de documents de travail de l'OED sur le site web www.worldbank.org/oed/gppp/

Chapter 1

1. The Bank's capacity to give grants to global programs is limited by its earnings, which come from two major sources—the returns on its investments and the interest charges on its loans to borrowing countries. In FY05, the DGF, which is funded from the Bank's gross administrative budget, allocated $50 million to CGIAR, $76 million to 46 other global programs, $34.5 million to 10 regional programs, and $19.8 million to the Institutional Development Fund. While the Bank's governors may also authorize exceptional grants out of the Bank's net income, these are typically for country programming trust funds such as West Bank and Gaza, Kosovo, and East Timor, and most recently for the Low-Income Countries under Stress (LICUS) trust fund.

2. Nineteen of the 26 programs have had program-level evaluations. For CGIAR, there were over 700 reports.

3. Stakeholders are parties who are interested in or affected, either positively or negatively, by the program. Partners are a subset of the stakeholders.

4. The phase 1 report (OED 2001d) details how these programs were identified. The Global Fund to Fight AIDS, Tuberculosis, and Malaria (GFATM) became operational in January 2002 and thus is neither included in the figures cited here nor reviewed in this report.

5. These figures exclude HIPC and IFC trust funds. The total funds held in trust by the World Bank Group, including HIPC were US$7.1 billion at the end of FY04.

6. GFATM Web site: http://www.theglobalfund.org/en

Chapter 2

1. These expenditures refer to FY04 or to the most recent fiscal (FY) or calendar year (CY) for which data are available. See table H.1, "Phase 2 Case Study Programs at a Glance." The quality and coverage of the information on sources and uses of program funds vary widely across programs and OED takes no responsibility for their accuracy. See chapter 6 for further discussion of this issue.

2. While the arrival of GFATM has not changed DGF allocations in any significant way, it has changed the global shares of expenditures going to health and environment, as indicated earlier.

3. The generic term "lending" is used to refer to IBRD lending, IDA credits, and IDA grants. When the lending instrument is critical to determine global and country linkages with Bank operations, it is discussed explicitly.

4. As shown in table H. 8, OED assessed the extent to which each program has been undertaking each of the 12 activities listed in figure 2.2. OED categorized these 12 activities according to the Bank's 4 strategic foci for global programs: (1) providing global public goods, (2) supporting international advocacy, (3) coordinating multi-country programs and (4) mobilizing substantial incremental resources, introduced by the Bank in March of 2003.

5. The Stop TB Partnership and the Global Forum are also conducting similar activities for tuberculosis

and a few other diseases (in the case of the Global Forum, through fostering public-private partnerships). However, their financing for these activities is so small at the global level that OED has not included them in this category. Indeed, staff of both programs told OED during consultations on the case studies that current levels of funding for health research, including their own, are too small.

6. In commenting on the draft phase 2 report, Bank management acknowledged that, in practice, it is difficult to differentiate CGIAR Center investment activities that regular Bank instruments could support from the so-called complementary investments (at the country level that the countries or donors could finance), *because the two share common characteristics irrespective of financing source*. There is often similarity between the activities of some CGIAR centers that the Bank finances out of DGF funds and activities that the Bank could finance at the country level out of loans and credits. This challenges the subsidiarity principle that the Bank has correctly adopted in the use of the limited DGF funds.

7. See Annex C, table C.4, for the DGF subsidiarity criterion not to "compete with, or substitute for, regular Bank instruments." The CGIAR Centers also mobilize funding from local donors for country-level activities that the donors think the countries are unable to carry out or to carry out well.

8. Health research in this report is broadly defined to include the development of new vaccines and drugs, surveillance, epidemiological research, testing and monitoring responses to various interventions, and multisectoral factors underlying the containment of communicable and noncommunicable diseases that particularly afflict the poor in developing countries.

9. GEF also finances regional-level investments.

10. Public intervention in immunization has been justified on three grounds: (1) the spread and incomplete course of treatment in the absence of public provision; (2) some options (such as vector control and information) are pure public goods; and (3) on equity grounds, since immunization-preventable diseases disproportionately affect the poor. While most non-informational services involved are private (rival and exclusionary), there are substantial social externalities associated with immunization. For example, polio vaccination is unique because it exhibits both characteristics of public goods. The oral vaccine allows the virus to multiply in the child's intestine and is released in much larger quantities in excreta. The attenuated virus competes in the environment with the wild virus, which is responsible for polio, making benefits both non-rival and non-exclusionary, and therefore a public good. See Hammer 1996.

11. The objective of the program is to position the Bank through constructive engagement in such countries where normal instruments and budget provisions cannot apply. This includes countries that have just emerged from a conflict, have no functioning government, have arrears on previous loans and credits, or have just become new members. More than 90 percent of the program's expenditures have been devoted to country-level investments—primarily small-scale pilot reconstruction activities such as conflict mitigation, internally displaced persons and refugees, rehabilitation of social sectors, start-up support for land mine clearance, economic recovery, and private sector governance and capacity building. These activities contribute to national peace and security, with potential spillovers into regional and even global peace. While global peace and security are global public goods, OED has concluded that the magnitude and scope of most of the Post-conflict Fund's activities are too small and country-specific to have a significant impact on global, or indeed even regional, peace and security.

12. The Stop TB Partnership has a small drug facility associated with it, which is reported to have treated 1.5 million patients. However, the financing for the drug facility has been uncertain and does not include financing for infrastructure or for institutional development of the type that large World Bank loans and credits include. The Bank has committed $104 million in a tuberculosis control project in China and $142 million in India, compared with the TB Drug Facility's annual expenditures of $16 million. UNAIDS similarly provides training for monitoring and evaluation coordination, but its financing is small relative to the Bank's $1.41 billion in commitments to HIV/AIDS projects between 1990 and 2004.

13. GFATM was established in part because developing countries seemed unwilling or unable to borrow or to receive donor grants to address communicable diseases on the scale the global community prefers.

14. See table H.12 for the list of partners represented on the governing bodies of the study programs.

Chapter 3

1. As indicated in figure ES.1 in the summary, "providing global public goods" and "supporting international advocacy" are direct references to the Bank's global public goods and corporate advocacy priorities, as enunciated in the Bank's *Strategic Directions Paper for FY02–04* (World Bank 2001b).

2. OED 2002c, pp. 57-59. Reprinted in this volume as Annex D.

3. The GEF, established in 1991, provides additional grant and concessional funding to meet the agreed incremental costs of actions related to biological diversity, climate change, international waters, ozone-layer depletion, land degradation, and persistent organic pollutants. The GEF is the financial mechanism for global conventions and protocols under the United Nations in these areas.

4. The MLF is the financial mechanism created in 1990 by the London Amendment to the Montreal Protocol to help developing countries meet the agreed incremental costs of eliminating the production and consumption of ozone-depleting substances (ODS).

5. The negotiations for the mechanisms were noteworthy because they established the principle of "common but differentiated responsibility" between countries. The financing mechanisms were precedent-setting because industrialized countries acknowledged that developing countries should be refunded the "full agreed incremental costs" of providing global environmental benefits.

6. In the health sector, for example, the World Bank recently estimated that client countries would need $15 to $30 billion more per year in 15 to 20 target countries to achieve the health MDGs by 2015, whereas only $6.7 billion is spent annually on health. Scientists have estimated that $30 billion is needed to protect the world's biodiversity in 21 hotspots covering less than 2 percent of the world's surface. GEF's annual disbursements of $400 million plus were distributed among six focal areas, including biodiversity.

7. Some developing-country representatives to the WTO are in favor of setting up a separate funding mechanism to finance such activities in individual countries. Donors, including the World Bank, do not support this position.

8. Reflecting the challenges of linking global programs with country operations, OED obtained quite different responses to the IF case study from the team in charge of the program in the Poverty Reduction and Economic Management (PREM) Network and from the Bank's country economists. The latter acknowledged the importance of integrating trade into the overall development strategy of the least-developed countries, but stress the competing demands on limited country capacity and on the Bank's resources in relation to other donors' priorities, such as health and education.

9. WHO indicated, for instance, that it spent the equivalent of $10 million in support to developing-country governments to prepare applications for GFATM.

10. OED's *2002 Annual Review of Development Effectiveness* also pointed out that the MDGs "represent risks to the Bank and to the larger development community—risks posed by the cynicism that failure (or only partial success) could engender. Such cynicism is a danger, given that health and social sector goals the development community had set for itself over the past quarter century . . . remain either unattained or only partially attained" (OED 2003c).

11. See Annex C, table C.2.

12. Even evaluations of GEF have stressed the difficulties of mainstreaming GEF objectives in Bank country operations.

13. The preparation of sector strategies is the responsibility of the Bank's networks (ESSD, FSE, HDN, INF, and PREM) and of the sector boards within each network. Since the Bank created its thematic networks in 1997, Sector Strategy Papers have been expected to scan the universe of relevant players in each sector and to discuss existing or potential partnerships, based on the Bank's comparative advantages. See table H.8 for the list of recent sector strategies and OED sector studies relating to the case study programs.

14. ESMAP activities in the 1980s contributed most of the information on environmental issues in energy that influenced strategy and policymaking in the early 1990s, and ESMAP staff wrote the Bank's rural energy strategy.

15. OED interviews of Bank and IMF staff and AERC current and past board members.

16. A recent variant on this case indicated that as long as health programs bring external grant funds with no domestic budgetary implications, the IMF sees no issues. However, most such grant programs also imply increased domestic expenditures, either public or private or both. See Piot 2003.

17. OED 2002b. Management has responded to this criticism by observing that FSAP should still promote coherence to good practices even though "not all countries can or should implement good practices in all respects, at least in the near term"—an observation with which OED concurs.

18. Nonetheless, in chapter 2 OED classified these 2 programs among the 16 programs that provide primarily national public goods, since their primary focus is to strengthen country-level capacity in relation to national financial markets. As in the case of other programs, the programs' current resources are too small relative to the demand for their services to make a significant global impact.

Chapter 4

1. The guidelines were recently revised in November 2003. (See World Bank 2003b.)

2. These criteria are based on OED's standards of best practice, as identified in OED 1995, pp. 23–24.

3. While the Global Water Partnership's mission is to support countries in the sustainable development of their water resources, comprehensive integrated water resource management is complex and intensely political. Reforms require more than the "articulation of prioritized, sequenced, practical, and patient interventions." Findings of the World Bank's Water Resources Sector Strategy (World Bank 2004).

4. This is an area in which the efforts of programs such as UNAIDS may be bearing fruit. An agreement announced at the 2004 spring meetings of the World Bank and IMF noted that the major OECD donors would improve coordination of their country-level efforts to fight AIDS. Following an approach advocated by UNAIDS, they would use a single action program in each country for coordinating donations, a single authority for receiving the donations, and a single system for monitoring and evaluating how the money is spent.

5. It is generally agreed, for instance, that the transaction costs of organizing the Integrated Framework for Trade-Related Technical Assistance (IF) have been considerable. In interviews with OED, some have wondered whether it is adding sufficient value to developing countries beyond what the Bank could have done through economic and sector work on trade. Others have argued that the Bank would not have been able to devote an average of $300,000 per study from its administrative budget to the analysis of trade in small African countries. Moreover, IF's other reported benefits include increased demand from middle-income countries for technical studies, which is bringing more resources to the Bank's research department for trade-related research and putting the trade issue back on the international agenda.

6. That is, programs such as GEF, MLF, and the Prototype Carbon Fund, which finance investments similar to those financed by the World Bank, have used a results-based framework. Their projects have concrete objectives, specific schedules with discrete endpoints, well-defined responsibility for various aspects of the project implementation, and well-identified outcomes. Among programs providing country-level technical assistance, ESMAP adopted a results-based management framework, including output and outcome indicators, in FY02, and WSP in FY04.

7. The 2002 evaluation of the Cities Alliance is among the best program-level evaluations to date. This assessed the relevance, efficacy, and efficiency of the Cities Alliance during its first three years against its four stated objectives, its three strategies, and the six guiding principles laid out in its Charter, and followed a results chain (inputs => outputs => outcomes => impacts) so far as was practicable, given the program's recent provenance.

8. The 2003 UNICEF-managed external evaluation of Understanding Children's Work observed that, when agreeing on an open project design, the participating agencies did not apply their usual standards of results-based management and did not include a critical set of intermediate results and indicators. The evaluator therefore could not assess the effectiveness of the program results. The other two partners dispute these findings. While the 2003 IF evaluation assessed effectiveness, some of the program's staff indicated that the program would have benefited from a critical evaluation of the diagnostic studies in the IF evaluation.

9. On the other hand, CGIAR has historically been an outlier in its lack of regular system-level evaluations and of systematic mechanisms to reflect these evaluations' findings in design and implementation.

10. In the case of research programs with long gestation periods, such as in agriculture and health, the pressure to demonstrate immediate results can distort resource allocation. In other cases, which do not involve such long-term activities, demonstrating immediate results may well be essential.

11. In its first three years of operation up to June 30, 2003, PPIAF funded the drafting of 25 sets of laws and regulations; facilitated the design of 30 public-private infrastructure transactions, such as management contracts, leases, auctions of telecom licenses, privatizations, and concessions; made recommendations leading to the implementation of 14 different sector reform strategies in 11 countries; funded the creation or strengthening of 20 regulatory institutions; and funded training courses, primarily in the field of regulation, attended by more than 1,500 participants (PPIAF data).

12. Conservation of biodiversity is difficult to measure or document, except when conserving charismatic animals such as the panda. In addition, measuring water-quality improvements in international waters can take up to 10 years; reduction in the production of ozone-depleting substances or carbon dioxide is inherently easier to measure.

13. Some GEF programs use satellite imagery and GIS techniques in their monitoring and evaluation, as do some of the more advanced middle-income developing countries. In Brazil and Indonesia, this helps to track forest fires and manage forests. Such information is not being synthesized to show how effective GEF is in helping developing countries to improve what they do in aggregate terms—that is, to improve country and global outcomes.

14. The divergence between perceived global and local costs and benefits is a major issue, as are the challenges of assessing the incremental costs for GEF financing and developing incentives for local populations to produce global benefits.

15. Even so, some evaluations do not evaluate the quality of either the governance or the secretariats of the program.

16. Global Forum for Health Research 2002. Some commentators on the earlier draft of this paper considered this estimate out of date. Global Forum is making a new assessment, and results are not yet available.

17. GEF evaluations suggest that there is scope to improve mainstreaming of environment concerns in Bank operations. This essentially means shifting the view of the environment from an externality and a separate sector to an integral part of development. However, a broader interpretation of mainstreaming also implies the integration of GEF priorities and strategies into the Bank's various sectoral strategies (for example, environment strategy, energy strategy, forest strategy) or in the client's own strategies (such as PRSPs). This integration could also take place at the individual project level, blending GEF priorities and strategies in the project's objectives and expected outcomes.

18. Moreover, because these programs are financing incremental expenditures, over and above what the countries can and do undertake, to realize global benefits, there is greater likelihood of the sustainability of at least the underlying national benefits, even granting that there are a number of conceptual and measurement issues with regard to the concept of "incrementality."

19. The eight countries receiving $36.801 million, or more than half of all PCF funding since the program's inception, are Somalia ($6.607 million), Kosovo ($5.782 million), Afghanistan ($5.175 million), the Democratic Republic of the Congo ($4.855 million), Burundi ($3.993 million), Haiti ($3.714 million), Sudan ($3.398 million), and East Timor ($3.275 million).

20. Development Alternatives, 2002. The PostConFund has made available nine evaluation reports of its larger grants. However, many completed grants (mostly small- to medium-size grants for which the Fund's procedures typically do not require an independent assessment) still lack enough basic reporting to demonstrate their impact.

21. Initial results from one survey indicate that more than $4 billion of investments are linked with Alliance-funded activities. Approximately $1.5 billion are from investments already committed, and $2.5 billion are prospective investments in various stages of preparation or appraisal. More than $2.3 billion are from World Bank loans and credits (Cities Alliance 2003).

22. *info*Dev's 2002 evaluation concluded that its capacity building grants (of up to $250,000) to help recipients design, test, and apply innovative uses of information and communication technologies (ICTs) have had little impact at the country level beyond the direct beneficiaries. Rather, its biggest success has been its advocacy of access to ICTs. Since *info*Dev now operates in a crowded field with many alternative sources of supply, the evaluation concluded that *info*Dev must reinvent itself and "focus on its knowledge activities in order to capitalize on its initial success and stay ahead of the growing pack of ICT-for-development programs" (da Costa, Wilson, and Fillip 2002). In response to these concerns, the new *info*Dev man-

agement and team have embarked on a restructuring of *info*Dev's programs and priorities.

23. In 2003, for example, the Trust Funds Quality Assurance and Compliance Unit found examples of Bank-executed activities financing what should have been recipient-executed civil works in the case of WSP, a practice that has now been stopped. The 2001 report of *info*Dev's Technical Advisory Panel found that *info*Dev spent a great deal of its resources screening project proposals, then applying very little supervision or monitoring once these were approved, noting that this appears to have been based on the assumption that correct choice leads to successful projects.

24. These estimates are based on a World Bank classification of its lending activities. A more detailed assessment of the precise amounts committed and disbursed for HIV/AIDS is under way in OED's forthcoming evaluation on the Bank's HIV/AIDS assistance. The data presented here may diverge from the data presented in that report because of differences in definitions, diseases, and periods covered.

Chapter 5

1. The Business Sector Advisory Group found a similar diversity of private-sector corporate governance models, with a particular dichotomy between the "shareholder" tradition in Anglo-American countries and the "stakeholder" tradition in continental European countries and Japan. They concluded that regardless of model, these four underlying principles were part of a well-functioning corporate governance system, and enshrined these in the OECD Principles of Corporate Governance, endorsed by ministers at the OECD Council meeting in May 1999. OED is grateful to Anne Simpson, manager of the Global Corporate Governance Program, for bringing this to our attention.

2. This is not to say that the stakeholder model is always preferable or appropriate. Both FSAP and FIRST, for example, argue that it is not desirable to have stakeholders represented on their Liaison Committee and Steering Committee, respectively.

3. CGAP's director is also ex officio. Four members of the restructured Executive Committee were explicitly sought from the former Policy Advisory Group to ensure continuity in the new governance structure.

4. When programs have in-house secretariats, who determines performance is a complex issue. In some cases, managers' performance evaluations are completed as if they were employees of the organizations in which the programs are housed. In other cases, feedback is obtained from the board—another aspect of the "two masters" problem.

5. For example, the evaluations of the Global Forum and of the Global Water Partnership did not review either board governance or the secretariat, although there was an earlier external review of GWP board governance. The third system-level review of CGIAR did not review the secretariat.

6. The UNAIDS evaluation suggested that the program secretariat intensify its support to national governments, civil society, and the private sector in the preparation of funding proposals. The highest governing body of UNAIDS, the Program Coordinating Board, clarified the roles and functions of the various program actors. Citing the "sub-optimal" impact of the Roll Back Malaria Partnership, and noting that the program's loose governance structure had introduced inefficiencies in decisionmaking and hampered accountability within the partnership, the evaluation proposed specific changes: (a) the establishment of an RBM Governance Board to set the strategic direction of the partnership and oversee the RBM Secretariat's activities; (b) de-linking WHO Technical Malaria functions from the RBM Secretariat; (c) multipartner working groups to develop guidance on strategies for going to scale with RBM interventions; and (d) four interagency, inter-country teams in the Africa region to coordinate technical and programmatic support to countries. With respect to the Stop TB Secretariat, the evaluation noted that the location of the secretariat in WHO benefits both parties, despite some administrative frustrations. The technical relationships between the WHO and the Stop TB Partnership Secretariat are strong and do not compromise the partnership's independence.

7. Because of unforeseen circumstances, GDN lacked an active chairman over an extended period, resulting in a lack of clarity about accountability and responsibilities for program governance. Program agendas were not determined in sufficient consultation with board members. Board members were therefore insufficiently consulted on certain aspects of the program. OED's meta-evaluation found similar problems with CGIAR's Executive Committee. Verbatim minutes, which CGIAR used to keep, are kept no longer. Minutes of GDN board meetings are also not available from their Web site.

8. The Stop TB evaluation observes: "The Board is struggling to handle the volume of business . . . given the current conjunction of a number of strategic issues and pressure of work-planning activities, the Board had planned to hold a third Board meeting in 2003, in tandem with the 2003 Partners' Forum, until the latter was postponed. It has now substituted a teleconference, although this cannot deal adequately with the range of items originally intended" (Institute for Health Sector Development 2003, p. 55).

9. For example, the evaluation of Stop TB observes that the aim of securing long-term annual financing of $20–$30 million to sustain the Global Drug Facility, starting in 2004, is unrealistic, and that alternative options are needed.

10. The scientific achievements of CGIAR centers and their contribution to development continue to be internationally recognized, as for example by the 2004 World Food Prize awarded to CGIAR scientist Dr. Monty Jones. Yet the CGIAR's spending on productivity-enhancing agricultural research declined in real terms by 6.5 percent annually between 1992 and 2001, and larger developing countries have caught up with, and sometimes surpassed, the CGIAR scientifically.

11. The committee meets annually, reviews TDR's scientific, technical, and operational issues, and reports its findings directly to the Joint Coordinating Board. The committee consists of 15 to 18 scientists and other technical personnel that serve in their personal capacities to represent the range of biomedical and other disciplines required by TDR activities. The members of the Scientific and Technical Advisory Committee, appointed to serve for three years, are selected on the basis of their scientific or technical competence by the Executing Agency, in consultation with the Standing Committee, and with the endorsement of the Joint Coordinating Board. Stakeholders stressed the challenges of maintaining the competence of the committee members and the quality of the advice they provide.

12. Task forces, now disbanded, were funded and managed by their respective lead agency(ies) and include representatives of the relevant partner agencies. The Advocacy and Communications Task Force was chaired by UNICEF; the Implementation Task Force was co-chaired by WHO; the Financing Task Force was chaired by the World Bank; and the Research and Development Task Force was co-chaired by WHO, NIH, and Chiron Vaccines. http://vaccinealliance.org/home/General_Information/About_alliance/Governance/ whoweare.php#wg

13. In several countries, board members require insurance because of their expected responsibilities and liabilities due to board accountabilities.

14. FIRST requires an annual financial contribution of $2 million for membership, CGIAR requires $500,000, and PPIAF and Cities Alliance require $250,000. According to FIRST, the program's steering committee felt that representation should be limited to keep the board's size manageable. This was deemed important because decisions are made by consensus. FIRST argues that, since discussions were at a very early stage regarding the type of contribution, it remained unclear whether the country in question would ultimately have chosen to participate.

15. Cities Alliance is an example. CGIAR does this, but sometimes regions decide to disqualify nonpaying members from being eligible to serve on the Executive Committee, even when nonmember, nonpaying private sector and NGO representatives were invited.

16. One notable example comes from an interview with a cabinet official who was not consulted during the design of a country-level study. Because the ministry's role is integral to outcomes related to child labor, including the need to expand access to primary schooling, the program should have at least informed the Ministry of the program's policy-related components attached to the study's statistics-gathering function.

17. WHO has recently announced its commitment to the "3 by 5 Plan," which would provide three million people living with AIDS with antiretroviral medicines by the end of 2005. Dr. Lee Jong-wook, the Director-General of WHO, in a speech in September 2003 to African health ministers, emphasized the urgent need for treatment for people living with HIV/AIDS. WHO stresses that treatment must be offered as part of a strategy that includes prevention and care. The Bank has similarly begun to finance antiretrovirals (ARVs) in some countries.

18. Private firms working through partnerships, for example, are suspected of merely seeking future profits and markets, trying to control the agendas of international organizations, or to benefit from tax deductions and subsidies for their new products.

19. According to Lucas (2000), there has been an "honest recognition by the public sector" of the

"unique, unrivalled monopoly of the pharmaceutical industry in drug and vaccine development . . . (and that) they own the ball. If you want to play, you must play with them." New developments in biotechnology are making drug and vaccine discovery and development increasingly expensive, as are changes in intellectual property rights. Concomitantly, extensive consolidation of the pharmaceutical industry has led to reduced competition. Although public-private partnerships in health research of relevance to the poor have increased considerably, the commercial development of research results into affordable products would require large investments.

20. The GAVI Board includes the multinational pharmaceutical manufacturer Wyeth Pharmaceuticals, as well as the Serum Institute of India. Wyeth represents the developed-country manufacturers of patented multivalent vaccines. The Serum Institute of India represents the manufacturers' association of 30 developing countries, and its members supply 60 percent of all the cheaper monovalent vaccines to developing countries. Both groups have an interest in promoting their own vaccines. Although GAVI's original mandate was to promote new vaccines and to support traditional, less expensive vaccines, GAVI initially (and with good intentions) stressed the patented multivalent vaccines, which require fewer vaccinations but cost more per vaccine. The goal in doing so was to reduce demand on vaccine-delivery systems in developing countries, promote the production of the newer vaccines, and develop a market by replacing old vaccines. Some developing countries, such as India, indicated at the outset that they would find it financially and politically difficult to deliver multivalent vaccines in "GAVI-covered" areas and cheaper vaccines elsewhere, on grounds of cost and equity. Other countries, such as Ghana, accepted the new vaccines but later indicated to GAVI that they could not sustain spending on them. Timely and reliable supplies of both types of vaccines have been issues.

21. In particular, targets 17 and 18. See table H.7.

22. State-funded U.S. land-grant institutions, by contrast, are expected to routinely report research conducted through public-private partnerships to the university offices, which engage patent lawyers to negotiate contracts for such research.

23. The Bank did not have a policy when a private sector representative was brought on the CGIAR executive council, or earlier made chairman of the private sector committee and given resources and a seat at the CGIAR table, or when Syngenta became a member.

24. Each fiscal year, two to five regions are approved to begin funding at regional levels. Initially regions where Conservation International had a historic presence were approved, whereas now regions where they have not been active are being approved.

Chapter 6

1. While ODA has been stagnant for a decade, the share of ODA allocated to health has increased. Although TDR's research funding has not increased much, and although global health research expenditures are nowhere near the $3 billion annually recommended by the Commission on Macroeconomics and Health, recent evidence (assembled by the Global Forum, but incomplete at the time of writing) suggests that public health research expenditures have increased since the early 1990s. Some of this increase is directed at the research on communicable diseases in poorer countries and the poorer populations. A report on the major consultation conducted by the Initiative on Public-Private Partnerships for Health issued at the time of issuance of this report indicates that a significant amount of funds have been pledged to new not-for-profit ventures in the last 5 years to research on diseases of the poor. But product development requires a long-term commitment, and current donors may have reached the limit of their funding, given other responsibilities, priorities, and the like.

2. Whether official development assistance would have declined without the support of global-program constituencies, and whether it will increase in the future, is impossible to know.

3. India and the Eastern Mediterranean regional office (EMRO) of the WHO, for example, have made commitments to achieve the 2 percent target of their health spending going to health research (information provided by the Global Forum for Health Research).

4. OED acknowledges that some flexibility may be needed for defined periods of time if the Bank helps to put in place strong boards, oversight, and well-designed financing plans; but in most cases these have been absent. The DGF eligibility criterion continues: "Where grant programs belong to new areas of activities (involving, e.g., innovations, pilot projects, or seed capital), some flexibility is allowed for the Bank's financial leverage to build over time, and the target for

the Bank grant not to exceed 15 percent of total percent of total funding will be pursued after allowing for an initial start-up phase (maximum 3 years)." <http://wbln0018.worldbank.org/dgf/dgf.nsf/DOCs/Eligibility+Criteria?OpenDocument>

5. While PostConFund grants have contributed to activities at key junctures in a number of countries and helped position the Bank in the reconstruction process by providing quick and flexible funding, issues have arisen with respect to several DGF criteria for the use of Bank earnings, such as leveraging DGF funding with other sources and arm's-length relationship from the Bank. The DGF's provision that the Fund should eventually comply with the criteria was vague and has not been sufficiently followed up. Since more than half of the Fund's grants have gone to eight of the most urgent conflict areas, the Fund appears to serve as a quick channel to respond to specific issues through targeted country-by-country grants. But these grants do not sufficiently generate broader cross-country lessons and do not exploit the program's full potential to serve the Bank and its partners strategically.

6. Indeed, OED recommended in the CGIAR meta-evaluation that donors should contribute their share of the in-house secretariat costs in order to promote greater efficiency and accountability to all donors in terms of costs and performance. (OED 2003b, p. 106.) This would also bring CGIAR in line with the DGF's own guidelines (issued in June 2000) on the burden-sharing of in-house secretariat costs, which other in-house programs already comply with.

7. Another example of different treatment concerns how DGF grants are transferred to different in-house programs. CGAP and the Post-conflict Fund's annual DGF allocations are transferred into a Bank-administered trust fund that does not have to be disbursed in the fiscal year in which the allocation was received. Other in-house programs' annual DGF allocations are transferred as internal budgetary allocations that must be spent by the end of the fiscal year.

8. IF, which has six international agency partners and 42 meetings, seems to have had higher start-up costs than programs like FSAP, which has similar objectives but fewer partners. Hence the share of resources actually going to activities that benefit developing countries, in the form of research, diagnostic studies, and technical assistance, seems to have been smaller in IF's case (GDN has had similar weaknesses). Recipient countries have complained about the lack of follow-up activities at the country level.

Chapter 7

1. This is also one of the six criteria for approving a global program at the initial concept stage that Bank Management established in April 2000, and one of the eight eligibility criteria for grant support established by the DGF Council in September 1998.

2. Developing countries cited CGIAR, GEF, and GFATM as examples of programs that seriously address issues over the long term, with a dedicated set of resources and expertise.

3. As the largest actor in the water sector globally, the Bank was the leader in establishing the GWP, which aims to promote integrated water-resource management, an idea that staff argue was ahead of its time. However, the Bank has subsequently lost interest in the partnership, and links between the program and the Bank have become very weak. This affects both the future effectiveness of the partnership and the quality of the Bank's engagement in water resource management.

4. Only the Coordination Unit of FIRST is housed in the Bank. While a Bank managing director currently chairs the governing body, he is not the permanent chair.

5. This would exclude trust fund-financed external consultants, even if they are only representing a busy senior Bank manager who is the Bank's formal representative on the governing body. There is likely to be insufficient reflection of Bank institutional perspectives and concerns when programs are overseen by persons with little Bank institutional perspective.

6. But the Bank is not exiting from the carbon trading business, in which it has just established two new and quite different funds from ProCarbFund.

7. GDN is a DGF Window 1 program that receives long-term support, while World Links is a Window 2 program scheduled to exit in FY04.

8. Management has indicated that it agrees with the main findings, conclusions and lessons from the OED case study of GDN. While GDN is worthy of Bank support, it is important to address its strategic weaknesses, including mission and objectives, governance structure, financing, other matters of organizational status, and Bank oversight.

9. World Links may also fall into this category, provided its objectives are clarified and Bank oversight and

its own governance improve. Continued support to both World Links and GDN could then give them time to develop independent identities and demonstrate results, which would justify long-term donor support.

10. Except in rare cases, even new "long-term development" programs that receive DGF grants for the first time should start out in Window 2, and not be promoted to Window 1 until they have demonstrated acceptable performance on the eight DGF criteria.

Chapter 8

1. While the four Development Committee criteria do not provide an adequate basis for ex ante selectivity or ex post evaluation, they are the set of criteria in figure ES.1 that comes closest to providing a basis for assessing each program, and align roughly with the central chapters in this report. "An emerging international consensus that global action is required" is one aspect of relevance covered in chapter 3. "A clear value added to the Bank's development objectives" relates broadly to outcomes and impacts covered in chapter 4. "The need for Bank action to catalyze other resources and partnerships" is an important aspect of governance, management and financing covered in chapters 5 and 6. "A significant comparative advantage for the Bank" is a vital dimension of Bank performance covered in chapter 7.

Annex C

1. OED 2001a, p. 21. "Partnerships and participation" were originally listed as two separate evaluation issues in the evaluation strategy document. "Monitoring and evaluation" is now interpreted more broadly to include not only an assessment of each program's monitoring and evaluation procedures but also the findings of previous evaluations about each program's outcomes and impacts, and their sustainability.

Annex E

1. Interview with Mohamed El-Ashry.

2. Analysts have justified public intervention in immunization on three grounds: (1) the spread and incomplete course of treatment in the absence of public provisions; (2) some options are pure public goods (vector control and information); and (3) on equity grounds, since such diseases disproportionately strike the poor. While most non-informational services involved are private (rival and exclusionary), there are substantial social externalities associated with immunization. For example, polio vaccine is unique because it exhibits the characteristics of a public good—the oral vaccine multiplies in the child's intestine and is released in much larger quantities in excreta. The attenuated vaccine then competes with the non-attenuated virus—making benefits both non-rival and non-exclusionary (see Hammer 1996).

3. GAVI's objective is 90 percent immunization coverage for all developing countries nationally, and at least 80 percent coverage in every district, by 2010. The program estimates that the total incremental cost, beyond the current expenditures by developing countries, of achieving such coverage ranges from $226 million using the traditional monovalent EPI (Expanded Program Immunization) vaccines to $352 million with new multivalent vaccines.

4. Obviously this does not mean that they have had no impacts, only that impacts are undocumented.

5. This followed its first evaluation in 1991, the 1992 Dublin Conference on Water and the Environment, and the 1992 Rio de Janeiro Conference on Environment and Development. The Rio-Dublin principles emphasize universal access (rather than universal coverage) and a participatory and demand-responsive approach to investments in water and sanitation—as does the Global Water Partnership, which has a broader scope for dealing with managing water resources.

6. The Bank is also working in close partnership with other international agencies under a new global umbrella effort, the Global Facilitation Partnership for Transportation and Trade.

7. Several stakeholders suggested that the evaluation did not sufficiently address (a) the steps needed to strengthen country-level operations and scale up work; (b) the steps needed to improve synergy and coordination between the secretariat and co-sponsors for country-level capacity building, the potential for U.N. reform, or increased synergy with MAP and the GFATM; and (c) how to measure increased cosponsor commitment and activities at the global and country level. (See the September 2002 stakeholder workshop discussions on the draft final report of the five-year evaluation of UNAIDS.) Some stakeholders reported that the UNAIDS evaluation focused too much on the secretariat's role and too little on analysis of its current and future structure. They also criticized the relative inattention to factors that

contributed to the success or failure of national HIV/AIDS responses. Some interviewees felt that the evaluation did not provide strategic recommendations, and that there was insufficient clarity or analysis of the monitoring and evaluation of the program. The lack of country-based evidence makes it difficult to assess how well country-coordinating mechanisms work or to attribute their success to UNAIDS. The OED team frequently encountered the issues of scalability and sustainability of the approaches being promoted, even when multiple channels are being used to make up for the limited public sector capacity for service delivery.

8. WHO, one of the partners, announced its "3 by 5" plan to provide anti-retroviral therapy to 3 million of the 42 million people currently affected by 2005.

9. The value that global programs add to the Bank's country operations is not always clear, because the links between various global programs and the Bank's country-level analytic work and lending are unclear. Stakeholders expressed frustration with the weak links between the Bank's sector staff, who manage global programs, and its country directors and regional task managers, who manage its country health-sector operations. The links vary among programs and regions, though. For example, there are better links between TB activities and Stop TB in China and India than there are on malaria activities and RBM in India. Systematic, global monitoring of the links between individual global programs and country operations is urgently needed. Better links—that focus on results and that leverage the Bank's influence and country experience—are themselves needed.

10. The OED review of Bank project documents found that every tuberculosis-related investment uses the DOTS approach, and therefore creates links between the Stop TB program and Bank lending.

Annex I

1. Management understands from OED that the Report's first four recommendations are directed to Bank management and that the fifth relates to OED itself. The sub-bullets under the recommendations are meant to be explanatory and do not represent additional subrecommendations.

2. Two managing directors chair the Council, and its members are vice presidents from networks, Regions, and corporate areas.

REFERENCES

Note: Please refer to the individual case studies for a full list of references consulted for each study.

Basu, Kaushik, and Zafiris Tzannatos. 2003. "The Global Child Labor Problem: What Do We Know and What Can We Do?" *The World Bank Economic Review* 17 (2).

Barrett, Christopher B. 2001. "Natural Resources Management Research in the CGIAR: A Meta-Evaluation." OED, World Bank, Washington, D.C. Photocopy.

Bezanson, Keith, and Francisco Sagasti. 2001. *Financing International Public Goods: Challenges, Problems and a Way Forward.* Sussex, U.K.: Institute for Development Studies for Swedish Ministry of Foreign Affairs, Department of International Development Cooperation.

Cities Alliance. 2003. *2003 Annual Report*. <http://www.citiesalliance.org/citiesalliance homepage.nsf/Attachments/auualrepo rt03/ $File/03-annual-report.pdf>

Cooper, Richard M. 2001. "Financing International Public Goods: A Historical Overview and New Challenges." In *Global Public Policies and Programs,* C. D. Gerrard, M. Ferroni, and A. Mody, eds. Washington, D.C.: World Bank.

da Costa, Eduardo, Ernest Wilson III, and Barbara Fillip. "*info*Dev External Evaluation 2002: Final Report." World Bank, Washington, D.C. Photocopy.

Davis, Michael, and Andrew Stark, eds. 2001. *Conflict of Interest in the Professions*. Oxford, U.K.: Oxford University Press.

DAC (Development Assistance Committee). 2002. *Glossary of Key Terms in Evaluation and Results-Based Management.* Paris: OECD.

Development Alternatives. 2002. *Covering New Ground: Evaluation of the Post-conflict Fund.* Washington, D.C.

DGF (Development Grant Facility). 2001. "Governing Global Programs: Challenges, Principles, and Practice." Washington, D.C.: World Bank.

Eicher, Carl, Mandivamba, and Rukuni. 2002. "The CGIAR and Africa: Past, Present and Future." OED, World Bank, Washington, D.C. Photocopy.

Etzioni, Amitai. 2001. *The Monochrome Society*. Princeton, NJ: Princeton University Press.

Fox, James W., Mark Havers, and Klaus Maurer. 2002. "Evaluation and Strategic Review of the Consultative Group to Assist the Poorest." World Bank, Washington, D.C.

Gardner, Bruce. 2002. "Global Public Goods from the CGIAR: Impact Assessment." OED, World Bank, Washington, D.C. Photocopy.

GEF (Global Environment Facility). 2002. "Focusing on the Global Environment: The First Decade of the GEF—Second Overall Performance Study." Washington, D.C.

_____. 1998. "Study of GEF's Overall Performance." Washington, D.C., World Bank.

Gerrard, Christopher D., Marco Ferroni, and Ashoka Mody. 2001. *Global Public Policies and Programs: Implications for Financing and Evaluation.* Washington, D.C.: World Bank.

Global Forum for Health Research. 2002. "The 10/90 Report on Health Research 2001–2002." Geneva. <http://www.globalforumhealth.org/ pages/index.asp>

Hammer, Jeffrey. 1996. *Economic Analysis of Health Project.* Policy Research Working Paper WPS 1611. Washington, D.C.: World Bank.

Hellman, Thomas, and Manju Puri. 2000. "The Interaction Between Product Market and Financing Strategy: The Role of Venture Capital." *The Review of Financial Studies* (13) 4: 959–84.

Hewitt, Adrian, Oliver Morrissey, and Dirk Willem te Velde. 2001. *Financing International Public Goods: Options for Resource Mobilization.* London: Overseas Development Institute.

Institute for Health Sector Development. 2003. *Independent External Evaluation of the Global Stop TB Partnership.* London.

ITAD. 2002. "Five-Year Evaluation of UNAIDS." Hove, U.K.

Katyal, J. C., and Mruthyunjaya. 2003. "CGIAR Effectiveness—A NARS Perspective from India." OED Working Paper. Washington, D.C.

Kaul, Inge, Isabelle Grunberg, and Marc Stern. 1999. *Global Public Goods: International Cooperation in the 21st Century.* New York: Oxford University Press for the UNDP.

Lele, U. 2003. "Biotechnology: Opportunities and Challenges for Developing Countries." Paper presented to the American Agricultural Economics Association, Montreal, July 29, 2003.

Lele, U., N. Kumar, A. S. Husain, A. Zazueta, and L. Kelly. 2000. *The World Bank's Forest Strategy: Striking the Right Balance.* Washington, D.C.: World Bank.

Lucas, Adekotumbo. 2000. "Public-Private Partnerships: Illustrative Examples." Paper presented at the Workshop on Public-Private Partnerships in Public Health, Endicott House, Dedham, Massachusetts, April 7–8th, 2000.

Macedo, J., M.C.M. Porto, E. Contini, and A.F.D. Avila. 2003. "Brazil Country Paper for the CGIAR Meta-Evaluation." OED Working Paper. Washington, D.C.

McDermott, Richard. 1999. "Why Information Technology Inspired But Cannot Deliver Knowledge Management." *California Management Review* (41) 4.

Musgrave, R. A. 1998. "Merit Goods," in J. Eatwell, M. Milgate, and P. Newman, eds., *The New Palgrave Dictionary of Economics*. London: Macmillan.

OED (Operations Evaluation Department, World Bank). 2003a. "Efficient, Sustainable Service for All? An OED Review of the World Bank's Assistance to Water Supply and Sanitation." Washington, D.C.

______. 2003b. *The CGIAR at 31: An Independent Meta-evaluation of the Consultative Group on International Agricultural Research.* Washington, D.C.

______. 2003c. *Annual Review of Development Effectiveness: Achieving Development Outcomes: The Millennium Challenge*. Washington, D.C.

______. 2002a. "Grant Programs: Improving their Governance." OED Precis 224. Washington, D.C.

______. 2002b. "The Highly Indebted Poor Countries (HIPC) Debt Initiative: An OED Review." Washington D.C.

______. 2002c. *The World Bank's Approach to Global Programs: An Independent Evaluation*, Phase 1 Report and Annexes." Report No. 26284-GLB. Washington, D.C.

______. 2001a. "The World Bank and Global Public Policies and Programs: An Evaluation Strategy." Washington, D.C. <http://www.worldbank.org/oed/gppp/evaluation_strategy.html>

———. 2001b. *Bridging Troubled Waters: Assessing the Water Resources Strategy since 1993*. OED Study Series. Washington, D.C: World Bank.

———. 1995. "Monitoring and Evaluation Plans in Staff Appraisal Reports in Fiscal Year 1995." Report No. 15222. World Bank, Washington, D.C.

OED, OEG (Operations Evaluation Group, IFC), and OEU (Operations Evaluation Unit, MIGA). 2003. *Power for Development: A Review of the World Bank Group's Experience with Private Participation in the Electricity Sector*. OED Study Series. Washington, D.C.: World Bank.

Pardey, P. G., and N. M. Beintema. 2001. *Slow Magic: Agricultural R&D a Century after Mendel*. Washington, D.C.: International Food Policy Research Institute.

Piot, Peter. 2003. "AIDS: The Need for an Exceptional Response to an Unprecedented Crisis." Presidential Fellow Lecture, Washington, D.C, November 20, 2003.

PPIAF (Public-Private Infrastructure Advisory Facility). 2003. *Annual Report 2003*. <http://ppiaf.org/Reports/PPIAFAR2003.pdf>

Samoff, Joel, and Nelly P. Stromquist. 2001. "Managing Knowledge and Storing Wisdom? New Forms of Foreign Aid?" *Development and Change* (32): 631–56.

Scholte, Jan Aart. 2000. *Globalization: A Critical Introduction*. New York: St. Martin's.

Standing, Guy. 2000. "Brave New Words? A Critique of Stiglitz's World Bank Rethink." *Development and Change* (31):737–63.

TDR, Third External Review Committee. 1998. *Final Report: Third External Review of the UNDP/World Bank/WHO Special Programme for Training and Research in Tropical Diseases (TDR)*. <http://www.who.int/tdr/publications/publications/pdf/exrev.pdf>

UNAIDS. 2003. "Report of the Fourteenth Meeting of the Programme Coordinating Board of UNAIDS."

Vaillancourt Rosenau, Pauline. *2000. Public-Private Partnerships for Public Health.* Cambridge, Mass.: MIT Press.

Wegner, Stephan, Rafael Dominguez, and Fernando Manibog. 2003. *Power for Development: A Review of the World Bank Group's Experience with Private Participation in the Electricity Sector*. OED Study Series. Washington, D.C.: World Bank.

Wilson, John S., and Tsuehiro Otsuki. 2002. "To Spray or Not to Spray: Pesticides, Banana Exports, and Food Safety." World Bank Development Research Group, Washington, D.C.

World Bank. 2004. *Water Resources Sector Strategy: Strategic Directions for World Bank Engagement*. Washington, D.C.

———. 2003a. "Getting Serious about Meeting the Millennium Development Goals: A Comprehensive Development Framework Progress Report." Washington, D.C.

———. 2003b. "Independent Evaluation: Principles, Guidelines, and Good Practice." World Bank Development Grant Facility Technical Note. Washington, D.C.

———. 2001a. *Global Development Finance 2001*. Washington, D.C.

———. 2001b. "Strategic Directions for FY02–FY04." Washington, D.C.

———. 2000. "Poverty Reduction and Global Public Goods: Issues for the World Bank in Supporting Global Public Collective Action." DC/2000-16. Washington, D.C.

———. 1999. *The World Development Report 1998/99: Knowledge for Development.* New York: Oxford University Press for the World Bank.

WHO (World Health Organization), Commission on Macroeconomics and Health. 2001. "Macroeconomics and Health: Investing in Health for Economic Development," Geneva.